Choosing Schools

Choosing Schools

Consumer Choice and the Quality of American Schools

Mark Schneider

Paul Teske

Melissa Marschall

PRINCETON UNIVERSITY PRESS

PRINCETON AND OXFORD

Published by Princeton University Press, 41 William Street, Princeton, New Jersey 08540
In the United Kingdom: Princeton University Press, 3 Market Place, Woodstock, Oxfordshire
OX20 1SY

Library of Congress Cataloging-in-Publication Data

Schneider, Mark, 1946–
Choosing schools : consumer choice and the quality of American schools / Mark Schneider,
Paul Teske, Melissa Marschall.
p. cm.
Includes bibliographical references (p.) and index.
ISBN 0-691-05057-0 (cl : alk. paper)
1. School choice—United States. I. Teske, Paul Eric. II. Marschall, Melissa, 1968–
III. Title.
LB1027.9.S32 2000
379.1'11'0973—dc21   00-027872

This book has been composed in Berkeley Old Style.

The paper used in this publication meets the minimum requirements of ANSI/NISO
Z39.48-1992 (R1997) (*Permanence of Paper*)

www.pup.princeton.edu

Printed in the United States of America

1   2   3   4   5   6   7   8   9   10

Contents

List of Figures

List of Tables

Acknowledgments

As in any major piece of research, the authors have accumulated substantial debts.

First of all, without the support of the National Science Foundation (grant number SBR9408970) this work would not have been possible. In addition, for varying periods during the course of this research, Paul Teske was supported by a Spencer Foundation/National Academy of Education Post Doctoral Fellowship and Mark Schneider was a Visiting Scholar at the Russell Sage Foundation. The work reported in chapter 9 was supported by the Manhattan Institute. We wish to acknowledge the support of all these institutions.

Second, we need to acknowledge the contributions of Christine Roch to this project. Although she came to the project too late to be a full coauthor of this book, she is a coauthor of most of the data-based chapters (chapters 4–9 and chapter 11).

Among the many other scholars who also helped in this work, we want to thank Robert Huckfeldt for his help in the network component of this study; Claudia Goldin and Gary Field for their insights into the efficiency issue; Jeff Henig and Ken Meier for their careful criticisms and comments on many of the individual components of this research; Diane Ravitch, Joseph Viteritti, and Sy Fliegel, for their extremely helpful insights into the operation of the New York City schools in our sample; and the many administrators in all four school districts in our sample for insights into the operation of their particular units, and also for their help in keeping our analysis "grounded" in the very real world of schools and education.

Choosing Schools

Introduction

School Choice, Parent Incentives, and the Use of Information

This book is about school choice, which has been a topic for discussion, debate, and action in academia, think tanks, and government at all levels. Many books and articles explore different aspects of choice, and some issues related to choice have been fought out in the editorial pages of the *Wall Street Journal*, the *New York Times*, and other mass media. Unfortunately, the debates about choice have often degenerated into acrimony.

We hope that this book provides a balanced perspective to the unfolding debates over choice and what we can and should expect from it. We believe that our work has several elements that can help to structure and inform the analysis of choice.

First, while many studies of choice focus on schools as "suppliers" of education, our main focus is on the behavior of parents faced with choice. Thus, we expand the study of choice from a focus on the supply side of education to the demand-side, represented by the behavior of parents, who in many ways are the "consumers" of education.[1] Clearly, every analysis of choice that focuses on schools must make certain assumptions about the behavior of parents in different settings. We explore the assumptions about parent-consumer behavior more thoroughly than previous studies of choice.

Second, school choice is a highly charged ideological battleground. While there is widespread agreement that schools in the United States need improvement, there is equally wide disagreement about the extent to which choice can produce it. Often, as in other policy domains in which the stakes are high and in which basic ideological issues about the role of government and the role of markets conflict, debates often resemble a battle more than a scientific enterprise. Proponents and opponents of choice often take one-sided and extreme views of what choice will do for American schools, ignoring the subtleties of different approaches to choice and what we should legitimately expect choice to accomplish. For example, John Chubb and Terry Moe, whose work has probably done more to ignite the current interest in choice than anyone else's, have gone so far as to argue that: "reformers would do well to entertain the notion that choice *is* a panacea. This is our way of saying that choice is not like other reforms and should not be combined with them as part of a reformist strategy for improving America's public schools. Choice is a self-contained reform with its own rationale and justification. It has the capacity *all by itself* to bring about the kind of transformation that, for years, reformers have been seeking to engineer in myriad other ways"

(Chubb and Moe 1990a, 217; emphasis in the original). In contrast, many critics see choice as not only making impossible demands on parents but also as destroying the very fabric of schools and communities, eliminating the shared experiences and common institutions necessary for healthy democracies.

Without a strong empirical foundation, little can be done to counter what we think are unreasonable expectations and arguments and to transform the battle over choice into a meaningful dialogue about the steps needed to improve America's schools.

We seek to create such a constructive dialogue by providing a durable foundation upon which expectations about the behavior of parents can be built. The work we present in this book is based on empirical data gathered by interviewing over 1,600 parents in four school districts. These individual-level data are supplemented by school-level data, our own observations of schools in these districts based on numerous field visits, and in-depth interviews with administrators at the schools, districts, and central school bureaucracies. This was a large undertaking, occupying the better part of four years of work.

As in any large-scale analysis of something so complex as education, humility is always appropriate. Similarly, in looking for the effects of something so complex as school choice, beginning with a set of reasonable expectations is critical.

We do not believe that school choice is a panacea for the ills of education. Although many other analysts also reject the extreme claim, many of them also believe that choice is not worth the effort and the risks it entails. It is here that we part company.

We believe that choice is capable of unleashing powerful forces that can have positive effects on parents, schools, and communities—and we believe that the evidence we present in this book shows this to be true. But we must always remember that choice is not operating in a vacuum and that choice is not a cure-all for the ills of urban education and communities. While schools are one of the most important public institutions found in any local community, the number of hours children spend in school is limited, and the social forces and conditions that children face in their communities can easily overwhelm any school-based activities. As we report in this book, choice has done good things in the school districts we study, but many of these positive effects are "on the margin"—that is, the effects are both substantively important and statistically significant, but they are often limited. And we must always remember that choice is not a uniform reform, but rather a class of reforms that differ in many important features. Again, as we report in this book, certain aspects of choice reform seem to be associated with better outcomes than others. Thus as choice proliferates, we must always keep in mind that there are differences in the forms of choice that are being implemented, and that different forms of choice will have different effects.

Thus, we must have reasonable expectations about how much of an effect it can and will have. In turn, the "story" we tell in this book is nuanced and complex—but no more so than the process of education and parental choice that is the subject of our analysis.

In this chapter, we start to explore the many facets of school choice. In the next few pages, we introduce many of the themes that structure this book. Not surprisingly, given the complexity of these issues, we return to these themes repeatedly, enlarging our examination of them and exploring them in increasingly greater detail. While we begin with overarching themes to provide the reader with a more precise roadmap of what follows, the last section of this chapter previews the ensuing chapters.

Why Choice?

Choice has emerged as a tool for transforming schools that are widely perceived as failing. There are innumerable articles and books that have documented the perceived failure of America's schools. Gerald Bracey summarizes the thrust of this argument nicely:

> The conventional wisdom is now firmly established: American students can't hold their own against their peers in other nations. They can't read, they can't do math, they are abysmally ignorant of science. That has been the message of countless stories in the media. (1998, 64)

While Bracey himself disputes the factual basis for this "conventional wisdom," he provides compelling evidence documenting the widespread discontent with the performance of American schools today. In addition to any factual basis for the belief that our schools are failing, discontent with the schools and the way they are governed is part of the growing anti-government, promarket rhetoric that is in the ascendancy today.

Reflecting these sentiments, many scholars argue that the organization of schools is a product of the "dead hand" of the past and hopelessly out of date. For example, Paul Hill, an astute critic of American schools, has argued that by the 1920s, in response to decades of intense immigration, the dominance of assembly line production techniques, and the sway of scientific management, the system of education in the United States had taken the shape that is evident today. Critics often call this the "factory model" of schools (Hill, Pierce, and Guthrie 1997).

Linda Darling-Hammond (1997) describes some of the components of this model in the following terms: "The large age-graded departmentalized schools were designed for the efficient batch processing of masses of children in the new age of compulsory education and large-scale immigration." The emphasis in the factory model is on rote learning and a standardized curriculum, with students moving on a "conveyor belt" from class to class, period to period, and grade to grade, with little concern for the needs and preferences of individual students or their parents.

According to these critics, despite remarkable changes in technology and demography, the factory model of education established nearly a century ago has changed little and the gap between what the country needs from its schools and what the schools deliver is widening. In response, a highly visible and increasingly powerful school reform movement has evolved.

As this reform movement has developed, its advocates have begun to articulate the characteristics of a good school. Not surprisingly, their vision differs radically from the factory model. Ravitch and Viteritti describe the alternative that today's reforms seek to create:

> a universe of distinctive schools—small, autonomous, and unburdened by a large administrative structure, not unlike the parochial schools that currently dot the urban landscape . . . In fact, the most effective schools—whether public, private, or parochial—share the same characteristics: They are relatively small, devote relatively fewer resources to administrative overhead, have high expectations for all students, have a common curriculum in which all students participate, and strong sense of mission and a well-defined culture. (1997, 13)

In this vision, good schools focus on student learning and the needs of children by personalizing education and creating long-term relationships between teachers and families—that is, what James Coleman referred to as "effective communities," united around shared values and communal organization. But there is a link between these community-based processes and outcomes: good schools are also organized to encourage high performance and they are given incentives to use resources efficiently, where success, rather than failure, is rewarded.

Some reformers see choice as a fundamental building-block of the vision articulated by Ravitch and Viteritti. For example, Brandl (1998) argues that choice creates the kind of commitment best sustained in freely chosen small communities. In contrast to the factory model of education, Brandl argues that choice among smaller autonomous schools maximizes the conditions for participation and, by allowing parents to select schools on the basis of the values they hold, creates effective communities.

Similarly, Hill, Pierce, and Guthrie (1997) identify several mechanisms that link choice to a broad set of desirable results:

- Schools of choice can influence students' attitudes, effort and motivation in ways that "regular" schools cannot.
- Schools of choice have more authority and legitimacy.
- Choice holds schools accountable to promises made, thereby allowing the development of effective school communities that link teachers and administrators together.

- Through their act of choice, parents have endorsed the school they have chosen as better than the alternatives, leading to higher levels of satisfaction and a stronger commitment to the school.

As the image of a good school and the connection between choice and desirable school outcomes has developed, the differences between this alternative vision and the practice of present schools have come more sharply into focus.

However, promises of reform and the reality of outcomes can differ. And while the theorists of choice promise many positive outcomes, we are concerned with the empirical reality of those claims. As we explain in chapter 3, we examine the relationship between choice and outcomes by exploring the effects of public school choice in a small number of school districts. We employ a quasi-experimental research design matching a central-city district with choice to a similar district without choice, and a suburban district with choice to a comparable district without choice. This powerful research design allows us to examine the effects of choice better than most other studies have been able to do.

Choice and School Reform

Given both the complex challenge of providing education in our society, and the vast differences in communities seeking to improve their schools, we always must keep in mind the fact that school choice is not a uniform initiative. Instead, choice refers to a wide range of school reforms. One of our first tasks is to try to make sense of these reforms and to place the school choice programs we study in this firmament.

As we discuss in much more detail in chapter 1, although many reforms seek to shift the balance of power away from centralized decision makers, they emphasize different means by which to accomplish this. For example, some reforms leave the bulk of school decision making to educational officials, but seek to alter accountability in ways that bind schools to certain performance standards and increase the ability of parents to demand higher standards from their schools. Other reforms seek to give parents and students more power by taking the school assignment decision away from central school administrators and granting parents and students the right to make this important choice themselves. Still other reform initiatives go beyond this, empowering parents to increase their control over a broader range of educational policies and decisions that affect their children. Of course, there are also reforms that seek to alter the balance of power between school officials and parents through all of these means.

In this book we focus on reforms that give parents the ability to choose the school their child attends. However, we also show how this set of reforms can produce much wider changes in parent behavior and school performance.

The Expansion of Choice

The act of choosing a school for one's child is not new in the United States. For years, many American parents have used their residential location decisions as a way to choose their children's schools. Indeed, many location decisions are made with the quality of the local schools in mind. But, once a family has chosen a place to live, parent choice over public schools has usually been limited by the intersection of geography and bureaucratic decision rules—after a family located in a given neighborhood, the children were sent to a zoned neighborhood school, determined by a school planner.

Changing this traditional method of assignment is at the core of choice reforms and a variety of choice mechanisms have emerged. These range from magnet schools (perhaps the most widely implemented form of choice) to the abolishment of neighborhood catchment areas within school districts (intradistrict choice) to allowing children to choose schools across district lines (interdistrict choice) to vouchers (the most "market-like" mechanism now being discussed in the domain of education). In the next chapter, we discuss the evolution of these models of choice in more detail and link the expansion of choice to other fundamental changes in school practices.

Not surprisingly, the controversies surrounding school choice are also myriad. For example, from a supply-side perspective, the issue of including parochial schools in choice programs has led to constitutional, legal, and political disputes. In addition, the question of regulating the selection process in order to maintain or achieve racial balance in schools has spurred debates about the stratifying effects of school choice (Bridge and Blackman 1978; Murnane 1986; Clewell and Joy 1990; Elmore 1991a; Wong 1992; Martinez et al. 1995).

More recently, issues related to the demand-side of choice have emerged, although similar to supply-side issues, they have been largely raised on ideological grounds and have to date received little empirical attention. These issues focus on parents as "citizens/consumers" and consider how their behavior might change in response to the introduction of choice. Opponents of choice in particular argue that disparities in parents' resources, involvement, and cognitive abilities will play a crucial role in determining both who will participate in choice and how parental choice will ultimately affect educational outcomes. Another critical issue in this debate revolves around the aspects of schools parents will emphasize once empowered with choice. Our objective in this book is to address these issues by developing the logic underlying the demand-side of school choice in greater detail and testing them empirically.

The Rhetoric of the Market

Choice is not only congruent with current thinking about what makes good schools, it is also congruent with the rhetoric of the free market that is ascendant in the United States today. Not surprisingly, many current proposals for school reform endorse the idea of a "market for education" and stress market mechanisms to deal with the problems of public schooling.

Many scholars are visceral in their negative reaction to the use of market organizing principles applied to schooling. In this book, we try to come to grips with market models that have been associated with choice reforms. While the intellectual challenges of developing a market for education have led many to reject this approach, we take the notion of markets for local schools seriously.

Although we consider other models of school organization, we start with a basic market-model, and build upon it in our analysis of school reform. While we embrace many of the assumptions embodied in the market-model, we also recognize that there are fundamental differences between the way in which schools are organized and the way in which markets are organized.

First, there are limits to how far market metaphors can go in describing the system of education. We therefore tend to think of school reforms as unleashing "market-like forces" and creating "quasi-markets" for education. We also take seriously Henig's (1994) critique of the market metaphor to structure school reform and his argument that we must rethink school choice. Thus, we address these fundamental issues of markets and schooling in chapters 1 and 2. While we recognize that there are many problems in applying market models to schooling, we remain relatively optimistic about the way in which market-like processes can create pressure on the schools to be more responsive and more efficient. In this approach, we agree with Hanushek (1997) who has argued that whatever reforms are instituted, schools must be assessed and rewarded (or punished) in a meaningful way and that market-like processes are among the best ways to enforce this type of accountability.

What Benefits Might Flow from Choice?

We believe that by creating the conditions for competition, choice can put pressure on schools to be more efficient providers of education. Choice can do this by providing incentives for schools to increase the quality of the product they deliver and to respond to the interests of the community they serve.

To the extent that schools fail to attract students because their product is defective or out-of-date, and to the extent that schools lose their monopoly power over enrollments, competition can work to either weed out the weakest schools or force them to improve in order to survive. Just as bankruptcy and the forces inherent in Schumpeter's concept of creative destruction are widely recognized as the mainspring of economic progress in market economies, we must recognize that the closing of schools due to insufficient enrollments is not a failure of choice but a part of the process leading to better schools. While bankruptcies or school closings clearly affect negatively the individual firms or schools that go out of business, the effects of such closings are positive at the systemic level—other units respond by improving their products in the face of these deficiencies.

Thus, choice can produce pressure for all schools in a school system to deliver a better service more efficiently. Economists call this "productive efficiency." Moreover, because education is a complex, multidimensional good, parents differ in the attributes of education they value most. In a system of choice, parents should be able to place their children in schools that emphasize the aspects of education they embrace. This increases "allocative efficiency"—the matching of consumer preferences with the goods and services they consume.

In addition, by granting more parents the ability to choose the schools their children attend, choice can reduce one major inequality that presently exists in most urban education systems: the disproportionate opportunities available to economically advantaged parents. In today's system of schooling, wealthy families already have extensive choice over the schools their children attend. They can choose among good schools in different suburban areas or they can choose to pay tuition to send their children to private schools. A system of public school choice will equalize these opportunities somewhat by giving less well-off parents an expanded set of options and more opportunities to match their preferences with what schools offer.

Finally, we also think that choice can improve the quality of education through another mechanism that is not often thought essential to the operation of markets: parental involvement. One consistent finding of educational research is that quality education cannot be delivered by schools acting alone—in order to succeed, schools need the involvement and energies of parents. To use the terminology we develop in chapter 2, education is a good that requires "coproduction" between school personnel and parents. By increasing parental involvement, choice can create the conditions for improved school performance.

In theory, then, choice can increase productive efficiency; it can increase the match between what parents want and what schools deliver; and it can help create the conditions for effective school communities and higher parental involvement. However, while theoretically choice *can* do all these things, we must have reasonable expectations regarding the size of these benefits. And we must remember that choice may also have negative consequences that must be identified and balanced against any gains.

The Double-Edged Sword Of Choice

Many critics argue that choice is likely to produce undesirable outcomes. In particular, one of the major mechanisms that makes choice work—engaging the talents, interests, and energy of parents to find better schools for their children—may also lead to one of the most frequently identified problems with choice: the unequal distribution of those parent characteristics across the population. In the ideal world, all parents would sort themselves into different schools based on those preferences, creating the conditions for the development of effective school communities, which would then in turn deliver a quality education. However, in the real world the question of stratification cannot be brushed aside lightly. In fact, it represents one of the central issues in the debate over school choice and we devote an entire chapter to this issue. However, let us just introduce briefly a scenario in which the benefits and costs of choice can be quickly identified.

By giving parents a greater say in the schools their children attend, we can think of choice as a means of overcoming what social scientists call "coordination failures." This idea is critical to the field of information economics and microeconomists often use it to explain some market failures. Kreps (1990, 578), for example, defines coordination failures as situations "where parties desirous of making a particular exchange must search for potential trading partners and where the need for search discourages certain otherwise beneficial trading activity." One type of market failure results from insufficient information on the part of some market participants about what other participants are doing. In well-functioning markets, these coordination problems are usually resolved over time (see, e.g., Schneider and Teske 1995).

Let us elaborate this idea and transform it from rather abstract economic reasoning to more concrete thinking about the schools.

In any school district, some number of parents will care more about the schools than other parents. These more involved parents are willing to demand better schools, to participate in school events, and to engage in other activities to get better schools and a better education for their children. But since education is a coproductive activity and since one of the most important ingredients in producing a quality education is an effective school community, these parents know that they need to find a school in which there are shared beliefs about education.

If these parents are dispersed in relatively small numbers throughout all schools in a district, they may fail to reach a critical mass in any given school. A coordination failure results because these parents have no way of finding other parents who share their beliefs and their willingness to participate in the school activities. If low-quality schools result, these concerned parents might exercise their exit option by enrolling their children in private schools or, if they have the geographic mobility, leaving the school district entirely. Thus, in a school system organized around traditional attendance zones and low levels of parent involvement in the schools (conditions found in many central cities), coordination failures among parents may drive down the quality of all the schools in the system and lead to high rates of exit to private schools or suburbs. They may also lead to higher levels of dissatisfaction among those parents who cannot exercise the exit option.

But consider this scenario: a school district establishes a set of "alternative" schools. These alternative schools could be structured in a variety of ways—for example, they could be thematic or they could stress different pedagogical techniques. And rather than automatic assignment, these are schools of choice—parents who believe that these techniques or themes meet the needs of their children would be allowed to choose from among them.

Thus, these schools act as places in which more concerned parents or parents with specific preferences for different types of instruction can now enroll their children. In this scenario, schools act as coordinating devices where parents can be more certain that the parents of other children in that school share both their greater concern for schooling and other basic values and preferences regarding schooling. As parents "coordinate" their behavior and preferences, the schools can better develop a mission based on shared beliefs. The greater level of parent involvement and cooperation allows schools themselves to respond by altering their organizational structure and devising new forms of activity for parents.

In short, these alternative schools not only act as coordinating devices for concerned parents, but are also better situated to alter governing structures in ways that enhance their effectiveness and efficiency. If schools can respond with programs that match the more focused preferences of parents, the possibilities for improved outcomes are clear. In a sense, these possibilities reflect "peer group" effects, where the peer groups include not only the students in classrooms, but the parents as well.

But within this process lays the foundation for one of the most fundamental criticisms leveled against choice—that choice will siphon off parents who are the most concerned about education and the most willing to engage in coproductive activities to increase the quality of education. And many scholars believe that as these parents concentrate their children in alternative schools, they will withdraw their support of the remaining traditional schools, which in turn will become even worse. Thus, it is possible that as active parents concentrate in a few schools, a minority of students become better off, while the majority suffer.

This argument almost always carries class and/or race components. If interest in education and a propensity to demand more from schools is a function of parental education, then choice may lead to "stratification," concentrating parents with the best education and the highest socioeconomic status in a few schools, and leaving the children from lower socioeconomic backgrounds in the worst schools. This stratification argument usually has a segregation component as well—that choice will create a process in which black, Hispanic, and children from other racial minority group children will end up in one set of schools and white children in others.

We consider this stratification/segregation argument to be absolutely critical to the analysis of any school reform and one that must be addressed in any study of school choice. Therefore, we return to it frequently throughout this book. And, we provide better evidence than we have seen anywhere else on the extent to which choice actually creates a situation in which one set of schools is "left behind."

Overview of the Book

We hope that we have made clear in these opening pages the basic ideas that motivate our analysis and why they are important. In the chapters that follow, we flesh out these ideas in more detail. The book consists of three main sections. In the first section, which includes chapters 1–3, we develop in more detail our perspective on school organization, and how choice reforms schools. We also examine the institutional arrangements of the choice plans characterizing the districts in our study and describe the research design we employ to test hypotheses about the functioning and outcome of the schools and school systems in our study.

In chapter 1, we examine the historical development of different choice reforms and how they vary. We note that all forms of choice share one common characteristic—expanding the set of schooling options from which parents can choose. However, they differ quite dramatically in terms of their governing structures, the accountability measures and systems they use to evaluate performance, and the extent to which they encourage and facilitate the active involvement of parents.

We begin by evaluating three different models of school governance. These models emphasize democratic, bureaucratic, or market approaches of schools as fundamental organizing principles. We explore how these governance models compare in terms of the effectiveness of the organizational forms and the outcomes that flow from them.

In chapter 1, we also argue that the original theoretical lens through which many school choice programs were viewed emphasized the supply-side of education. From the supply-side, creating more schools, breaking the geographically defined monopoly of schools, and forcing the schools to compete with one another would in itself create many desirable outcomes. From a simple market perspective, supply side competition alone should increase the efficiency of schools and make them more responsive to the interests of their "clients."

Examining the supply of education and the organizational aspects of schools is critically important for understanding the workings of local markets for education and for understanding why so many people are so unhappy with so many schools. However, in chapter 2 we argue this supply-side focus of education is too narrow. Most school reforms seek either explicitly or implicitly to shift power from the supply-side to the demand-side of schooling. And, as we have argued above, there is growing evidence that the active participation of parents in the working of the schools is necessary to create effective school communities in which more learning occurs. In short, we argue that a focus on schools as institutions must be matched by a concern for the involvement of parents in both the choice of schools and schooling processes.

Thus, in chapter 2 we outline our approach to parents as "consumers" of education. Fundamentally, we believe that choice reforms concerned with changing the supply-side of schooling must be based on a solid understanding of parental behavior—because this is the foundation on which successful reforms must be built. In developing our theory of how the incentives and behavior of parents interact with and depend upon features of the supply-side of schools, we pay particular attention to information and other transaction costs, since these have been shown to play a critical role in the functioning of both private markets and non-market organizations (Kreps 1990; Miller 1992; Ostrom 1990; Schneider and Teske 1995; Williamson 1985). We examine a number of different perspectives in comparing the kind of information we should expect parents to have about the schools and the kind of information they actually *need to have* in order for choice to work.

We thus devote considerable space in this book to building a theory of how school choice should function under different conditions and the various outcomes we should expect under these conditions. But, we are empirical social scientists who believe that ultimately every set of theoretical expectations must be tested using the best data and methods possible. We believe this is particularly important for school choice, since many previous studies have made assertions often in excess of what the data support and since debates continue to be waged primarily on ideological grounds. In chapter 3, we outline the research design and data collection approach we employed for our analysis of school choice.

The remainder of the book is organized in two clusters of empirical analysis. In part 2, we explore factors that precede, and to some degree structure, the choice process. For example, in chapter 4, we explore the preferences different parents have for the various dimensions of education. This is a fundamental issue, since many critics of choice argue that if parents are granted the authority to choose their child's school, many will choose poorly. In particular, the argument is often that poor and/or minority parents do not have a preference for rigorous academic standards and will choose schools based on other criteria. This obviously feeds back into the concern about stratification and segregation that some argue is associated with choice.

Our empirical analysis is concerned with the validity of this claim. We find that parents of lower socioeconomic status are in fact *more* interested in the bedrock values of schooling; compared to their more highly educated counterparts, these parents want schools that provide students with solid academic fundamentals so that their children will do well on academic tests. We explore the implications of these findings, but we believe that our results should help settle one of the debates about the preferences of parents from lower socio-economic status. However, having a preference for good schools doesn't mean that all parents have the same ability to find out which schools are good.

In chapters 5 and 6, we explore how different parents search for information about schools. In chapter 5, we look at how parents evaluate a range of information outlets, and we show that parents with higher socioeconomic status are much better positioned to gather information more efficiently than other parents. These differences are reinforced in chapter 6, when we look specifically at how parents create different networks in which discussions about the schools take place. Simply put, our analysis shows that even though parents of lower socioeconomic status may have a preference for academically good schools, they may not have the means of finding out which schools match those preferences or deliver a quality education.

In general, the three chapters in part 2 focus on the conditions that exist prior to choice. For example, we assume that parents form preferences for different aspects of schooling before they encounter the situation in which they may or may not need to choose a school for their child. We recognize that there may in fact be some reciprocal causation—that is, if parents choose a school with a distinctive mission or "product," over time, they may begin to value that aspect of education more highly. In this scenario, preferences are shaped by choice, rather than the choice being shaped by the preference. While we recognize this possibility, we believe that the flow of causation is predominately in the other direction—that is, preferences precede choice. Similarly, while, on the margin, choice may affect how parents construct networks of educational discussants, we believe that the construction of information networks is a function of the social environment in which parents are embedded and that this environment is created independently of choice.

In part 3, we look at parent behaviors that are theoretically more likely to be affected by choice. In this section, we also link the demand- and supply-sides of this market-like setting by examining how schools themselves respond to choice.

There is a fundamental debate about how much information parents have about the schools and how much they need to have in order to make school choice work. Given this, we begin with an exploration of the level of information parents have about the schools. Many proponents of choice argue that choice gives parents the incentive to become more informed about the schools. In chapter 7, we explore information levels of parents in districts with and without choice.

Another theme in this section focuses on the effects of choice on efficiency.

We recognize that efficiency is a broad term, encompassing many dimensions. As noted in the opening section of this chapter, one of our major concerns lies in identifying the effects of choice on two specific types of efficiency: *allocative efficiency* and *productive efficiency*. By allocative efficiency, we mean the tightness of the fit between what parents want from the schools and what they get. Education is a multidimensional good and, as we document in chapter 4, parents may legitimately want different things from the schools. Allocative efficiency is increased to the extent that the school a child attends is performing well on the aspects of education that the parent holds important. In chapter 8, we explore how choice and information levels can increase levels of allocative efficiency. We also explore the extent to which a better school match provides greater satisfaction for parents. In chapter 9, we explore how choice affects the productive efficiency of schools.

In chapter 10, we turn explicitly to an examination of segregation and stratification in the schools and how these have been affected by choice. As we noted earlier, while choice may increase the ability of parents to coordinate their behavior and to increase the quality of education their children receive, many scholars and policy makers are worried that this will leave many students and schools behind. We show that the gains in efficiency in District 4 did *not* come at the cost of neighborhood schools. That is, choice was a positive sum experience without adverse distributional consequences for the traditional schools in the district. Given the concern that critics of choice have about the increases in segregation and stratification that may result from choice, this is one of the most important findings in our work. It suggests that the dynamics of competition may be enough to overcome possible negative distributional consequences of choice.

In chapter 10 we also look at the issue of stratification in the context of school choice in our suburban district. Here we are particularly interested in whether choice has accomplished its goal of establishing racially balanced schools and also whether it has succeeded in increasing performance levels among students from racial minority groups. We find supportive evidence on both counts.

Schools are not only central institutions in the daily life of students, they are also central institutions in the daily life of communities. In chapter 11, we look at how choice can influence the stock of local social capital. We show that choice can increase parental involvement in the voluntary organizations and events that are essential to effective schools; that choice can increase the trust between parents and teachers; and that choice can increase the level of interaction between parents. We argue that all these behaviors are components of social capital and that choice, by increasing local social capital, not only can build stronger schools, but might help build stronger communities.

Finally, in chapter 12, we focus on a subset of parents in our sample that is not exclusively examined in previous chapters of the book: parents who have elected private schools for their children. Although we discuss private school parents in the chapters in part 2 (those investigate the characteristics of parents prior to choosing), we exclude them from other chapters in part 3 to avoid confusing our analyses of public school choosers. Yet choosing private schools over public ones is an option exercised by large numbers of parents in our sample and in the nation as a whole. And it is not an option taken lightly, as it involves parents paying a fee for their children's schooling in addition to whatever taxes they pay to support the public schools. Thus in this chapter, private school parents take center stage as we compare them to public school parents across a host of dimensions that have informed our analysis in other chapters. We find evidence that public school choice may be a way to retain or bring back parents who otherwise might opt for private schools, as public school choice affects the broader market for education.

Finally, we conclude the book by summarizing our results and placing our findings into the existing literature. As we noted earlier, scholars and public officials are hotly debating many aspects of school choice. We believe that these debates often do not serve to move policy forward and that the positions people stake out are often immune to empirical evidence. In our last chapter, we revisit some of the issues we think are central to the study of choice and use the patterns we have empirically documented in our work to move the debate to firmer ground.

PART ONE

Chapter 1

Reinventing the Governance Structure of Education: School Choice as Educational Reform

While most parents agree that a good education is critical to the quality of their child's future, and considerable empirical evidence supports this, there is great disagreement about which aspects of education matter the most. While we as a society want good schools, and devote considerable resources to achieving this goal, we aren't exactly sure what works best. Adding to this problem is the fact that debates about education are often colored by broader ideological disagreements. This creates a volatile combination of ingredients that has produced conditions ripe for intense political conflict. And, it explains the waves of educational reform that continue to sweep through the nation's schools.

While school reform has been a relatively constant phenomenon during this century, its form has been anything but constant. In the past, most educational reform movements focused on curriculum and teaching methods. Today's reforms, however, center more on issues of governance (Chubb and Moe 1990; Clune and Witte 1990; Henig 1994; Smith and Meier 1995; Anhalt et al. 1995; Ravitch and Viteritti 1997). A core belief underlying many new reform proposals is that education cannot be improved unless new actors are brought into the decision arena, changing the way in which educational policy decisions are made, shifting power toward parents, and exposing overly bureaucratized school systems to some form of market discipline. As these beliefs have crystallized, school choice has become one of the most controversial reforms of the century.

The Many Forms of School Choice

Although current debates over choice fail to acknowledge this, by some definitions, choice is neither particularly new nor particularly rare. The movement toward choice actually traces back several decades. While one can debate the exact starting point, without doubt the implementation of alternative schools in the 1960s and 1970s marked a substantial increase in the number of non-neighborhood schools across the country. Various other forms of choice have appeared since then, including magnet schools, open enrollment programs, and the rapidly expanding charter school movement. While all of these choice reforms focus on public schools, the movement for choice has expanded even further in recent years to include publicly funded vouchers that encompass both public and private schools (as found, for example, in Milwaukee and Cleveland). More important than the increasing variety of choice programs have been the expanding goals of this reform, particularly in the 1990s. Rather than simply allowing parents to choose schools other than their zoned neighborhood school, choice has come to represent a tool for generating systemic changes in the way schools and school systems operate.

The Evolution of Public School Choice

In recent decades, a variety of mechanisms have emerged within the public school sector to allow parents greater choice over the schools their children attend.[1] Since many scholars have produced "catalogs" of school reform and discussed their various theoretical underpinnings, we feel no need to replicate this work.[2] However, there are several themes in the evolution of choice that need to be highlighted in order to set the stage for the work we present in this book.

Henig (1998) has recently reviewed the different forms of choice currently found in the United States, and estimates the number of students and school districts affected by each form of choice. Based on these estimates, Henig argues that rather than an "oddity," public school choice of one kind or another actually is quite widespread. For example, in the National Household Education Survey conducted by the National Center for Education Statistics in 1993, approximately 40 percent of parents surveyed said that they had exercised the most traditional form of school choice—residential location—to gain access to good schools. Even more interesting however, is that an additional 20 percent said they exercised other forms of choice in selecting their children's schools (National Center for Educational Statistics 1997). In addition, many parents exercised informal routes to enrolling their children in a public school other than the one to which they were assigned; for example, by using administrative appeals.

The Evolving Forms of Choice

Henig begins his study of the evolution of choice with alternative schools, which were among the first public schools of choice to be widely introduced. Although the first alternative schools appeared during the Progressive Era, their numbers expanded rapidly during the cultural upheavals of the 1960s. During that decade, alternative schools became a means of both serving the special needs of students and experimenting with new pedagogical techniques. Because there is no set definition of alternative schools, estimates of the number of schools and students vary widely. Nevertheless, there is widespread agreement that large numbers of students are affected: Steel and Levine (1994), for example, argue that there are over 2,000 alternative schools in over 1,000 districts serving as many as 10 million students. Amy Stuart

Wells (1993) cites even higher numbers: between 3,000 and 6,000 public alternative schools.

In the 1970s and 1980s, magnet schools emerged as a new form of choice, largely in response to demands for desegregation. Many school districts created magnet schools to attract students from across the district and thereby achieve racially balanced schools while at the same time retaining students (mostly, white students) who might otherwise flee the public schools. Blank, Levine, and Steel counted over 1,000 magnet schools in 138 districts in 1982, and in a follow-up study in 1991, 2,433 magnet schools in 230 school districts serving 1.2 million students (Blank, Levine, and Steel 1996). Not surprisingly, magnet schools are found mostly in large and racially heterogeneous central cities. Based on the 1990 National Education Longitudinal Survey, Gamoran (1996) found students in central cities almost three times more likely to attend magnet public high schools than the national average.

While many students were given the right to choose through the development of alternative and magnet schools, these forms of choice were designed to work mostly within the traditional structure of education. They did very little to alter the relationship between students, parents, teachers, and administrators. In contrast, many reforms that have emerged in the last decade not only allow parents to choose schools, but also seek to shift power to parents across many different aspects of schooling and create more effective school communities. In many ways then, the choice movement has become far more ambitious in its mission and goals during the 1990s.

This transformation of the choice movement did not take place overnight. Rather, as choice options developed, some were eventually combined with new types of schools (e.g., mini-schools, new varieties of alternative schools). Many of these schools had well-defined pedagogical and curricular approaches and unified, overarching missions. Open enrollment choice plans were the first such reforms to make this transition to a more comprehensive educational movement, aiming to restructure school governance and the systemic transformation of school systems.

As with other school reforms, there is no strict definition for open enrollment and consequently there is no consensus about how many schools, districts, or students it encompasses. Henig estimates that there may be up to 1,200 districts serving close to 8 million students operating under some type of open enrollment program.

Early open enrollment programs (such as the ones we study in this book) affected schools within a single district (that is, they fostered intradistrict choice) and, while these programs were started for a variety of reasons, some were designed to stimulate innovation. Indeed, as we show in chapter 3, choice via open enrollment in New York City's District 4 was a conscious attempt to create a new atmosphere in a district where many schools were clearly failing. Over time, choice as a means of creating more effective school communities and instilling a sense of parental ownership of the schools became more manifest and a whole variety of innovations eventually flowed from open enrollment in District 4.

Interdistrict open enrollment plans, explicitly designed to affect the way in which schools are run, have become more common in recent years. Minnesota's Open Enrollment Program was one of the first such programs. Phased in between 1987 and 1990, this program allowed students to apply for schools in other local school districts. Local districts may deny applicants from entering their district only if space is unavailable or the racial balance in a school will be disturbed.

Several cities have adopted similar interdistrict choice programs. For example, in 1983, St. Louis adopted its plan as part of a settlement evolving out of desegregation litigation (LaPierre 1987). In 1993, at least partially in response to the success of choice in District 4, New York City adopted open enrollment across its thirty-two community school districts, though in practice such choice has been limited by lack of space in attractive schools.

While open-enrollment plans can lead to changes in the power relations in school systems, in recent years, the challenge to the school establishment inherent in choice reforms has escalated. This greater challenge stems from the growing use of vouchers and the rapidly expanding number of charter schools. Both reforms are clearly aimed at increasing the role of parents in school decision processes—and both are also designed explicitly to change the balance of power within the schools.

Vouchers

As is well known, the intellectual foundation for vouchers can be traced directly to Milton Friedman's early formulation (1962; chapter 6), a proposal rooted firmly in microeconomic theory. Efforts to launch an educational voucher program were frustrated for decades and despite hard work by federal officials anxious to develop empirical evidence about the consequences of vouchers, only one school district—Alum Rock, California—ultimately proved willing to engage in such an uncertain venture. Studies of the Alum Rock experiment are legion and there is still debate about the extent to which it succeeded. Indeed, there were so many conditions placed on the experiment that many voucher proponents argue Alum Rock was not really a legitimate test of vouchers (Mecklenberger and Hostrop 1972; Cohen and Farrar 1977; Salganik 1981; Henig 1994).

While interest in vouchers percolated among the policy community for years, John Chubb and Terry Moe (1990a) created the intellectual foundation for the current push for vouchers. Chubb and Moe's argument for vouchers gained widespread attention because they linked choice to a compelling theory of politics and democracy; broadening the audience, they based their analysis on empirical work and they developed an implementation plan for vouchers. In turn, Chubb and Moe succeeded in redefining vouchers from a conservative, microeconomic theory, to a broad-based practical approach to fixing the ills of education (Henig 1994, 87).

Chubb and Moe see vouchers as the means of freeing schools from the overly restrictive environment of the present bureaucratic organization. Specifically, they believe that vouchers have the capacity to create a publicly funded school system that is "almost entirely beyond the reach of public authority" (1990a, 216). In their plan, the entire school system would be driven by consumer choice and the quality of schools would be dependent upon the intelligence and diligence of parents. According to Chubb and Moe, "when it comes to performance, schools are held accountable from below, by parents and students who directly experience their services and are free to choose. The state plays a crucial supporting role here in monitoring the full and honest disclosure of information by the schools—but it is only a supporting role" (1990a, 217). The bottom up design of public schooling would purportedly force schools to be responsive to the needs and interests of students and parents rather than central administrators.

Though the full voucher system envisioned by Chubb and Moe is yet to be implemented in any school district in the United States, voucher programs are spreading rapidly. For example, privately funded scholarship programs serve over 13,000 students in more than 30 cities, including Dayton, Indianapolis, Milwaukee, New York City, San Antonio, and Washington, D.C. (Peterson 1998, 8). The Cleveland program is the first state-funded program to allow students to choose religious schools. And after several years of struggle in the court system, Milwaukee was able to expand its publicly funded voucher program to include religious schools in 1998.

Recall that the original impetus for vouchers came from Milton Friedman and other economists who were not interested in the "black box" that explains how markets and competition actually affect educational outcomes. Thus, they did not identify specific institutional processes that link vouchers to evidence of educational change and improvements. However, as vouchers spread, researchers from other disciplines began exploring the mechanisms linking vouchers to school communities. So while many arguments in favor of vouchers stop on the supply-side, arguing that schools will have to compete and offer distinct and better educational products, research documenting how vouchers can transform schools and create more vibrant school communities involving parents and students in decision making is now emerging. In contrast, the arguments in favor of charter schools have almost always been built on the idea of parental involvement as a key ingredient to more effective schools.

Charter Schools

While Friedman and, more recently, Chubb and Moe provided a strong intellectual foundation for the voucher movement, no such central theory exists for charter schools. Rather, the charter movement is evolving as a bottom-up reform, with a wide range of schools, themes, and approaches. One thing is clear: the number of charter schools is rapidly increasing. Minnesota adopted the first charter school law in 1991 and California followed in 1992. According to the Center for Education Reform, in 1999, there were close to 350,000 students attending about 1,700 charter schools in more than half of the states.

According to Bryan Hassel (1998), there are important differences between charter schools and vouchers. First, they differ on the issue of accessibility: in the ideal, charter schools would not select students on the basis of academic performance, sports, or other dimensions, but would instead be open to all students and, if oversubscribed, admission would be by lottery. Second, unlike voucher schools, which may require parents to pay at least a portion of the regular tuition, charter schools cannot charge tuition. Charter schools also differ from voucher school programs when it comes to accountability standards. While voucher programs set only minimal standards for schools, under charter reforms individuals or groups must petition some authoritative organization and be granted a charter in order to operate a school. A chartering agency can establish relatively rigorous standards and can close low-performing schools for failure to meet the terms of their charter. Thus, there is more central control in the charter school movement than in voucher programs, which rely almost exclusively on the "market" and parental choice to discipline schools.

To date, analysis of charter schools has largely focused on the legislative and political processes governing their creation. There is growing consensus regarding the components of good charter legislation. Perhaps the most important is the existence of multiple agencies, apart from the local school board, that are authorized to grant charters. Another critical element is whether or not limitations are placed on the number of charter schools that can be created. In addition, charter schools must have legal and fiscal autonomy and exercise control over their staffs. Based on restrictions in the number of schools and range of chartering agencies, it is possible to distinguish between "weak" and "strong" state charter legislation. Indeed, many states have weak charter laws and no charter schools.

The variation in state law makes it hard to define a typical charter school. In some cases, laws are clearly designed to make marginal changes in schooling arrangements, while in others the intention is to create a set of autonomous schools freed from centralized control, designed to meet the needs of parents and to increase their involvement in the educational process.

While charter schools have many distinctive curricula and philosophies, small size is common. In addition, charter schools are schools of choice and typically have high levels of parental involvement due to outreach activities. Some even require that parents become involved in certain school activities. Thus, charter schools are more responsive to the interests of parents and provide alternative models that might spur imitation and emulation by public schools. Empirical evidence has shown that parental satisfaction is high in charter schools and parents choose charter schools that match their interests.

In their study of parent attitudes toward charter schools, Vanourek et al. (1998) found that parents most frequently cited the following reasons for choosing charter schools: small size, high standards, educational philosophy, opportunities for involvement, and quality teachers. And, teachers choose charter schools for similar reasons.

Charter schools have emerged as a popular form of school choice partly because the ideals of the charter movement appeal to people with a broad range of ideological perspectives. Conservatives see charters developed under "strong" state laws as a step toward a more comprehensive voucher system that includes private schools. Liberals often see limited charters developed under "weak" state laws as a way to gain the flexibility of private schools without moving toward private vouchers.

An Evolving Theory of the Effects of Choice

While alternative schools, magnet schools, open enrollment programs, vouchers, and charters all expand the range of options available to parents, the earlier reforms stayed within the structure of the existing educational establishment and did not necessarily stimulate systemic change. However, we believe that recent reforms explicitly couple choice with broader challenges to existing institutional arrangements, seeking to empower parents not only with choice but with other rights as well. Today's choice reforms are viewed as essential to school governance and the creation of effective schools.

As we noted in our introduction, contemporary reforms share a vision of good schools and school systems that emphasize small, autonomous schools and a desire to create more "effective" school communities that bring parents, students, teachers, and administrators into cooperative, supportive relationships. But the emphasis on community ultimately and intimately links to reformers' concerns for high student performance; high performance becomes an aspect of schooling that is intertwined with the school's community, culture, and mission (Ravitch and Viteritti 1997).

Choice is often perceived as a means to achieve these goals by creating the incentives and pressures necessary to force schools to improve their performance. Unlike choice in a true market setting however, school choice is linked directly to the notion of governance, participation, and community (Brandl 1998; Hill, Pierce, and Guthrie 1997).

Choice as a Means of Changing School Governance

Chubb and Moe (1990) energized the discussion of choice by forging a clear link between choice, markets, and the power relationships between stakeholders in education. They argued that while school reform often has been considered an "insider's game," played by bureaucrats, administrators, and teachers, and fought over what appears to be technical issues such as testing, curriculum, and tenure, the bedrock issue is actually governance: who has the right to participate in decision making? Following Chubb and Moe, we start by exploring how choice affects fundamental governance arrangements.

We begin by developing three ideal types or models of how power relationships can be structured in the delivery of public services, and specifically education. These models, which we label as democracy, bureaucracy, and markets, each invest stakeholders with different powers and responsibilities and consequently emphasize different mechanisms in the functioning of schools.[3]

Our goal is to link power relationships to the organizational effectiveness of schools so that we may better assess how choice reforms are actually tied to the outcomes reformers seek: a functioning school community, higher levels of satisfaction, and improvements in performance. We believe that by focusing on the distribution of power in these three governance arrangements, we can understand how the organization of schools affects their outcomes. To examine the link between these different models of governance and the outcomes of schooling, we build on James Q. Wilson's (1989) analysis of organizational structure and effectiveness.

While Wilson believes there is no single best way to organize bureaucracies, he identifies three fundamental issues—*critical task*, *mission*, and *autonomy*—that he argues determine the effectiveness of various modes of organization. The *critical task* of any organization is the set of activities that, if successfully performed, permit it to cope with the environmental problems and issues it faces. An organization's *mission* relates to the way in which it defines its critical task. According to Wilson, when this definition is widely accepted and endorsed, the organization has a strong sense of shared mission. Finally, *autonomy* deals with the level of authority granted to (or sometimes asserted by) the organization and its members in making and implementing decisions.

Although schools may not always have an easy time identifying their critical environmental problems and the set of tasks needed to address these problems, for many schools an even more difficult challenge is achieving consensus. Given the complexity of education and the diverse interests of education stakeholders, dissent may develop around any set of actions a school pursues. This divisiveness can cripple the sense of mission and intensify conflicts. However, in order to develop a sense of mission, schools must cultivate the support of their staffs, parents, and students. This is often easier when schools are free to develop their own approach or theme to learning and when parents have the ability to choose a school for their children. When school officials, parents, and students can take pride not only in what the school is doing, but also in how it is doing it, they begin developing norms of commitment, trust, and reciprocity that ultimately enhance school effectiveness (see, e.g., Miller 1992).

Even if a school can define its critical task and cultivate a sense of mission, without sufficient authority to act and sufficient resources to implement plans, schools remain essentially powerless. Therefore, an essential ingredient in the organizational arrangement of any effective school is the autonomy to actually define tasks, allocate resources, and undertake actions necessary to infuse this definition with a sense of mission. Without autonomy, outside forces may implicitly define the critical task and mission of the school in an inappropriate manner. In short, for schools to be effective they ultimately need a degree of autonomy to take the actions necessary to address critical environmental problems.

These three elements of effective organizations are similar to those identified in research focused on schools, specifically what is broadly known as "effective schools" research. Stimulated by the work of Coleman and colleagues (1966; 1982; 1987), this body of research emerged in the mid-1980s seeking not only to identify school attributes that improve student performance, but also to understand how and why they do so. The critical school-level variables most often cited are a clear school mission, administrative autonomy, a cohesive curriculum, high expectations for students, instructional leadership, instructional time that maximizes students' opportunity to learn, parent contact and involvement, and widespread student rewards (Purkey and Smith 1983; Rowan, Bossert, and Dwyer 1983; Hallinger and Murphy 1986; James and Levin 1987; Hill, Pierce, and Guthrie 1997). Clearly, the factors identified by this research parallel both the vision of choice that reformers now articulate and the factors that Wilson identifies for effective governmental organizations.

In the rest of this chapter, we utilize Wilson's framework to evaluate the effectiveness of the different structures of school governance—democracy, bureaucracy, and market.

The Democratic Model for Organizing Schools

The notion of democracy based on the power of the vote is a familiar image. In the democratic model of education, voters and the officials they elect exercise primary power over schooling. Arguably, this system already exists in the United States—in fact, since education is provided by local governments, one could argue that we have a large variety of such systems in place. In many communities, voters directly elect members of the local school board and often vote on school budgets. In many cities, citizens also elect public officials who then appoint the top-level education decision makers. In the U.S., it is difficult to conceive of a publicly funded educational system that does not rely on at least some of these democratic elements of governance.

But there are questions about the applicability of the democratic model to schools. One issue relates to the kinds of educational decisions that should be made via the democratic process. Should this process simply provide a general framework, leaving school-level actors wide latitude to make more specific decisions, or should democratic processes govern these more detailed decisions as well? For example, who should decide which books to buy? Which courses to offer? Which teachers to hire?

A much more fundamental question concerns how the democratic model actually works in practice. Chubb and Moe (1990) provide a critique of the democratic process as it has developed in American school systems. One basic problem is that few people vote in local school elections. With a generally inattentive public, instead of real control by citizens, Chubb and Moe argue that powerful interest groups control the electoral process and subsequent school policy. In education, these powerful groups include teacher's unions, administrator's unions, or highly organized citizen groups who want to push a particular agenda within the schools. These groups often are able to impose their own ideals and preferences, rather than those of the majority, on the public educational system.

In many cities, especially large ones, the connection between voting for mayors and members of the city council, and their subsequent appointing of educational officials, is often quite tenuous, preventing clear-cut educational accountability. Mayors can blame school officials, these officials can blame the constraints elected officials put on them, and all local actors can blame state legislatures for not providing them with enough resources. The resulting "blame game" makes it difficult for average citizens to sort out the issues and, understandably, many do not even bother to try.

Elections and Participation in Mission, Task, and Autonomy

Given these processes, how does democracy affect a school's abilities to identify its critical tasks, develop a sense of mission, and achieve a level of autonomy appropriate to its needs?

In the ideal version of this democratic model of decision making, different groups in the community debate, discuss, and compromise on what kinds of education they want the public schools to deliver. Elections determine a slate of officials who represent these viewpoints in near proportion to the citizenry. Elected and top appointed officials then allocate resources to schools to help them meet their critical tasks. However, as noted earlier, democracy usually does not work in this manner. Low voter turnout, unclear lines of accountability through public officials, and information asymmetries allow well-organized groups to wield disproportionate influence. There may also be conflict between citizens without school-aged children, who as taxpayers are expected to help support the schools, and parents with children in the schools. Knowing they do not have a broad mandate, well-organized minority groups of whatever sort often attempt to use their political power to "hardwire" many issues, defining and constraining the actions of school-level officials.

Since these critical tasks are often defined in a top-down manner, it becomes difficult for schools to build a sense of mission around tasks they have not developed. Within a jurisdiction, all schools are assigned the same critical tasks from above, leaving little room for flexible responses to different environments. Schools are forced to implement the programs deemed appropriate by the majority, as long as these programs do not violate any constitutional or broader statutory concerns. But, and this is critical, a mission imposed from above is less likely to be embraced by a wide range of school-level actors.

Clearly, heavy reliance on policies generated through this democratic process limit school-level autonomy. In fact, a major goal of the democratic model is to *limit* autonomy by making key decisions in the voting booth and placing principal discretion in the hands of elected officials. Unless voters vote on every issue and the vote represents more than the usual blunt instrument, strong top-down control of schools by elected and high-level appointed officials results, leaving little room for school level autonomy.

The advantage of the democratic method is that it provides the opportunity for a majority of citizens in a jurisdiction to direct educational policy in a manner consistent with their preferences. In a system where public school costs are largely paid by local taxpayers, this is understandable. However, the reality of democratic politics for local schools often is quite different, and most analysts would agree that attempts at micromanagement of the schools through the democratic method of governance have not worked in the past and are unlikely to succeed in the future.

The Bureaucratic Model of Organizing Schools

While the democratic control of schools has produced a whole host of present-day failures, political intervention in the schools is not new. Earlier this century, it was common practice for political machines to treat schools as a source of patronage. Eventually, the Progressive Movement began to dislodge urban machines. As part of this movement, Progressive advocated decision making by professional educational administrators instead of politicians, and created a highly centralized bureaucratic model of schooling.

Democracy and bureaucracy are clearly intertwined, since bureaucratic organizations are charged with implementing policies developed via the democratic process. While we often accuse bureaucrats of creating their own rigidities, in fact, rules and constraints are often imposed upon bureaucrats by various actors in the democratic process (Wilson 1989). Indeed, Moe (1989) argues that political groups try to build their concerns and issues into the very structure of organizations and organizational processes, in order to constrain and control future outcomes. Chubb and Moe (1990a) argue that democratic processes have imposed a range of constraints that tend to blunt the initiatives of even the most well-meaning and entrepreneurial school-level actors. Thus, while the democratic and bureaucratic models are theoretically distinct, in the world of education, they have been intimately linked.

Under the bureaucratic model of education, schools are organized hierarchically and function within a broader system of checks and balances. This bureaucratic organization has been common in the United State for several decades. Indeed, the basic bureaucratic structures, rules, and practices of schooling have changed so little throughout this century that scholars often argue that they "have imprinted themselves on students, educators, and the public as the essential features of a 'real school'" (Tyack and Cuban 1995, 7).

The bureaucratic model of education emerged largely in response to the growing need to educate the masses of immigrant children arriving in the United States at the turn of the century and was "perfected" under the push for scientific management and Progressive reforms. Schools saw their critical task as one of establishing the most efficient means by which to prepare immigrant children for jobs in the rapidly industrializing economy. To accomplish this, they sought to provide a melting pot for the wide array of social, ethnic, and racial identities of immigrant students and to ensure that each student received the same basic education.

The Progressive reforms tried to depoliticize the frequently corrupt educational administration found in many cities that was a result of democratic ideas gone awry. Progressives often were able to replace untrained school board officials with professional administrators, analogous to city managers, who were expected to run school districts in a business-like manner, emphasizing principles of neutrality, responsiveness, and accountability. Thus, in the 1930s, experts schooled in the scientific management approach had succeeded in implementing their model of efficiency, uniformity, and standardization, starting the "one best system" of education in the United States.

Tensions were built into this structure. For example, while administrators emphasized accountability as the critical goal of educational establishment, the rise of professional administrators led to increasing demands for autonomy and discretion from school boards. In addition, the principles of hierarchy and standardization often came into conflict with the goals of responsiveness and efficiency. One element was clear: the organizational form of schools established under this reform movement came to depend increasingly upon the existence of a large bureaucracy (Knott and Miller 1987).

The bureaucratization of education insulated schools from external forces, while at the same time reduced the discretion of schools and their personnel. As Chubb and Moe (1990a, 46) note, "In a political environment permeated by diverse, threatening interests and powerful opponents, bureaucratization was the key to the Progressives' strategy of imposing their own values and protecting them from future subversion."

As bureaucratization proceeded, public education became subject not only to state and local controls, but to a vast array of federal laws, regulations, and court orders as well as. In addition, schools found that they must be responsive to several nongovernmental actors, including teachers' unions and civil rights organizations. As Hill (1995, 13) explains, all of this restricts the freedom of schools to develop effective programs:

> In many localities, court orders determine how much schools will spend, whether students will attend school in their own neighborhoods or elsewhere for racial balance, what services parents of children with disabilities can demand, and whether or not local districts can offer special programs for particular kinds of youngsters with particular needs. In many big cities, labor contracts (with teachers, administrators, and custodians) determine when schools will open and close, who will administer them, who will teach in them, and the limits of adult responsibility.

Therefore, although public schools are founded, financed, and operated mainly by state and local governments, they are not fully governed at this level. In fact, for a system that is so decentralized in terms of financing, schools across the United States illustrate a remarkable degree of uniformity and conformity in terms of decision-making processes regarding curriculum, teaching methods, staffing, student assignment, and student evaluation.

Bureaucratic Accountability in Mission, Task, and Autonomy

In this bureaucratic approach, central administrators, rather than individual schools, generally have the authority to make decisions about how to cope with environmental problems facing schools. Critical tasks are thus defined at the district level in an effort to prevent corruption, promote uniformity in standards and procedures, and ensure equal treatment across schools and interests. The assumption is that professional administrators are best positioned to identify the critical tasks of schools, formulate procedures for how they may be performed, and monitor how well schools execute these tasks.

Because accountability and neutrality are the driving principles of the bureaucratic model, centralized decision making is logical, as accountability and neutrality are more easily maintained and monitored. In addition, the critical task of ensuring all students receive the same basic education is easier under these centralized arrangements, where administrators play the greatest role in defining the mission of schools.

Throughout the twentieth century, as school systems, particularly in central cities, grew larger and more complex, the centers of decision making became more remote and detached from schools. Thus, the bureaucratized structure has prevented individual schools from identifying and pursuing their own mission.

The range of mandates and regulations imposed upon public schools also limits their autonomy. As Chubb and Moe (1990a, 46) remark: "True accountability for the schools—real discretion in important matters of policy—is the antithesis of the bureaucratic job and the ultimate threat to bureaucratic security." As a result of these constraints, the bureaucratic organization of schools leads to low marks on all three dimensions defining effective organizations and has limited the ability of schools to function as effective organizations.

Under centralized, bureaucratic administration, students are assigned to schools most often on the basis of their residential location. Consequently, students are often forced to attend schools they may not like. The inability to choose schools means students (and their parents) may have little in common with each other except residential propinquity. In reality, their preferences, needs, and demands may be quite diverse and schools must cope with these differences. Still, no matter how close schools actually come to meeting these demands, unsatisfied parents and students have little recourse other than moving to another school district or opting out of the public schools by paying tuition for private schools—choices that are unrealistic for many parents.

Moreover, in these bureaucratic systems, schools have almost no control over their faculties, arguably their most important resource. Instead teacher assignments to schools are typically determined centrally and/or by seniority. The inability of schools to choose teachers presents obstacles to providing coherent and appropriate educational programs and pedagogical approaches. Seniority rules and tenure systems exacerbate this problem by making it more difficult to remove ineffective, unmotivated, or uncaring teachers.

These bureaucratic incentive and reward structures emphasize top-down accountability to and compliance with the preferences of elected and appointed school officials. They do not emphasize bottom-up responsiveness to the preferences of individual teachers, parents, and students, who are the most meaningful, daily actors in the educational process.

Market-Like Approaches to the Organization of Schools

In the last few decades, the problems with large professionalized bureaucracy have been well documented and reform movements have sought to correct the problems of overly rigid bureaucratic structures (e.g., Osborne and Gaebler 1992). For example, the recent effort to "reinvent government" recognizes that past reforms have made many bureaucratic organizations excessively rule-bound. Reinventing government reforms have sought to fix these problems by making bureaucracies responsive to the demands of their "customers" (see Ruhil et al. 1999).

In the domain of schools, it has become common for advocates of choice to talk about the "market model" of schooling. However, as we make clear at several points in this book, we do not find this terminology fully satisfactory, since there are complexities and variations in the organizations of markets that are neglected by this term. Instead, here we use the term "market-like." In the next chapter we discuss in more detail the limitations of a market for schools that make the terms quasi-market or market-like more appropriate (also see Henig 1994). Our third model of governance thus incorpor; many but not all characteristics of markets.

While most forms of school choice are not exactly like private markets, they are based on mechanisms found in markets, especially decentralization, competition, and consumer sovereignty (Chubb and Moe 1990a). To the extent that these mechanisms are built into choice programs, market-like outcomes should flow, as parent-consumers are able to not only choose the schools their children will attend, but also determine where a share of society's educational resources will flow. Advocates hope that this demand side pressure will force all schools to compete for students, leading to better schools as winning schools thrive, as others emulate them, and as failing schools "go out of business."

As we noted in the historical review at the start of this chapter, choice allows parents to select the school their children attend. Under many choice plans, some or all resources devoted to a student flow to the chosen school. Thus, choice implicitly empowers parents to allocate resources across schools. If the supply-side of choice gives school-level actors greater autonomy in providing flexible educational programs, then schools have incentives to offer different pedagogical approaches and themes to meet the diverse needs and preferences of parents. With these dynamic elements built into the demand- and supply-sides, to the extent that the market model is appropriate, several identifiable positive outcomes should follow.

First, these market-like processes should lead to allocative efficiency—that is, parents should get more of what they want from the schools, and presumably experience greater satisfaction. But market-like competition among schools should also lead to greater productive efficiency. Competitive pressures provide schools with incentives to use the best available technologies to produce the highest quality product at the lowest cost. The process of natural selection further reinforces these incentives: if the quality of education produced by a school is markedly inferior to that of competitors, parent-consumers will opt out in favor of competitors, leading inefficient schools to change their programs or even shut down (Chubb and Moe 1990a, 190).

While we will investigate some implications and evidence of allocative and productive efficiency in later chapters, here we review briefly some important issues related to the institutional arrangements of markets that give rise to these outcomes. For competition to exist, there must not only be a sufficient number of schools available on the supply-side, but these schools must also represent distinctive educational options. After all, if all schools in a city are the same there would be little need for parental choice—one school could easily be substituted for another. At issue then is whether the range of quality schools can be expanded to adequately meet the needs and preferences of parent-consumers who comprise the demand-side (Hill, Pierce, and Guthrie 1997).

Suppliers must also know something about consumer preferences (Willms and Echols 1992; Levin 1989). In practice this is a dynamic process, relying on feedback. The extent to which allocative efficiency is achieved therefore depends in part on how well schools can identify, adapt to, or affect consumer tastes and preferences. In a market-like arrangement for schools, institutional structures should be in place to gauge parent preferences and needs. In fact, for schools to compete with each other they must not only identify parent-consumer demands, but they also must have the capacity and resources to act upon these demands, which requires flexibility and the means to be innovative. And, to keep up with changing demands and technologies, schools must have some control over budgetary resources, teacher selection, and the actual work that they do.

Choice in School Mission, Task, and Autonomy

As noted above, a fundamental limitation of the traditional bureaucratic model of schools is the highly centralized and standardized structure that prohibits schools from defining their own mission. Under the choice model, each school has the ability to identify its own distinctive objectives and organize in ways that maximize its ability to achieve these objectives. In effect, each school has the authority to specify its own contracts with parents and students. These contracts, which may be more or less explicit, articulate the school's mission, spelling out such things as the instructional emphasis of the school, its admission practices, and the teaching approach it embraces. With more flexibility, choice schools will be able to attract teachers who subscribe to this mission. Greater control over budgets, internal structures, and processes provides schools with the necessary autonomy to cope with their external environment and focus on performing their critical tasks.

Equally important is the extension and expansion of choice on the demand-side. Without choice, schools would be unable to establish the cohesiveness needed to pursue their missions and would be limited in their ability to organize in ways that best enabled them to perform their critical tasks. Thus, choice plays a critical role in enabling schools to establish a common mission. As Raywid (1989) notes, the extent to which teachers, parents, and students subscribe to the school's mission determines how well the school performs like a functional community.

From the perspective of teachers, choice provides schools with the capacity to minimize, if not eliminate, major sources of teacher dissatisfaction that exist under the traditional, bureaucratic model of schools. By granting teachers more responsibility and enhancing opportunities for professional development, choice increases autonomy and responsibility, which in turn diminish the negative aspects of teaching.[4] Moreover, the establishment of conditions that permit teachers to behave as professional educators increases the ability of schools to meet their critical tasks, thereby enabling them to deal with their environmental problems.

Like all of these methods of governance, choice has limitations. Most notably, the need for supply-side changes often has not been fully recognized. Some analysts argue that in many communities reforms that simply increase parental choice will not be sufficient. As Hill and Grover (1993, 248) note: "Choice, though important, is inadequate by itself as a school reform. The fundamental task in school reform is how to supply good schools, especially in the inner cities, where the schools are failing children. Giving parents the opportunity to demand good schools may be part of a reform strategy, but we've seen no evidence that demand itself calls up good schools from the vast deep. It doesn't."

We agree that increasing the supply of good schools and the range of choices they deliver for parents are critically important. In chapter 3 we show that this can in fact happen—at least in one district we studied, choice was associated with the creation of a number of thematically diverse "mini-schools," many of them quite excellent.

We also agree that simply giving parents the ability to choose these higher quality schools is not the whole story. Instead, granting parents greater control over entry and exit decisions is only one mechanism to empower them in education—parental involvement (or voice) in their schools is another. As we noted earlier in this chapter, school choice reforms have increasingly coupled this voice element with other more market-oriented measures in order create more effective schools. We believe that the two go hand-in-hand and that the effects of choice on mission, task, and autonomy actually foster more meaningful and sustained parental involvement in their schools. Because economists and other proponents of the market model have failed to look inside the "black box," they have not paid sufficient attention to *how* choice and related processes lead to gains in efficiency and performance. We address this limitation in the next chapter, where we develop our model of education reform in greater detail.

Conclusion

In recent years, a wide range of school reforms has attempted to provide parents with more choice, shifting greater power in the educational process in their direction. These reforms vary widely and debates about which are most appropriate are likely to continue. But they share at least one important element in common. While decision making processes derived from the democratic model and the bureaucratic model will always be somewhat necessary to govern American public schools, shifts in power toward parents provide a more bottom-up, consumer-driven model of public education. In theory, this shift can create a better match between what parents want and what they get from their schools, as well as better schooling outcomes.

Even though the market model may not apply fully to public schools, the central elements of this model—choice, consumer sovereignty, decentralization, and competition—can. Competition implies some innovation in the supply and organization of schools and in the products and services they deliver. Market mechanisms have a genius for matching the supply- and demand-sides in a decentralized manner that serves consumers' preferences.

In this chapter we have been concerned mostly with exploring the arrangements affecting the supply of schools and how those arrangements influence the tasks, mission, and autonomy that are developed at the school level. In the next chapter we shift our attention to parents (and by extension their children), who represent the demand-, or consumer, side of schooling. Specifically, we analyze the assumptions about parental decision making that must be met in order for choice to function effectively. From there, we recombine the two sides of the equation, illustrating the essential role that parent involvement plays in the creation of effective schools.

Chapter 2

Parent Behavior and the Demand Side
of School Choice

In chapter 1, we discussed the ways in which school choice changes the relationship between schools, parents, and students. While early school choice reforms were mostly concerned with expanding parents' ability to choose the schools their children attend, over time the choice movement evolved a theoretical perspective that calls for enhanced parental involvement and control over a whole host of other school-related activities.

As we explored this evolution, our main focus was on with the institutional arrangements affecting the schools themselves, including, for example, the number and range of schools. In short, we were concerned with changes in the supply-side of what many analysts call the market for schools created by choice. However, school reforms seek to energize this market-like arena not only by changing the behavior of schools, but also by changing the demand behavior of parents—giving them incentives to become better "shoppers" and unleashing the competitive forces associated with comparative shopping in an expanded and diversified market.[1]

Fundamentally, then, arguments in favor of school choice rest on the assumption that positive effects will flow from interactions between actors on the supply- *and* demand-sides of market-like settings. However, scholars and policy makers actually know very little about how parent-consumers learn about the quality of the schools. In particular, little is known about what sources parents use to gather information, how good that information is, and how parents use that information to find appropriate schools for their children. Scholars also know very little about the extent to which school choice actually affects the incentives of parents to become more involved in and informed about their schools. And, scholars know very little about how resulting patterns of behavior are influenced by demographic factors, such as racial and socioeconomic characteristics of parents. In this chapter, and indeed, throughout most of this book, we focus on these demand-side questions.

This change of focus is important for two fundamental reasons. First, the presence of multiple suppliers alone does not necessarily improve market outcomes. Consequently, arguments calling for an expansion in the number of schools from which parents can choose are simply not sufficient. Informed activity on the demand-side of markets is as critical to the functioning of markets as is competition on the supply-side. Second, regardless of the form or forms of choice society ultimately adopts, the resulting market for schools will, in many ways, be quite different than private goods markets. Thus, we need to clarify how the idea of markets helps our understanding of school reform.

Market Models Help, But . . .

It should be clear by now that we believe there is considerable value in using the market concept as an organizing principle for the study of school choice. The most important elements of that concept for choice are competition, decentralization, and consumer sovereignty. We believe that school choice can unleash these forces to improve the efficiency and performance of our schools. But (and this is a big but), we are uncomfortable with the simple (and often simplistic) application of the (often underspecified) market model to schools that is all-too-often advanced in support of school choice. We believe that proponents of choice frequently argue that choice will create "markets for schools" and they argue that these markets will increase school performance and efficiency without fully exploring the implications of this argument. Certainly giving parents more choice over their children's schooling should create more market-like environments in which parents get more of what they want from the schools and where competition increases pressure on the schools to do a better job. But, the term *market* is so loaded with implications that vary from observer to observer, that we need to develop the idea of a market for schools in more detail.

Markets and Schools

Generally, market approaches work best for the repeated trading of simple, homogeneous goods by many buyers and sellers. In such cases, reputations can develop, monitoring can be easily employed, relatively complete information exists on both sides, and transaction costs are low (Williamson 1985; Kreps 1990; Miller 1992; Schneider and Teske 1995). Markets also work best when there is easy entry and exit by suppliers. For private goods markets, the basic model is fairly robust to the relaxation of these assumptions.

However, education is a highly complex public good with multiple attributes, and any market for schools is characterized by incomplete information, a limited number of providers, and high transaction costs. Consequently, as Hill (1995, 129) notes: "The choice of a school is more akin to the choice of a family doctor or pastor than to the choice of a car dealer or grocery store." Moreover, elementary and secondary education is at least partly a public good since it is paid for jointly through taxes. The typical tight market linkage between direct payment and service received is attenuated—for example, individual parents cannot withhold payment for education, as they might be able to do for other goods, to put pressure on the supplier to meet their needs.

The fact that most parents care about their own child's education is obvious. However, many people also care about the education of other children with whom their children interact in classroom settings and with whom they will interact in the economy and polity of the future. Since a quality education is dependent on the coproductive behavior of students, teachers, parents, and other children, we must also push beyond the market model—which is built purely on individual behavior—to a concept of school communities, which we discuss at the end of this chapter.

Other dimensions of education must also be considered. For example, most parents are comparing a variety of school attributes at the same time—including good teachers, safety, high test scores, and the fundamental values of education a school embraces. In addition, rather than frequent shopping trips to a supermarket, parents typically have only one opportunity per year to choose their school—repeat choices are limited by the difficulty and disruption of changing schools during a given school year. Indeed, even annual changes of schools are disruptive.

Finally, information asymmetries abound, and because education is a highly complex good, the "production process" for educating children is not well understood even by experts. As we note in chapter 9, there is a large academic "industry" that is at loggerheads trying to identify the effects of different aspects of schools on student performance and earnings. If highly trained analysts have trouble agreeing about what aspects of schooling matter, how can parents feel well informed or confident that they are making the right choice?

In short, if we want to think of education as being delivered in a market, it is at the very least a complicated market, with important "nonmarket" elements. And simple market metaphors or vague references to the market model that appear in the literature gloss over these complexities and fail to explore the resulting complications adequately.

We want to bring more analytic force to bear on the demand-side of the market for schools by studying the complexity of parent demand. However, as we have just noted, parental demand for schools needs to be distinguished from parental demand for breakfast cereal. In exploring the difference in demand behavior, we first establish the importance not only of informed consumer behavior, but we also identify the need to explore the distribution of informed behavior across parent-consumers.

Moving Beyond the Market Model in the Search for Information

It is well known that in a market setting with only one supplier, consumers have little incentive to search for information because they have no choices. Similarly, a sole supplier has little incentive to be efficient or responsive to the demands of its clients. However, even in a market setting with multiple suppliers, if consumers have little information about services, suppliers still have few incentives to improve the quality of their product or avoid other inefficient monopolistic practices (Scitovsky 1950; Tirole 1994). Research has shown that more desirable outcomes emerge when even a relatively small subset of consumers search for information about the quality and prices of goods provided by alternate suppliers (Wilde and Schwartz 1979; Wilde 1981; Rhoades 1985; Teske et al. 1993; Tirole 1994). The question we investigate here is whether parent-consumers can increase the efficiency, productivity, and responsiveness of schools by engaging in more extended searches for information and acting on this new information.

Advocates of school choice often draw analogies to private markets, assuming that choice stimulates parents to shop around and gather information about the schools. In turn, these more informed consumers (parents) demand that suppliers (schools) improve the quality of the service they deliver (education). This analogy to the private market is far from perfect (see especially Henig 1994). The reasons for this imperfect fit are important to us. We identify several basic aspects of public goods that weaken the analogy between school choice and markets, and develop them in more detail throughout this chapter.

First, the flow of information about local public goods, including schools, differs from the flow of information about private goods. For many private goods, comparative price information is available simply by walking up and down the aisles of a supermarket or department store. Widely disseminated publications, such as *Consumer Reports*, provide unbiased information about the durability and quality of consumer goods. By contrast, information about local schools is more costly to gather, the nature of the good is more complex, and the quality of the product is harder to assess (Schneider 1999). Consequently, the level of ambient information in the school environment is lower and the distribution of information about educational products is uneven. In many market studies, researchers have found that while a subset of consumers is well-informed, most consumers have very low levels of information about the quality of goods. In addition, research has also shown that rather than gathering exhaustive information, consumers often use shortcuts to collecting information. We believe that these two findings even more accurately describe public goods markets.

Second, the basic assumption that consumers are "atomistic" actors operating independently of social networks and influences is seriously flawed when applied to markets for public goods. In fact, this assumption is an oversimplification of reality even in private markets (see Granovetter 1985; chapter 6 in this book). The kinds of networks in which individuals are embedded and the subsequent flows of school information to which they are exposed may be even more central to understanding how these education markets will work than in the analysis of private markets. Moreover, to the extent that networks are important to the flow of information about schools, systematic biases may exist in networks due to racial and socioeconomic stratification in schools.

Third, in the process of choosing a school, parents' search behavior and their "purchase" decisions are more complex than the private market exchange. For schools to be effective, parent participation and involvement is essential—that is, choosing a school is not a "single shot" event or "spot purchase," but instead the first step in creating strong schools. This complexity is compounded by the collective nature of schooling and its centrality to a democratic society.

As Henig notes, schools can provide a framework for a collective experience and a common reference point for parents—cementing the ties that bind citizens together. In private markets, individual consumer choice simultaneously creates efficiency and maximizes the welfare of both individual participants and society as a whole. But Henig also argues that school choice represents a retreat from "responsibility to a broader collectivity" (1994, 9) and the erosion of democratic capacity. Thus while choice and markets in the private sector operate in a mutually beneficial relationship, many critics argue that choice in schools will fundamentally erode the ability of individuals to work together in democratic settings. This is an important question in analyzing parental behavior (see chapter 11).

Thus, while much research on consumer search behavior in private markets focuses on activities before the purchase, in the domain of education, the purchase decision is far from the final action. The coproductive requirements of education and the link between schools and communities make parent behavior after the choice of a school as important as the act of choosing itself.

We believe in the organizing and analytic power of the market as applied to the study of school choice, but we recognize that the market metaphor is limited by at least these conditions. Thus, while we believe that we must go beyond the market to address these concerns, we begin our analysis by following the basic model of consumer behavior. After establishing this basic benchmark, we move beyond this simple model to investigate the complexity of school choice.

Information Levels and Consumer Behavior in Public and Private Markets

Though efficient markets, both public and private, clearly need a core of informed consumers, there is a difference between saying that there must be a *core* of informed consumers and saying that *perfect* information must exist or that *everyone* in the market must be informed.

Virtually all markets, even the most competitive ones, operate without complete information. While the institutional arrangements of competitive private markets reduce the costs of gathering information, research has demonstrated that the level of consumer information about private goods sold in competitive markets is surprisingly low (see, for example, Claxton et al. 1974; Fiske and Taylor 1984; Bloch, Sherrel, and Ridgway 1986; Bettman 1986; Cohen and Chakravarti 1990; Kardes 1994; Tybout and Artz 1994). Yet even with limited information many of these markets are quite efficient (Stigler 1961; Friedman 1962; Nelson 1970; Akerlof 1970; Wilde and Schwartz 1979; Wilde 1981; Rhoads 1985; Kardes 1994).

According to economic theory, markets with a greater number of informed consumers are more likely to provide desirable outcomes. The factors leading to a cadre of informed consumers of education are defined at both the level of the individual and at the level of institutions. At the individual level, existing research on school choice has already documented some of the factors related to informed choice—education and involvement levels of parents, and parents' experience with choice. While individual-level characteristics are exogenous to the schools, other factors are the product of the institutional design of the local school system—for example, the range and type of choice presented. Other factors affecting information levels among parents are the products of the actions of the schools themselves—for example, the extent of school outreach activities.

Many institutional theories are driven by the idea that the incentives built into different institutional arrangements will affect individual decision processes. This suggests that individual parents will engage in more thoughtful and purposeful choice processes when school systems are designed to make their choices matter more. As evident from the following quote, Chubb and Moe make this link the cornerstone of their argument for school choice:

> In a system where virtually all the important choices are the responsibility of others, parents have little incentive to be informed or involved. In a market-based system, much of the responsibility would be shifted to parents (their choices would have consequences for their children's education), and their incentives to become informed and involved would be dramatically different. (1990a, 564)

Coons and Sugarman make the same point, but much more colorfully: "In a system with no options, ignorance might be bliss. In a system based on choice, ignorance is ruin" (1978, 188).

The connections among choice, incentive, and behavior have great intuitive appeal; however, the empirical evidence supporting these links is actually sparse. Consequently, identifying the effects of incentives on parent behavior is a central task in our investigation of choice. Moreover, while most studies of consumer choice focus on individual-level decision making, we expand the analysis of choice behavior beyond the individual. We ultimately seek to identify how the characteristics of markets and the social context of school choice interact with individual capacities and behaviors. Thus we move from a simple model of individual-level choice to the exploration of links between the micro-(individual) level of choice and the macro-

(institutional) level performance of markets (see also Teske et al. 1993; Lowery et al. 1995).

A Basic Individual-Level Model of School Choice

Our model of school choice begins with a simple set of assumptions that parallel those embodied in basic rational choice models of decision making. We then add complexity to this model by integrating observations and findings from studies in several other disciplines and by examining individual-level processes surrounding the complicated decision-making context of school choice.

Our model has four basic components. First, we recognize that education is a complex multidimensional good. We expect parents can articulate their general preferences over different aspects of the educational product of the school, including the school's goals, teaching approach, or philosophy. Parents should also have preferences over other related factors, such as the location of the school and the demographic characteristics of the student body. Like most models of markets, we assume that parents' preferences for different aspects of education and schooling are based on a variety of personal and societal factors—and are therefore exogenous to the market itself.[2]

Second, we expect parents facing choice to learn about the schooling options available in their district, utilizing the information sources they find most useful and easiest to access. This information can be gathered and integrated in a variety of ways. Here the institutional arrangements of the market for schools begin to matter. From a simple benefit/cost perspective, the amount of search and subsequent information parents have about their options should be contingent upon whether or not they have choice: parents with choice have greater incentives to gather more information about the schools than do parents without choice.

Third, we expect parents to make a choice that enrolls their child in a school that is performing well on the educational attributes they find important. For example, other things equal, parents who value ethnic diversity in their children's schools should enroll their children in a school with a diverse student body, while parents who value academic performance should enroll their children in a school with high test scores. The institutional rules of choice in any given school district (e.g., racial balancing, minimum academic test score requirements) may not allow parents to achieve their first choice. In this case they would presumably try to achieve their second choice, and so on.

The fourth component is a feedback mechanism between the choice process and the parents. We argue that parents gain a greater sense of empowerment by being involved in the choice process, which should influence their subsequent involvement with the schools. This feedback adds complexity to a school choice process already complicated by the public good nature of education and the importance of trust and coproduction between parents, children, teachers, and school officials. As we will demonstrate, these characteristics make the task of choosing schools quite different than shopping for cereal in the local supermarket.

Choice at the Individual Level

The simple model of choice just described centers on the individual as decision maker. Simon notes that any realistic model of rational behavior must "describe a person who is limited in computational capacity, and who searches very selectively through large realms of possibilities in order to discover what alternative actions are available, and what the consequences of each of these alternatives are" (1986, 295).[3] One of our goals is to specify the factors that affect the ability of individuals to engage in this "procedural" or "boundedly rational" behavior and to identify whether school choice affects the incentives of parents to behave rationally.[4] However, while traditional economic models assume full information, our work incorporates the idea that citizens can utilize shortcuts to get enough information to make appropriate choices

Do Citizens Have Less Information than Consumers?

While social scientists have long noted that citizens have scant information about public goods (see, for example, Althaus 1995; Graber 1989; Iyengar 1989; Sniderman, Brody, and Tetlock 1991; Zaller 1992; Popkin 1991; Lupia 1992, 1994; Lindeman 1996), many models of competitive private markets assume that consumers have full information. Yet, empirical evidence regarding information levels in private markets indeed points in a different direction—and one more similar to the situation for public goods and politics than many would realize. According to Kardes: "The typical consumer is exposed to a relatively small subset of available information about products and services, and the consumer attends to an even smaller subset of information to which he or she has been exposed. Not all information is encountered, and not all encountered information is attended to and processed" (1994, 400).

Many studies of information search also find that "consumers have surprisingly little enthusiasm for the pursuit [of information], even when buying expensive or socially risky goods" (Bloch, Sherrel, and Ridgway 1986, 119). In short, even in private goods markets, consumers typically spend little time gathering and analyzing information about the products and services they purchase (see, e.g., Fiske and Taylor 1991; Bettman 1986; Cohen and Chakravarti 1990; and Tybout and Artz 1994).

Fewer studies have examined the nature of the information held by individuals making choices in public goods markets. There is, however, considerable research documenting the scant information citizens hold regarding their electoral choices. Dating back to at least as early as Lazarsfeld, Berelson, and Gaudet's classic study in 1944, political scientists have shown that most citizens have extremely poor information about their political choices. The evidence is so consistent that Bartels (1996, 194) suggests "The political ignorance of the American voter is one of the best documented data of modern political science."

Since electoral politics are removed from the daily world of most citizens, some analysts have argued that the knowledge of candidates might be lower than their knowledge about the *policies* of government that may directly affect them. As Kuklinski et al. (1996, 4) note, research on citizen knowledge has been "overwhelmingly" weighted toward the study of processes, institutional structures, and the names of politicians, and "researchers have rarely asked for factual knowledge about policy." However, in their exploration of citizen knowledge of specific policies, Kuklinski, Metlay, and Kay (1982) found that even following the accident at the Three Mile Island nuclear power plant, few citizens were well informed about basic issues of nuclear power. In more recent work examining citizen knowledge of welfare, Kuklinski et al. (1996) find a citizenry woefully misinformed about basic aspects of that policy. More generally, Zaller dismisses the suggestion that citizens are likely to learn more about matters important to them, arguing that the "tendency appears not to be very great or very widespread" (1992, 18; see also Price and Zaller 1993; but see Delli Carpini and Keeter 1996).

Not surprisingly, these issues have emerged in the study of school choice. A recent Twentieth Century Fund report argued that parents are not "natural 'consumers' of education" and that "few parents of any social class appear willing to acquire the information necessary to make active and informed educational choices" (Ascher, Fruchter, and Berne 1996, 40–41).

In contrast to Ascher, Fruchter, and Berne's broad indictment of parental search behavior, a more common argument about parent information levels focuses on potential race and class biases in both the flow of information and quality of subsequent decisions. Bridge concisely (1978) articulates this point, calling the lack of information the "Achilles' heel" of voucher systems and arguing that "If socially disadvantaged target groups lack the information to make informed decisions, they will make choices based on educationally irrelevant grounds (e.g., emotional responses to hucksters' advertising), and the social equity objectives of the program will be missed" (506).

Indeed, data from the Alum Rock demonstration program showed that awareness of the voucher program was lower among parents with less formal education and those who had lower expectations for their children's educational attainment. And, a survey of parents in Montgomery County, Maryland (Henig 1996) found that, even among parents whose children attended magnet schools, many, especially minority parents, responded that they had never heard the terms "magnet school" or "magnet program."

Thus, many analysts who criticize choice argue that because less-educated parents will have the greatest difficulty making informed decisions, choice will exacerbate social stratification (see Boyer 1992; Bridge 1978; Catterall 1992; Levin 1989; Rose-Ackerman 1992; Henig 1994).

The Benefits and Costs of Gathering Information about Public Goods

One explanation for such low citizen information levels is that the search for information is costly. All decision making involves both benefits (decision accuracy) and costs (cognitive effort), and individuals can be viewed as "cognitive misers" seeking to minimize costs while maximizing rewards (see, for example, Simon 1986; Fiske and Taylor 1991; Sniderman, Brody, and Tetlock 1991; Lodge and Stroh 1993). This view of individuals has led many social scientists to explore the role of decision aids—shortcuts and heuristics—in helping individuals acquire the information they need to make informed choices.

Shortcuts to Decisions

The idea of shortcuts to decisions is not new. For example, Popkin's concept of the "reasoning voter" roots the question of information acquisition in a benefit/cost framework (Popkin 1991). Central to his argument is the concept of "low information rationality," which refers to a method of economically combining learning and information from past experiences, daily life, the media, and political campaigns (1991, 7). The reliance on heuristics and information generated as a by-product of other aspects of life make citizen choices much more rational than are typically portrayed.

Similarly, Kuklinski and Hurley (1994) argue that there is growing evidence that the use of heuristics, specifically taking cues from political elites, serves citizens well. Underlying this "new optimism" is the "idea that ordinary citizens can make good political judgments even when they lack general political acumen or information about the specific issue at hand by taking cues from political actors" (1994, 730). Lupia and McCubbins (1998) also address this issue, criticizing the commonly held belief that individuals need the equivalent of encyclopedias in order to make reasoned choices. Lupia argued that: "As an alternative to the costly acquisition of encyclopedic information, voters may choose to employ information shortcuts. For example, voters can acquire information about the preferences or opinions of friends, coworkers, political parties or other groups, which they may then use to infer how a proposition will affect them. The appeal of these information shortcuts is that they generally require relatively little effort to acquire" (1994, 63).

Lupia and McCubbins (1998) extend this position, arguing that in contrast to "encyclopedic knowledge," citizens can acquire "ability knowledge" even with selective attention and cognitive limits. Lupia and McCubbins argue that "by forming simple and effective strategies about what information to use and how to use it, people can make the same decisions they otherwise would if they were expert" (1998). In this approach, people who lack detailed information not only use simple cues, but are also systematic, selective, and strategic about the cues they do use (See Payne, Bethran, and Johnson 1993; Simon 1957; Beach and Mitchell 1978, on effort and accuracy in problem solving).[5]

Unfortunately, this relatively straightforward benefit/cost approach to low information rationality is complicated by characteristics that define the local market for schools. First, in markets for public goods, such as education, understanding the distribution of consumer knowledge is particularly important because these markets are often stratified by race and class and are almost always defined by limited geographic scope (Schneider 1989). There may, in effect, be multiple markets for local public goods, and differences in consumer information levels and behavior across these submarkets may be critically important.[6] In addition, equity concerns in the use of public goods are far greater than in private markets or even the electoral arena. This makes a demand-side focus of the market for public goods even more important.

Institutional Arrangements and the Benefits and Costs of Information

Another complexity in modeling individual choice behavior is that the calculation of benefits and costs is driven by the extent of alternatives in a market. In any market with limited choice, consumers have few incentives to gather information, because there are minimal benefits flowing from the (often costly) search. Because so many private markets are competitive, the incentives for choice in these markets are often taken as given. Yet in public goods markets, incentives for choice vary widely, and clearly are a function of the institutional design of the market and the degree of effective choice provided.

In the domain of schooling, incentives to engage in the search for information vary across the range of options parents have. In neighborhood school systems based on zoning, the incentives for searching are minimal. In contrast, in market-like systems, such as voucher programs, the incentives for gathering information are high. Rather than assuming that there are incentives to gather information, we must recognize that such incentives are contingent on the school system in which a parent is located.

This returns us to Chubb and Moe's position on existing levels of ignorance about school performance: parents with no choice over their children's schools may have little information about school performance because there are no benefits from engaging in search activity. Thus, we need to model parental search behavior as a function of institutional design and the differential "stakes" that parents have to become informed about schools.

What Drives the Search for Information?

The study of individual choice often resembles a cross-disciplinary debate between economists with their model of rational choice versus psychologists and sociologists with alternative models and lists of biases they argue must be addressed. Many of these conditions are a function of the cognitive ability of individuals facing choice and the complexity of the choice facing those individuals.

We believe that individuals can manage complex decision tasks by using heuristics (or "rules of thumb") to simplify the decision making process and minimize effort. Heuristics affect the way in which individuals both gather information and combine information to make decisions. The use of heuristics, however, may lead to systematic biases in decisions, thereby reducing accuracy.

Behavioral decision researchers have demonstrated that people have a repertoire of strategies for solving problems of varying complexity.[7] These strategies are acquired through some combination of training and past experience with decision making. Thus, when selecting decision rules, decision makers use a strategy that is sensitive to effort, as well as other costs and benefits.

Psychologists suggest that some individuals will not necessarily respond to the kinds of incentives provided by school choice (Tversky and Kahneman 1986; Payne, Bettman, and Johnson 1993). While incentives can lead individuals to pay more attention to alternatives and to work harder to make good choices, if their decision strategy is flawed, incentives by themselves may not lead to better decisions. While there are many theoretical schemes that seek to identify the factors affecting this search for information, we structure our approach around the basic framework developed by Delli Carpini and Keeter (1996).

Ability, Motivation, and Opportunity in Information Gathering

Delli Carpini and Keeter (1996) argue that individuals' information about politics and public policy is a function of their ability to process information, their motivation to get information, and their opportunity to use the information. There is little society can do to change the fact that some individuals simply have more education, time, and skills to devote to finding and utilizing effective information. As Rose-Ackerman (1992), Henig (1994), Levin (1991), and others have noted, the ability to gather information to make effective school choices is not uniformly distributed across society, which may increase socioeconomic stratification and racial segregation.

Motivation is somewhat more complicated. In their studies of consumer motivation, Beatty and Smith (1987) found that search is influenced by the perceived benefits of search, demographics, and previous product knowledge. The same kind of individual variation is also found within any institutional setting governing schools: some individuals will be more motivated to learn about their children's education under any circumstances. Proponents of choice argue that choice increases the average level of parent information, because choice links levels of information and desired outcomes.

Opportunity relates more to the supply-side of the equation. In private markets, Beatty and Smith (1987) found evidence that marketplace factors, such as store distribution, influence consumer information search. While the public schools we visited in our study make some information about their programs and performance available, they do not advertise and most do not engage in any systematic outreach efforts. And much of the information needed to evaluate the schools is often difficult to compile and to interpret. For example, it literally took us months to assemble a data base on the performance of schools in New York City.

Opportunity is driven by context. For example, the suburban context in which our New Jersey survey respondents live may provide parents with better opportunities for interacting with school officials, in part because the social "distance" between teachers and parents is much shorter compared to the inner-city districts we studied. At a minimum, in the suburban districts, differences in the level of education of teachers and the average citizen are much less than in the inner city (in District 1 only 17 percent of parents have any college education, in District 4 only 7 percent; in contrast, 58 percent of parents in Morristown and 65 percent of parents in Montclair have at least some college education). This may reduce the barriers to seeking out information from institutional sources.

Opportunity is also a function of the attitude of the schools toward the community. Here the city/suburban difference may be less important than the ethos and commitment of the schools in a district. For example, serious efforts at community outreach have marked the evolution of school choice in New York's District 4. Among its many outreach tools, the district has produced attractive brochures (in both Spanish and English) describing the school options parents have. In addition, the district encourages parents to attend school fairs, where schools provide information about their programs. Parents and perspective students are encouraged to visit the schools that interest them most and ask questions. More generally, in many other districts, parent information centers have been found to be highly effective in disseminating information to parents at a low cost.

How Many Informed Consumers Are Needed to "Make a Market"?

Obviously, increasing levels of parental information about schools is important. A larger number of informed consumers should increase the efficiency of any market. However, we believe that the debate regarding sufficient levels of information and the effects of choice on information levels may itself be misinformed.

Chubb and Moe, Coons and Sugarman, and others seem to imply that choice will lead to better schools by creating the conditions under which *all* parents will have incentives to become informed about schools, thereby generating competitive pressures on schools. We argue that this perspective overstates what we should *expect* from the average parent. But more importantly, we think this perspective overstates what is *necessary* to generate competitive pressures and desirable outcomes.

Competitive markets do not need *all* consumers to be informed; rather, competitive pressures can result even if a relatively small subset of consumers engage in informed, self-interested search. In this light, we argue that one of the major benefits of the creation of school choice in inner-city school districts is the creation of conditions that allow a set of parents, who we term "marginal consumers," to play an enhanced role in choosing and governing the schools.[8] As in any market-like setting, these marginal consumers create pressure on all suppliers in the market to improve performance.

But efficient performance isn't the only consideration in education. Many scholars are concerned that if only some parents become informed and then school choice gives them the opportunity to act on this information, these parents will make choices that will ultimately harm the children of less informed parents. Specifically, many analysts argue that these more informed parents will choose the best schools and leave the uninformed behind in the worst ones. We believe that this argument ignores the possibility that competition can force other schools to improve. Thus a critical question, which we address later in this book, is whether or not these informed consumers do in fact increase the efficiency of educational outcomes for everyone or just for themselves.

Providing education through market-like mechanisms is clearly complex. Important theoretical concerns abound and many of these issues have been addressed by scholars in different disciplines who do not normally "talk" with each other. The difficulty of studying school choice is made even more complex because ideological issues often affect the investigation of the relationship between school choice and the quality of education. One further complication that we add to this mix is the importance of the social context of school decision making. We must recognize that parent-consumers are not always autonomous actors, but are instead subject to social influence when making decisions.

Information and the Socially Embedded Decision Maker

Although economists generally have treated information gathering as an activity conducted by autonomous individuals, a growing number now recognize that the ability of consumers to learn from the behaviors of others is relevant for many markets (see, e.g., Leibenstein 1950; Becker 1974; Pollak 1976; Becker 1991; Bikhchandani, Hirshleifer, and Welch 1992; Banarjee

1992; Ellison and Fudenberg 1993; Hirshleifer 1993; Cosgel 1994; Smith and Sørenson 1994a, 1994b). However, much of this work on social learning still implicitly assumes that consumers have considerable autonomy over the acquisition and use of information. We believe it is necessary to more explicitly add social context and social interactions to the study of individual behavior by examining social networks.

Social Networks and Information Flows

While network analysis is now increasingly used by economists, political scientists, and market researchers, sociologists first employed this perspective to study how information is structured and conveyed.[9] Baron and Hannan examine the different underlying assumptions of network theory:

> Social network analysts reformulate economic theories by supplanting atomistic notions of information and action with tangible network structures of social relations. Economists tend to treat information as a commodity, which actors can accumulate (by purchasing it in a market or through investment), and they focus on distinctions between public and private information. Sociological accounts, in contrast, see the availability, nature, and value of information as *products*, often unintended, of social relations. In this view, it may not be possible to de-couple the information from its social structural base; nor would the information be available to actors, regardless of their level of investment or search, absent the social connections that provide access to the information in the first place. (1994, 1132–33)

Sociologists developed network analysis first for "closed" organizations, and gradually expanded their analysis to more open social systems (see, e.g., Cartwright 1965; Knoke and Kuklinski 1982; Marsden, Cook, and Kalleberg 1994). Granovetter (1985) provided the justification for greater attention to the socially mediated ways in which individuals obtain information and make choices. He argued: "Actors do not behave or decide as atoms outside a social context, nor do they adhere slavishly to a script written for them by the particular intersection of social categories that they happen to occupy. Their attempts at purposive action are instead embedded in concrete, ongoing systems of social relations" (1985, 487).

This insight leads to two key assumptions of the network approach. The first is that any individual typically participates in a social system involving many other actors who are "significant reference points in another's decisions" (Knoke and Kuklinski 1982, 9). The nature of the relationships between a given actor and other network members may affect that focal actor's perceptions, beliefs, and actions. The second assumption is that there are empirical regularities in the patterns of relations of network members, which produce differences in the quality of individuals' networks.

An important question is the degree to which individuals can choose their networks, perhaps in response to choice, or whether their social context strictly defines with whom they interact. In chapter 6, we examine the construction of discussion networks centered on schools.

Implications of the Level and Distribution of Knowledge about Schools

This general discussion of information has several important implications for our exploration of school choice. First, a combination of factors drives parents' decision process. Among the most important factors are the context of choice, the incentives to choose, and the individual characteristics of parents. Second, it is likely that, rather than acquiring a complete set of information about all schools and all dimensions of education, most parents use various shortcuts to making decisions. Some of these shortcuts are more efficient than others in terms of generating accurate information at a relatively low cost. Thus, in later chapters, we examine the use of different sources of information by parents, the use of various heuristics, the use and makeup of educational discussion networks that parents have, and the two-step flow of information from more informed parents to others. Third, even given increased benefits built into extended choice, not all parents will become informed about their options. In subsequent chapters, we explore how these patterns affect the efficiency and the equity implications of the market for education.

Information levels, the distribution of information, and the role of social networks all add complexity to the study of school choice from a market perspective. These complexities all precede the act of choice. However, there is another aspect of schooling that follows the act of choice that must be built into any study of school choice.

The Importance of School Communities: What Happens after Choice Matters

What happens between citizen/consumers and producers over time affects the quality of many public goods, especially education. The notion that schools are communities where individuals continue to interact beyond the initial "market choice" must be integrated into the development of any model of the educational process. Specifically, we think that there are two processes that must be integrated into the model of choice.

First, coproduction among citizens and between citizens/consumers and providers is needed for the successful provision of many public goods. In addition, trust between citizens/consumers and providers is essential in the repeated interactions and coordination necessary for the production of complex public goods.

Because much of the educational process takes place at home, schools are unlikely to succeed without the active assistance of parents, both in school activities and at home. The goal of coproduction is to make the relationship between parents, students, and teachers more cooperative and interdependent (see, e.g., Gittell 1980; Henig 1994, 187; Marschall 1998; Ostrom 1996).

As Ostrom (1996, 1079) points out: "If students are not actively engaged in their own education, encouraged and supported by their family and friends, what teachers do may make little difference in the skills students acquire."

Coproduction is important in the provision of public goods other than education, including community policing efforts (for example, Neighborhood Watch and Crime Stoppers), or sanitation removal programs that depend on curbside recycling or residents transporting waste to specific areas for collection. Although scholars initially viewed coproduction as a means to increase efficiency in the delivery of public goods, recently attention has shifted to how coproduction can improve the quality of public goods and services (e.g., Percy 1984; Brudney 1984). While the term coproduction is not used often by charter school proponents, clearly the intense involvement of parents sought by charter schools seeks to achieve the benefits of coproduction.

Coproduction, and the trust that follows, can help stimulate participation, develop a more knowledgeable citizenry, and enhance public confidence in governmental processes and institutions (see Berry, Portney, and Thomson 1993). Through the participatory experiences inherent in coproduction, individuals receive training on how to become better citizens (Gittell 1980). In a wide range of production processes, trust can reduce costs and enhance the level of social capital necessary to the functioning of markets and democracy (e.g., North 1990; Putnam 1993; Fukuyama 1995).

Do similar processes hold in school choice? We believe that trust between parents, children, teachers, and administrators is critical for high-quality education, especially since much of school activity takes place out of view of parents and can not be monitored fully (on the importance of these aspects of transactions see Williamson 1985; Kreps 1990; in the context of school choice see Coons 1992). Thus, we argue that the role of coproduction, trust, and social capital must be built into the application of market models to the choice process (see chapter 11 below).

Coproduction and Trust Can Shape More Effective Schools

The importance of coproduction and trust requires scholars to go beyond the market model to understand how institutional arrangements influence activities inside and outside of schools. Here we link these concepts with the discussion of effective schools we presented in chapter 1.

Children learn from their teachers, but they also learn from other children in their classes and from their parents. The broader community also has a stake in this learning process. These facts require parents to become more involved in schooling and highlight the importance of shifting power away from central administrators toward school building, classrooms, and homes (e.g., Chubb and Moe 1990). Simple market metaphors do not capture these fundamentally important elements.

We believe that schools should be viewed as *communities* in which all members must take a more active role. And successful choice reforms encourage these interactions. In addition, parents should have a voice in the structuring and functioning of their child's school. In short, school reforms must be evaluated from a perspective that considers choice *and* voice.

While many analysts fear that choice will break apart communities, the kind of parental participation that choice requires can contribute to community development. Activities that provide opportunities for discussion and deliberation and allow citizens to engage in face-to-face interaction foster norms and values that enhance the ability of groups and individuals to work toward collective goals (Ostrom 1990; Axelrod 1984; Olson 1965).

Choice and Voice Affect School Mission, Task, and Autonomy

In chapter 1 we explored how the democratic, bureaucratic, and market models of governance in education affect the missions, tasks, and autonomy of schools. Here, we need to analyze how school systems that encourage parental choice and voice in the school community compare to these models.

The school mission is strongest in an organizational form that emphasizes community, since the process of identifying and sustaining the purpose of schools rests in the hands of those closest to the educational process. Teachers, parents, and students are given the right not just to choose their own schools, but to actively participate in shaping a whole set of school attributes in accordance with their ideas. Because both parents and school personnel contribute to providing the "educational product," the school environment is characterized by mutual support and assistance.

As Coleman (1990) points out, the incentives of parents to aid, complement, and reinforce schools in their missions are not only an asset for children, but also an asset upon which schools are heavily dependent. When schools have parental support they are more likely to function as communities since social norms are broadly shared and consistently reinforced.

The strong sense of mission afforded by the community organization of schools enhances their effectiveness, which in turn can improve student outcomes. In addition, coproduction built on choice and voice provides enough flexibility to enable parents and school personnel to respond to emerging needs. By relying on the reciprocal responsibilities of the schools' students and adults, schools are better situated to perform their critical educational tasks. Henderson (1987, 1) argues that "the evidence is now beyond dispute: parent involvement improves student achievement. When parents are involved, children do better in school, and they go to better schools." Henderson also cites many studies that show that, in addition to home involvement, parents must also be involved at all levels in school, especially parents in low-income and minority families.

Finally, when emphasizing choice and voice, it follows that schools must have sufficient autonomy to make decisions about the critical elements of schooling. Though many agree that schools should always be subject to state and federal laws regarding such things as safety, health, and civil rights, for pedagogical and organizational matters, it is also widely believed that schools should be accountable to the people most affected by their performance—parents, students, and the local community.

No single institutional structure is likely to work best in all settings and there are problems with the coproduction model. While choice systems can force parents to choose a school, they cannot necessarily force parents to become an integrated element of a stronger school community (even though some choice schools require explicit parent involvement). This approach depends in part on the resources available to both institutions and communities. Civic capacity—which Henig defines as "the ability [of communities] to build and maintain an effective alliance among institutional representatives in the public, private, and independent sectors to work toward a common community goal" (1994, 220)—is particularly important. A community characterized by a vibrant civic arena already possesses many of the kinds of resources that are needed to make the choice and voice model function properly.

Another problem is that coproduction requires considerable change in relationships between stakeholders. While individual teachers may find many benefits ensuing from greater parental involvement, this involvement may correspond to interactions that are less predictable than under a more bureaucratic approach. As Wilson (1989) notes, resistance on the part of organizational members, such as teachers and administrators, is particularly common when innovation entails redefining core tasks or relations.

Despite these challenges, coproduction and choice and voice reforms hold the potential for improving America's schools. However, these reforms illustrate the continuous and complex interactions that are necessary when the supply- and demand-sides of the market model of education are brought together.

Conclusion

In this chapter we have argued that the demand-side of reforms such as school choice is just as important as the supply-side. However, much less is known about the demand-side of school reforms. The ways in which school choice alters parents' incentives and in turn affects their behavior is the focus of most of this book.

As we examine the effects of school choice, we begin with a basic microeconomic approach to consumer information, yet recognize that microeconomics typically focuses on the "average" consumer. We also incorporate insights from psychological theories suggesting that not all individuals react in the same manner, or even react at all, to the incentives provided by school choice.

Empirical evidence suggests that consumers (and citizens) with higher education and greater involvement with a product are more likely to have better information. When these patterns appear for public goods, the resulting stratification by race and class can affect the quality of these public goods and the larger society.

Although economists have recently studied how people economize on search costs by simply following the actions of others, they do not have a monopoly on the study of information flows. In stark contrast to the economic approach that focuses on how and why individuals invest in information, sociologists treat information as a by-product of social interactions. Thus, social network analysis has been employed to explore the ways people acquire information as part of their daily lives. The empirical literature on networks also shows that individuals vary greatly, often in predictable ways, in their ability to use social networks to their advantage. We briefly examined the specific literature on school choice and decision making to assess the degree to which these general economic, psychological, and sociological theories have been employed and tested in the study of school choice.

Finally, we put the supply- and demand-sides together again and argued that while the market metaphor is useful in examining school choice decision making, it is incomplete. Several factors make education different from many other services sold in private markets. As partly a public good, schooling is characterized by only an indirect link between the payment for and the receipt of the service, which blunts some of the power consumers have over private goods, such as the ability to withhold payment. To be successful, education requires trust between the parents and the professionals who teach their children and run their schools and, more generally, education requires coproduction. Together, these factors require a rethinking of the market metaphor. Recognizing the complexity of these interactions allows the creation of a theoretical framework for assessing the relationship between information gathering in making a school choice and subsequent decisions by parents to become more involved in their children's education.

As we move to the empirical analyses presented in this book, we do so with an appreciation of the market model for analyzing school choice. This appreciation is tempered by the reality that no simple model can explain all the issues that a complex phenomenon such as schooling raises. However, we believe that by using the model as a baseline we can gain insights about school choice. Throughout the empirical analysis we present in this book, we constantly seek to develop more complex models of the behavior of parent-consumers in the settings that aim at creating a market for education.

But first we turn to a discussion of our research design and our research settings.

Chapter 3

Studying Choice: The Research Design

In chapter 1, we analyzed the design of school choice—looking at the supply-side of the school choice market. In chapter 2, we looked at the factors that influence parent behavior—which define the demand-side of the market. In this chapter, we focus on the school districts included in our study and discuss some of the details of our study design and methodology.

We first describe our quasi-experimental research design and its strengths and weaknesses for studying school choice. We then introduce the history and present conditions of the districts we study. From there, we focus on the specific institutional arrangements characterizing school choice in each of our urban and suburban districts. Because our concerns focus on the effects of choice not only on students and schools but also on parents, we rely heavily on survey research. Therefore, in the final section of this chapter, we discuss the survey instrument we designed and administered to a sample of 1,600 parents across the four school districts in our study.

Research Design

Theoretically informed arguments in favor of school choice can be traced back at least to Milton Friedman's work in the 1950s. In response to the intellectual impact of Friedman's arguments and to other challenges facing the schools, school choice began to move from theory to practice as a policy innovation beginning with a series of reforms implemented by a number of school districts in the late 1960s. As noted in chapter 1, many choice reforms came from the introduction of magnet and specialty schools into school districts in which residential catchment zones remained the norm for most students. However, a few school districts (most notably, Cambridge, Massachusetts; Montclair, New Jersey; and District 4 in New York City) introduced more systemic choice programs that have now been in place for around twenty-five years.

We took the existence of these established choice programs as an opportunity to implement a powerful research design that would enable us to isolate the effects of school choice on a number of demand-side phenomena. In addition, we wanted to study choice in more than one district, in order to evaluate whether, and how, school choice affects a range of parent behavior, including information gathering, parental participation, in school events and interaction with school officials.

In the natural sciences, experimental methods and replication in different settings provide the most powerful research tools for identifying relation-ships. In the social sciences, powerful experimental techniques are usually not available, since the random assignment of individuals, schools, or com-munities into control and experimental groups is often impractical and un-ethical. Since some school districts implemented choice while others did not, the evolutionary diffusion of school choice created the conditions for a natu-rally occurring quasi-experiment, with possibilities of replication. Seizing the opportunities this presented, we matched districts with choice to similar dis-tricts without choice, using one pair from a central city and one pair from a suburban setting. By controlling for many (but admittedly not all) relevant conditions affecting choice, our quasi-experimental design allows us to iden-tify the effects of various contextual and institutional features on the behavior of parents. See table 3.1.

In each pair, we matched a district with a long-standing choice program to a demographically similar district with little or no choice. By comparing parental behavior within each matched pair, we can focus on the effects of choice. And by conducting this analysis in two pairs of schools, we can analyze the robustness of our findings.

We recognize that there are limitations inherent in the cross-sectional na-ture of this research design and, subsequently, that the internal validity of this research design may be challenged. For example, in any reform situa-tion, there is an intimate relationship between the behavior of citizens de-manding or responding to change and the behavior of officials implementing or enforcing change. Because it is often difficult to establish temporal order, cause and effect relations cannot be exactly determined (for example, to what extent did parents force the changes in the institutions versus to what extent did parent behavior change in response to the institution of choice?) and the potential for spurious relationships cannot be wholly controlled.

One means by which to address these threats is to explicitly account for all possible events occurring during the period of study that could potentially affect the individuals in our study and thereby provide a means to test rival explanations. To do this, we would need to examine the same set of parents from the late 1960s or early 1970s (the period just before school choice was

Table 3.1
The Quasi-Experimental Design

District Type	District Location	
	Central City	Suburban
Choice	Community District 4, New York City	Montclair Public Schools, Montclair, New Jersey
Nonchoice	Community District 1, New York City	Morris School District, Morristown, New Jersey

implemented in Montclair and District 4) to the present. In addition, we would need data for all schools and programs in each of the four districts over the same time period. These over-time data would establish temporal order, thereby enabling us to analyze more exactly how the introduction of school choice affected parental behavior.

While this kind of time series design has advantages, it too has limitations. For example, given the twenty-five year-time period of choice, many parents would move or drop-out of the sample, leaving us with a severe attrition rate—a problem endemic to any longitudinal study, but worse in studies of low-income central city populations. Finally, over-time data on school-level measures such as test scores are often wrought with problems of availability and consistency (for example, New Jersey's efforts to track school performance over time have been sporadic and New York City has changed its test instrument several times; see chapter 9). In short, every research design represents a set of trade-offs, but by employing a quasi-experimental design and by including two sets of matched districts, we believe that we have gained considerable leverage in reducing many of the problems of standard cross-sectional designs.

Our quasi-experimental approach, then, compares the behavior of parents from similar demographic backgrounds operating in school districts with quite different institutional arrangements governing how children are placed in schools. To take full advantage of this quasi-experimental design, where appropriate in the empirical analyses we present in subsequent chapters, we replicate each of the analyses we conducted in any pair of districts using data from the other pair. This allows us to explore the robustness of our findings by testing their sensitivity to changes in the context of school choice. In addition, we can closely examine the effects of choice on different racial and socioeconomic groups and address the equity issue, one of the questions central to the debate over school choice.

The Research Sites

In selecting our research sites, we wanted districts in which choice was well-established. The Carnegie Foundation Study of School Choice (Boyer 1992) identified three such districts across the nation: Community School District 4 in New York City; Montclair, New Jersey; and Cambridge, Massachusetts. Because we had limited resources, we chose to do a more in-depth analysis of two of these districts rather than a more superficial study of all three. We chose District 4 and Montclair partly because both are located in the New York metropolitan area and partly because of the clear suburban/central city dichotomy.

Given our quasi-experimental design, we needed to find appropriate "controls"—school districts without choice that we could match with the choice ("treatment") districts. After looking at census data and school district profiles, we chose Community School District 1 in New York City and the Morris School District in Morristown, New Jersey, as the control districts. District 1, like District 4, is comprised largely of low-income minority parents (most of whom are Hispanic) in a compact inner-city district. Morristown, New Jersey is a suburban town with similar income levels to Montclair, but which employs a strict neighborhood attendance zone or catchment approach to school assignment. (These zones are periodically redrawn to ensure racial balance.)

Community school districts in New York are responsible for K–8 education, while New York's central board of education has responsibility for the high schools. Choice in Montclair takes place at the K–8 level, since there is only a single high school in the district. Similarly, there is only one high school in Morristown. Given this, we focus on parents of children in grades K–8 in all four districts. Demographic information (along with the number of schools and students) for each of the four school districts is presented in table 3.2.

Because roughly 10 percent of parents in the United States (and about 20 percent of parents in both the two New Jersey counties and the New York City school systems) choose to send their children to private schools, we decided to interview parents of both public and private school children. Private school parents have made an explicit choice to opt out of the local public schools and voluntarily pay tuition to send their children to private schools. In establishing many of the basic conditions of parent choice behavior, we include private school parents in our analyses. As we move to more

Table 3.2
Population Demographics for the Four Research Sites

	District 4	District 1	Montclair	Morristown
Total Number of Students	13,806	12,519	5,850	5,080
Public Students	91%	85%	82%	73%
Number of Public Schools	50	24	10	9
Hispanics	57%	39%	4%	9%
Blacks	36%	10%	36%	17%
Whites	5%	37%	56%	70%
Asian	1%	13%	3%	4%
Students in poverty	40%	29%	7%	6%
Income <20,000	NA	NA	16%	21%
Employed	83%	83%	95%	97%
High School Degree or More	48%	63%	88%	86%
Single Parent	44%	50%	11%	23%
Female	50%	55%	54%	53%

Source: School District Data Book Profiles, 1989–90.

Note: Since both districts are administrative units for the NYC school system rather than, e.g., census designated units, some demographic data are not available (NA).

complicated issues of parent behavior, we focus more tightly on public school parents, excluding private school parents from the analysis. In chapter 12, we specifically address how private school parents differ from their public school counterparts on these behaviors.

The Research Venue: Profiles of the Four Districts

Before looking more carefully at the actual design and structure of the two choice programs, we first describe the research sites in more detail. Each of the four districts has its own history that has influenced the evolution of schools and school choice. We developed these district sketches using previously written material (which were much more extensive for District 4 and Montclair, since they have been studied more), and by our visits to each district and discussions with district officials.

The Evolution of Choice in District 4: A School Choice Innovator

District 4 is located in East or "Spanish" Harlem, one of the poorest communities in New York City. The district serves roughly 14,000 students from prekindergarten through the ninth grade. In the early 1970s, the district's performance was ranked the lowest of thirty-two city public school districts in math and reading scores. Choice was part of a response to this poor performance.

Fliegel (1990) described the evolution of school choice in District 4 as resulting from "creative noncompliance" with New York City rules and regulations. The factors shaping the emergence of the choice program in District 4 can be traced back to the late 1960s when the administration of New York City's public school system was decentralized to allow for greater community control of K–8 education. Thirty-two separate community school districts were established, each of which was governed by an elected community school board, an appointed district superintendent, and the central board of education.

District 4 took full advantage of decentralization, as a reform-minded school board almost immediately forced out their "old guard" superintendent and replaced him with Anthony Alvarado, a charismatic leader of Puerto Rican ethnicity. Alvarado pushed the envelope of his powers as superintendent to reform the schools and energize the district's students and residents. He realized that he first needed to create conditions conducive to change before attempting radical reform. Consequently, Alvarado established a supportive coalition of teachers, principals, parents, and members of the central bureaucracy. For example, he appointed five minority principals (four Puerto Ricans and one African American) to run predominantly black and Hispanic schools in the district (Kirp 1992; Gittell 1973). This move won him immediate credibility among minority parents, as did his development of an extensive bilingual education program.

Alvarado sought out staff who shared his beliefs and hired a number of young, energetic teachers (many of whom did not have city licenses) to generate enthusiasm and build upon his sense of mission (Harrington and Cookson 1992, 177). He then launched his alternative schools program and began selling the idea to these reform-minded teachers and innovators. In 1974, Deborah Meier and her colleagues, perhaps the best known District 4 innovators, established the first alternative school—Central Park East. This school, and Deborah Meier herself, played a crucial role in the reform process by establishing a precedent for academic excellence.

During Alvarado's ten-year reign as superintendent of District 4, thirty alternative schools were established. Rather than reforming existing schools, Alvarado's plan was to revolutionize the schools by creating entirely new ones that were formed largely in bottom-up fashion by those closest to the educational task (teachers, principals, parents), who would participate in their governance (Meier 1987).

With these alternative schools, District 4 began to cast aside the tradition of zoned, bureaucratically controlled schools. However, the necessary flexibility to run these alternative schools did not exist under the formal arrangements of the New York School system. The Board of Education, the New York State Regents, and the teachers union, the United Federation of Teachers (UFT), all defined the legal context under which schools were forced to operate. To circumvent some of these rules and regulations, Alvarado and the district administrators often turned to unofficial means and "creative noncompliance." This required imagination, initiative, and a willingness to take substantial risks (Meier 1991, 266). Alvarado and the director of alternative schools, Sy Fliegel, took on this entrepreneurial role (see Schneider and Teske 1995 for more on the role of public entrepreneurs). For example, to enable principal-directors to exercise greater control over staffing, the seniority system often had to be side-stepped, and teachers recruited by word-of-mouth rather than through official means (Kirp 1992).

The creation of new schools, rather than the reform of existing ones, required additional funds and facilities. Alvarado's solution to facilities shortages was to locate the alternative schools in existing buildings, breaking the "one school, one building" model. By the mid-1980s, District 4's fifty-one schools occupied twenty buildings (Meier 1991). In addition to facilities, the alternative schools needed financial resources to support their educational programs. Alvarado gave alternative schools more flexibility in spending their funds, and also sought external support. The federal Emergency School Aid Act (ESAA) was providing federal money in the 1980s to support desegregation in alternative schools. Alvarado aggressively seized such funding, and at one point in the 1980s, won more federal money per pupil for District 4 than any other school district in the nation (Kirp 1992; Harrington and Cookson 1992).

As the number of alternative schools in District 4 increased, the differences between schools became apparent and Meier (1995, 94) suggests that it became "hopeless" to tell parents or teachers that their assignments would be determined bureaucratically. Thus, in 1982, the district decided to provide all parents with choice. The concept of the neighborhood school was completely eliminated at the junior high level at this time. By 1995 there were twenty junior high schools in District 4, with an average enrollment of approximately 172 students. As table 3.3 illustrates, the alternative junior high schools in District 4 represent a very diverse range of curricular themes.

Although choice is universal at the junior high level in District 4, it is more limited at the elementary level. In 1995, there were ten alternative elementary schools from which parents could choose, but these existed alongside sixteen neighborhood schools. Parents who did not actively choose one of the alternative schools were assigned to a neighborhood school depending on the catchment zone in which they lived.

Table 3.4 provides some descriptive information about the neighborhood and alternative elementary schools in District 4. Note that the alternative schools are not only organized around specific curricular or pedagogical themes, but also have considerably smaller enrollments than the neighborhood schools.

Table 3.3
District 4 Junior High Schools

School No.	School Name	Grade Level	Enroll- ment	School No.	School Name	Grade Level	Enroll- ment
JHS 805	East Harlem Bridge	7–9	176	IS 72	East Harlem Tech	7–8	NA
JHS 806	New York Prep	7–9	188	IS 802	Performing Arts	7–8	224
JHS 814	Creative Learning Community	7–9	164	IS 804	Science and Humanities	6–8	171
JHS 818	Rafael Cordero Bilingual School	7–9	192	IS 812	College of Human Services	7–8	61
JHS 819	Maritime Academy	7–9	186	IS 813	Northview	7–8	122
JHS 821	Academy of Environmental Science	7–9	260	IS 816	Central Park East Secondary School	7–8	165
JHS 823	Harbor School	7–9	185	IS 820	Manhattan East	6–8	212
JHS 831	Hurston Academy	7–9	57	IS 822	E. Harlem Career Academy	7–8	193
JHS 832	Health and Biomedical	7–9	232	IS 826	Isaac Newton	7–8	235
JHS 833	Julia De Burgos	7–9	163	IS 828	Manhattan West	7–8	80

Source: 1994–95 Annual School Reports, New York City Board of Education.

Table 3.4
District 4 Elementary Schools

Neighborhood Schools			Alternative Schools			
School No.	Grade Level	Enrollment	School No.	School Name	Grade Level	Enrollment
PS 7	PK–6	452	PS 801	Bilingual Arts	1–6	290
PS 50	K–6	534	PS 807	E. H. Block	K–6	NA
PS 57	PK–6	709	PS 808	Schomburg	K–6	206
PS 72	PK–6	713	PS 809	Central Park East II	PK–6	205
PS 83	K–6	460	PS 810	Hostos Academy	K–7	159
PS 96	PK–5	515	PS 811	Bilingual Learning Center	K–6	191
PS 101	PK–6	440	PS 815	Central Park East I	PK–6	261
PS 102	PK–6	490	PS 825	Talented and Gifted	3–6	295
PS 108	K–6	519	PS 827	River East	PK–6	229
PS 109	K–6	272	PS 829	Harbor Academy of	2	49
PS 112	PK–2	574		Environmental Studies		
PS 121	PK–6	379	PS 830	Bilingual Bicultural Mini	K–6	547
PS 146	K–6	597				
PS 155	K–6	497				
PS 171	PK–6	614				
PS 206	3–6	580				

Source: 1994–95 Annual School Reports, New York City Board of Education.

District 1: Limited Choice

The Lower East Side of Manhattan is home to Community School District 1, the other central city district in our study. While the student population of District 1 shares many of the characteristics of District 4's, the Lower East Side is a relatively more diverse community—both economically and ethnically—than East Harlem. This area has traditionally been, and continues to be, a place where newly arrived immigrants to the United States initially settle.

Most recently, immigrants from the Caribbean, Central and South America, and East Asia have come in large numbers. Since the late 1980s the community has also begun to experience some gentrification as a result of the influx of higher income residents who are unable to find housing in the more established neighborhoods nearby. While this influx of more advantaged residents provides benefits to the neighborhood, almost none have been transferred to the public schools. A comparison of the demographic characteristics of the District 1 community as a whole to those of the school-aged population reveals striking differences. For example, while the District population is 39 percent Hispanic and 37 percent white, the student population is 63 percent Hispanic and 11 percent white. In addition, 49 percent of students are living in poverty as compared to 29 percent of the District 1 population. This pattern results because white and higher income residents have chosen not to send their children to the district's public schools (Ubinas and Lawrence 1990). Both student achievement and enrollment exhibited steady declines throughout the late 1980s (e.g., District 1 lost nearly 1,000 students between 1985 and 1990), and District 1 ranked at the bottom of New York City's thirty-two community school districts in 1990 on standardized tests.

As a result of these educational problems, increasing numbers of parents—particularly those who recently moved into the district—found private school alternatives. In 1990, about 2,500 students who live in District 1 attended private and parochial schools in the Lower East Side community (Ubinas and Lawrence 1990). In addition, many other parents were able to register their children in better schools outside the district.

William Ubinas, district superintendent from 1990–1994, realized that a major overhaul of the district was necessary to reverse these trends. One idea was to introduce a choice plan in the district, establishing some alternative schools to develop distinctive instructional programs, create a broad range of opportunities and activities to facilitate parent involvement in schooling, and build partnerships with community, business, and university affiliations. The reforms also included initiatives to increase principal and school-level autonomy.

Unlike Alvarado in District 4, Ubinas found it difficult to build a coalition of supporters for reform, partly because of District 1's conflictual political history. District 1 was created out of the Two Bridges School District, one of most active districts in New York City's fights over school decentralization in the 1960s. Recent activism has been characterized by interneighborhood conflict and rivalry between the majority Hispanic population, multicultural liberal groups, and a sizable minority of Hasidic Jewish families, who play a significant role in district politics despite the fact that almost all send their children to private schools. This rivalry is played out in contested school board elections, in the struggle for control over the board, and in the appointment of the superintendent.

Thus, Ubinas could not garner sufficient political support for his reform and a new school board forced him out of office. Although his ambitious goals were unrealized, he did create a few alternative schools (see table 3.5) and many schools developed new programs, especially in bilingual education.

In sum, some restructuring has taken place in District 1, though the extent of choice remains small and the infrastructure of the reform effort weak.

Thus while both of the New York districts are geographically compact, have large numbers of students from very poor families (more than eight of ten students are eligible for free lunch), and have student populations drawn

Table 3.5
District 1 Elementary and Junior High Schools

School No.	Grade Level	Enrollment	School No.		Grade Level	Enrollment
PS 15	K–6	253	PS 140		PK–8	505
PS 19	PK–8	734	PS142		PK–6	523
PS 20	K–6	916	JHS 22		7–9	617
PS 34	K–6	418	JHS 56		7–9	1,193
PS 61	PK–6	274	JHS 60		7–9	400
PS 63	PK–6	351		*Alternative Schools*		
PS 64	PK–6	322	PS 315	Lower East Side	PK–6	126
PS 97	PK–6	491	PS 361	Children's Workshop	PK–4	105
PS 110	PK–6	561	PS 363	Neighborhood School	PK–4	173
PS 134	PK–6	470	PS 364	Earth School	PK–6	131
PS 137	PK–6	654	JSH 25	Marta Valle	7–9	35

Source: 1994–95 Annual School Reports, New York City Board of Education.

overwhelmingly from racial minority groups, the two districts differ dramatically in terms of their political environments and the success of their efforts at implementing school reform.

As a result of its entrepreneurial efforts to develop choice, District 4 has developed a reputation in the city and in the nation as an innovative, successful district. There is a sense of mission evident among parents, teachers, and administrators. Parents from other districts try to send their children to District 4 schools. In contrast, District 1 has faced considerable political turmoil and administrative turnover, and many parents opt out of these public schools.

The New Jersey School Districts

Montclair and Morristown, New Jersey, two suburban communities within commuting distance of New York City, represent our second paired set of school districts.

Montclair, New Jersey

Montclair, New Jersey is located less than fifteen miles from New York City. Despite its close proximity to the nation's largest city, and the fact that many residents commute to New York, Montclair's population of 38,000 gives it a "small town" feeling. The town has become increasingly affluent in recent years: In 1990, Montclair's median housing value was $267,000 and its median household income was over $52,000. Montclair's residents are well educated—about 47 percent hold college degrees.

In addition to being affluent, Montclair is also an example of a racially mixed suburb. The black population increased from 24 percent in 1960 to 29 percent in 1980 to 36 percent in 1990. As we discuss below, race relations have not always been smooth in Montclair. However, today, despite the increasing proportion of minorities in the community, residents have not abandoned the public schools. In fact, the private school enrollment in Montclair (18 percent) is significantly lower than the county average (21 percent).

In contrast to District 4, choice was not implemented in Montclair because its schools were failing. Indeed, as the Carnegie Foundation Report (1992, 31) notes, Montclair has always been a high-performing district with an involved parent population. Instead, Montclair adopted school choice in 1976 as a means to voluntarily accomplish desegregation. As African Americans began moving into the community in larger numbers throughout the 1960s, housing patterns became increasingly segregated. This led to a racial imbalance in school enrollments, since school boundaries were drawn according to neighborhoods. Racial unrest in Montclair and neighboring towns intensified during the late 1960s. According to long-time residents, tensions among African Americans and whites ran high, and cross burnings were not unheard of (Carnegie Foundation 1992).

During this period many white parents in Montclair took their children out of the public schools. This "white flight" intensified with the implementation of a forced busing plan in the early 1970s. Rather than improving the racial balance of the public schools, the busing plan actually had the reverse effect.

Under the threat of losing state funding, Montclair developed magnet schools in 1976 to desegregate (Carnegie Foundation 1992, 31; Clewell and Joy 1990, 5). Under this initial plan, Montclair developed a "talented and gifted" program and opened it in an African American neighborhood. At the same time, in a predominately white neighborhood, Montclair began a program that stressed traditional approaches to learning, emphasizing "the basics" (Carnegie Foundation 1992, 31). In addition to creating these magnets, district boundaries were also redrawn (Clewell and Joy 1992, 5).

While this initial plan partly succeeded, some parents perceived inequalities between the magnet and traditional schools. Thus, in 1985 Montclair eliminated the concept of the neighborhood school and moved to a magnet school program. Each school had its own distinctive curricular theme and/or pedagogical approach (see table 3.6). Though some of the themes have changed over time, the basic plan has remained intact since 1985.

Morristown, New Jersey

Although Morristown is overall an affluent suburb, families with a wide range of income still populate the community. There is a high degree of spatial segregation: highly affluent areas surround a core neighborhood that

Table 3.6
Montclair Elementary and Junior High Schools

School Name	Grade Level	Enrollment	School Name	Grade Level	Enrollment
Bradford Academy	PK–5	302	Rand	PK–3	270
Edgemont Montessori	PK–5	342	Watchung	PK–5	450
Hillside School	3–5	606			
Nishuane	PK–2	674	Glenfield Middle	6–8	567
Northeast	PK–5	344	Mt. Hebron Middle	6–8	677

Source: New Jersey Department of Education 1993 School Report Card.

is substantially poorer and populated by racial minorities. The schools in Morristown are quite good—with academic performance levels that are actually higher than in Montclair. In general, Morristown's schools have not attracted much national attention—with one exception. Morristown played a small but important role in the fights over school desegregation that were touched off by the *Brown v. Board of Education* decision in 1954.

Segregated schools were banned by the New Jersey Constitution and in 1965, the New Jersey State Supreme Court gave the state commissioner of education the right to desegregate schools by combining districts. In 1971, Morris Township sought to end a century-old practice of sending its students to Morristown High School located in Morristown. The township wanted to sever ties with Morristown and build its own high school. This decision resulted from the growing affluence in Morris Township, which totally surrounded Morristown, a low income, minority area. However, the New Jersey Supreme Court in *Jenkins v. Township of Morris School District* (58 N. J. 483) ruled against this action and the commissioner of education forced the merger of the town and the township into a single district.

After the merger, residential zones were created for neighborhood schools to address the segregation problem. The three school zones are cut out, like wedges of pie, to racially balance schools. Though these zones are peri-

Table 3.7
Morristown Elementary and Junior High Schools

School Name	Grade Level	Enrollment	School Name	Grade Level	Enrollment
Alexander Hamilton	3–5	282	Thomas Jefferson	3–5	278
Alfred Vail	K–2	323	Woodland Avenue	K–2	302
Hillcrest	K–2	320			
Sussex Avenue	3–5	296	Frelinghuysen JHS	6–8	750

Source: New Jersey Department of Education 1993 School Report Card.

odically adjusted to maintain balanced, once the zones are set they are strictly enforced.

The Various Forms of Choice

Choice is not a single reform, but rather a class of reforms with different rules and institutional arrangements. Here, we examine the choice mechanisms in each district. These include the rules that determine who can choose, how many alternatives they have, how school or district selection criteria or objectives limit or enhance the ability of parents and students to match their preferences, and what resources are available to assist parents with choice.

We identify five institutional arrangements in our four districts and array them in table 3.8 along a continuum from most to least restrictive. The districts and school levels (elementary, junior high, or both) corresponding to each of these types of choice are also listed in table 3.8.

Neighborhood Schools

Neighborhood schools are found in three out of the four districts in our study. In this traditional arrangement, students are assigned to schools based on residential location with designated catchment zones. Although these zones may be adjusted in order to accomplish racial balancing or other objectives (as in Morristown), once located in a particular zone, parents have little control over this process, unless they are able to move or pay for private schools.

Controlled Choice

Controlled choice, which describes the full site magnet program in Montclair, generally refers to choice programs with mandates for racial balancing.

Table 3.8
Institutional Arrangements of the Four Research Sites

Neighborhood Schools	Controlled Choice	Option-Demand Choice	Universal Choice	Private Schools
Morristown (Both)	Montclair (Both)	District 4 (Elementary)	District 4 (Jr. High)	District 1
District 4 (Elementary)		District 1 (Both)*		District 4
District 1 (Both)				Montclair
				Morristown

*Note: there is only one alternative junior high school in District 1 and its enrollment was thirty-five students at the time of our study.

These programs are often characterized by a "universal" design whereby all schools in a district become schools of choice from which all parents *must* choose. However, the choice mechanism differs in important ways across controlled and universal choice programs. Under controlled choice, district officials regulate parents' choices to ensure that all district schools are similar with respect to racial and/or other demographic characteristics of students.

As Rossell (1995, 43) explains, controlled choice is one of the most recent innovations in the four-decade evolution of school desegregation policy. While this innovation relies on the voluntary actions of a school district's parents and students to accomplish desegregation, it also includes a mandatory back-up plan to ensure that desegregation is actually accomplished. It is a compromise between parents' desires for greater choice and school administrators' desires (or mandates) to desegregate by controlling assignments. The hope is that magnet schools with different themes will attract students with similar interests, but who are diverse in racial background and/or socio-economic status.

As shown in table 3.6, Montclair's controlled choice program includes two junior high magnet schools (gifted/talented and science/technology) and seven elementary magnet schools. At the elementary level, the themes are reflected by gifted and talented programs at two schools, a Montessori school, a science and technology school, an international studies school, a family and environment school, and an information technology school.

The district office in Montclair disseminates a considerable amount of information about the schools and the process of choice. The fifty-page *Parent to Parent* handbook explains the magnet system, outlines the curriculums offered, and lists all important events, services, resources, and opportunities for parent involvement. A second booklet, *Montclair's Magnets*, provides parents with additional information about each school, including registration procedures and requirements. Montclair also publishes a newsletter, various "fact sheets," and fliers for all school and district sponsored events.

In selecting schools, parents indicate their top two choices to the district office, which assigns students to schools. In addition to the parental preferences, several factors are taken into account: placement of siblings, gender and racial balance of schools, and available space. Parents who move into the district midway through the school year are assigned to schools based on available space (Clewell and Joy 1990, 7). Since the schools are nearly uniformly good, about 95 percent of parents receive their first choice (Strobert 1991, 56–57). Because the district provides transportation for all students, distance does not limit parental choice.[1] Between 60 and 80 percent of students take buses to their schools.

Option-Demand Choice

The second type of choice listed in table 3.8, *option-demand*, refers to explicit programs adopted by local school districts to expand the range of educational alternatives available to parents and students. Unlike controlled and universal choice, under the option-demand system these choice alternatives exist alongside neighborhood schools. Option-demand thus does not eliminate the traditional schooling arrangements but instead implements change by offering a limited set of alternatives to a smaller group of parents and students.

The majority of choice programs currently in place across the United States are option-demand. While they vary somewhat, the characteristic feature of option-demand choice is a two-stage selection process. The first stage involves the decision to opt out of the zoned neighborhood school. At the second stage, parents/students select their preferred school from the set of possible alternatives.

The distinction between these two levels of choice is critical in studying equity issues that frequently emerge in school choice debates. Option-demand choice essentially creates a separate sector of public schools, and since parents self-select under option-demand choice, for several reasons these programs may be vulnerable to adverse outcomes such as stratification. First, option-demand choice places more responsibility on the individual parents and students, which may result in biases in who exercises choice, as some parents have access to more and better information (Bridge and Blackman 1978; Henig 1994; Wells 1993b; Murnane 1986). In addition, some parents are more capable of making informed choice as a result of greater involvement and participation in their children's education (Wells 1993b; Witte 1993; Coleman and Hoffer 1987).

A second reason option-demand systems are associated with stratification relates to institutional aspects of school choice. In particular, the nature of the alternative schools established, and the process schools use to admit students, may lead to systematic biases. Alternative schools may be disproportionately targeted at particular "types" of students (for example, bilingual schools are often designed to attract a certain type of student—in New York districts, Hispanics).

As option-demand choice places greater responsibility on individual parents and students in making schooling decisions, it also increases the importance of institutional and contextual features that can either reinforce or diminish existing biases in who participates in choice. Specifically, the number and type of alternative schools established, the existence of public transportation, the presence of information, and rules specifying how students are accepted into schools all play important roles.

Both of the option-demand programs we study are found in the New York City districts. District 4 has an option-demand system in place at the elementary school level, while District 1 has one alternative school at the junior high level and four at the elementary school level (see table 3.9).

Although the option-demand choice programs in these two New York City districts are quite different, they share some common features. To begin with, they are both located in geographically compact areas in Manhattan, serviced

Table 3.9
Neighborhood and Alternative Elementary Schools Summary

	District 4		District 1	
	Neighborhood	*Alternative*	*Neighborhood*	*Alternative*
Number of Schools	16	11	13	5
Number of Students	8,345	2,432	8,682	570

Source: New York City Board of Education Annual School Report, 1994–95.

by the city's vast public transportation system. Second, since both districts are overwhelmingly Hispanic and black, neither district regulates the racial composition of schools. In fact, alternative schools in both districts are relatively free to formulate their own selection criteria.

The biggest difference between the two programs is the length of time they have existed. District 1 has only recently begun to experiment with choice, while District 4 has used choice since the early 1970s. The size and depth of the two programs are also quite different. District 1's program has only a limited number of alternative schools in place that serve only about 8 percent of elementary students and less than 2 percent of junior high students. In contrast, District 4's alternative schools enroll nearly 21 percent of the elementary student population. The range of options is also much broader in District 4, including schools that specialize in bilingual education, science and technology, programs for talented and gifted students, the performing arts, and the humanities.

The choice process is also supported by much more information in District 4. Each year the director of option schools issues a handbook, available in both Spanish and English, that describes the choice process and each of the alternative schools. A comparable resource does not exist in District 1, where parents instead must acquire and assemble information on their own.

Universal Choice

Although we noted previously that controlled choice programs are often characterized by a "universal" design, they differ in important ways from universal choice programs. Most importantly, controlled choice programs are associated with voluntary desegregation schemes and mandatory requirements to achieve racial balancing. Universal choice programs, on the other hand, do not share the explicit goal of desegregation and are generally much less regulated than controlled choice programs. The one universal choice program in our study operates at the junior high school level in District 4.

As table 3.3 reports, the universal choice program in District 4 includes twenty alternative junior high schools, from which students must make an explicit choice based on a booklet they receive in sixth grade. Parents and students attend orientation sessions led by the directors of various alternative schools (Wells 1993a, 55). The district runs a parent information center where both English and Spanish are spoken. During recruitment, the parent information center also holds evening meetings where parents receive information about the schools, have a chance to listen to presentations by school representatives, and have question and answer sessions with school directors and district personnel.

In March, sixth-grade students and their parents must fill out an application indicating their top six choices. Junior high schools mail out acceptance letters to students in May. According to district officials, 60 percent of the students in the district are accepted into their first-choice school, 30 percent into their second choice, and 5 percent into their third-choice school.[2] The remaining 5 percent are placed in schools that are thought to be most appropriate for them (Boyer 1992, 52–53). To ensure that all students have viable choices, administrators in District 4 monitor the popularity of the various alternative schools, closing or restructuring less popular schools (Wells 1993a, 55).

Private Schools

Obviously parents in each of the four school districts in our study also have the option to send their children to private schools. Although about 10 percent of students in the U.S. attend private schools, the proportion is much greater in the geographic region we study. In table 3.10 we report the percentage of private school students in each of our four research sites and the corresponding county- or system-wide average. To get an idea of the variation across districts within counties or systems, we also include the standard deviation for the county or system mean in parentheses.

When choosing private schools, parents are not restricted to schools that are located in their districts. Instead, they can select private schools in neighboring districts, neighboring boroughs, or even in neighboring counties. Though most parents choose private schools within relatively close proximity to their homes, our sample included parents who enrolled their children in schools quite distant from their homes.

Given the urban character of our research sites, parents in all four districts

Table 3.10
Proportion of Private School Students in District and County Schools

	District 4	District 1	NYC	Montclair	Essex County	Morristown	Morris County
% Private School Students	9.0	14.7	20.5 (10.0)	18.3	20.9 (5.2)	26.4	20.8 (8.4)

Note: Standard deviations are in parentheses. Data based on the 1990 census figures. See the School District Data Book Profiles, http://govinfo.kerr.orst.edu/sddb-stateis.html.

have a wide range of private schools from which to choose. Prestigious, nonsectarian schools are available in each setting, for example, Brearly and the Dalton School in New York City, the Villa Walsh Academy and the Morristown Beard School in Morristown, and the Montclair Kimberly and Barnstable Academies in the Montclair area. In addition, sectarian options— Catholic, other Christian, and Jewish schools—are widely available, and a number of Muslim schools are beginning to emerge.

We found some patterns in the kinds of private schools chosen by parents in each district. In District 4, an overwhelming majority of private school parents in our sample (more than 90 percent) had selected Catholic schools, and the remainder chose nonsectarian schools. On the other hand, only about 60 percent of our sample of private school parents in District 1 sent their children to Catholic schools (about 13 percent selected Yeshivas, 8 percent Christian schools, and 19 percent nonsectarian schools). The distribution of private school parents in Morristown is similar to District 1's— about 65 percent choose Catholic schools, 25 percent non-sectarian schools, and 8 percent Yeshivas. Finally, in Montclair, the majority of private school parents in our sample (60 percent) enrolled their children in nonsectarian schools (30 percent are in Catholic schools and 4 percent in both Christian and Jewish schools).

Surveying Parents in the Four Research Sites

With this background information in place, we now provide an overview of the survey instrument we designed and administered to parents. In addition, we also discuss some important methodological issues that emerge in our attempts to test empirically various components of the theoretical framework laid out in chapters 1 and 2.

Our goal in designing the survey was to tap as many dimensions as possible about the nature and extent of parents' involvement with the schools. Consequently, our survey instrument includes several different components, including the following:

- The form and frequency of parent involvement in school activities.
- The school attributes parents find most important for their child's education.
- The sources parents find most useful in acquiring information about their schools.
- Who parents talk to about schools.
- Parent accuracy regarding objective conditions of their schools.
- Parent satisfaction with their schools.

We also asked parents to provide us with background information about themselves, their children, and their schools so that we could control for possible differences in their knowledge and behavior that stemmed from individual-level attributes rather than institutional arrangements.

In the winter of 1995, we pretested our survey on a sample of parents who lived in one of the most demographically heterogeneous school districts on Long Island. This pretest enabled us to identify and correct problems with question wording and allowed us to tighten the instrument to ensure that respondents would not have trouble completing it within the thirty minute benchmark we had established.

After consulting several survey experts, we chose to interview 400 parents in each district. We contracted the Polimetrics Research and Survey Laboratory at Ohio State University to actually conduct the telephone interviews. To construct the sampling frame, Polimetrics identified the zip codes in each of the four school districts and cataloged all listed telephone numbers for each zip code. From this, a list was developed using random generation of the last two digits of the appropriate telephone exchanges, so that unlisted numbers were included as well. Next, all known business and fax numbers were eliminated. Finally, a random sample was taken from the remaining numbers.

To be eligible to be interviewed, each respondent needed to live within the school district, have at least one child between grades kindergarten through eight, be the adult responsible for making schooling decisions, and be able to identify the school his or her child attended (which could be either private or one of the public schools in the district). The actual interviews were conducted in the spring (March–June) of 1995. The interviewers were given extensive training and a set of bilingual interviewers was on hand to conduct interviews with Spanish-speaking parents. Interviews were monitored randomly and supervisors verified 15 percent of completed interviews in order to ensure quality. Our goal was to obtain 400 completed interviews in each of the four districts.

To focus on the schools controlled by the districts, we constructed the sample frame around parents who lived in the district with children in grades K–8.[3] To randomize which child's school we would ask questions about, we asked respondents to focus exclusively on the experience of the child in grades K–8 whose birthday came next in the calendar. Our school-specific questions were thus based on only one child and his/her school. In table 3.11 we report the call dispositions for each district.

Table 3.11
Disposition of Survey Telephone Calls

	District 4	District 1	Montclair	Morristown
Completed	400	401	408	395
Refusals	113	522	109	174
No Final Disposition	225	1,642	281	343
Nonhousehold	5,237	17,883	5,268	12,913
Ineligible	5,722	13,469	3,935	5,918

Comparing District Sample and Population Characteristics

In table 3.12 we report the demographic data for our sample of New York City parents[4] and once again we provide population figures for ease of comparison.

In both of the New York districts our sample of public school parents has a larger proportion of minorities and disadvantaged parents than the district population as a whole. However, private school parents included in the population figures likely account for most of these differences. As table 3.12 indicates, compared to the public school parents, our sample of private school parents in both districts is significantly more likely to be white, well educated, and married. In District 1, 26 percent of the respondents sent their child to private school, considerably higher than the 17 percent in District 4.

Looking at the characteristics of parents in our sample, we find that they were overwhelmingly female because the proportion of single mothers in these districts is high and because we asked for the "main school decision maker" in the household. Our public school respondents in both districts were predominantly Hispanic (68 percent and 71 percent, respectively) and reported that they did not work for pay outside the home (62 percent and 57 percent).[5] Private school parents in District 4 were also predominantly Hispanic, however, in District 1 the majority were white.

Table 3.12
Demographics for NYC Districts and Samples

	District 4			District 1		
	Population	Sample (Public)	Sample (Private)	Population	Sample (Public)	Sample (Private)
No. of K–8 Students*	14,043	333	67	9,252	295	106
No. of K–8 Schools*	50	46	22	24	24	25
Hispanics	57%	68%	43%	39%	71%	32%
Blacks	36%	26%	22%	10%	11%	8%
Whites	5%	2%	21%	37%	10%	45%
Asian	1%	1%	6%	13%	2%	7%
Indigent	40%	NA	NA	29%	NA	NA
Income <20K	NA	67%	24%	NA	66%	20%
Employed	83%	38%	70%	83%	43%	75%
H.S. Degree or More	48%	65%	79%	63%	65%	71%
Single Parent	44%	61%	34%	50%	46%	26%
Female	50%	90%	76%	55%	87%	78%

Source for district information: School District Data Book Profiles, 1989–90.

*Figures are based on the 1994–95 school report cards.

NA: Since both districts are administrative units for the New York City school system rather than, e.g., census designated units, some demographic data are not available.

Though not reported in table 3.12, in both districts the median age of respondents was the same, thirty-eight, and more than half the respondents had only one child in grades K–8. Additionally, about half of the respondents in Districts 1 and 4 reported attending church on a weekly basis.

Comparing across districts we find that more black respondents were surveyed in District 4 and more white respondents were surveyed in District 1. Although the same percentage of public school parents (65 percent) reported having graduated from high school, 25 percent of District 1 public school respondents reported graduating from college as compared to only 13 percent of the respondents in District 4.

Turning now to our two New Jersey districts, the differences between the population demographics and those of the public and private school samples tend to be smaller than in New York (see table 3.13). Not surprisingly, parents in the suburban New Jersey districts are quite different from parents in the central city districts. They are predominantly white, employed, and hold at least a high school degree. In both districts, these patterns are even starker with respect to the sample of private school parents. The most significant differences between the public and private school respondents are racial: in both districts a much smaller proportion of blacks attend private schools, while whites are overrepresented in private schools. It is interesting to note that, similar to the New York districts, more parents in the nonchoice district (Morristown) sent their children to private schools than did parents in the choice district (Montclair). We surveyed 114 (26 percent of the sample) pri-

Table 3.13
Demographics for New Jersey Districts and Samples

	Montclair			Morristown		
	Population	Sample (Public)	Sample (Private)	Population	Sample (Public)	Sample (Private)
No. of K–8 Students*	4,232	356	51	2,551	286	109
No. of K–8 Schools*	10	10	14	9	9	28
Hispanics	3%	3%	4%	7%	7%	6%
Blacks	31%	34%	16%	13%	16%	2%
Whites	63%	57%	75%	76%	70%	84%
Asian	2%	1%	0%	3%	5%	4%
Indigent	6%	NA	NA	5%	NA	NA
Income <20K	16%	8%	4%	21%	14%	1%
Employed	59%	80%	71%	58%	71%	65%
H.S. Degree or More	88%	98%	92%	86%	94%	93%
Single Parent	11%	23%	20%	23%	22%	9%
Female	54%	78%	80%	53%	76%	78%

Source for district information: School District Data Book Profiles, 1989–90.

vate school parents in Morristown and only 44 (11 percent of our sample) in Montclair.

Methodological Issues

Because our analytic and theoretical goals are varied and complex, it follows that our methods for analyzing our date are also varied and, at times, quite complex. In many of the chapters that follow, we take full advantage of our quasi-experimental design, testing relationships in one pair of districts and then replicating the analysis in the other. In the course of such replication, we show both general trends that hold across city and suburban settings and also interesting differences that distinguish parent behavior in the two contexts. In some cases, the differences we find are a function not simply of the different city/suburban contexts, but also of the different institutional arrangements that characterize the four school districts.

As we argued earlier, our comparative approach allows us to identify and isolate the effects of choice on parental behavior in the different contexts. However, for some of the issues we study in this book, our focus is on exogenous, structural characteristics that are not a function of context or institutional arrangements. In these cases, we pool the four research sites together in order to achieve a more representative sample. For example, we use this pooled approach to analyze parent preferences for school attributes, which are exogenous to the choice process.

Parents of Private School Students

About 20 percent of the parents in our sample had chosen private schools for their children. We were faced with the issue of how to analyze their choice behavior. Given the frequency and corresponding importance of private school choice in the United States, we did not want to exclude private school parents from our survey or from the analysis. However, we wanted the main focus of our study to be public schools. Having parents of private school children in all the analyses that follow added too much complexity to our analyses. In addition, we ran into a serious data problem—the objective information that private schools make available to the public is much more limited than the information that public schools must report. This problem is particularly acute in New Jersey. Thus some of the analyses we report for public school parents would simply be impossible for private school parents.

Our decision to include private school parents represents a compromise between their importance to any study of choice and the difficult challenges they present when merging them in with public school parents. In a few of our empirical analyses that provide the foundation for our more complex studies of choice behavior, we include both public and private parents and compare them (for example see the study of values that parents hold about education in chapter 4). When we move to more complicated analyses we focus only on public school parents. However, since so many of the issues we identify affect the behavior of private parents as well, we devote chapter 12 to an explicit study of private school parent behavior.

Two-Stage Modeling

Our focus is on how different institutional arrangements (a macrolevel condition) affect microlevel parent behavior. This leads to a difficult measurement problem in the study of New York parents and in our study of private school parents. In New York, both school districts run option-demand systems at the K–6 grade level, and choice is therefore a two-stage process. In the first stage, parents choose to choose. In the second stage, they choose the school their children will attend.

In any option-demand system, parents are self-selecting to enter the choice process. This can create serious biases in statistical analysis because the parents who are choosing to choose may not be (and in fact most likely are not) randomly drawn from the population, creating a "nonrandom selection" problem. While this problem has been recognized by some social scientists studying school choice, most previous work has not done enough to control for this problem. Using recent work in econometrics and political science, when necessary we employ a two-stage estimation procedure to correct for the nonrandom selection process of option-demand choice systems.

The same nonrandom selection process is clearly evident in any study of private school parents. However, as will become clear as the book develops, this selection bias problem is *not* a problem for *every* type of behavior we study. Essentially, the problem emerges when the behavior we are studying may also affect who has exercised the option to choose.

The clearest example is the relationship between choice and social capital that we address in detail in chapter 10. Let us assume that parents who have a higher propensity to become involved in school affairs are also more likely to exercise their option to choose. If we are interested in seeing whether or not choice leads to more involvement, as many advocates of choice argue it does, then we must control for the propensity to become involved that *preceded* choice. Only if we explicitly model the selection bias can we then identify the *independent* effects of choice on creating higher levels of involvement.

On the other hand, consider an issue such as satisfaction. Is it the case that some parents are predisposed to being more satisfied with their schools? Further, are these same parents also more likely to end up choosing alternative schools? We think not. Rather, we believe that parents' satisfaction with their schools depends on the schools themselves. In other words, satisfaction is determined by characteristics of schools and thus succeeds the choice process. It is therefore not necessary to control for selection bias when measuring the effects of schools on parents' levels of satisfaction.

Modeling the Selection Bias

We draw heavily on the work of Achen (1986), who demonstrates that ordinary regression fails to produce unbiased estimates of treatment effects in quasi-experiments when the "assignment" to different conditions is not random (see Heckman 1978; Heckman, Holtz, and Dabos 1987; Lord 1967, 1969; LaLonde and Maynard 1987). Consequently, in addition to modeling the behavioral outcome we must explicitly model the assignment process.

Thus, the first stage of these selection bias models consists of estimating an explicit assignment equation, where the dependent variable is a dichotomous variable indicating whether or not the parent chooses to choose—in our terminology, whether or not the parent was an "active chooser." We model this dichotomous "active chooser" variable against a host of demographic variables (e.g., education, race, church attendance) that might systematically affect the propensity of a parent to choose. This stage can be done in a straightforward manner by applying a linear probability model. We employ Goldberger's (1964) two-step weighted estimator to correct for the problems of Ordinary Least Squares (OLS) regression with a dichotomous dependent variable. Before calculating the weights, the predicted values outside the 0–1 interval from the OLS regression are reset to these bounds. It should also be noted that in order for the system of equations to be estimated, at least one variable in the assignment equation must be excluded from the outcome equation. This variable provides the necessary statistical leverage to estimate the system, so its coefficient in the assignment equation must be nonzero.

For the second-stage, the forecast values of the treatment variable (the dependent variable from the assignment equation) are inserted into the outcome equation. When the dependent variable in this equation is continuous, ordinary regression can be applied. The resulting coefficients are Two Stage least squares (2SLS) estimates. The only remaining step when our dependent variable is continuous consists of correcting the standard errors of the coefficients. To accomplish this, we first denote the variance of the residuals from our OLS regression ω^2. Next we generate a new forecast value for the dependent variable by using the second-stage coefficients and the original variables. We then compute the variance of the new set of residuals, σ^2, by taking the difference between the two equations. The standard errors of the 2SLS coefficients are corrected by multiplying each standard error by the square root of σ^2/ω^2.

If the dependent variable in the outcome equation is dichotomous, additional steps are necessary. Once again we insert the forecast values of the treatment variable into the outcome equation. After applying OLS to the outcome equation we compute a new forecast value for the dependent variable using the regression coefficients and the original variables, and predicted values outside the 0–1 interval are reset to the bounds. Next we apply Goldberger's two-step weighted estimator to the outcome equation. The coefficients of the final estimation are the two stage general least squares (2SGLS) estimates, but again, the reported standard errors are wrong. To correct them we first denote the variance of the residuals from the final stage regression as ω^2. We then multiply each standard error by the square root of $1/\omega^2$. We report these corrected coefficients and standard errors in our tables. Note too that once these corrections are implemented the R^2 statistic is no longer meaningful and is not reported for any of our selection bias models.

This complex approach embodies one of the best and most straightforward statistical techniques that social scientists have to control the biases that may be built into the option-demand system. This approach may also be used to estimate the effects of private schooling on appropriate behavioral variables.

Fortunately, in universal choice systems such as found at the intermediate school level in District 4 or at all grades in Montclair, all parents must choose and the nonrandom assignment problem caused by self-selection does not emerge.[6] When we seek to identify the effects of choice in these universal choice districts, we will employ a relatively simple dummy variable approach to identify the effects of choice.

Conclusions

In this chapter, we have outlined our basic research approach. We have argued that the diffusion of school choice throughout the nation presented the opportunities to measure the effects of choice using a quasi-experimental design. We believe that this design allows us to identify the effects of choice more closely than other researchers have been able to do in the past. Moreover, because our study encompasses two central city districts, we can address the most critical issue in the debate about school choice—will choice work in lower-income inner-city populations? And, since the United States is increasingly a nation of suburban residents, we believe that our results from New Jersey are equally important.

PART TWO

Chapter 4

The Distribution of Preferences:
What Do Parents Want from Schools?

School choice is designed to shift power to parents, enabling them to shop around for their child's school. Under traditional neighborhood school arrangements, the combination of residential location and bureaucratically determined catchment zones essentially creates a monopoly situation for parents.[1] School choice breaks this relationship and can transform the selection of schools for parents from a passive process to an active decision task. In this newly configured task, the parent-consumer is presented with multiple options and the opportunity to choose a school that maximizes the fit between her preferences in education and what the school offers. To the extent this match actually occurs, choice improves allocative efficiency in the quasi-market for schools.

As we have argued, while school choice began as an institutional reform designed to transform the supply-side of schooling, it has important consequences for the demand-side behavior of individuals, by providing new incentives for parents. Once we view school selection as an active process, we can identify a set of steps parents must negotiate in order to make an appropriate decision.

In the most basic terms, to make a good school choice, parents must:

- have a set of preferences about education and schooling;
- gather information about the set of schools available to their children;
- make trade-offs between the attributes of these schools;
- choose the school that best fits their preferences.

Once the school choice is made, parents should:

- monitor the performance of the school to make sure their choice was in fact a good one;
- seek a different school for their children if the choice was not correct.

And, as we will argue later in this book, as a by-product of the choice process, parents should:

- participate actively and regularly in their children's schools.

While all but the last of these steps describe a "rational" approach to studying choice among competing options, we must remember that all choice processes are context dependent—that is, the nature of the choice is conditioned by the size and complexity of the choice set. And, there are several factors that make school choice a particularly complicated decision context.

Education is a multidimensional product. Parents and society ask schools to accomplish multiple goals, and parents weigh different aspects of the mission of schools quite differently. For example, while schools are designed primarily to transmit knowledge and skills, we also expect them to train children to be good citizens and to promote the values held by society (with all the complexity and conflicts these terms hold). In addition, we often expect schools to deliver many social welfare services, ranging from recreation to nutritious food to a safe haven from threatening city streets. In many cases, we also expect schools to provide athletic and social opportunities for children.

Schools are also engaged in a complex "production process," where the product, education, is so multifaceted that even experts disagree considerably about both the importance of the various educational inputs and the outputs of the process. For example, ever since the famous Coleman report (Coleman et al. 1966), intense debates have raged over the relative importance of social status versus educational expenditures in student performance. Empirical evidence first dismissed the importance of educational expenditures and the "inputs" money buys (e.g., smaller classes, better trained teachers), but the accepted wisdom now seems to be endorsing the importance of these factors of production (for example, compare Hanushek 1986 with Card and Krueger 1992; see also chapter 9). Despite this recent shift, this debate has been going on for decades with little sign of abatement.

Moreover, even if experts ultimately agree that higher expenditures are important, there remains the unsettled question about what allocation of those expenditures will maximize educational performance. Should a parent weigh more heavily the number of experienced teachers, the average class size, or the number and range of different courses of study?

While there is intense disagreement about the relative value of different inputs to schooling, the outputs of education are not much easier to measure. Should we be measuring test performance? If so, which tests should be used? Are these tests culturally biased? Is it the absolute levels of performance that matter or the "value added" by the school? If it's the value added, how do we "control" for the unequal starting points of students in different schools?

More recently, a new debate over *what* children learn versus *how* they learn has emerged, which Hirsch (1996) calls the conflict between "product" and "process." Here the debate can verge on the esoteric, conducted with much conviction but without strong foundation. Do children learn better in highly structured classrooms emphasizing discipline dress codes? Do children learn better in single-sex schools? Do children learn better if values are emphasized? And, what works best for one child may not work at all for another.

Given the intensity of the debate over these issues and the lack of agreement among experts, both evaluating and choosing schools are difficult tasks for parents. However, the quality of parent choice helps structure the quality of the quasi-market for schools that choice creates.

While choice can be judged on many dimensions, given our concern for the demand-side of schooling, the matching of preferences and product, which economists call allocative efficiency, is particularly important. That is, one of the most important dimensions on which to evaluate whether or not choice works is the degree to which it allows parents to enroll their children in the schools they believe are right for them.

Given the fundamental importance of preferences, both for different models of choice and the evaluation of allocative efficiency, we begin our empirical investigation with the first step of this process: determining what parents want from the schools their children attend.

In this chapter, we look at the attributes of schools parents value and the distribution of those values across the different types of parents. We begin by looking at the preferences (and in later chapters, behaviors) across parents of different ethnic identification, socioeconomic status, geographic location (city versus suburb), and school sector (private versus public).

What Do Parents Want?

Like so much of the analysis of school choice, the rhetoric surrounding the discussion of parental values and the effects of the distribution of their preferences on schools has often outpaced the empirical evidence. A key issue is, given choice, whether or not parents will select schools on educationally sound dimensions or on noneducational dimensions that they (according to some critics, erroneously) value.

Moe summarizes this debate, observing that a common criticism of parental choice is the idea that "parents cannot be counted on to make choices by reference to sound educational criteria or values." He continues by noting that critics often argue that "parents—especially low-income parents—supposedly care about practical concerns, such as how close the school is or whether it has a good sports team, and put little emphasis on academic quality and other properties of effective schooling" (1995, 26–27; also see, e.g., Carnegie Foundation for the Advancement of Teaching 1992).

Such critiques have two dimensions. First is the general indictment that *many* parents will fail to choose schools based on educational quality. If this is true and parents base their choice on ancillary or irrelevant school characteristics, schools will have incentives to emphasize the "wrong" performance criteria—for example, the number of football games won rather than the number of students reading at grade level or going to college. To the extent this occurs, school choice could prove disastrous for the quality of learning across the country, as bad schools would drive out good ones as large numbers of parents choose schools for the wrong reasons.

Second is the corollary criticism that *only certain types* of parents are prone to choosing schools for the wrong reasons. As evident in Moe's statement, this concern is often phrased in terms of the particular susceptibility of low-income parents to embrace nonacademic (and "wrong") school attributes.

Thus, the second dimension involves the assumption that only *some* parents (particularly low-income parents) will fail to choose schools based on academic criteria. This raises the concern commonly referred to as "skimming" or "creaming"—the stratification of high- and low-performing schools along socioeconomic dimensions that results from the different preferences of high- and low-income parents. As high-income parents focus on academics, while low-income parents concentrate on nonacademic factors, children of low-income parents are left behind in low-performing schools. This bias in the selection process could fuel cumulative intergenerational inequality[2] (Wells 1993a; Levin 1989; Kozol 1991; Cookson 1992).

Despite intense debate on this issue, empirical evidence is not very strong. The Carnegie Foundation (1992) found that, compared to high-income parents, low-income parents do not select schools on the basis of academic excellence. There is also evidence that in some settings, it is parents' concerns for the racial/ethnic composition rather than the academic performance of the student body that motivates their choice.

For example, in his study of the Montgomery County magnet program, Henig (1996) found a tendency for minority families to request transfers into schools located in lower-income neighborhoods (see also Smith and Meier 1995). Henig also found that white families were most likely to seek transfers into schools with low proportions of minorities, while minorities were most likely to seek transfers to schools with higher proportions of minorities (1996, 106). Similarly, Armor and Peiser (1998) found that in Massachusetts, where there is extensive interdistrict choice, "sending districts" were more likely to be of lower socioeconomic status than "receiving districts"—that is, students exercising choice were much more likely to choose schools in more affluent districts (also see Fossey 1994).

These concerns have been reinforced by the course-taking patterns of students in different types of high schools. Data from the Department of Education show that in public high schools, where students have the freedom to choose from a range of courses, white and Asian-American students take more academic courses than black and Hispanic students (see Ravitch 1996; Bryk, Lee, and Holland 1993). This evidence suggests that the "shopping mall" approach of many contemporary public high schools can result in both lower enrollments in academically focused courses and increased stratification as some minority groups disproportionately choose nonacademic courses. This pattern, according to critics of choice, will be replicated across entire school systems perpetuating existing divisions across race and class.

In contrast, Witte's data show that low-income parents in the Milwaukee voucher program cite academic quality as the most important reason for using vouchers (see Witte, Bailey, and Thorn 1993, 1994). Several other studies have also demonstrated that parents emphasize academic values in their choice of schools across a range of choice settings. For example, in the Massachusetts interdistrict choice program, parents cited high academic standards, curriculum, and facilities most frequently as the most important reasons for moving their children (Armor and Peiser 1998). Vanourek et al. (1998) show most students in charter schools stressed academics—they listed "good teachers" as the most important attribute of charter schools, followed by "they teach it until I learn it," and "they don't let me fall behind." Similarly, in their study of the Cleveland Scholarship Program, Greene, Howell, and Peterson (1998) found that the decision to apply was motivated largely by academic concerns.[3]

Perhaps the longest running study measuring parental attitudes and interests in schools is the annual Phi Delta Kappa/Gallup Poll, which started in the late 1960s. One of the most consistent findings from recent polls is that parents give higher grades to their own schools than to the nation's schools in general.[4] When asked why their own schools were better than the nation's schools, in the 1995 study, the single reason most often chosen (by 79 percent of the parents) was that their own school placed more emphasis on high academic performance than did other schools. Following this (at 74 percent) were concerns about safety. But just below safety were a whole host of academic issues: the percent going to college (69 percent), varied academic courses (68 percent), fewer dropouts (68 percent), and better teachers (67 percent). While better sports and athletic programs were also noted by 67 percent of respondents, parents strongly endorsed academic values.

A recent study on both parents and students done by Public Agenda demonstrates that racial minorities are just as likely as whites to value academics. Their nationwide study of the attitudes of high school students found that "contrary to some conventional wisdom, minority youngsters are less dismissive of traditional academic course work than their white counterparts." Moreover, Public Agenda reported that "minority teens—both black and Hispanic—are more likely than white students to consider a strong academic background as the chief component of future career success" (1997, 31). Parents of black high school students, also surveyed by Public Agenda, echoed similar sentiments.

Recently Delpit (1995) has argued that low-income individuals and members of racial minorities now endorse academic values more strongly than others. Delpit describes a newly emerging rift pitting progressive white reformers who emphasize the teaching of values and the creation of a "humanized" open classroom, against black reformers, who emphasize success on tests and other skills. Black reformers argue that high performance on these tests is critical because it allows students from lower-socioeconomic strata to pass through what Delpit calls the "gatekeeping points" to the middle class.

According to Delpit:

> Many liberal educators hold that the primary goal for education is for children to become autonomous, to develop fully who they are in the classroom setting without having arbitrary, outside standards forced upon them. This is a very reasonable goal for people whose children are already participants in the culture of power and who have already internalized its codes. . . . But parents who don't function within that culture often want something else. It's not that they disagree with the former aim . . . They want to ensure that the school provides their children with discourse patterns, interactional styles, and spoken and written language codes that will allow them success in the larger society. (1995, 28–29)

Hirsch (1996) echoes these concerns, arguing that our schools do little to improve the educational prospects of poor children because progressive education emphasizes process (how children learn) over product (what they learn). Hirsch argues that a veritable war has broken out in schools over this debate, in which even the placement of student chairs in rows or semicircles takes on major significance.

While there is a clear ideological dimension driving this debate, the stakes for children are high. According to Ravitch (1996), the two organizations that administer college-entrance exams, the College Board and the ACT, agree that the single most important predictor of student performance on their tests is the number and rigor of the academic courses students take. Thus, the endorsement of traditional academic programs by minority students and parents is clearly instrumental—a means to pass one of the gatekeepers of academic success.

While this debate is often cast in class terms, there is an inevitable racial dimension. Here the issue is crystal clear: if whites and racial minorities want different things from schools, given choice, greater segregation will result as parents of different racial groups choose separate schools.

Some analysts have taken the argument concerning the distribution of values even further, arguing that school choice undermines the democratic foundation of society more generally. Carnoy (1993, 187) and Henig (1994, 222) both argue that school choice will increase the social stratification between parents who are more involved and interested in their children's education and those who are not, fundamentally reducing the ability of communities to address collective problems.

More broadly, Henry Levin (1989) argues that:

> It is widely recognized that democratic and capitalist societies must rely heavily upon their schools to provide an education that will preserve and support the fundamental political, social, and economic institutions that comprise those soci-

eties and that make it possible to change those societies in a democratic fashion. . . .

. . . schools must provide students with a common set of values and knowledge to create citizens who can function democratically. They must contribute to equality of social, economic, and political opportunities among persons drawn from different racial and social class origins. . . .

To a large extent these requirements suggest that all students be exposed to a common educational experience that cannot be left to the vagaries of individual or family choice. (1989, 6–7)

Studying the Distribution of Values

Like so much of the debate about school reforms, the analysis of preferences and choice is often driven by ideology and, consequently, often the "data" to support different positions remains anecdotal. In this chapter, we examine the attributes of schools parents judge important and investigate what, if any, differences emerge along racial or socioeconomic dimensions. We assume that given expanded choice, parents will seek to maximize their preferences over these school attributes in selecting their schools. If significant class and race differences appear in parents' values, then choice may in fact lead to more segregated schools and further fragmentation in the shared experiences that Levin and others feel are crucial to the functioning of our democratic society.

We first review existing literature in more detail before turning to our data. We believe that the study of parental preferences for different attributes of schools revolves around several questions, of which the most important are:

- Which attributes of schools do parents value?
- Do different types of parents value similar school attributes?

These questions lead directly to the question of what differences in parents' preferences are most important. The literature has identified the following questions as important:

- Do parents who have chosen private schools differ from parents who have chosen public ones?
- Do parents participating in public school choice programs have different values than nonparticipating parents?
- Are there city/suburban differences in parental preferences?
- Do parents of different socioeconomic status and different racial identities value academic quality equally?

The Distribution of Preferences

In our study, we presented parents with a list of eleven attributes of schools and they were asked which of these attributes was the most important to them. Interviewers read the following statements to parents: "Different parents believe that different things are important for their child's education. We are interested in knowing which things you think are important. In this next section I will read to you a list of some of the things that parents believe are important in a school and I'd like to know what you believe to be most important to your child's education." They were then told: "From the following list of qualities about schools, first tell me which is the most important to you" and were read a list of eleven attributes: quality of teachers and staff, a student body that is mostly the same race as [child's name], values of the school, a racially diverse student body, safety, economic background of students, location, high math or reading scores, special programs, discipline code, and class size." After selecting an attribute as most important, respondents were then read the list again, this time without the previously named attribute and again they were asked to name the attribute they thought most important. This procedure was repeated four times and the order in which the list was presented to the respondents was randomized to control for any order effects. In contrast to other studies that allow parents to rank multiple dimensions of schools as important, in our approach parents were forced to choose what they considered the single most important dimension of schools, then the next most important, etc.

We begin by reporting the distribution of the school attributes valued by parents as a whole; we then move on to see if different types of parents differ in their preferences.

Our results are congruent with the growing body of work showing that parents consistently emphasize the importance of the academic aspects of schools.[5] As evident in figure 4.1, the quality of teachers is by far the school attribute that is most frequently cited as important, followed by high scores. Fully 39 percent of the parents in our sample mentioned teachers as *the* most important attribute of schools. Teachers are perhaps the most important "input" into the educational production process and parents overwhelmingly want good teachers. Note that the second most frequently mentioned attribute of schools is high test scores—a measure of the "product" of the schools. Thus, the two aspects of schools most frequently mentioned as important are both academic in nature.

After these academic aspects of the schools, safety was the next most frequently cited attribute of schools.[6] Parents clearly value academically good schools that are also safe schools. Note that "values" ranks as the fourth most important school attribute. As we will see later, the concern for the ethical teachings and moral principles embodied in the term values is a dimension on which there are substantial differences between different types of parents. Finally, the "lifestyle" attributes of schools (diversity, the economic background of students) rank far below other fundamental dimensions of schools.

This pattern illustrates that overall, most parents believe academic condi-

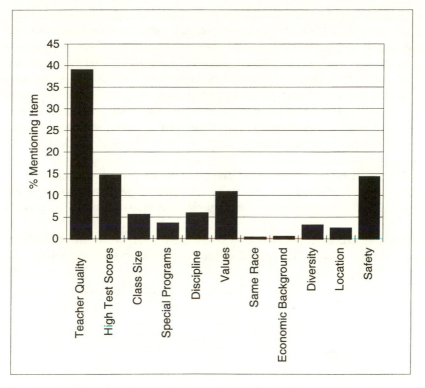

Figure 4.1   What Do Parents Find Important in Schools?

tions are the most important attributes of schools. But what about the concern that some parents will choose poorly because they value the "wrong" attributes in education? To investigate this possibility, we turn next to patterns across different types of parents.

We begin with an investigation of the distribution of attitudes across parents of different socioeconomic status. We use education as an indictor of socioeconomic status (SES) rather than income, because while these two measures are highly correlated, education tends to have a larger effect on attitudes and behavior toward schools than does income (e.g., Martinez et al. 1995).[7] Note that in the next few sections of this chapter we present simple descriptive bivariate patterns—that is, the relationship between values and parental demographic variables one at a time. Later in the chapter, we present a multivariate analysis to sort out the independent effects of each demographic variable.

Does the Level of Education Affect the Values Parents Hold?

In figure 4.2 we present data on the importance of different attributes of schools held by parents of different education levels. The sample is divided into those parents who have any college education and those who do not. There are striking differences between these groups. Note that parents without college education are much less likely to emphasize the importance of teachers than are college-educated parents. In contrast, parents without college education are more likely to emphasize objective test scores—these parents may be more attuned to the importance of doing well on the tests that act as gatekeepers. In addition, compared to college-educated parents, less-educated parents may recognize that their own resources may not be sufficient for assuring their children's academic success if ther children do not perform well on these exams.

Not surprisingly, less-educated parents are much more likely to emphasize safety and discipline. The emphasis on safety is primarily a function of the reality of the neighborhoods in which these predominately inner-city parents live.

Interestingly, note too that college-educated parents are more likely to mention the values of the school as important. This we believe reflects the

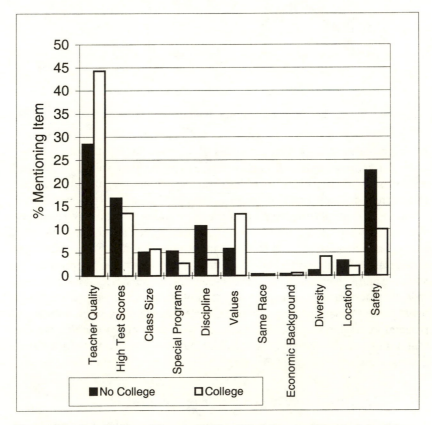

Figure 4.2   Does College Education Affect What Parents Value in Schools?

emerging culture wars that Delpit refers to in her work—more highly educated parents have the "luxury" of endorsing values as a product of the educational process, while parents with high school education emphasize the
importance of objective indicators of scholarly performance.

Does Race Make a Difference?

Figure 4.3 displays rankings of school attributes by the racial identity of
respondents. We report the pattern across the four largest ethnic groups in
our sample: whites, Hispanics, blacks, and Asians. As evident in that figure,
whites are more likely to emphasize the importance of teachers than are
other ethnic groups, but less likely to emphasize high scores. Note that white
parents are also much more likely to emphasize values than are other parents. These differences again reflect Delpit's insight—children from minority
groups need to get through the "gates" established by academic tests. In
contrast, safety and discipline are concerns of black and Hispanic parents,
though this may be a function of their concentration in New York City.

Private versus Public School Parents

Much of the work comparing the school attributes valued by parents has
focused on differences across parents who have selected private schools and
those remaining in public schools. This body of work is strongly affected by
the fact that private schools in the United States are predominately parochial
schools run by the Catholic Church. Paralleling this long-standing interest in
public versus private schools, research focusing on public schools of choice
has recently emerged.

The U.S. Department of Education's School Finance Project (1983) found
that private school parents mentioned three primary reasons for choosing
private schools: academic quality (42 percent), values or religious instruction
(30 percent), and discipline (12 percent). In contrast, public school parents
highlighted assignment to school (28 percent), transportation (24 percent),
and academic quality (17 percent). The stronger emphasis on values and
academic quality by private school parents, a consistent theme in empirical
work on parental attitudes, has been linked to the superior performance of
private school students.

Hirschoff (1986) argues that the curriculum, instructional methods, or
even general atmosphere of public schools may be in conflict with religious,
political, moral, or cultural values of some parents. But even in the absence
of such conflicts, Hirschoff identifies ideas, values, skills, attitudes, and
knowledge that schools seek to impart to their students. "Even though public
schools are not as restricted in teaching secular values as they are in teaching
religious beliefs, most commentators believe that they must, at least as to
controversial issues, maintain neutrality. Such a neutrality would not be as

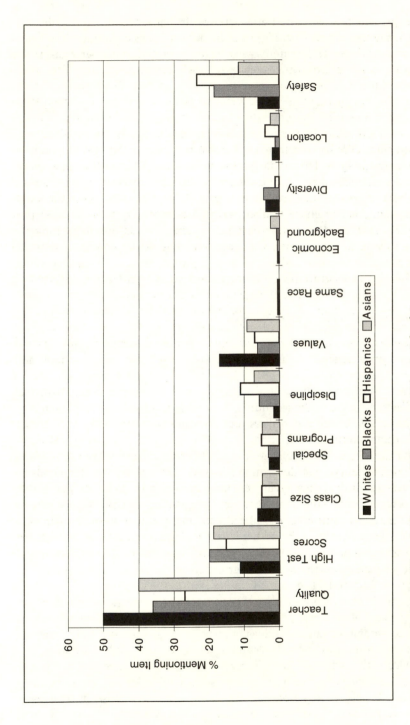

Figure 4.3   Does Race Make a Difference in What Parents Value in Schools?

helpful to parents seeking to inculcate specific values in their children as would a private school that could actively espouse those values" (42). These differences have also been noted by Bryk, Lee, and Holland (1993) and Ravitch (1996), who demonstrate how these values affect course-taking patterns of public and private school children.

Figure 4.4 demonstrates that school attributes embraced by parents in our sample correspond to this public/private dichotomy. Most notable is the extent to which private school parents stress values: these parents are more than three times more likely than public school parents to cite values of the school as most important. Note too that private school parents are more likely to mention special programs and diversity, while public school parents are significantly more likely to mention safety than are private school parents.

City/Suburban Differences

Given the nature of our data set, an additional comparison of interest is between city and suburban parents. While other dividing lines among parents have received more scrutiny, the city/suburb distinction has been less studied. In one of the few studies, Lee, Croninger, and Smith (1996) surveyed 1,042 households in three counties in the Detroit metropolitan area

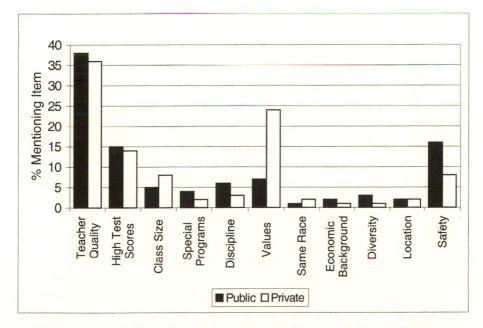

Figure 4.4   Do Public School and Private School Parents Differ in What They Value in Schools?

(including the city of Detroit). They asked respondents a series of questions regarding their attitudes and opinions about schools. Respondents rated the relative importance of seven school qualities they would consider when deciding where to send their child to school. Two nonacademic qualities of schools were rated highest: school safety (mean 5.11 out of 7) and moral and ethical values of schools (mean of 4.8), followed by strong academic course requirements (4.79), a varied set of course offerings (4.36), strict discipline (3.68), and proximity to home or work (3.23). In comparing responses across parents residing in Detroit and parents residing in surrounding suburbs, Lee, Croninger, and Smith (83–84) found Detroit residents placed somewhat higher values on school safety (5.36 versus 5.04) and strict discipline (4.04 versus 3.58) and lower values on course variety than suburban residents (4.09 versus 4.43).

In figure 4.5, we report the pattern in preferences for parents in New York and New Jersey. Consistent with Lee, Croninger, and Smith (1986), New York parents are much more likely to emphasize safety and discipline than are suburban parents—this is clearly a function of the characteristics of the different geographic domains. In contrast, New Jersey parents are much

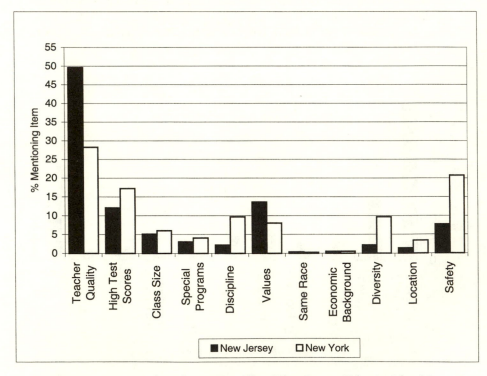

Figure 4.5 Does Residential Location Affect What Parents Value in Schools?

more likely to emphasize the importance of teachers, while New York parents are more likely to mention high scores.

Choosers versus Nonchoosers

While differences between private and public schools have attracted attention over the past fifteen years, research on differences across choosers (public or private) and nonchoosers has only recently emerged.

Witte's work in Milwaukee shows that parents cite academic values as the most important reason for using the voucher program—followed by discipline and the general atmosphere of the school (also see Greene et al. 1998). Research on *private* voucher programs (reported in Moe 1995) also tends to support the importance of academics in motivating choice. For example, Beales and Wahl (1996) report that almost 90 percent of parents in Milwaukee school choice programs cited academic quality as "very important" in their decision to enroll.[8] This was followed by concerns for discipline, the general atmosphere of the school, and financial considerations. At the bottom of the list was "other children in the chosen school." Similar results were found in studies of San Antonio (Martinez et al. 1995) and Indianapolis (Heise, Colburn, and Lamberti 1995), where educational quality was cited as the most important factor among parents participating in choice.

In figure 4.6, we see only marginal differences in the ranking of fundamental academic dimensions between choosers and nonchoosers. Two nota-

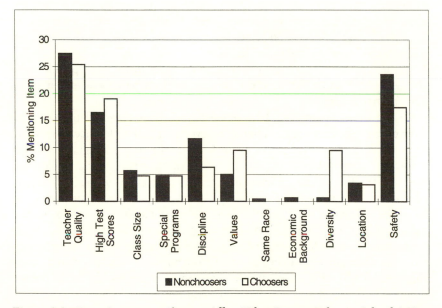

Figure 4.6   Does Status as a Chooser Affect What Parents Value in Schools? New York Only

ble differences do emerge however. First, nonchoosers are more likely emphasize safety and discipline, again a function of conditions in the schools. Second, choosers are more likely to stress values and diversity. This last finding is not surprising since many alternative schools in New York are organized around multicultural themes.

The Bivariate Relationships: What Do Parents Think Is Important in Their Schools?

In the simple descriptive analysis presented thus far, academic concerns, especially teacher quality, are the most frequently cited aspect of schools parents find important. However, some interesting differences across parents do begin to appear. But, few of these provide evidence that stratification by class or race will emerge if parents are allowed to choose schools according to the dimensions they find important. For example, while there are differences in which parents find discipline and safety important, these differences are rooted in the life experiences of the parents—less-educated parents in New York's public schools are more concerned about safety than other parents. This is a reaction to reality—compared to both private schools and the conditions of middle-class suburbs, New York parents have every reason to emphasize safety and discipline.

Some patterns support Delpit's argument about the preferences of lower-income and minority parents for performance on standardized tests. Parents from racial minorities and with lower socioeconomic status are consistently more likely to emphasize test scores when compared to white parents and those with higher education. And they are more likely to emphasize test scores above even the quality of teachers.

We also find that preferences for school values distinguish parents who choose private and alternative public schools from parents who remain in neighborhood schools.

Clearly, the demographic characteristics underlying these relationships are interrelated. Socioeconomic differences overlap racial differences, which in turn overlap the city/suburban distinction. In the next section we sort out these inter-relationships using a multivariate probit analysis, which allows us to isolate the independent effects these factors have on what parents value in education. Rather than display results for all eleven school attributes, we focus on test scores (because they are a critical measure of school performance and central to debates about whether different parents value academic performance—see Moe 1995; Delpit 1995); values (because of their importance in distinguishing choosers from nonchoosers); discipline and safety (because of the difference in their distribution across different parents grouped by location and by education); and diversity.

A Digression on Our Multivariate Models

Before we undertake a multivariate analysis of the factors affecting the likelihood that a parent mentions a specific school aspect as important, we need a brief digression to define our approach to the empirical work in both this and subsequent chapters. In most of the empirical modeling we develop in this book, we use a set of core independent variables. These core variables include fundamental demographic characteristics of the parents we interviewed. These characteristics include racial identification, education level, employment status, gender, frequency of church attendance, and length of residence in the district. Studies have shown that these factors influence parent attitudes toward schools, expectations about education, and involvement and interest in schooling. We often employ these demographic measures as control variables so that we can focus on the organizational and institutional variables that are our primary concerns. However, some of these variables, especially education and racial identification, also assume important substantive meaning, especially given concerns about stratification and segregation so common to debates about choice.

In addition to these core demographic variables, we also include indicators of geographic location in our models. The specific indicators vary according to the question at hand. For example, as in the analysis that follows, we want to control for the different environments found in the central city and suburban districts in our study. Thus, a simple dummy variable for New York versus New Jersey suffices. In other analyses, however, we want to isolate more carefully the effects of different schooling environments on parent behavior. In these cases, we introduce specific dummy variables for each district so we can, for example, identify the extent to which choice in District 4 is associated with different patterns of parent behavior compared to parent behavior in District 1, controlling for specific demographic conditions. Similarly, we can compare the effects of choice in Montclair to the lack of choice in Morristown.

In addition to specifying the broad choice environment in which a parent lives, we often specify the type of chooser (if any) a parent is. Here, depending on the specific question under consideration, we might use a set of dummy variables that indicate whether or not a parent has chosen a private school and whether or not the parent has chosen a public school. Moreover, depending on the specific question at hand, we sometimes distinguish between universal choosers and option-demand choosers.

While these variables are found in almost all our empirical models, in some cases we add a set of unique variables that may have important effects on the behavior we are studying. In these instances, we discuss the rationale for including them in the specific analyses at hand.

We begin our empirical investigation with perhaps the most simple model we present in the book. Here we model what is important to parents as a function of our core variables. Specifically, we specify the following probit model:

Prob (Y) = f (racial identification, education, choice status, central city/suburban location, employment status, gender, church attendance, length of residence)

Where:

Y = the importance of a school attribute measured by whether or not parents cited it first (school attributes considered here include high scores, values, discipline, safety, and diversity).

Racial identification: a set of dummy variables corresponding to Asian, black, or Hispanic races.[9]

Education: a set of dummy variables representing the highest level of education achieved: less than high school graduate is the excluded category, high school graduate (high school = 1), and college experience (college = 1).[10]

Choice status: two dummy variables; parents choosing private schools (private = 1) and parents choosing public alternative schools (chooser = 1).

Central city versus suburban location: a dummy variable indicating residence in New York City or suburban New Jersey (New York = 1).

Employment status: a dummy variable indicating whether the parent works outside the home (working = 1).

Gender: a dummy variable indicating whether the parent is female (female = 1).

Church attendance: a categorical variable measuring the frequency of a respondent's church attendance (1 = never; 2 = hardly ever; 3 = couple of times per year; 4 = every few months; 5 = monthly; 6 = every other week; 7 = weekly).

Length of residence: a continuous variable measuring the number of years a parent has lived in the district.

As the dependent variable here is dichotomous (the parent mentioned an attribute or not), we use probit analysis. And, given the difficulty in interpreting "normal" probit coefficients, we translate these coefficients into the change in probability that a parent mentions a specific attribute corresponding to a unit change in the independent variable.

With this background material in place, we return to our substantive issue: determining the independent effects of our core variables on parental preferences for different aspects of schooling.

What Is Important to Parents?

Given the intense debate about school performance and the purported difference in the weight placed on it by parents of different educational status, we begin with an investigation of this attribute. We measure academic quality of the school using student scores on standardized math and reading tests.

Table 4.1, column 1, reports the change in the probability of citing high scores as important.

The multivariate analysis confirms the independent effects of many of the conditions displayed in the earlier figures. Rather than reflecting the common belief that individuals with lower social status do not value academic performance highly, the results reflect the emerging debate described by Del-

Table 4.1
The Change in the Probability of an Aspect of Schools Being Named Important

	High Scores	Values	Discipline	Safety	Diversity
Asian	.04	−.03	.08*	.08	***
	(.05)	(.03)	(.05)	(.07)	
Hispanic	.01	−.04**	.04*	.11*	.00
	(.03)	(.02)	(.02)	(.03)	(.00)
Black	.06*	−.04*	.04*	.14*	.00
	(.03)	(.02)	(.02)	(.03)	(.00)
College	−.04**	.05*	−.01	.00	.02**
	(.02)	(.02)	(.01)	(.02)	(.01)
High School	.05*	−.06**	.00	−.06*	.01
	(.02)	(.03)	(.01)	(.03)	(.01)
Private	.00	.14*	−.01	−.02	−.02*
	(.02)	(.03)	(.01)	(.02)	(.00)
New York	.04*	−.03	.03*	.05*	.00
	(.02)	(.02)	(.01)	(.02)	(.00)
Chooser	.02	.06	.01	−.02	.07*
	(.04)	(.05)	(.02)	(.03)	(.04)
Employed	.01	−.01	−.01	.00	.00
	(.02)	(.01)	(.01)	(.01)	(.00)
Female	.00	−.02	.00	.03	−.01
	(.02)	(.02)	(.01)	(.02)	(.01)
Church Attendance	−.007**	.01*	.01*	.00	.00
	(.004)	(.00)	(.00)	(.00)	(.00)
Length of Residence	.00	.00	.00	.002**	.00
	(.00)	(.00)	(.00)	(.001)	(.00)
Observed "P"	.15	.11	.06	.14	.03
Chi square	28.51	110.71	75.46	118.21	47.28
Prob.	.004	.00	.00	.00	.00
No. of Cases	1572	1572	1572	1572	1518

Note: Coefficients are the change in probability of a respondent saying a condition is important on the first reading.

  *probability <. 05

 **probability <. 10

***Because Asians predicted "failure" perfectly, 54 cases were dropped from this particular analysis.

pit and Hirsch. Our data show that parents who have high school diplomas but no college, and who identify themselves as black, are all significantly more likely to rank test scores as the most important attribute of schools. This analysis suggests that low-income, inner-city parents are quite aware of the evolving stakes associated with testing and want a more traditional academic curriculum.

This finding is reinforced by the distribution of parents who find values important. As is evident in column 2 of table 4.1, white parents are significantly more likely to rank values as important than are black or Hispanic parents. And parents with high school diplomas, but no college, are also less likely to emphasize values. Not surprisingly, the biggest predictor of parents' preferences for school values is the public/private distinction: private school parents are much more likely to emphasize values than are other parents, a result congruent with previous research.

On the importance of discipline (see column 3 of table 4.1), we find that parents from minority groups are much more likely to emphasize discipline than are white parents. Not surprisingly, discipline is more frequently cited as important in New York than in New Jersey.

Finally, the factors influencing the importance of safety are similar to those for discipline. That is, white parents are less likely to find safety important, as are parents in New Jersey.

The Importance of Racial Composition in School Choice

There are differences between parents of different racial and educational backgrounds in the importance they assign to the academic dimensions of schools. The next question we examine is whether or not there are differences in their preferences for the racial composition of the student population. Critics of school choice argue that parents will select schools on the basis of race and create segregated schools (Bridge and Blackman 1978; Murnane 1986; Wong 1992). How important is the racial composition of schools to different types of parents?

We asked each parent to evaluate two dimensions of the racial composition of their child's school. First, we asked how important it was to her that her child attend a school populated mostly by students of the same race as her child. Second, we asked how important it was to her that her child attend a racially and ethnically diverse school.

We find that parents hardly ever cite racial similarity as a relevant criterion in evaluating the quality of schools. Less than 1 percent of parents we surveyed ranked race as important, and consequently, we are unable to investigate further the effects of race and class on who evaluates race as an important criterion. While we acknowledge that this low percentage most likely underrepresents the true level of parent concern with race, as they report what they believe to be socially acceptable responses, it may also signify a declining role of race as a motivation for choice (see Henig 1994, 115).

Diversity in the student population was more important to more parents than was racial similarity: close to 3 percent of the parents in the survey ranked this as the first most important attribute of a good school. We recognize that this highly skewed distribution causes the same problems that led us to reject analyzing the pattern of responses for the same race dimension, but we believe it is necessary to analyze the importance of the racial composition of schools on at least one dimension. On the diversity dimension, we find that parents with a college education are significantly more likely to emphasize this dimension than are parents with less education (see column 5 of table 4.1). We also find that public school choosers are more likely to find diversity important, which may reflect the importance of bilingual/bicultural themes in many of the alternative schools in New York City and the strong commitment to racial balance in Montclair.

There Are Differences among Parents and These Differences Make a Difference

We believe that our data make clear that parents of different socioeconomic and racial backgrounds do indeed value different attributes of schools. However, these differences are not the ones most often noted. Parents of lower socioeconomic status and parents who identify themselves as racial minorities want something different from their schools than do white parents or parents with higher education levels. Lower socioeconomic status and minority parents are more likely to value schools that perform the bedrock function of providing a safe environment and the fundamentals of education. They desire such fundamentals to increase the likelihood that their children can pass the gatekeeping points on the path to economic success. An emphasis on values, including diversity, is perhaps a luxury that middle-class and white parents can better afford.

Sharp (1996) has recently identified cities as critical sites for "culture wars"—arenas in which fundamental divisions in the values people hold are acted out. Not surprisingly, local schools, certainly the most expensive and arguably the most important public good cities provide, have emerged as an arena in which these divisions are played out.

Our work shows that the concerns that school choice will lead to increased segregation because parents will focus on race in choosing schools are misplaced. Segregation in schools is the product of a variety of strong forces, perhaps the most important being residential patterns. We believe that the distribution of preferences for same race schools will have little or no effect on these already strong patterns of segregation in the schools.

However, there are still numerous issues beyond the distribution of preferences that affect the relationship between choice and stratification and segregation. In the next set of chapters, we examine the role that information, and the ways parents gather and use information to make schooling decisions, plays in affecting who gets what from their schools.

Chapter 5

How Do Parents Search for Information?

Clearly, parents must have at least some information about schools if they are to make an appropriate choice of school for their children. In this and the next few chapters, we examine how different types of parents in different settings search for and use information about schools. We begin by identifying the sources parents find useful in their search for information. We continue this study of information in the next chapter, where we focus on the role of social networks in the flow of information. Later in the book, we examine the accuracy of the information parents have about their children's schools and examine how parents use information when choosing schools.

While the acquisition and use of information by parents is central to the study of school choice, the issues involved are more general. Indeed, the flow of information is basic to debates about increasing citizen/consumer choice over any public good, not just schools. In fact, many analysts argue that citizen information levels are fundamentally important to political activities other than the choice over public goods. And Delli Carpini and Keeter go so far as to argue that an "informed citizenry is an implicit requisite for any theory of democracy" (1991, 583).

Despite the importance of an informed citizenry, beginning at least as far back as Lazarsfeld, Berelson, and Gaudet (1944), political scientists have demonstrated that most citizens know very little about politics and public policy. Many analysts argue that low information levels result from simple benefit/cost calculations. For most citizens, the costs of gathering information about politics and public goods is high relative to the benefits of such information. Faced with this adverse calculation, most citizens simply remain uninformed. The effects of this calculation have been found in a variety of political and policy domains (see, e.g., Lupia and McCubbins 1998), including education (see especially Chubb and Moe 1990a).

On the cost side, basic information about schools is often not widely circulated and, even if available, is often difficult to interpret. For instance, linking the kinds of data usually reported by schools or school boards (for example, the number of teachers or expenditures per pupil) to actual school performance is a task that has engaged the talents of large numbers of highly trained econometricians. Moreover, indicators reflecting what parents care about are often difficult to identify. For example, most parents want good teachers, but what indicators reflect the actual quality of the teaching staff—seniority? advanced credentials? salary?

On the benefit side, once settled in a house or apartment, there may be very few payoffs for gathering information about schools: it may make little sense to have extensive knowledge about the quality of a public good if your "consumption" decision (the school your child attends) is dictated by a bureaucratic decision rule such as the attendance zone in which you live.

Even if institutional arrangements increase the incentives parents have to gather information, the costs of information processing remain high. Cognitive effort is a scarce resource and the computational power of the decision maker is always limited (Simon 1986, S210–S211). Thus, all decision making involves a trade-off between decision accuracy and cognitive effort (see, for example, Fiske and Taylor 1991; Sniderman, Brody, and Tetlock 1991; Lodge and Stroh 1993).

According to Delli Carpini and Keeter, some conditions in American society have changed in ways that might increase levels of citizen information. Most notably, rising education levels in America may lead to increased levels of citizen information. Nie, Junn, and Stehlik-Bawy (1996) note that education is the single variable that studies of political participation most often highlight as increasing levels of individual political participation and involvement—factors closely tied to higher levels of political information. Education not only reduces the cognitive costs of gathering and using information, but it also increases the likelihood that an individual is surrounded by others with a high level of education. More highly educated individuals are more likely to be embedded in better networks—and good networks can be a highly efficient shortcut to quality information (Huckfeldt and Sprague 1995).

The growing pervasiveness of mass media is another environmental change that leads some analysts to expect higher levels of information. This "information explosion," which has taken many forms, the most recent being the introduction of the Internet, can greatly reduce the costs of gathering information.

However, critics have argued that the beneficial effects of both education and the information explosion can be overstated. Many argue that higher levels of formal education have not necessarily produced a more informed citizenry. Other analysts argue that even if there has been an information explosion and a growing availability of relatively low-cost information, the diffusion of these conditions has not been uniform across the population—rather, they argue that the information explosion has created a world of "haves" and "have-nots," with the development of an information-poor segment of the population that overlaps with a population that is already low on other valued resources.

In addition, the information explosion may have actually increased the costs of information. Given what Shenk (1997) calls "data smog," it may become increasingly important for citizens to develop strategies to sift through large volumes of information. In turn, the distribution of information and the ability to engage in search for information may overlap the distribution of other valued skills and resources, increasing rather than decreasing levels of inequality in access to public goods.

In our work, we show how many of these issues play out in the domain of school choice. We begin our study of how people of different educational levels, demographics, and institutional environments gather and use information by focusing on how parents evaluate different sources of information about the schools.

Searching for Information

We emphasize two distinct dimensions inherent in all human decision making-cognitive effort and decision accuracy. We assume that individual decision makers attempt to minimize cognitive effort while trying to make accurate decisions. They employ cost/benefit strategies acquired through some combination of training and experience with decision making.

These concepts have motivated many studies of decision making, including the adaptive decision-maker model developed by Payne, Bettham, and Johnson (1993; also see Beach and Mitchell 1978; and Simon 1957 on effort and accuracy in problem solving). In this approach, individuals manage complex decision tasks by using heuristics (or "rules of thumb") to simplify the decision-making process and minimize effort. According to Sniderman, Brody, and Tetlock: "Heuristics are judgmental shortcuts, efficient ways to organize and simplify political choices, efficient in the double sense of requiring relatively little information to execute, yet yielding dependable answers even to complex problems of choice" (1991, 19).

The choice of heuristics, and more generally, the costs and benefits of decision making are a function of the characteristics of the individual *and* of the choice situation. Perhaps the most important characteristics of the individual relate to the individual's cognitive skills and involvement with the "product" about which the person is choosing. Clearly, education and the resulting skills are among the most critical individual-level characteristics determining an individual's ability to gather and process information. Well-educated people have consistently been found to have more efficient methods for gathering and processing information.

To the extent that more-educated and less-educated individuals rely on different sources of information, and to the extent that these sources of information vary in their usefulness, school choice might increase stratification. Given the enduring concern for racial segregation in the schools, we need also to be concerned about the distribution of information search procedures across racial groups.

While these are characteristics of individuals, the context of choice itself can affect information search. Decision theoretic research has shown that the number of alternatives and other factors affecting the cost of information influence the choice process and the accuracy of individual decisions (see

Rona and Schneider 1996). Nevertheless, little research has examined how the characteristics of different school systems, including choice mechanisms, affect the choice process.

We investigate the extent to which institutional incentives built into the choice process affect search processes. Do parents who are given the opportunity to choose search for information any differently than other parents?

Sources of Information

Price and Zaller (1993) identify several sources that individuals can turn to for political information. First, they argue that individuals can use the news media. This argument is based on the "intuitive notion that people exposed more frequently to news media will be more likely to learn about current events" (135).

A second pathway to information relies on interpersonal communication (Huckfeldt and Sprague 1995; Robinson and Levy 1986). The importance of learning from others in politics was recognized early on by the Columbia School. Pioneering studies by Lazarsfeld, Berelson, and Gaudet (1944) identified a two-step flow of information from mass media to the individual. This flow is mediated by opinion leaders who enjoy the social power that holding and transmitting information gives them (See Knoke and Kuklinski 1982. Also see Atkins 1972; Chaffee and McLeod 1973; Sieber 1974; Richmond 1977; and Levy 1978). Thus, citizens rely on interactions with opinion leaders to provide valuable political information, such as recounts of campaign speeches, at a reduced cost. The idea of opinion leadership continues to play an influential role in political science; recent work relies on the idea that voters can rely on a small subset of informed citizens when making political decisions (Zaller 1992; Popkin 1991; Lupia 1992, 1994).

Lupia has demonstrated how voters can use interpersonal sources to gather information about when voting on referenda—a situation that resembles the school choice decision task.

> Voters in large electorates who consider their opportunity costs may decide that the acquisition of "encyclopedic" information is not a worthwhile activity. As an alternative to the costly acquisition of encyclopedic information, voters may choose to employ information shortcuts. For example, voters can acquire information about the preferences or opinions of friends, coworkers, political parties or other groups, which they may then use to infer how a proposition will affect them. The appeal of these information shortcuts is that they generally require relatively little effort to acquire. (1994, 63)

The process Lupia describes draws on both the two-step flow of information documented by Lazarsfeld, Berelson, and Gaudet and the network studies done by Granovetter, Huckfeldt and Sprague, and others. Building on this argument, we believe that parents can use both strategies in their search for information about schools, that is, they can use formal sources of information or they can use networks.

Previous work has documented that parents use social networks as shortcuts to information about schools (Witte 1991a; Witte, Bailey, and Thorn 1992; Wilson 1992; Boyer 1992; and Glenn, McLaughlin, and Salganik 1993). But, research has also shown that there are significant differences in the way these networks of information are constructed. Most notably, studies of Alum Rock found that higher-income parents had higher quality ties to information networks than did lower-income parents—thus, the concerns of critics that school choice will exacerbate social class differences may have an empirical foundation.

Patterns of Parent Search Behavior

We approach the study of information and social class by looking at patterns in the sources parents use for gathering data about the schools. Much previous research asked individuals to report on how frequently they engaged in a type of search activity (for example, how often they read the newspaper or talked to someone about politics). In our approach, we asked parents to evaluate how useful they found particular sources of information. Specifically, we asked parents to evaluate the usefulness of ten different information sources: newsletters from the school or district, friends, the mass media such as TV, teachers, staff, coworkers, children, other parents, community centers, and politicians. All sources were evaluated according to a four-point scale: not at all useful, not very useful, very useful, and extremely useful.

Following Price and Zaller and others, we identify two major categories of information sources that are available to parents. We begin with a category in which the sources of information are relatively "close" to our respondents. These sources of information include interpersonal communications between a parent and both friends and parents of other children in her child's school. These sources are cheap and easy to use—information can be passed around as part of a person's daily rounds, one can assess the reputation of the source from repeated interaction, and difficulties caused by differences in social background are minimal. However, the information a person receives depends on the "quality" of her friends—if a parent is surrounded by poorly informed individuals, these interpersonal sources of information may yield little reliable or accurate information.

Further removed from the daily life of most parents, the other major avenue for gathering information is "formal" sources of information. Looking at the media first, we quickly discovered that in the world of schools, not much information about school performance is carried in the mass media. For example, using the Nexis/Lexis databases, we searched for all references to school performance in the districts in our study over the last ten years and came up with just a handful of articles. In addition, very few of these articles carried specific information about school performance—many were general, or focused on the internal politics of the school board. Consequently, we expanded our focus on formal sources of information to include the use of community-based sources of information—community centers and politicians.

In addition, we considered a specific subset of potential information providers within the school system: school newsletters, teachers, and school staff. These are expert, detailed sources, but the social distance between them and parents can be quite large (this is especially true among the parents of lower socioeconomic status in New York City).

We created counts of usefulness within each of these three categories—summing the number of information sources of each type that a parent found to be either extremely or very useful. We begin with the sources of information closest to parents: The "social" scale combines two variables—the usefulness of friends and parents of other children in the same school. We then move to our category "school-based" sources of information, combining responses on three variables: the usefulness of newsletters, teachers, and staff. Finally, we construct a "formal" scale that counts the number of the "external" and relatively impersonal sources of information parents found either extremely or very useful: mass media, politicians, and community centers.[1] We also combined these separate measures into a single scale, counting the total number of sources of information parents found very or extremely useful.[2]

In the next sections, we look at the patterns of information sources parents find useful across specific groups of parents defined by their demographics and their opportunities to choose schools. We then turn to a multivariate analysis to sort out the independent effects of these factors.

Do Parents of Different Education Levels Find Different Sources of Information Useful?

Given the centrality of education levels to theories of information search, we begin our empirical investigation by examining how parents with different levels of education evaluate different sources of information. In this initial stage of analysis, we divide parents into four groups: those who did not complete high school, those with high school diplomas but no college, those who attended but did not complete college, and those with a college degree. In figures 5.1 and 5.2, we display the relationship between parent education level and the evaluation of the usefulness of different sources of information. We believe that these figures show an important pattern in how parents of different education levels evaluate sources of information.

Figure 5.1 shows a *negative* relationship between education and the total number of sources parents find useful—as education levels increase, the number of sources of information parents find useful declines. While this

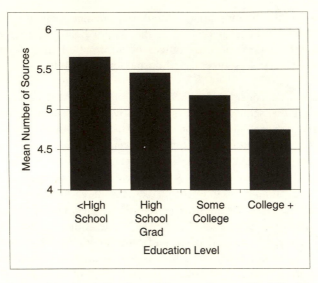

Figure 5.1   Total Number of Sources Parents Find Useful,
by Education Level

may at first seem strange—well-educated parents actually use *fewer* sources
of information—the reason for the direction of this relationship is made
clear by looking at parental evaluations of the different categories of sources
of information. In figure 5.2, we find the same decline in the evaluation of

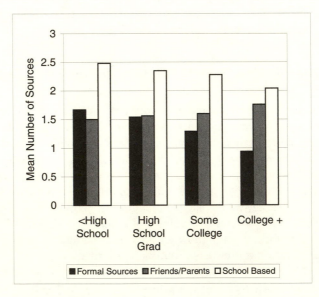

Figure 5.2   Sources of Information Parents Find Useful, by
Education Level

school-based sources of information and of the usefulness of formal sources as education levels increase. But note that parents with higher education levels find friends and parents with children in their child's school *more useful*.

Parents are embedded in networks of information that are highly stratified by education: highly educated individuals are likely to talk about schools with other highly educated individuals and less-educated individuals are likely to talk about schools with other less-educated individuals. In general, then, highly educated individuals are surrounded by people with more reliable information about the schools. In this milieu, highly educated parents have access to an efficient pathway to information: in their daily contact with friends, neighbors, and other parents, they can gather reliable information about the schools relatively cheaply from the other highly educated people they meet. In contrast, less-educated individuals are tied to educational discussants with lower levels of education and with less reliable information. Given that this pathway to information does not produce reliable information, less-educated parents search for information more widely.

Of course, regardless of the quality of their networks, parents may also choose to rely on school-based sources of information. While these sources of information should produce reliable information (teachers and staff should have accurate information about the schools), the costs of relying on these sources may be high. First, there may be considerable social distance between school officials and parents. Second, there are clear institutional roles that may distance teachers from parents (for example, teachers may not share the incentives with parents to identify failing programs) and there are logistical constraints that limit the extent and frequency of contact. For example, contact with a teacher or a staff member may require a formal appointment at the school building.

Similarly, a reliance on formal, external sources of information represents trade-offs. Media sources can be entertaining, but, as noted above, our research into the stories the media carries about schools showed little useful information about individual school performance.

Thus, while there are clearly different pathways to knowledge about the schools, the most efficient and reliable sources of information may be those used by more highly educated individuals—for them, reliable information can be gathered fairly cheaply in their daily social interactions with other well-educated parents.

Do Parents of Different Races Find Different Sources of Information Useful?

In addition to the issue of stratification by class (as measured in our analysis by education), debates over school choice also focus on racial differences. In this section, we examine racial patterns in the pathways to information parents use for gathering information.

Given the overlap between race and class, the patterns evident in figures 5.3 and 5.4 should not be surprising. Compared to other racial groups,

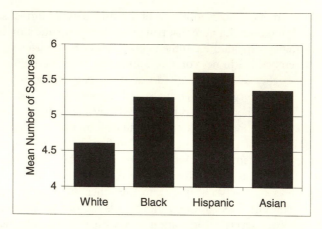

Figure 5.3   Total Number of Useful Sources, by Race

whites report the lowest total number of sources of information and tend to find both formal and school-based sources of information less useful. While the differences are not as large, compared to black and Hispanic parents, Asian parents tend also to find fewer sources of information useful and they are less likely to find school-based and external sources of information useful.

Not surprisingly, these patterns reverse when we look at the usefulness of other parents and friends. Here, white parents and Asian parents are more

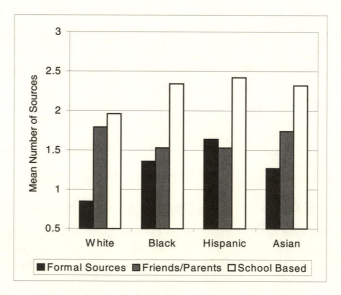

Figure 5.4   Useful Sources, by Race

likely to find these sources of information useful than are black or Hispanic parents. We believe that the underlying reasons for these patterns are similar to those that we have already identified—interpersonal networks of information are not only defined by education; they are also defined by race. In addition, parents identifying themselves as black or Hispanic tend to be in smaller networks that are often of lower quality than the networks of white parents.

Thus, race and class matter in parents' evaluation of the usefulness of different information sources. Next, we examine whether or not the institutional incentives provided by choice affect the information pathways parents employ.

Do Institutional Arrangements Matter?

Theoretically, the search for information is driven by both the personal characteristics of individuals *and* the environment in which individuals operate. According to its proponents, school choice increases the incentives of individuals to search for information. While we address later the *quality* of the information parents in different school districts possess, here we focus on the pathways to information: do parents in choice districts find different sources of information useful? As with the previous analyses, we begin with a simple bivariate presentation of the data—later we will employ a multivariate model.

Here we see variations on the themes from the previous analysis. Comparing the overall pattern displayed in figure 5.5, we see that parents in New York City are more likely to find more sources of information useful than are parents in the New Jersey suburbs. And repeating the pattern shown previously in Figure 5.6, we find that parents in New York are more likely to find

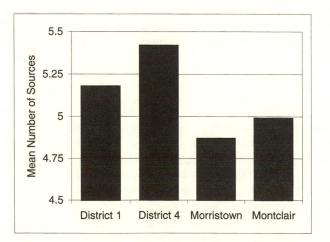

Figure 5.5 Total Number of Useful Sources, by District

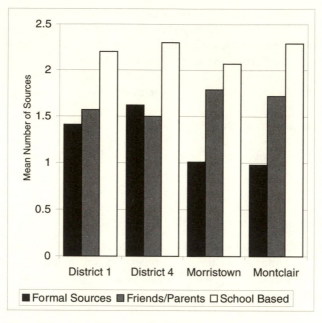

Figure 5.6   Useful Sources, by District

formal sources of information useful, and, also not surprisingly, less likely to find friends and other parents useful. These patterns are predictable from the race and education data we presented earlier.

However, consider the pattern in parents' evaluations of the usefulness of school-based sources. Here, the data show a clear effect of choice—parents in both choice districts are more likely to find school-based sources of information useful than are parents in the "matched" district. This may indicate that choice has succeeded in making parents feel more like "owners" of their schools, reducing the distance and barriers between parents and schools.

Does Individual Status as a Chooser Matter?

Here we examine the information sources parents of different choice status find useful. In figures 5.7 and 5.8, we display levels of usefulness in the following four categories: (1) parents whose children attend neighborhood public schools; (2) parents who are in universal choice settings; (3) option-demand parents; and (4) parents who have chosen private schools for their children. We look at the usefulness of each of the four categories of information sources by individual choice status.

Figure 5.7 shows that the total number of sources of information that parents find useful declines when we compare parents whose children attend neighborhood public schools to parents in public school choice environ-

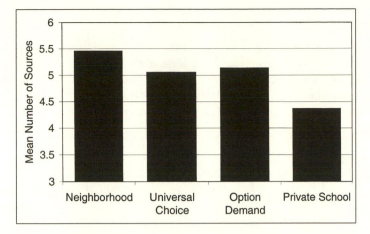

Figure 5.7   Total Number of Useful Sources, by Chooser Status

ments. In addition, we observe an even greater difference in comparing the number of useful sources named by parents whose children attend neighborhood public schools to the number of sources named by private school parents. This decline is driven almost entirely by the lower use of school-based sources by private school parents (see figure 5.8). In contrast, parents whose children attend neighborhood schools are more likely to use more formal sources including the mass media and school-based sources. In general, however, differences in the evaluation of information sources by parents categorized by chooser status do not point to any consistent pattern.

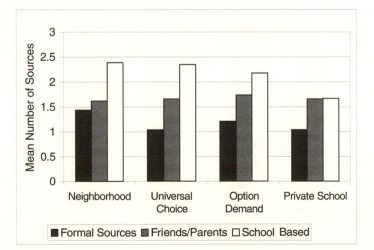

Figure 5.8   Useful Sources, by Chooser Status

Sorting Out Effects: A Multivariate Analysis

We have seen some effects of race, education, institutional structure, and individual chooser status on the usefulness of the various pathways to school information. Now, given the overlap between race, class, and location, we try to sort out the independent effects using a multivariate regression framework. We present the results of four separate estimates of the following form:

Usefulness = f (education, race, institutional factors, controls)

Where:

Usefulness is measured by the scales in each of the four domains identified above (total sources; friends/parents; school-based sources; external sources).

Education is the total number of years of education completed. Note that here we are moving away from the categories used in the earlier section for the bivariate visual presentation to a continuous variable more suitable for multivariate analysis.

Race is a series of dichotomous variables representing the self-reported racial identity of the respondents.

Institutional factors is represented by (1) a dichotomous variable representing whether or not the parent is an universal chooser; (2) an interaction term between the universal chooser variable and a dichotomous variable representing whether the respondent lives in New York; (3) a dichotomous variable representing whether or not a parent is an option-demand chooser; (4) a dichotomous variable indicating private school parents.

Control variables include the core measures used in the models throughout this book: length of residence in the district, to capture the possibility that experience with different sources of information over time can change the perception of usefulness; the frequency of church attendance, which can affect the flow of information in a variety of ways; employment status; and gender. We also include a dichotomous variable representing whether the respondent lives in New York or New Jersey.

Table 5.1 reports the model estimates for each of the four measures of usefulness. We estimated the total number of sources using multiple regression and the models of each specific information domain with ordered probit. In tables 5.1a, 5.1b, and 5.1c, we present the changes in predicted probabilities that we calculated using the ordered probit coefficients reported in table 5.1.

In the first column of table 5.1, we report the effects of these conditions on the total number of useful information pathways. The results confirm most of the bivariate patterns. Ceteris paribus, there are significant effects of race on the total number of sources found useful—parents from minority groups, on average, find a greater number of sources of information useful. Examining the institutional variables in the model, we find that private

Table 5.1
The Impact of Demographic and Institutional Factors on Sources of Information
That Parents Find Useful

	Total	Social	School Based	Formal
Black	.464**	−.440**	.363**	.433**
	(.123)	(.097)	(.085)	(.081)
Asian	.758**	−.022	.572**	.364*
	(.239)	(.198)	(.171)	(.155)
Hispanic	.658**	−.264*	.440**	.455**
	(.140)	(.110)	(.096)	(.092)
Education	−.013	.030*	−.015	−.020*
	(.015)	(.012)	(.011)	(.010)
Gender	.193	.135	.176	.004
	(.111)	(.089)	(.074)	(.073)
Work	−.285**	.024	−.115*	−.254**
	(.098)	(.078)	(.067)	(.064)
Church Attendance	−.073**	−.018	−.030	−.049**
	(.020)	(.015)	(.013)	(.013)
Length of Residence	.001	.005	−.004	.002
	(.006)	(.005)	(.004)	(.004)
New York	−.095	−.339**	−.105	.187*
	(.129)	(.103)	(.088)	(.085)
Active Chooser	−.138	.293	−.153	−.230
	(.220)	(.181)	(.151)	(.145)
NY—Univ. Chooser	−.527*	−.214	−.320	−.169
	(.253)	(.188)	(.175)	(.164)
Universal Chooser	−.064	−.150	.095	−.095
	(.128)	(.109)	(.088)	(.084)
Private	−.805**	−.124	−.686**	−.227**
	(.117)	(.095)	(.079)	(.077)
Threshold 1		−1.29**	−1.974**	−1.008**
		(.215)	(.198)	(.183)
Threshold 2		−.531**	−1.112**	.055
		(.23)	(.193)	(.182)
Threshold 3			−.193	.885**
			(.192)	(.183)
Constant	5.447**			
	(.278)			
Chi^2	14.67**	99.58**	218.01**	238.99**
F(13,1551)				
Adj R² = .10				
N = Sample Size	1565	1565	1565	1565

Notes: We estimated the Total Sources used with multiple regression, and the other three models using ordered probit. Standard errors are in parentheses. The threshold values correspond to the cutpoints on the standardized normal distribution used to calculate the predicted probabilities for each category of the dependent variable.

*p < .05
**p < .01

Table 5.1a
Changes in Predicted Probabilities of Finding 0, 1, or 2 Categories of Social
Sources Useful

		0	1	2
Base Probability		.03	.11	.86
Variable	*Change*			
Black	No to Yes	.05	.07	−.12
Asian	No to Yes	.00	.00	.00
Hispanic	No to Yes	.02	.04	−.07
Education	12 to 15.5 Years	−.02	−.03	.05
Work	No to Yes	.00	.00	.01
Church	Every Other Week to Every Few Months	.01	.01	−.02
New York	No to Yes	.03	.06	−.09
Private	No to Yes	.01	.02	−.03

school parents cite significantly fewer sources of information useful than public school parents as do universal choosers in New York compared to their neighborhood school counterparts. Note too that working parents and parents who attend church more frequently also find fewer sources of information useful. We return to the meaning of these overall findings below, but first, we report the results of our analysis of the effects of parental characteristics on the evaluation of each of the different domains of information. These analyses help explain the aggregate relationships that we observe in the first column of table 5.1.

Table 5.1b
Changes in Predicted Probabilities of Finding 0, 1, 2, or 3 Categories of School
Sources Useful

		0	1	2	3
Base Probability		.04	.14	.32	.51
Independent Variable	*Change*				
Black	No to Yes	−.02	−.06	−.06	.14
Asian	No to Yes	−.03	−.08	−.11	.21
Hispanic	No to Yes	−.02	−.07	−.08	.17
Education	12 to 15.5 Years	.01	.02	.02	−.04
Work	No to Yes	.01	.02	.01	−.05
Church	Every Other Week to Every Few Months	.01	.02	.02	−.05
New York	No to Yes	.01	.02	.01	−.04
Private	No to Yes	.10	.13	.03	−.26

Table 5.1c
Changes in Predicted Probabilities of Finding 0, 1, 2, or 3 Categories of Formal
Sources Useful

		0	1	2	3
Base Probability		.27	.40	.23	.10
Variable	*Change*				
Black	No to Yes	−.12	−.04	.07	.10
Asian	No to Yes	−.11	−.03	.06	.08
Hispanic	No to Yes	−.13	−.05	.07	.10
Education	12 to 15.5 Years	.05	.00	−.03	−.02
Work	No to Yes	.09	.00	−.05	−.04
Church	Every Other Week to Every Few Months	.07	.01	−.04	−.04
New York	No to Yes	−.06	−.01	.03	.04
Private	No to Yes	.08	.00	−.04	−.03

Notes: Changes in predicted probabilities were calculated for each category of the dependent variable (finding *school sources* useful, finding *social sources* useful, and finding *formal sources* useful) while holding continuous variables constant at their mean. For dummy variables, Black, Asian, and Hispanic were held at 0 (no). Work, New York, and Private were also held at 0 (no). Changes in the independent variables correspond to a 0 to 1 change for dummy variables, a change from 1 standard deviation below the mean to 1 standard deviation above the mean for other variables.

Confirming our earlier analysis, blacks and Hispanics are significantly less likely to find friends and other parents useful sources of information about the schools (see the second column of table 5.1). Looking at table 5.1a, we see that the probability of finding neither other parents nor friends useful more than doubles for blacks and increases by over 50 percent for Hispanics, compared to the baseline probability calculated for a white parent. Thus, even after controlling for other conditions, when it comes to gathering information about the schools, black or Hispanic parents find social contacts less useful than other parents. In contrast, the usefulness of social contacts increases with education. These findings mirror the patterns from our bivariate comparisons—and they provide further evidence that race and class affect the nature of the information parents receive through interpersonal discussion.

Note too that parents in New York are much *less* likely to find friends and other parents useful than are New Jersey parents. Institutional factors have no significant effect on this variable.

In the third column of table 5.1, we move to the next "ring" of contacts—those based in the schools. Confirming our earlier bivariate results, note the strong and consistent effects of racial identification. We calculate that parents from any of the three largest racial minority groups in our sample are about 30 percent more likely than white parents to report that three school-based sources of information are useful.

Also, note that once we control for race, universal choosers in New Jersey are no longer significantly likely to rely on school-based information sources. However, universal choosers in New York are significantly less likely (at p < .07) than others to find contacts in the schools useful. This difference may indicate that school officials in Montclair have been more effective in reaching out to parents than officials in District 4. Replicating the results of our bivariate comparisons, private school choosers are much less likely to find school-based sources useful.

Moving to the more formal information sources in the fourth column of table 5.1, we again find strong racial effects—black, Hispanic, and Asian parents are all significantly more likely than whites to report that newspapers and television are useful in their search. In contrast, the usefulness of these sources of information declines with education, ceteris paribus. Parents in New York are 40 percent more likely to find useful all three categories of formal sources.

Note too that private school parents are less likely to find external sources of information useful—if public schools attract little mass media attention, private schools attract even less.

Conclusion

Two basic themes motivated the analyses in this chapter. First, we begin to address one of the fundamental issues underlying debates about school choice: do parents of different socioeconomic status find different sources of information useful? Second, we ask if the institutional arrangements of choice affect parents' evaluation of the usefulness of different information sources.

On the first point, we found that education and race matter a great deal. The effects of education are consistent, although not as large as the literature on political knowledge would have predicted: as education increases, parents rely on their more highly educated friends to supply them with information about schools and they find other sources, particularly formal sources of information (television, newspapers, etc.), less useful. We believe that social contacts provide a more efficient pathway to school information than does the media for these more-educated parents. However, less-educated parents, who do not have easy access to highly educated contacts, may be forced to rely on media and other sources. Considering the overlap between race and education, it is not surprising that many of these patterns exhibited by parents with lower levels of education were also present for black and Hispanic parents. We believe that these patterns are indicative of the ability of higher-socioeconomic status parents to construct efficient school discussion networks, creating a way of getting useful information about the schools "on the cheap"—a point we explore in more detail in the next chapter.

In contrast to the importance of education and race, choice only marginally affects the pathways to parental information sources. Our most consistent findings have been for parents whose children attend private schools. They are strikingly less likely to find formal sources of information useful— in part because these sources carry virtually no information useful to their choice process. Somewhat more surprisingly, they are also less likely to use teachers, staff, and school newsletters. Given the relatively low visibility of private schools, private school parents are much more on their own than are public school parents. The overall pattern of responses from private parents suggests that their search processes are different, and that further analyses are needed.

For us, however, the critical issue is how public school parents, particularly in choice settings, gather school information. Thus, in this next chapter we examine in greater detail how public school parents rely on social networks to provide them with information about schools.

Chapter 6

Building Social Networks to Search for Information about Schools

In the last chapter, we demonstrated that parents use many different sources of information to learn about schools—and we showed that one of the most important is talking with friends and neighbors. Other researchers have also found that parental networks play an important role in the flow of information about schools (for example, Wilson 1992; Carnegie Foundation 1992; Glenn, McLaughlin, and Salganik 1993; Beales and Wahl 1995; Heise, Colburn, and Lamberti 1995). This is a relatively low-cost strategy to learn about the schools, since information can be exchanged in the course of normal, day-to-day interactions. However, there is a downside to this strategy—friends and neighbors may have no better information about schools than parents. In this chapter, we continue our analysis of the flow of information about schools by focusing more closely on how parents can construct better school discussion networks.

How Do People Construct Networks?

Though network analysis typically focuses on how individual behavior is *constrained* by the social context in which an individual is embedded, we believe this view of networks is too limited. Building on the work of Ronald Burt (especially Burt 1992), we argue that individuals can act *strategically* to increase the quality of their networks and at least partially transcend the constraints of their immediate social context. In our approach, parents can make strategic choices about whom they include in their networks. In this chapter, we model these strategic choices as a function of individual characteristics and the institutional incentives provided by choice.

Strategies of Network Construction

The simplest strategy parents can follow is to rely upon information provided by those individuals, such as family members or close friends, encountered during the course of their daily rounds. But, some parents may encounter problems that cannot be solved by accessing these network members, and in response, they may choose to adopt more costly information-gathering strategies. For instance, they can try to increase their information by enlarging their network. While size does not guarantee quality, many analysts agree that a bigger network is, generally, a better network.

However, the strategy of increasing network size may fall victim to the law of diminishing returns—the costs of managing large networks can go up without a commensurate increase in the value added by new members. Thus, rather than simply increasing her network's size, a parent may instead choose discussants strategically, talking with individuals from whom she is likely to receive better information, increasing network quality while keeping costs down.

One manifestation of this strategy would be to seek out experts who could provide reliable information about schools without radically increasing the size of the network. But there is also another, less-obvious strategy that parents can use: they can strategically select discussants who are likely to have access to different sources of information than existing network members. To use Burt's term, parents can find network discussants who span "structural holes." In this chapter, we examine which parents use these strategies and compare the effectiveness of these strategies for improving the efficiency of networks.

We begin our discussion by focusing on the attributes of potential discussants that may affect whether or not others rely on them for information. We focus first on the role of expertise. We then examine how the position of a discussant in a parent's network can act as a signal of the likelihood that a discussant will provide nonredundant information—and thus also provide a valuable guide to choosing discussants that increase a network's efficiency.

Creating Efficient Networks: The Role of Experts

Relying on experts is an important strategy in all types of informational searches. A large literature documents the importance of expertise in consumer choice behavior (see, for example, Birnbaum and Stegner 1979; Birnbaum and Mellers 1983; Petty, Cacioppo, and Goldman 1981; Anderson 1990). Research has also documented the importance of expertise in political choices (e.g., Zaller 1992), and in the flow of information about public policies (Lupia 1994). In the domain of schooling, research has similarly demonstrated that educational "elites," such as teachers and school officials, provide parents with valuable information about schools (Glenn, McLaughlin, and Salganik 1993).

In addition to formal experts, research suggests that lay experts can also play an important role in providing information about schools. For example, Glenn, McLaughlin, and Salganik in their study of school choice in Massachusetts report that "each neighborhood has . . . informal leaders . . . who have a knowledge of how to maneuver within the system and share that expertise with their neighbors" (1993, 55). Much like the public opinion leaders identified by Lazarsfeld and his colleagues (1944), these informal leaders mediate the flow of information from more formal sources of information to parents.

While expertise provides a valuable guide to efficient network construction, individuals may consider other characteristics of potential discussants. As parents seek new information, redundancy may also guide evaluation of discussants and the construction of efficient networks. Thus, by considering a discussant's potential position in their network—where position acts as an indicator of the likelihood that a discussant will provide new information—parents can also increase the quality of their networks.

But who creates high-quality networks?

Network Quality: Weak Ties and Structural Holes

We examine network quality through two different, but closely related, measures. As noted in chapter 2, one of the most important measures of network quality is the strong tie/weak tie distinction developed by Granovetter (1985; also see Knoke 1990; Huckfeldt and Sprague 1991; Schneider et al. 1997a). Granovetter defined the strength of ties by the frequency of interactions between individuals—the more frequent the interaction, the stronger the tie. Granovetter's insight was identifying the "weakness of strong ties"—that networks built around weak ties are more likely to contain more new information and to span different networks than are networks built largely around strong ties.

While the definition of a weak tie relies on the relationship between individuals and their discussants, Burt (1992) specifies a more dynamic notion of this relationship by considering the importance of the position of a source or discussant in an individual's entire network. Burt introduced the idea of a structural hole that occurs "between two [discussants] who provide nonredundant network benefits" (11). The idea of a structural hole is similar to Granovetter's strong tie/weak tie distinction—discussants in a network who have access to different sources of information are more likely to provide better information. But according to Burt, weak ties provide greater benefits because they are more likely to span a structural hole. Perhaps most importantly, Burt suggests that individuals can *strategically* construct their networks to include nonredundant contacts to maximize network information.

While Burt's work is focused on corporate managers, we believe that this insight about active network construction can apply to parents shopping for information about schools. We do not argue that parents are aware of who is a potential "weak tie" or who is likely to "span a structural hole" but rather that parents can increase the efficiency of their networks by choosing discussants that they believe will provide nonredundant information.

We recognize that not all parents are equally able to construct efficient networks. As in the analyses of other aspects of parent behavior we present in this book, the strategic construction of efficient networks may be a function of the personal characteristics of individuals, as well as the incentives provided in the environment to engage in informational searches about schools.

Eliciting and Analyzing Information about Networks

Scholars debate the precise methodology by which to generate information about networks of discussion (see Marsden 1985; Burt 1987; Arabie and Wind 1994; Huckfeldt and Sprague 1995; Schneider et al. 1997a). In our study, we asked respondents to give us the first names of up to three people with whom they had discussed their children's education during the last six months, excluding their spouses and their children's teacher. For each person named, we elicited information about the "locus" of the relationship, e.g., was the discussant a friend, a relative, a coworker? We also asked the respondent to supply demographic information about the discussant and the frequency of discussions with each discussant. This approach in effect produces two data sets: one based on the responses of the 1,600 main respondents, the other based on the over 2,000 respondent-discussant dyads that respondents supplied to us. In contrast to the analysis in other chapters of this book where we focus on individual respondents, here we study patterns from the second data set, the dyads. In addition, we focus only on public school parents.

In chapters 4 and 5 we combined responses from parents in all four districts into a single data set. However, it quickly became apparent to us that networks differed quite dramatically across the central city-suburban divide. Consequently, we begin these analyses by exploring networks in the New York school districts and then replicating our analyses in New Jersey.

How Big Are Education Networks in New York City?

Increasing the number of discussants is the simplest strategy parents can use to increase the quality of their education networks—and so we begin by studying network size. In Table 6.1, we present the distribution of the number of discussants in each of the New York districts. Even a quick look shows that these networks about education are quite small. About 40 percent of respondents had no discussants (the modal category) and an additional 18 percent had only one educational discussant. While these numbers may seem low, the pattern of education discussants in New York City follows the pattern of networks that other analysts have found built around "important matters." For example, Marsden (1987) found that nearly a quarter of the respondents to the General Social Survey network battery had either no or just one discussant.

While the typical network in New York is small, 40 percent of the parents we interviewed reported discussing education issues with either two or three discussants. This leads to our next question: what factors support the construction of larger networks? First and foremost, if the opportunity to choose motivates parents to gather more information about schools, then the size of education networks should be larger in districts with choice than in districts without choice. However, a quick interdistrict comparison shows no signifi-

Table 6.1
The Number of Discussants Reported by Parents in New York

Number of Discussants	District 1	District 4
0	38%	41%
1	18%	16%
2	20%	20%
3	24%	22%

Note: Percentages do not total 100 percent because of rounding error.

cant differences between the mean number of discussants in District 4 and District 1. But, the effects of institutional structure must be studied along with the characteristics of individual parents. To sort out these effects, we present a multivariate analysis of the factors affecting network size in table 6.2.

In this model, we include the set of demographic factors that constitute the "core set" of control variables that we use throughout this book. In addition, we measure the employment status of the parent and the frequency

Table 6.2
Who Constructs Larger Networks?
The Number of Discussants as a Function of Individual Characteristics and District Location: New York Only

Independent Variable	Coefficient	Standard Error
Hispanic	−.611**	.175
Asian	−1.012**	.355
Black	−.226	.191
District 4	−.144	.096
Years of School Completed	.092**	.016
Length of Residence	.010	.006
Attends a Place of Worship	−.081**	.022
Work	.033	.101
Comes Home Unhappy	.226*	.095
χ^2 (9)	112.88***	
Cut 1	.281	.280
Cut 2	.791	.281
Cut 3	1.403	.283
N	607	

Source: School Choice Survey.

Notes: We report ordered probit coefficients and standard errors. Cut 1 etc. refer to cut-points on a standardized normal distribution that are used to calculate predicted probabilities for each category of the dependent variable.

*p < .05

**p < .01

***p < .001

with which the parent attends a place of worship, since parents with either of these characteristics have a potentially wider set of opportunities for finding discussants. We also control for the length of residence in the district since research has shown that levels of information about the schools and the number of friends and contacts a person has both increase with longer residence in a district.

In addition to these core variables, we include a measure of whether a child is having problems at school, since this may encourage the parent to seek out more people with whom to discuss the condition of the school in order to identify the causes and possible solutions to the problem.[1]

Our first result is a negative one: there is no significant difference between the size of parental networks in District 1 and District 4—choice does not affect this behavior pattern. However, parent education levels, problems at school, and church attendance all affect the size of the network. Note also that there are racial effects—parents who identify themselves as Hispanic or Asian have networks that are significantly smaller than parents who identify themselves as white.[2]

In table 6.2a, we report the percentage point change in probability for each parent talking to zero, one, two, or three discussants. In the ordered probit analysis presented in that table, we see that parent racial identification and educational status have the largest effects on the size of their networks. For example, parents who identify themselves as Hispanic or Asian are more than 20 percentage points less likely to talk to three discussants than are other parents. Education levels also have a large effect. For example, parents with high levels of education are 40 percentage points more likely to have three discussants than are the least-educated parents in our sample. Reinforc-

Table 6.2a
Changes in Predicted Probabilities of Network Size

Variable	Change in Variable	Change in Probability for Number of Discussants			
		0	1	2	3
Hispanic	No to Yes	.201	.038	−.028	−.211
Asian	No to Yes	.378	−.004	−.104	−.270
Years of School Completed	12 to 15 Years	−.099	−.020	.008	.116
	No Years to 17 Years	−.554	.007	.140	.408
Attends a Place of Worship	Every Other Week to Every Few Months	.055	.014	−.005	−.065
	Weekly to Never	.160	.032	−.022	−.170
Comes Home Unhappy	No to Yes	−.071	−.017	.007	.082
Base Probability		.240	.182	.239	.339

Notes: The changes in predicted probabilities were calculated while using the coefficients reported in table 6.2. Independent variables were held at their mean.

ing the findings of our last chapter, well-educated parents are more likely to have larger networks, not only because they can better manage the costs of maintaining such networks, but also because their discussants are more likely to have better information about the schools.

While having a larger network is one way to gather valuable information, next we examine whether or not parents make strategic choices about the overall composition of their education network.

To Whom Do Parents Talk about Education?

To study the strategic construction of networks, we consider the loci of the discussants with whom parents talk about schools. Figure 6.1 shows the distribution of the 756 discussants named by our New York parents across nine loci. (Note that discussants can be placed in more than one category and therefore the percentages do not add to 100 percent.)

As is evident in figure 6.1, when people talk about schools they most often talk to their neighbors and other parents who have children in the same schools as theirs. This communication is easy and "cheap": interactions are

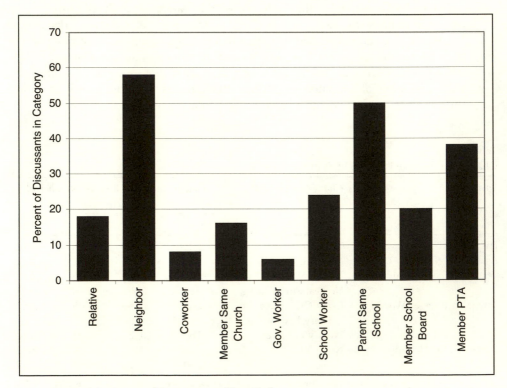

Figure 6.1   Locus of Discussants, New York

natural and the social distance between the respondent and the discussant is minimal. Norms of trust, honesty, and reciprocity are likely to develop as these adults engage in repeated interactions. Respondents may view the information about the schools they receive through these discussions as not only cheap but also quite useful, because the parent and her discussant share so many life circumstances.

But there is a cost to these discussions with neighbors and other parents— because interactions are stratified by education levels and segregated by race, they may not provide new or quality information about their child's school (Schneider et al. 1997a). However, there are two loci where discussants are still socially close to parents but are potentially more well-informed about school matters than other neighbors or parents: discussants who are members of the PTA or the community school board. Discussants drawn from these two milieu have obviously made a decision to become more intimately involved with the schools than most parents and can be thought of as relatively expert in school matters. Compared to school officials, these individuals are community residents and the social distance between them and respondents is small.

In our sample, approximately 37 percent of discussants belong to the PTA and 19 percent sat on the local school board. These numbers alone suggest that parents are engaging in some strategic selection of discussants. Parents can also include in their networks individuals that have high levels of formal involvement in the delivery of public services. Parents were asked if their discussants worked for the schools or if they worked for government. About 25 percent of discussants worked for the schools. In contrast, government workers generally were one of the least likely sources of discussants.

However, we found few differences in the overall patterns of the loci of discussants across parents in the two New York districts, suggesting once again that the incentives built into choice are not sufficient to change basic network patterns.

From Whom Do Parents Get the Most Useful Information?

Next, we examine the relationship between the loci of a discussant and whether a parent finds the information provided by a discussant useful when making decisions about schooling. We believe that examining the "usefulness" of the discussants who occupy different loci provides us with an initial indicator of who parents rely on most when making decisions about schooling and of the benefits associated with including a particular discussant in a network.

We measure "usefulness" by relying on parents' responses to a question asking them to identify the discussant in their network who provides the most useful information. While we know it is unlikely that parents assess and compare fully the information provided by each discussant, we view a

Table 6.3
New York: Percentage of Parents Reporting That They Get the Most Useful
Information from Each Discussant, by Loci

Loci	Yes	χ^2
Same School Parent	28.57	.01
Same Church Member	29.37	.85
Coworker	25.97	.31
Relative	26.17	.50
Neighbor	28.51	.02
Community School Board Member	32.64	1.30
PTA Member	33.65	5.86*
School Worker	38.42	12.17**
Government Worker	30.16	.07

Source: School Choice Survey (dyads).

*$p < .05$

**$p < .01$

parent's response to this question as an indicator of the relative value of the information provided by a particular discussant.

The first column of table 6.3 shows the percentage of parents reporting that a discussant who occupies a particular locus provides the most useful information in the network. When examining table 6.3, recall that discussants can belong to more than one locus—neighbors can also sit on the community school board or they can work for the schools.

Clearly, parents are more likely to report that they get the most useful information from discussants who have expertise in education—both members of the PTA and individuals who work in the schools are significantly more likely to be identified as "most useful" than are discussants in other loci. On the basis of these results, it would be fairly easy to conclude that the search for information about schools closely parallels other forms of search: parents rely on information from discussants who are perceived to be experts and involved with the product.

However, we believe that the use of experts is just one of many factors affecting the construction of efficient networks. To identify these additional factors, we broaden our focus beyond the loci of the discussants to include the position discussants hold in a network, as well as the race and class of the discussants.

The Importance of Experts, Weak Ties, and Structural Holes

Building on Burt's (1992) exploration of the strategic construction of networks, we use two different measures to identify discussants who are likely to provide nonredundant information. First, we construct a simple measure of strength of the tie based on the frequency of interaction between the parent and discussant.[3] Second, we create a redundancy index that reflects the number of loci a discussant occupies that are different from the loci occupied by the rest of the discussants in that individual's network—in our view, discussants who occupy unique loci span structural holes.[4]

As a first step, we test the relationship between occupying a given position in the network and the usefulness of the information parents receive. Conducting the same bivariate comparisons as above, we find that 54 percent of the discussants who span at least one structural hole are identified as providing the most useful information in the network and 69 percent of the discussants that are weak ties are identified as "most useful." This finding is suggestive, but it is possible that many of these useful, nonredundant discussants are the same discussants parents identified as useful experts. Again using simple cross-tabulations, we found that lay experts are more likely to be weak ties (63 percent) and discussants who span structural holes are also more likely to be lay experts (53 percent) and to work in the schools (32 percent).[5]

This overlap makes sense. Given the limited number of community school board members and individuals who work in the schools, parents are more likely to have only one network discussant filling these loci. Thus, these experts are more likely to both span a structural hole and be a weak tie. Because this overlap raises the issue of whether expertise or redundancy is the more effective guide to increasing the efficiency of a network, we need to untangle the roles of expertise, strength of tie, and structural holes in a parent's network. In addition, reflecting our concern for segregation and stratification, we want to examine how race and class affect parents' decisions to rely on the information provided by a discussant. Consequently, we include in our analysis two additional measures: one that reflects whether a discussant and respondent belong to the same racial category and one that reflects whether they are of the same education category.

We estimate the following model:

Discussant provides the most useful information = f (structural holes, strength of the tie, formal expert, informal expert, difference in education, same race).

Where:

Discussant provides the most useful information is the same variable introduced above.

We expect that several different conditions will affect this variable:

Difference in education is a variable that has a value of one if the discussant has attended college and the respondent has not, a value of zero if both have the same level of education, and a value of −1 if the respondent has attended college and the discussant has not.

Same race is a dichotomous variable that takes on a value of one if the respondent and discussant report being of the same race and a value of zero otherwise.

Discussant quality is represented by a series of variables measuring the expertise of the discussant, the frequency of interaction with the parent, and whether or not the discussant spans a structural hole.

- *Expertise* is represented by two variables: (1) a dichotomous variable that takes on a value of one when the discussant works for the schools and a value of zero otherwise, and (2) a dichotomous variable that takes on a value of one when the discussant is a member of the PTA or sits on the community school board, zero otherwise.
- *Frequency of interaction* is the number of days a year the respondent reports interacting with the discussant.
- *Spanning a structural hole* is the number of original loci occupied by the discussant.

We also control for the total number of discussants in the network since our sample includes parents who have named either two or three discussants.[6]

To estimate this model we employ a probit estimation procedure that provides pseudo-maximum likelihood estimates and Huber standard errors. (See Skinner 1989 for a discussion of pseudo-maximum likelihood estimates.) The standard errors have been adjusted to take into account dependence among observations in defined clusters—where each cluster includes all the respondent-discussant dyads of a particular respondent (Rogers 1993; see also Huber 1967). We use this procedure rather than the standard probit analysis to account for the inclusion of the same respondent in multiple dyads.

These results are reported in table 6.4. In the first column is the percentage point change in the probability of identifying a discussant as most useful for a zero to one change in dummy variables and for a unit change in all other variables. In the second column is the percentage point change in probability that occurs when moving across the total range of each independent variable.

Position in a network matters: parents are substantially more likely to say that a discussant who spans a structural hole provides the most useful information in the network. Note, too, that expertise continues to act as an important predictor of the quality of information provided by a discussant. In addition, status plays an important role in the construction of networks in New York: a parent without a college education is ten percentage points more likely to rely on the information provided by a college educated discussant than is a parent who also has a college education.

Table 6.4
New York: Which Discussant Provides the Most Useful Information?

Independent Variable	Most Useful Information	Change in Probability of Most Useful by Min to Max Change in Each Independent Variable
Structural Hole	.080**	.348
	(.027)	
Works in Schools	.098*	.098
	(.051)	
PTA / School Board	.057	.057
	(.041)	
Frequency of Interaction	.0001	.042
	(.0001)	
Same Race	.003	.003
	(.044)	
Difference in Education	.099**	.188
	(.032)	
Total Number of Discussants	−.028	−.055
	(.040)	
Observed P	.298	
χ^2 (7)	34.77**	
Clusters	216	
N	443	

Source: School Choice Survey (dyads).

Notes: We report the results of a probit model. Numbers in parentheses are robust standard errors. Numbers above robust standard errors for the first two models indicate the effect of a change from 0 to 1 for the dummy variables and represent the effect of a unit change for the non-dummy variables. The Chi Square values we report are for the Wald test rather than the likelihood ratio test.

*p < .10
**p < .001

Who Constructs More Efficient Networks?

We argued earlier that information strategies are a function of individual ability. We now examine whether ability affects the likelihood that parents will strategically select discussants who are lay experts, span structural holes, or represent weak ties. We are particularly interested in assessing the relationship between the increased incentives provided by choice and the likelihood of strategic behavior.

We estimate a series of models taking the form:

Discussant quality = f (demographic factors, opportunities for contact, incentives).

The dependent variables are the same as those measures of *discussant quality* models. The independent variables are the same as those we included in the model we present in table 6.2, except we also control for the *total number of discussants*, since the sample includes respondents that have named either two or three discussants. Thus, in table 6.5, we report the results of four models: a probit analysis of whether a parent talks to a discussant that spans a structural hole, a regression model predicting frequency of interaction between the parent and discussant, a probit model predicting whether the parent talks to a discussant who is also a school expert, and a probit model predicting whether the parent talks to a discussant who is a lay expert. Again, for all four models, we rely on estimation routines that provide robust standard errors and that take into account dependence among observations in clusters.[7] As evident in table 6.5, choice has little or no effect on network construction, in part because so many aspects of social interactions and parent behavior are strongly rooted in broad social processes.

While we find weak support for the impact of individual-level factors such as length of residence in the community on the likelihood of constructing efficient networks, we find no effect for many standard demographic characteristics. This may be explained by the nature of the subsample used in this network analysis—in our analysis we include a select group of parents (those who have multiple discussants). And while a discussion strategic network construction is only relevant to individuals who have networks, respondents naming more discussants are more likely to be more well-educated than other parents.

To investigate whether these findings, based on the networks of parents who live in an inner-city environment in New York, are robust, we turn now to our suburban New Jersey parents.

The Construction of Networks in a Suburban Context

We begin again by examining the number of discussants with whom parents talk. As shown in table 6.6, parents in New Jersey talk to substantially more discussants than parents in New York—the modal number of discussants is three rather than zero. Here, as in New York, the number of discussants does not differ across the two districts. Again, white parents have larger networks than minority parents. And, as in New York, the size of networks increases with education levels (see tables 6.7 and 6.7a).

In figure 6.2 we present the distribution of discussants across the nine loci in New Jersey. There are few differences between the New Jersey districts, suggesting that the incentives of choice are not sufficient to change basic network patterns. However, differences are evident between New York and New Jersey—the clearest is the higher percentage of discussants who work for the schools and belong to the community school board in New York,

Table 6.5
New York: Who Talks to Experts, Weak Ties, and Structural Holes?

Independent Variable	Experts	Informal Experts	Strength of Tie	Structural Holes
Hispanic	.039	−.033	11.022	−.003
	(.065)	(.082)	(19.141)	(.061)
Asian	−.101	−.175	−66.340	−.002
	(.130)	(.144)	(15.645)	(.056)
Black	.019	−.026	21.305	−.070
	(.076)	(.085)	(18.999)	(.070)
District 4	−.065	−.104**	27.339**	.017
	(.046)	(.052)	(14.552)	(.043)
Length of Residence	−.002	.002	.370	.007***
	(.003)	(.004)	(3.338)	(.002)
Attends a Place of Worship	−.004	−.017	−3.000	−.012**
	(.010)	(.012)	(3.338)	(.010)
Work	−.010	−.054	−12.776	−.020
	(.047)	(.053)	(16.203)	(.042)
Total Number of Discussants	−.025	.018	−21.785*	−.223***
	(.045)	(.053)	(15.443)	(.044)
Education	−.006	.009	.294	.009
	(.008)	(.010)	(3.214)	(.007)
Comes Home Un- happy	.029	−.011	−24.758*	.027
	(.046)	.055	14.988	(.043)
Constant			159.758***	
			(58.707)	
Observed P	.243	.404		.417
Adjusted R^2	.01		.04	
χ^2 (9)	7.43	9.79	12.40***	39.20***
Clusters	248	248	248	248
N	629	629	626	629

Source: School Choice Survey (dyads).

Numbers in parentheses are robust standard errors. We estimate the likelihood of talking to an expert, lay expert, or discussant that spans a structural hole by using probit. Numbers above robust standard errors for the first two models indicate the effect of a change from 0 to 1 for the dummy variables and represent the effect of a unit change for the non-dummy variables. We model the strength of the tie by using multiple regression. The dependent variable is the number of days a year that the respondent reports talking to the discussant. In the case of the regression model, the Wald test is a model F test. F (9, 239) = 12.40, p < .05. The Chi Square values we report are for the Wald test rather than the likelihood ratio test.

*p < .1
**p < .05
***p < .01

Table 6.6
The Number of Discussants Reported by Parents in New Jersey

Number of Discussants	Morristown	Montclair
0	20%	19%
1	12%	13%
2	21%	21%
3	48%	47%

Note: Percentages for Morristown do not total 100 percent because of rounding error.

compared to the larger percentage of discussants who belong to the parent organizations in New Jersey. Note that a higher percentage of parents in New Jersey also consider a discussant who belongs to a parent organization as providing the most useful information in the network (See table 6.8). Thus, contacts with fellow parents have higher payoffs in this suburban setting.

This difference is likely due to the higher education levels of parents in New Jersey—since higher education often signals a greater familiarity with schooling issues, parents in New Jersey can get more information about

Table 6.7
Who Has Larger Networks?
The Number of Discussants as a Function of Individual Characteristics and District Location: New Jersey

Independent Variable	Coefficient	Standard Error
Hispanic	−.811***	.223
Asian	−.563**	.243
Black	−.352***	.110
Montclair	.060	.097
Years of School Completed	.063***	.019
Length of Residence	−.004	.007
Attends a Place of Worship	−.032	.022
Work	−.250**	.118
Comes Home Unhappy	.181*	.105
χ^2 (9)	59.58***	
Cut 1	−.248	.332
Cut 2	.167	.331
Cut 3	.744	.332
N	633	

Source: School Choice Survey. We report ordered probit coefficients and standard errors. Cut 1 etc. refer to cut-points on a standardized normal distribution that are used to calculate predicted probabilities for each category of the dependent variable.

  *p < .10
 **p < .05
***p < .01

Table 6.7a
Changes in Predicted Probabilities of Network Size

Variable	Change in Variable	Change in Probability for Number of Discussants			
		0	1	2	3
Hispanic	No to Yes	.289	.030	−.040	−.275
Asian	No to Yes	.210	.010	−.042	−.179
Black	No to Yes	.125	.015	−.017	−.123
Years of School	12 to 15 Years	−.074	−.013	.006	.081
Completed	No Years to 17 Years	−.400	.008	.084	.320
Work	No to Yes	.082	.015	−.005	−.093
Comes Home Unhappy	No to Yes	−.062	−.010	.005	.066
Base Probability		.278	.153	.226	.343

Notes: These changes in predicted probabilities were calculated while using the coefficients reported in table 6.7. Independent variables were held at their mean.

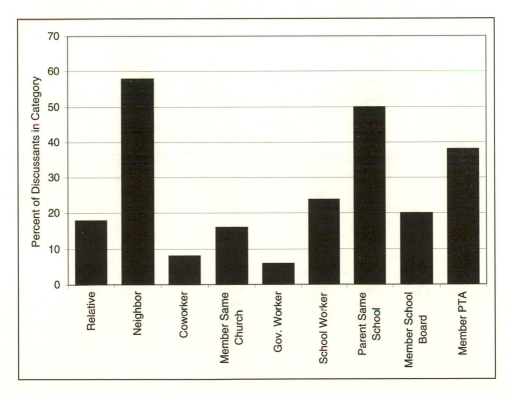

Figure 6.2   Locus of Discussants, New Jersey

Table 6.8
New Jersey: Percentage of Parents Reporting That They Get the Most Useful
Information from Discussants Occupying Each Loci

Loci	Yes	χ^2
Same School Parent	30.28	.46
Same Church Member	30.52	.75
Coworker	29.63	.99
Relative	28.10	.17
Neighbor	23.98	.92
Community School Board Member	40.19	6.21*
PTA Member	33.62	10.32**
School Worker	40.55	14.65**
Government Worker	29.63	1.00

Source: School Choice Survey (dyads).

*p < .05
**p < .01

schools simply by extending their networks to include other parents. Otherwise, parents in New Jersey, like their New York counterparts, rely on teachers, school board members, and members of the PTA for information about schools.

In table 6.9, we analyze the degree to which New Jersey parents rely on information provided by experts, weak ties, and discussants who span structural holes, replicating the model presented in table 6.4. We find clear evidence that filling structural holes is a useful strategy; after controlling for expertise, difference in education, race, and strength of the tie, New Jersey parents are more likely to say that a discussant who spans a structural hole provides the most useful information in the network. Parents are also seven percentage points more likely to consider a discussant as providing the most useful information in the network if the discussant is a member of the PTA or community school board. Discussants who are formal experts are also seven percentage points more likely to be identified as "most useful" (p < .10). However, in New Jersey we find a smaller role for status (p < .10), compared to the substantial effect for difference in education levels we found in New York.

We believe that this difference, similar to the difference in the use of members of parent organizations, is due to the higher levels of schooling in New Jersey and resulting degree of homogeneity in these suburban communities. In New Jersey, the mean education level attained by the respondents in our sample of parents was fifteen years with a standard deviation of 2.4. In New York the mean level of education was less than twelve years with a standard deviation of 3.6. This difference is also visible in our parent-discussant dyads: 90 percent of our New Jersey respondents who named two or three

Table 6.9
New Jersey: Which Discussant Provides the Most Useful Information?

Independent Variable	Most Useful Information	Change in Probability of Most Useful by Min. to Max. Change in Each Independent Variable
Structural Hole	.073***	.319
	(.018)	
Works in Schools	.067*	.067
	(.040)	
PTA/School Board	.074**	.074
	(.024)	
Frequency of Interaction	.0003*	.116
	(.0002)	
Same Race	.004	.004
	(.037)	
Difference in Education	−.063*	.127
	(.032)	
Total Number of Discussants	−.034	−.070
	(.035)	
Observed P	.307	
χ^2 (7)	42.87***	
Clusters	419	
N	1033	

Source: School Choice Survey (dyads).

Notes: We report the results of a probit model. Numbers in parentheses are standard errors. Numbers above robust standard errors for the first two models indicate the effect of a change from 0 to 1 for the dummy variables and represent the effect of a unit change for the non-dummy variables. The Chi Square values we report are for the Wald test rather than the likelihood ratio test.

*$p < .1$
**$p < .05$
***$p < .01$

discussants reported having attended college and report that 92 percent of their discussants attended college. In contrast, only 50 percent of the parents having two or three discussants reported having attended college in New York while they report that 70 percent of their discussants did so. Thus, in New Jersey, using "formal education" as a shortcut to choosing discussants is an ineffective tool for distinguishing quality among potential discussants, while in New York "formal education" allows parents to weed out potentially uninformative discussants.

In table 6.10, we again find that the incentives built into school choice do not affect strategic behavior, duplicating the pattern we found in New York.

Table 6.10
New Jersey: Who Talks to Experts, Weak Ties, and Discussants That Span Structural Holes?

Independent Variable	Experts	Lay Experts	Strength of Tie	Structural Holes
Hispanic	.126	−.009	−14.639**	−.093*
	(.131)	(.140)	(5.592)	(.081)
Asian	.173*	−.134	.255	−.053
	(.116)	(.099)	(15.141)	(.103)
Black	.068**	−.074	14.143*	.093**
	(.034)	(.049)	(8.180)	(.041)
Montclair	−.033	.020	−3.615	.014
	(.002)	(.042)	(5.560)	(.032)
Length of Residence	.003*	.007**	.879**	.0003
	(.002)	(.003)	(.420)	(.0023)
Attends a Place of Worship	.005	−.033***	.318	−.011
	(.005)	(.010)	(1.209)	(.007)
Work	−.004	−.085*	−1.662	.048**
	(.029)	(.049)	(5.473)	(.035)
Total number of Discussants	−.026	.022	8.971	−.178***
	(.026)	(.044)	(5.565)	(.035)
Education	−.004	.005	.033	.013**
	(.004)	(.009)	(.816)	(.006)
Comes Home Unhappy	.063**	.046	−8.265	.078**
	(.024)	(.047)	(6.744)	(.034)
Constant			13.875	
			(20.895)	
Observed P	.147	.504		.397
Adjusted R^2			.02	
χ^2 (9)	20.34**	28.16***	2.11**	50.35***
Clusters	424	424	423	424
N	1139	1139	1121	1139

Source: School Choice Survey (dyads).

Numbers in parentheses are robust standard errors. We estimate the likelihood of talking to an expert, lay expert, or a discussant that spans a structural hole by using probit. Numbers above robust standard errors for the first two models indicate the effect of a change from 0 to 1 for the dummy variables and represent the effect of a unit change for the non-dummy variables. We model the strength of the tie by using multiple regression. The dependent variable is the number of days a year that the respondent reports talking to the discussant. In the case of the regression model, the Wald test is a model F test. F (9, 422) = 2.37, p < .05. The Chi Square values we report are for the Wald test rather than the likelihood ratio test.

*p < .1
**p < .05
***p < .01

Conclusion

Choice does not affect how parents construct networks. Instead, the usefulness of interpersonal discussion as a source of information depends more on the individual characteristics of parents and the social environment in which they live.

In the last chapter we showed that parents who find interpersonal discussion a useful source of information are more likely to identify themselves as white or Asian, and that the usefulness of social contacts increases with education. In this chapter, we have shown that these same factors also influence the size of networks, a traditional benchmark of network quality. But we have also argued that in order to understand how parents use their networks to obtain information, we must also consider other strategies that parents may use to increase the efficiency of their networks.

Similar to work that shows how individuals can rely on information provided by political elites for campaign information or "market mavens" for information about consumer goods, we find that parents rely on educational elites who are likely to possess "expert" information to provide information about schools. Specifically, these experts work in the schools, serve on the school board, or belong to the PTA. If we had halted our investigation at that point, we would have concluded that individuals seeking to minimize information costs and maximize the potential benefits of their networks strategically select discussants who possess such expertise.

However, parents can use an alternative strategy when constructing their networks. They can rely on information provided by a discussant who is more likely to have access to different information than the other discussants in the network. Thus, parents can also construct an efficient network by relying on a simple rule: select discussants who are likely to provide nonredundant information. We find some evidence that the strategic position of the discussant in the network also matters.

In addition, we have shown that the social milieu in which parents live matters. In the New York districts, where fewer parents have college degrees than in New Jersey, parents are likely to rely on status, selecting discussants with higher education to provide information about schools. This strategy would provide far fewer benefits in suburban New Jersey, where variation in education is minimal compared to New York.

These patterns suggest that policies for informing parents about schooling options must take into account the social context in which parents live. Policies in low-income urban areas must acknowledge the greater importance of informing well-educated community leaders, as well as the importance of assuring parents easy access to individuals (and information) directly associated with the schools. As school choice diffuses, especially in central cities, outreach activities to inform parents are essential.

PART THREE

Chapter 7

The Distribution of Knowledge: How Much Do Parents Know about the Schools?

The goal of this section of the book is to identify the ways in which parents gather information about schools, with or without choice. In chapter 5, we examined the information sources parents utilize. In chapter 6, we focused on networks, an important source of information. In this chapter, we ask: what do parents actually know about the schools?

In the next set of chapters, we focus on the individual characteristics that shape information gathering, the context and information environment in which parents operate (e.g., central city versus suburban school districts), and whether choice changes parental behavior. In this chapter, we focus on the extent to which parental information is accurate. As in chapter 6, we find that the different information context of small suburban school districts versus large, urban districts accounts for the largest difference in parental information accuracy. For the question in which we are most interested, whether the incentive provided by choice affects parental information accuracy, we find mixed results. And, we find that specific individual characteristics related to race and class have weaker effects than predicted by the broader literature on information acquisition.

Some scholars have argued that because information on schools is difficult to obtain and hard to interpret, parental information levels will be low and, thus, parents will either not choose schools for their children or will not choose well. Indeed, many studies, beginning with those on the Alum Rock demonstration program, have found that parents usually know very little about the alternatives available to them. Because this is often assumed to be especially true for minorities and lower socioeconomic status parents, the equity implications are critical. Given the importance of information to any program of choice and given the lack of good information in the hands of parent/consumers, many scholars have argued that choice reforms are unlikely to succeed. Indeed, Bridge (1978) has called the low level of parent information the "Achilles' heel" of choice.

However, proponents of school choice argue that low levels of parent information are a product of the lack of incentives that parents have to become informed, and that choice will create strong incentives for parents to become informed consumers.

In this chapter, we address this issue by examining four basic questions:

- What and how much do parents know?
- Do parents who are given the opportunity to choose their schools have more accurate information than other parents?

- What other factors explain levels of information accuracy that parents have about schools?
- Are individual or contextual factors most important?

As we demonstrated in the last two chapters, the information environment facing parents in the central city districts is quite different from the environment parents in the suburbs face. Thus, we use the same strategy as in many previous chapters in this book: we examine parents in the New York and New Jersey districts separately. Because we are most concerned with the extent to which choice creates incentives for parents to become informed, using the matched pair component of our quasi-experimental research design, we compare parent information levels in the choice and nonchoice districts in each of the central city/suburban matches.

The Benefits and Costs of Information:
Individual and Systemic Factors

Earlier we argued that parent information levels should be a function of characteristics of the individual *and* the context of choice that parents face, rooting our argument in the ability, motivation, and opportunity framework for information acquisition developed by Delli Carpini and Keeter (1996). We expand their analysis of the acquisition of political information by merging their argument with broader evidence from consumer search.

The first term in the framework, *ability*, relates to individual characteristics. Research on how consumers of both public and private goods gather information suggests that individuals with more education and greater "involvement" with the product are typically more knowledgeable than less-educated and less-involved individuals (for example, see Kardes 1994 on private sector goods; see Bauch 1989; Bledsoe and Stoker 1992; Teske et al. 1993; and John, Dowding, and Biggs 1995 on public sector issues including schools). Since data about the schools are especially difficult to gather and interpret, individual characteristics, especially education, may affect the flow of information about schools.

Motivation is rooted in both individual characteristics and the nature of the choice environment. The issue here is whether choice can provide the motivation for some parents to become more informed. Without appropriate motivation, previous research documenting that most parents tend to have scant information about public goods is not surprising (e.g., Lowery, Lyons, and DeHoag 1995; Teske et al. 1995). For many analysts, low information levels are a predictable outcome of a simple benefit/cost calculation: the costs of gathering information are high relative to the benefits of such information. Faced with this adverse calculation, most citizens simply remain uninformed.

Not surprisingly, low levels of information about schools among parents have been linked to a poor benefit/cost ratio in that domain. According to the proponents of choice, the benefit/cost ratio of acquiring information about schools is reduced by the centralized control of school selection found in most school districts. It makes little sense for a parent to gather extensive information about the schools if the "choice" of the school has been dictated by bureaucratically determined school attendance zones. From this perspective, choice radically transforms the benefit/cost ratio of being informed.

Researchers have generated some evidence that the incentive to gather information provided by choice does indeed affect parent behavior (see, e.g., Glenn, McLaughlin, and Salganik 1993; Martinez, Kemerer, and Godwin 1993; Hudson Institute 1992; Witte 1991a; Witte, Bailey, and Thorn 1992). Perhaps the best evidence comes from the Alum Rock voucher experiment in the 1970s. There, researchers found that parents enrolled in the school voucher program were consistently more knowledgeable about the schools and their choices than were nonparticipants. And, parental information levels increased over time but dropped off rapidly when the program was terminated (Bridge and Blackman 1978, 27–45).

There may be other interactions between individual characteristics, the structure of choice, and motivation that have not been fully explored. For example, Archbold (1988), Moore and Davenport (1990), and Henig (1996) found less knowledge by minority and lower socioeconomic status parents for magnet schools and Chriss, Nash, and Stern (1992) and Bridge (1978, 512–14) found a similar pattern for voucher programs. On the other hand, some studies suggest that the interaction of choice and parent characteristics may in fact reduce the socioeconomic basis for differences in parental information levels. Most notably, both Bauch (1989) and Lines (1994) found that the information differences between groups of Alum Rock parents largely disappeared over time.

Beyond individual ability and motivation, the information environment itself shapes the opportunity for parents to become informed. While proponents of choice cite the benefits to parents from becoming informed, they have not examined as carefully the cost side. In the present system of education, the costs of acquiring information about schools can be high, creating another set of barriers for parents. Basic information about local schools is often not widely circulated and even when available, is not presented in a "user friendly" manner (Schneider 1999).

Often school officials seem to keep the costs of information gathering high on purpose. According to Henig (1994), some principals in the Alum Rock project simply refused to provide information about their schools. More recently, Wilson (1992) found that some of the most valuable kinds of school information were not generally available to parents in the areas he studied. Carver and Salganik (1991, 75) report that they were unable to gather information about test scores, grade retention, graduation, and college attendance rates from many schools of choice. And in our own fieldwork in New York and New Jersey, we encountered numerous problems in gathering data about schools.

Thus, education research has shown that parents' ability to collect information matters a great deal, but it is not *all* that matters. The motivation provided by the opportunity to choose and the information environment in which the choice task takes place also affect the flow of accurate information. In the analyses presented in this chapter, we identify the individual characteristics that are important to the level of information parents possess and also seek to identify if choice itself affects parental incentives to become informed about their children's schools.

How Accurate Are Parents about School Conditions?

To examine how much information parents in our research settings have, we examine multiple indicators of information. While we begin with a subjective indicator of parent information levels—do parents feel as though they had enough information to make a choice among the schools in the district?[1]—we also use multiple measures of parent knowledge about objective conditions in their children's schools. These objective indicators range from whether or not a parent could accurately name the principal of her child's school to detailed assessments of parent knowledge of three specific conditions in a child's school: the educational outcomes of the school (percent of students in the child's school reading at grade level), school resources in the classroom (average class size), and the diversity of the student body (percent of black and Hispanic children in the school). Many education experts argue that reading performance may be the single most important indicator of school performance. In addition, there is evidence that small class size, especially in the early grades, may have a substantial effect on academic performance. The other two measures assess how knowledgeable parents are about the demographic makeup of their children's schools, which should be easier to assess than test scores by using simple visual cues.

In our survey, we asked parents to estimate each of these conditions in their children's school. We used official reports to measure the actual level of these dimensions found in each school. We then computed "distance" scores that measure how close (in absolute value) a parent's estimate is to the actual performance of his child's school on each dimension.[2] For example, if a parent estimated that 60 percent of students in her child's school were reading at or above grade level and the actual performance level was 50 percent, the distance score would be 10.[3]

In table 7.1, we report the subjective evaluation of information, the percent of parents who have successfully named their children's principals, and the distribution of these distance scores for the four objective measures, broken down separately for parents in New York and New Jersey.

Table 7.1 shows that suburban parents are significantly more likely than

Table 7.1
Means and Standard Deviations of Information Measures in New Jersey and New York

District Location	Had Enough Info.	Knows Principal's Name	Distance Score for Reading	Distance Score for Class Size	Distance Score for Hispanic Percent	Distance Score for Black Percent
New Jersey	1.9**	75%**	14.8**	6.3	6.7**	8.2*
			(13.5)	(4.7)	(7.0)	(7.7)
New York	2.4	56%	24.0	6.2	17.6	15.8
			(16.6)	(6.4)	(14.6)	(14.2)
	N = 1588	N = 1565	N = 1206	N = 1264	N = 1330	N = 1324

*p < = .05
**p < = .01

their central city counterparts to feel they had enough information to make a choice of schools. This may reflect the higher feelings of competence that are associated with higher education (which the suburban parents have) but it may also be a function of reality—data about school performance is more widely available in the suburbs we studied than in New York.

As the rest of table 7.1 illustrates, suburban parents are also more likely to have more accurate information about their children's schools than are their central city counterparts.

Are Parents Nearly or Relatively Accurate?

Some scholars argue that the type of distance measure just reported is too severe a test for most citizens. For example, Delli Carpini and Keeter (1996) feel that researchers should not ignore "close calls." They found that citizen answers often cluster around the correct response and traditional coding schemes categorize these responses as "incorrect." The distance score method of measuring accuracy we use is not subject to this weakness that permeates much research on political knowledge (since we have created an interval level scale rather than a dichotomous correct/incorrect coding scheme). Still, to investigate the possibility that we might be underestimating parental information, we look at the percentage of parents who are "nearly correct" in their estimates.

Of course, the definition of "nearly correct" and "close calls" is subjective. Here we create boundaries around the actual performance score of a school equal to that score ±20 percent of that score (for example, if 50 percent of children in a school were reading at grade level, then a parent is counted as "correct" if her estimate is in the 40–60 percent range). As table 7.2 illustrates, the majority of parents in New York are not nearly accurate: less than 50 percent are in this range on all measures and only 25 percent for are near correct on their estimate of reading scores. As was the case in table 7.1, nearly twice as many parents in New Jersey are accurate than those in New York, using these "near correct" measures.

Table 7.2
Percent of Parents Who Are "Near Correct" and "Relatively Accurate" in New York and New Jersey

	Reading Scores	Hispanic Percent	Black Percent
	Near Correct / Relatively Accurate	Near Correct / Relatively Accurate	Near Correct / Relatively Accurate
New York	25% / 18%	39% / 27%	45% / 29%
New Jersey	47% / 45%	78% / 68%	70% / 61%
	N = 1206	N = 1330	N = 1324

In trying to be sure that we are characterizing the apparent low levels of information appropriately, we explored one more possibility. One could reasonably argue that parents don't need to know absolutely how well their children's schools are doing, but that relative rankings are important. Thus, we asked parents to rank their children's schools in relation to other schools in the district on a five-point scale: way below average, somewhat below average, about average, somewhat above average, and way above average. To code the accuracy of parental placement of their children's schools, we converted the performance of every school into a z-score using the mean and standard deviation of all schools in the district.

We then examine whether the parent placed her child's school correctly in the relative hierarchy of the district. To do this, if a parent said a school was "average" on a given dimension, and the school's z-score on that dimension was ± .33 we counted the parent as correct. If the parent said that the school was somewhat above (or below) average, then she was classified as correct if the school was between .33 and 1 standard deviation above (or below) the mean. A parent who said the school was way above (or way below) average was classified as correct if the school's z-score was ± 1. Using these cut points, as shown in table 7.2, less than 30 percent of New York parents are relatively accurate about all of these school conditions.[4] Again, for New Jersey parents, a higher percentage, greater than 45 percent in all cases, are more accurate about these school conditions.

Using these more lenient definitions, the number of "accurate" parents in a school district increases, but there is still a large gap between the number of knowledgeable parents in New York and New Jersey. And, we still are left with the fundamental task of identifying how individual characteristics and the incentives of choice affect this distribution. Since all of the accuracy measures we experimented with track closely with each other, and the results of the following analysis are similar using different measures, we continue our analyses by focusing on the clearest metric: the distance scores.

Contextual Effects on Parent Information Levels

To answer the questions posed at the start of this chapter, we need to be able to sort out the individual, contextual, and incentive-oriented aspects of information accuracy. Thus, we examine accurate knowledge in a multivariate framework based on Delli Carpini and Keeter's (1996) concept of individual knowledge as a function of parents' abilities, motivations, and opportunities to gather and process information.

In previous chapters, we used a set of core variables to understand parental behavior. Several of the core variables reflect individual ability to gather accurate information: parent education, "involvement" with the schools, and length of residence in the school district. Other core variables act as controls related to individual characteristics, including parental race, church attendance, employment, and gender. We include a variable measuring the size of a respondent's network, a measure that reflects the analyses in the last chapter and builds on recent studies confirming that friends and relatives are one of the most common information sources about schools (e.g., Rubenstein and Adelman 1994; Beales and Wahl 1996; Heise, Colburn, and Lamberti 1995). Opportunity focuses mainly on the information actually available in the institutional environment, which we test here with a dummy variable for the New York districts where information was less freely available. We also add a control variable for the size of the school, which may also influence the opportunity to gather accurate information. In this analysis, we are not yet focusing on the effects of choice, which we will do next by measuring information levels in each pair of the matched districts.

In table 7.3 we present the multivariate analysis of information levels, with

Table 7.3
Multivariate Analysis of Parental Information in City and Suburb

	Had Enough Info.	Principal's Name	Reading Scores	Class Size	Hispanic Percent	Black Percent
Asian	−.153	−.111	6.42	−1.18	3.08	6.98*
	(.299)	(.106)	(4.35)	(1.33)	(3.07)	(3.14)
Black	−.166	.022	.942	−.422	1.19	3.27**
	(.117)	(.042)	(1.43)	(.491)	(1.14)	(1.01)
Hispanic	−.063	−.072	−.746	.043	3.10*	5.97**
	(.137)	(.048)	(1.73)	(.627)	(1.30)	(1.21)
Years of Schooling	.016	.021**	−.367*	−.072	−.106	−.027
	(.015)	(.005)	(.185)	(.064)	(.141)	(.133)
Length of Residence	.029**	.002	.051	.011	.020	−.047
	(.006)	(.002)	(.074)	(.025)	(.056)	(.052)
Church Attendance	.022	.006	.055	−.052	.186	.049
	(.019)	(.007)	(.242)	(.082)	(.180)	(.167)
Employed	.095	.017	−2.73*	−.167	−1.49	−2.28**
	(.094)	(.033)	(1.17)	(.411)	(.90)	(.831)
Gender	−.057	.065	−2.12	−.501	.039	−.467
	(.115)	(.041)	(1.43)	(.486)	(1.08)	(.977)
New York Location	−.564**	−.069*	7.17**	−2.16**	7.44**	2.68**
	(.113)	(.038)	(1.43)	(.506)	(1.09)	(1.01)
School Involvement	.111**	.023	−1.61**	−.135	−.342	−1.06**
	(.044)	(.015)	(.55)	(.189)	(.420)	(.387)
Number of Network Discussants	.046	−.034	−.456*	.022	.128	−.056
	(0.37)	(.054)	(.233)	(.032)	(.088)	(.047)
Size of School	.0004*	−.001*	−.0011	.005**	.0034	.0006
	(.0002)	(.0007)	(.0025)	(.001)	(.0019)	(.0018)
Constant	2.9**	—	27.1**	22.6**	7.4**	12.2**
	(.30)		(3.8)	(4.6)	(2.9)	(2.7)
N. of Cases	1176	1177	916	964	1021	1013
F Statistic	9.3	$\chi^2 = 97$	9.8	4.9	18.1	14.9
Probability	0.000	0.000	0.000	0.000	0.000	0.000
Adjusted R-Squared	0.09	0.12	0.10	0.09	0.13	.011

*p < = .05
**p < = .01

our main focus on the differences between parents in New York and New Jersey. While the data showed large and significant differences, the question this analysis addresses is whether New Jersey parents have more accurate information because they have greater individual ability, or because their environment creates opportunities for them to become more informed.

Table 7.3 shows that New Jersey parents are significantly more accurate about all of our measures, except for class size.[5] Indeed, New Jersey location accounts for much of the power of these models. In contrast, most of the individual characteristics have insignificant and inconsistent effects on accuracy. Only one individual-level variable, parental involvement, shows significant effects leading to greater accuracy in at least half of the models. Thus, controlling for differences in the distribution of parent characteristics in the New York and the New Jersey districts, the suburban school districts provide greater opportunity for parents to access information.

Next, we turn to the two matched comparisons to examine the effects of choice on parental information accuracy. We first examine how accurate parents in District 4 are compared to those in District 1. We then compare levels of accuracy in Montclair and Morristown.

Cross-District Comparisons of Information Levels in New York

We start by comparing the bivariate accuracy measures across District 4 and District 1. The subjective measure of information adequacy shows that parents in District 4 do report feeling somewhat more informed (by about one-third of a category on a five-category scale). District 4 parents are also significantly more likely to correctly name their principals than are parents in District 1 (60 percent versus 45 percent). However, when we move to more detailed information in the distance scores, we find minimal differences between parents in each district—only for the percentage of Hispanic students do we find significantly more accurate information among District 4 parents.

Thus, while parents in the choice district report more accurate information on the most basic measures, this result is not sustained for more detailed information about school academic performance and racial diversity. However, we need to run multivariate models to assess the effects of choice, controlling for individual parental characteristics.

As noted above for the models in table 7.3, our multivariate model tests independent variables that assess the abilities, motivations, and opportunities of parents. Here we add a simple dummy variable for District 4 to assess the effects of choice. Ability is largely shaped by individual characteristics that we measure with variables from our core model. Motivation may also vary by individuals, but the incentive of choice should increase motivation for all parents who can or do actually utilize choice, in this case those in District 4. Opportunity focuses mainly on the information actually available in the institutional environment.

Table 7.4
Multivariate Analysis of Parental Information in New York Districts

	Had Enough Info.	Principal's Name	Reading Scores	Class Size	Hispanic Percent	Black Percent
Asian	−.523	.056	7.63	−3.06	−3.95	3.89
	(.522)	(.179)	(7.52)	(2.00)	(5.61)	(5.87)
Black	−.524*	−.114	−3.56	−1.90	−6.01**	1.38
	(.254)	(.089)	(3.43)	(1.08)	(2.61)	(2.49)
Hispanic	−.342	−.124	−4.03	−.926	−2.43	4.79*
	(.231)	(.080)	(3.10)	(.989)	(2.37)	(2.25)
Years of	.009	.020**	.016	−.213**	.071	.206
Schooling	(.020)	(.007)	(.264)	(.087)	(.202)	(.198)
Length of Resi-	.029**	.006*	−.004	−.009	.018	−.092
dence	(.009)	(.003)	(.116)	(.038)	(.088)	(.085)
Church Atten-	.039	.008	.330	−.009	.185	−.042
dance	(.029)	(.010)	(.398)	(.132)	(.296)	(.294)
Employed	.070	−.037	−2.35	−.176	−1.48	−3.40*
	(.140)	(.048)	(1.81)	(.620)	(1.39)	(1.35)
Gender	−.020	.099	−3.30	−1.30	.642	−.239
	(.214)	(.071)	(2.82)	(.889)	(2.05)	(1.99)
District 4	.173	.180**	2.09	−.205	−2.01	−1.34
	(.131)	(.044)	(1.72)	(.563)	(1.30)	(1.28)
Number of	.033	.060**	−.946	−.065	.155	.133
Network	(.058)	(.019)	(.756)	(.056)	(.585)	(.580)
Discussants						
School Involve-	.105	.028	−.223	−.095	−.357	−1.67**
ment	(.067)	(.023)	(.880)	(.287)	(.664)	(.657)
Size of School	.0001	−.00001	−.0004	.0004	.0048*	.0019
	(.0003)	(.0001)	(.004)	(.001)	(.0029)	(.0027)
Constant	3.0**	—	31.2**	24.5**	17.8**	15.1**
	(.43)		(5.8)	(6.7)	(4.3)	(4.2)
N. of Cases	592	596	434	487	547	490
F Statistic	2.1	$\chi^2 = 71$	1.1	1.6	1.5	2.5
Probability	0.01	0.000	0.35	0.10	0.11	0.003
Adjusted R-Square	0.02	0.09	0.01	0.01	0.01	0.04

*p < =.05
**p < = .01

In the first column of table 7.4, we examine whether parents felt that they had "enough information" about the schools in their district to make a choice. Some individual level effects are evident: longer-term residents are more likely to feel they had enough information and black parents are significantly less likely to report having enough information. However, choice does not seem to be a factor here; there are no significant differences between parents in District 1 and District 4.

We examine next what predicts whether or not a New York parent can name correctly their child's school principal.[6] Delli Carpini and Keeter (1996) argue that knowing the name of a national politician is often associated with other kinds of political knowledge—so knowing the name of the school principal may similarly indicate that parents possess other kinds of information about schools.[7] The second column of Table 7.4 reports the results of a probit analysis with naming the principal correctly ($= 1$) as the dependent variable. The coefficients reported are the change in the probability of correctly naming the principal associated with a one-unit change in the independent variable. Reflecting individual abilities, parents with more education are better able to name their principal, as are those with larger networks of education discussants. Most important, here we find a district effect, even controlling for these individual factors: parents in District 4 are significantly more likely to name their children's principal correctly than are parents in District 1. The effect of location in District 4 is larger than that of any of the other variables, and, we believe, reflects the ethos of District 4 in building ties between schools and the community.

We now turn to the school academic and diversity measures. Here we find that, in general, almost none of the individual-level ability variables affect the distribution of knowledge. Moreover, the district variable is not significant in any of these cases, suggesting that district-level choice does not affect this level of accurate knowledge. Indeed, with the exception of the model for the percentage of black students, the other three models are not significant at conventional levels. Thus, while central city parents in our choice district are more likely to know the name of their children's principal, they are not any more accurate on reading test scores, class sizes, or student body demographics than comparable parents in the nonchoice district.

While the general incentives have not increased most forms of knowledge, we now examine the knowledge of parents who have actually made an "active choice." This includes parents who have participated in option-demand choice in either District 1 or 4 and parents who are universal choosers with children in middle school in District 4.

The data in table 7.5 indicate generally that active choosers do not have more accurate information than other parents. Universal choosers are more likely to report having enough information and they are more likely to correctly name the principal than others, but they are not more accurate about the more specific school dimensions.

Thus, in New York, choice does not go very far in explaining levels of knowledge for most of these school measures. In the next chapter we return to role of active choosers, revisiting their incentives and motivation in a more detailed model of choice. But first we replicate the analysis just presented for parents in New Jersey in order to understand how choice affects parental knowledge in a more information-rich environment.

160 • Chapter 7

Table 7.5
Multivariate Analysis of Information Held by Active Choosers in New York

	Had Enough Info.	Principal's Name	Reading Scores	Class Size	Hispanic Percent	Black Percent
Asian	−.355	.045	3.56	−2.59	−1.28	5.90
	(.413)	(.143)	(5.68)	(1.91)	(4.21)	(4.53)
Black	−.408*	−.015	.311	−1.55	−2.68	4.54*
	(.206)	(.075)	(2.77)	(1.01)	(2.19)	(2.08)
Hispanic	−.260	−.064	−.918	−.744	.223	6.44**
	(.195)	(.067)	(2.47)	(.927)	(1.95)	(1.86)
Years of School-ing	.008	.027**	−.350	−.214**	−.042	.065
	(.019)	(.007)	(.241)	(.081)	(.188)	(.187)
Length of Resi-dence	.031**	.004	.067	−.013	.039	−.054
	(.008)	(.003)	(.107)	(.035)	(.082)	(.081)
Church Atten-dance	.044	.009	.225	−.043	.303	−.076
	(.028)	(.009)	(.368)	(.122)	(.278)	(.273)
Employed	−.010	−.023	−3.37*	.035	−2.92*	−4.07**
	(.130)	(.044)	(1.64)	(.572)	(1.29)	(1.26)
Gender	−.059	.133*	−1.94	−1.15	.097	.533
	(.186)	(.063)	(2.40)	(.824)	(1.80)	(1.74)
Option-Demand Choosers	.340	.030	2.38	3.40*	3.08	4.63*
	(.216)	(.074)	(2.78)	(1.60)	(2.15)	(2.02)
Universal Choosers	.435*	.152*	2.64	1.49	−3.38	2.01
	(.228)	(.076)	(2.87)	(1.55)	(2.24)	(2.13)
Number of Net-work Discus-sants	.038	.072*	−.865	−.065	.143	.127
	(0.53)	(.032)	(.667)	(.054)	(.97)	(.116)
School Involve-ment	.079	.036*	−1.15	−.275	−.395	−1.38*
	(.062)	(.021)	(.789)	(.267)	(.614)	(.604)
Size of School	.0002	−.002**	.0038	.0007	.007**	.0048
	(.0003)	(.000)	(.0036)	(.001)	(.0027)	(.003)
Constant	3.2***	—	29.7**	11.4**	14.9**	11.8**
	(.41)		(5.3)	(1.9)	(4.0)	(4.1)
N. of cases	603	598	438	454	590	510
F Statistic	3.0	$\chi^2 = 62$	1.3	2.1	2.4	4.1
Probability	0.001	0.000	0.23	0.01	0.005	0.000
Adjusted R-Square	0.02	0.08	0.00	0.01	0.01	0.01

*$p < = .05$
**$p < = .01$

Choice and Accuracy of Suburban Parents

In table 7.1, we showed that the base level of information is much higher among parents in New Jersey. The results presented in table 7.3 confirmed that this was not simply a function of higher socioeconomic status of suburban parents. Given the higher levels of knowledge in these smaller suburban school districts, does choice in Montclair lead to still greater accuracy?

Simple bivariate comparisons show that Montclair parents are significantly more likely than their counterparts in Morristown to report having enough information (by 0.7 points on the 5 point scale). While there are no significant differences in the ability to correctly name principals, Montclair parents are significantly more accurate than those in Morristown on two of the four measures: reading scores and the percentage of Hispanic students. There is no significant difference across these New Jersey parents in knowledge of the percentage of black children in the schools. In the case of average class size, Morristown parents are actually more accurate than Montclair parents. Thus, the bivariate evidence is mixed, but suggests somewhat more accurate information among choice parents.

We now turn to the multivariate results, utilizing the same independent variables as in the New York models. The basic bivariate results are robust. Table 7.6 suggests that parents in Montclair are more accurate about some facets of their children's schools than are parents in Morristown. For example, the first column of table 7.6 shows that Montclair parents are significantly more likely than those in Morristown to report having enough information in deciding on their children's schools, by almost 1 full point on a 5 point scale. As the results in New York showed, longer-term and more-involved residents are also significantly more likely to report having enough information.

The probit analysis in the second column of table 7.6 shows that Montclair parents are no more likely to know the principal's name than Morristown parents. Indeed, this model is the only one that is not significant at conventional levels of statistical confidence.

In contrast to New York, we do find evidence that choice affects levels of knowledge of school performance. As the analysis reported in the third column of table 7.6 illustrates, Montclair public school parents are significantly more accurate about reading scores than are Morristown public school parents.[8] This is a "strong" test because actual scores in Montclair show a wider range of variation than in Morristown, suggesting that it would be harder to be accurate in Montclair by simply guessing near the district mean. In addition, more-involved parents are more accurate about reading scores.

In contrast, Montclair parents are less likely to be accurate about class sizes than those in Morristown. Not surprisingly, those with children in smaller schools are more likely to be accurate about class sizes. Columns Five and Six illustrate that Montclair parents are significantly more accurate about the percentage of Hispanic children, but not the percentage of black children.

While the effects are not overwhelming, public school choice in the suburban districts we studied has produced an environment in which parents feel more informed about their schools and in fact are more accurate about test

Table 7.6
Multivariate Analysis of Parental Information in New Jersey

	Had Enough Info.	Principal's Name	Reading Scores	Class Size	Hispanic Percent	Black Percent
Asian	.653	−.351*	14.1*	1.85	8.14*	11.6**
	(.457)	(.185)	(6.8)	(.1.65)	(4.32)	(4.14)
Black	−.110	.027	2.02	−.564	3.73**	3.15**
	(.131)	(.049)	(1.64)	(.480)	(.938)	(.840)
Hispanic	.202	−.260*	−4.30	.482	4.41**	4.02*
	(.269)	(.107)	(3.57)	(.993)	(1.82)	(1.85)
Years of Schooling	.015	−.003	−.320	.106	−.474**	−.382*
	(.026)	(.009)	(.321)	(.093)	(.200)	(.175)
Length of Residence	.030**	−.004	.047	.045	−.051	−.028
	(.008)	(.003)	(.102)	(.029)	(.058)	(.052)
Church Attendance	.007	−.0007	−.338	−.019	.102	.218
	(.025)	(.009)	(.314)	(.089)	(.173)	(.158)
Employed	.165	.062	−1.13	−.529	.407	.023
	(.135)	(.050)	(1.69)	(.485)	(.969)	(.879)
Gender	−.040	−.002	−1.72	.071	−.356	−1.58*
	(.135)	(.050)	(1.66)	(.487)	(.917)	(.837)
Montclair	.967**	−.004	−5.87**	2.94**	−2.90**	1.67
	(.149)	(.054)	(1.88)	(.531)	(1.05)	(.96)
Number of Network Discussants	−.029	.007	0.46	.040	−.334	−.077
	(.047)	(.017)	(0.61)	(.032)	(.340)	(.301)
School Involvement	.103*	.016	−2.51**	−.374	.177	−.025
	(.060)	(.023)	(.80)	(.222)	(.451)	(.400)
Size of School	−.0001	.00002	−.0008	.009**	.004	−.010**
	(.0004)	(.0002)	(.005)	(.001)	(.003)	(.003)
Constant	3.4***	—	31.6**	5.4**	13.6**	17.2**
	(.46)		(5.7)	(1.7)	(3.48)	(3.1)
N. of cases	481	489	403	477	380	432
F Statistic	6.9	$\chi^2 = 15$	3.5	14	4.5	4.9
Probability	0.000	0.18	0.000	0.000	0.000	0.000
Adjusted R-Square	0.12	0.02	0.07	0.02	0.10	0.10

*$p < = .05$
**$p < = .01$

scores and the percentage of Hispanic children. Suburban parents motivated by choice may hold this more-detailed level of accuracy because of their greater ability to gather information, combined with opportunity that provides easier access to such information. From our visits to all of these districts, we think it is much easier for a motivated individual to get information about test scores in these New Jersey districts than in New York.[9]

Conclusion

The parents in our sample generally are not highly accurate about the objective conditions of their children's schools. Not surprisingly, parents in suburban districts are more accurate than urban parents, even when controlling for their higher socioeconomic status. The findings for suburban versus urban context are the strongest and most consistent in this chapter, and are consistent with findings from the network analyses in the previous chapter.

In contrast, the results for choice are mixed. Parents in Montclair are more accurate about some aspects of their children's schools, particularly reading test scores, than comparable suburban parents in Morristown. Ability and opportunity may combine to enable suburban parents to react to the incentives choice provides to gain more detailed information about school performance. But when we look at the central city districts, the incentives provided by public school choice produce few if any effects on levels of information accuracy. Except for knowledge of principals, central city parents with choice do not have consistently higher levels of accurate information than other urban parents. In fact, variation in knowledge of objective conditions of schools by urban parents is not explained well by most of the individual-level variables that other scholars have used.

This result may be a function of the barriers to gathering information about schools. It may simply be too difficult for low-income, largely single urban parents (many with limited English proficiency) to learn specific details about their children's schools, even given the added incentive of choice. The lack of easy information availability may overwhelm most other factors, whether related to individual ability or to changed motivation from the incentives of choice.

These results have clear implications. School districts, and especially those in urban areas, need to make determined and sustained efforts to provide the opportunity for all parents to gather useful information. Even if choice does provide some incentives for parents to increase their school knowledge, without outreach efforts by school districts, relatively higher socioeconomic status and more involved parents may be the ones to find the information they need to make good choices. In short, the efforts of school-based actors to supply information are critical to achieving positive results for schools that choice seeks to produce.

Chapter 8

Allocational Efficiency: You Can't Always Get What You Want—But Some Do

Extending parents the right to choose their own schools enhances efficiency in two ways: first, allocative efficiency increases when parental choice leads to a better match between what parent-consumers want and what they get. Second, productive efficiency increases when schools, the suppliers of public education, fall under competitive pressure to improve the quality of their product to attract and retain parent-consumers. In this chapter, we examine allocative efficiency.

We begin by addressing the following question: can parents make good choices given the levels of information they have? In the last chapter, we showed that parents, on average, do not have accurate information about the schools in their district. In this chapter we show that even in the absence of accurate information, there may be a matching process in which parents enroll their children in schools high on the dimensions of education they think are important.

This creates a puzzle: how can this matching take place in the face of such low levels of information?

To solve this puzzle, we discuss various shortcuts to information that might help parents identify good schools. We first examine a growing body of work that links visual indicators (e.g., broken windows) to objective conditions in communities (crime rates). After exploring the role of visual indicators, we shift our analysis away from the behavior of the "average" parent and consider instead a subset of parents who in fact are informed about the conditions of the schools. We demonstrate that there is a tighter match between what these parents want and the conditions of the schools in which their children are enrolled.

We then look at the effect of parent choice on levels of satisfaction with the schools—are parents who get what they want from the schools more satisfied with them? We then consider the efficiency and equity implications of a market for schools driven by these informed parents, who we argue play the role of the "marginal consumer" in the choice process.

Research Design Issues: A Focus on Elementary Schools in New York

As the debate over choice often centers on the ability of low-income parents to make appropriate choices, we begin by examining the two inner-city school districts in New York. We showed in the last chapter that the actual level of information held by parents is far lower in New York than in the suburban districts in New Jersey. Here, we focus only on parents with children in elementary schools. In addition to the theoretical justification for this decision, which is based on the differences in the choice protocols found at different grade levels, this focus is dictated by the preponderance of schools and grades at the elementary school level. While we interviewed more than 500 parents of public elementary school students in the two districts, only 121 parents of junior high school students were in our sample. Given missing values in the various indicators we use in this study, the replication of the results we report for elementary school parents using intermediate school parents would be based on as few as 41 parents in the analysis of school safety and at most 82 in the others.[1] Thus, we are better able to examine the issues of information and choice of public goods in the option-demand system used for elementary schools in the two districts.

In considering the matching process, we address the fact that education is a multifaceted good and parents differ on the attributes of schools they feel are important for their children (see chapter 4). Cognitive resources are limited and, as we saw in the last chapter, even the most involved parents find it difficult to learn about every dimension of the schools available to them. Thus, to study the matching process, we believe that levels of information and choice behavior must be weighted by the specific attributes of schools parents value. That is, if a parent feels that academic performance is important and multiculturalism is not, she should be more accurate on the first dimension than on the second, and the school she chooses for her child should be higher on the first dimension as well. This introduces an important new element to the search for accurate information, and one that moves us beyond the analysis presented in the last chapter. We now ask: how important is a particular aspect of a school to a parent?

Recall that in our survey, we presented parents with a list of school attributes that previous research demonstrated was important to parents (again, see chapter 4). These specific attributes fall into three domains. The first domain consists of attributes associated with the educational "product" of the schools: math and reading scores, teacher quality, and class size. The second domain reflects the reality of local schools in inner cities: safety and discipline. A third set of attributes focuses on the make-up of the student population in terms of race and income.

Rather than utilize the full range of measures of school conditions, in the analyses that follow we explore one indicator from each of these clusters: reading scores, the number of incidents in a school,[2] and the racial/ethnic diversity of the student population. In analyzing parental knowledge, preferences, and choice behavior, we combine the data from the two New York school districts, controlling for other characteristics of each district using a variety of methods described later.

Is Knowledge a Function of Parental Interest?

We examine the extent to which information accuracy is a function of the importance parents place on particular aspects of schooling. Similar to our approach in the previous chapter, we begin by modeling the distance between the estimate and the true condition as a function of the variables in our core explanatory model. But in this analysis we also include an indicator of whether or not a parent considered a particular aspect of schooling important.

While logically, parents who believe a particular dimension of schooling is important should be more accurate on that dimension than parents who do not rate the dimension important, the results in table 8.1 indicate that accuracy does not vary significantly by the importance parents assign to the issue.

Table 8.1
Do Parents Have Objective Knowledge of School Conditions?

	Reading	Incidents	Black Percent	Hispanic Percent
Asian	2.46	.34	−3.82	−6.29
	(7.60)	(2.40)	(5.36)	(5.82)
Black	−8.81(*)	1.21	−.22	−6.62(*)
	(3.75)	(1.39)	(2.83)	(2.97)
Hispanic	−7.40(*)	.87	3.39	−1.71
	(3.46)	(1.26)	(2.63)	(2.73)
Years of Schooling	−.08	−.15	.00	.09
	(.28)	(.10)	(.21)	(.21)
Length of Residence	.01	−.02	−.17	−.04
	(.13)	(.04)	(.09)	(.10)
Church Attendance	−.08	−.00	−.23	−.04
	(.43)	(.15)	(.30)	(.32)
Is Issue Important?	−3.34	−.48	−1.05	−1.78
	(1.89)	(.68)	(1.96)	(2.13)
District 4	2.23	.84	−1.70	−1.31
	(1.92)	(.69)	(1.36)	(1.43)
Constant	34.4(*)	7.53(*)	17.17(*)	20.59(*)
	(5.52)	(2.08)	(3.95)	(4.17)
No. of Cases	393	408	424	452
F Statistic	1.48	.87	1.96	1.44
Probability	.16	.54	.05	.18
Adj. R Squared	.00	.00	.01	.00

Source: Survey of parents in two New York City School districts.

(*) Significant at $p < = .05$.

Note: The dependent variable is the distance between the estimate of each condition and the actual objective condition in the school. The number in the first line of each entry is the regression coefficient, while the second number is the standard error of the estimate.

Indeed, replicating the results of the previous chapter, very few of the independent variables we measured have statistically significant effects on accuracy, and none of the four equations reach acceptable levels of statistical significance.

Matching Children with Schools

In the study of politics, some scholars argue that measuring information accuracy the way we have is too stringent a test—that despite low levels of information, citizens can still get "enough" information to make good choices (see, for example, Iyengar 1989; Sniderman, Brody, and Tetlock 1991; Popkin 1991; Zaller 1992; Lupia 1992, 1994; Althaus 1995; for choosing schools, see Bickers and Stein 1998). In their exploration of this issue, Lupia and McCubbins (1998) have suggested that rather than being overpowered by complex problems, people are actually quite good at observing the world around them and estimating the consequences of a wide range of actions. According to Lupia and McCubbins, while citizens rarely demonstrate detailed "encyclopedic knowledge" about public issues, they often demonstrate "ability knowledge."

We demonstrated in the last chapter that parents generally do not have encyclopedic information about schools, and we have just shown this is true even for parents who report that a particular dimension of schools is important to them. However, can parents still manage to enroll their children in schools that are high on the dimensions of education they value?

To investigate this, we look at the performance of the schools in which children are actually enrolled. Our analysis assesses the degree of the match between parents' preferences and the performance of the schools they chose for their children.

In this stage of our analysis, we use as the dependent variable the performance of a child's school relative to other schools in the district. Our procedure is straightforward. For each school, we collected information on reading scores, the number of incidents, and ethnic composition. We then converted each school's characteristics on each measure into a z-score, using the mean and standard deviation of the performance of all the public elementary schools in the district on that specific measure. After computing these z-scores within each district, we combined the observations from both districts into a single data set, allowing the analysis of comparative performance across different locales (on the use of z-scores for comparative analysis see, e.g., Schneider 1989).[3]

We focus on three objective measures of school performance—one measure in each of the domains of education with which we are concerned. We measure test scores as the percentage of students in the school reading at or above grade level, as measured by the New York City Chancellor's Achievement Test. For safety, we use the number of incidents in each school, as reported by the New York City Board of Education. Finally, as a measure of diversity we use the ratio of the percent of the student population that is white to the percent Hispanic.

All data are for the 1994–1995 school year, the period during which our survey was administered. Note that the reading scores and diversity measure are available for both neighborhood *and* alternative schools, while the incident data are available only at the level of the school building. Since a single building may house several alternative programs or combine both a traditional neighborhood school and one or more alternative programs, this level of reporting presents a measurement problem that affects our analysis.

Table 8.2
Do Parents Sort Themselves into the "Right" Schools?

	Reading	Incidents	Diversity
Asian	.61	.13	−1.20
	(.39)	(.24)	(.37)
Black	.18	.08	−1.41
	(.20)	(.14)	(.19)
Hispanic	−.02	.05	−1.24(*)
	(.20)	(.12)	(.19)
Years of Schooling	−.01	.00	.014(*)
	(.01)	(.01)	(.01)
Length of Residence	.02(*)	.00	.006(*)
	(.00)	(.00)	(.00)
Church Attendance	−.01	.01	.02
	(.02)	(.01)	(.02)
Is Issue Important?	.26(*)	−.13(*)	.25(*)
	(.10)	(.06)	(.13)
Accuracy(**)	−.02(*)	.10(*)	.00
	(.00)	(.00)	(.00)
Accuracy 2			−.01(*)
			(.00)
Constant	.01	−.66(*)	.76(*)
	(.32)	(.21)	(.31)
No. of Cases	347	408	373
F Statistic	7.91	57.10	14.93
Probability	.00	.00	.00
Adj. R Squared	.17	.53	.29

Source: Survey of parents in two New York City school districts.

(*) $p < = .05$

(**) Accuracy: The distance measure between the actual score and the score estimated by the respondent. In the diversity equation, there are two measures of knowledge: one the distance score for the percent black (Accuracy), the other for the percent Hispanic (Accuracy 2).

The dependent variable is the z-score of each school on the specific indicator of performance. The number in the first line of each entry is the regression coefficient, while the second number is the standard error of the estimate.

The results in the three analyses presented in table 8.2 all point in the same direction—even though the levels of information held by parents are low, *their actual choice of schools reflects their preferences*. For example, parents who say that high scores are important enroll their children in schools that are more than .25 standard deviation above the district mean in reading scores. Similarly, parents who value safety and those who value diversity also enroll their children in schools that are significantly better than the average schools in their district on these dimensions.[4]

This raises an intriguing puzzle: if parents in general do not have accurate information about these dimensions of schools, how can the matching process demonstrated in table 8.2 take place?

We explore two solutions to this puzzle, realizing that they could be working in concert. The first possibility is that many parents have developed a set of heuristics that allows them to identify schools high on the dimensions that they value without actually having detailed information about schools' performance on this dimension. For instance, parents may rely on the judgments of friends, family, and coworkers about the quality of schools when choosing. Or, they may rely on a set of visual cues to tell them what they need to know about schools (Bickers and Stein 1998).

A second explanation relies on a phenomenon that has been examined in the study of many private goods markets, and that demonstrates the important role of a small group of consumers who actually gather information about products. Thus while *on average*, information about products is low, a small group of buyers in markets tend to be more informed. These studies show that this small percentage of buyers can effectively drive a market toward a competitive outcome.[5] Paralleling this phenomenon in private sector markets, we demonstrate that the matching process evident in table 8.2 is driven by the behavior of a subset of parents.

Shortcuts to Decisions

Clearly, individual decision makers often rely on shortcuts in a range of decision domains, including politics and policy. Lupia has demonstrated the importance of relying on friends, coworkers, and groups as cue givers in a referendum on insurance reform in California (1994). Lupia and McCubbins (1998) argue that individuals develop strategies to screen out important information from the vast flows of information to which they are exposed (also see, for example, Fiske and Taylor 1991; Sniderman, Brody, and Tetlock 1991; or Lodge and Stroh 1993).

Following this line of argument, we could try to explain the matching process by demonstrating that parents rely on cues provided by others when choosing a school. However, there is little evidence that the majority of inner-city residents engage in extensive interpersonal communications about schools. Recall that in our study, we asked respondents to name up to three people with whom they talked about schools. As noted in chapter 6, among our sample of inner-city parents, the modal number of educational respondents in New York was 0 and the mean just over 1, suggesting that this is not a prime source of information.

Visual Cues to School Performance: Graffiti, Dirty Schools, and Performance

Urban analysts have argued that inner-city residents can use simple visual cues to measure the extent of underlying pathologies of urban life in a neighborhood. The importance of visual cues as an indicator of crime can be traced back at least to 1967, when Biderman et al. used survey data to show that fear of crime was strongly related to the extent of disorderly conditions in neighborhoods. But, the argument has been most closely associated with George Kelling, who developed the image of broken windows as an indicator of neighborhood decline (see, for example, Wilson and Kelling 1982; Coles and Kelling 1996).

The process Kelling has described is deceptively simple: if windows in a factory or a shop remain broken, a passerby walks away with the idea that no one cares about the neighborhood. In turn, more windows will be broken and the sense of disorder will intensify. In a self-propelling process, as the feeling of disorder intensifies, law-abiding individuals begin to avoid the area, thinking no one is in charge and that the area is dangerous. This leaves the area open to criminals—so, in fact, the area does become increasingly unsafe. Thus, in Kelling's view, small disorders can snowball into larger disorders and ultimately high crime rates.

Skogan (1990) has provided extensive survey data to support this link. He documents a consistent relationship between citizen fears, experiences with crime, and perceptions of neighborhood disorder on the one hand, with actual conditions of graffiti, gang-related congregations, prostitution, drunkenness, etc. While this body of work is mostly concerned with crime, the fundamental lesson is that individuals can use simple experiences to tell them about more complex phenomena.[6] The same kinds of linkages may exist between observable conditions in schools and the quality of education, as parents use visual cues to understand how well a school is "working."

To test this idea, we sent four researchers to inspect the physical conditions of each school building in each of the districts in our study. They reported on both the external and internal conditions of the school building, for example, gathering data on the general cleanliness of the facility and the presence of graffiti on the building and in the hallways.[7] Once we established that there were high levels of intercoder reliability, we averaged the evaluations across all of the researchers to create a single score on each of several physical dimensions.

In table 8.3, we report two sets of correlations between visible indicators of conditions in the school and objective measures of conditions that parents

Table 8.3
Shortcuts to Information: Objective Conditions Are Correlated with Visual Cues

	Percent Reading at Grade Level	*Number of Incidents*
Graffiti on Building	− .24(*)	.24
Graffiti in Halls	− .21(**)	.55(*)
Facility in Working Order	.27(**)	− .32(**)
	N = 62	N = 32

Source: Graffiti, cleanliness: visual inspection of school buildings. Reading scores, number of incidents: New York City school report cards.

Graffiti is a dichotomous variable (1 = yes there was graffiti). The facility indicator is a scale ranging from 1–10 based on a visual inspection of the general condition of the school building.
  (*) $p < = .05$
(**) $p < = .10$

value.[8] In the first panel, we report the correlations between observable conditions and reading scores for sixty-two schools and programs.

The data suggest that by simply walking past a school and noting the presence of graffiti or the condition of the school building a parent can infer school performance. Similarly, in the second panel of table 8.3, we show visual cues can again act as a shortcut to information about a valued condition: a clean school free of graffiti is likely a safer school.[9]

To further highlight the extent to which these objective conditions can signal the quality of a school, we compared the conditions found in schools at the extremes of the distribution of reading scores and incidents (see table 8.4.). Here, we look at schools that are ½ a standard deviation above (or below) the mean performance of the other schools in their district and compare the objective conditions in these two types of schools. The results further support the relationship displayed in table 8.3.

Consider first the relationship between visual conditions and academic performance: the worst performing programs were much more likely to be in

Table 8.4
Conditions in Schools at the Extremes of the Reading and Incident Distribution

	Schools with Worst Reading Scores	*Schools with Best Reading Scores*	*Most Unsafe Schools*	*Safest Schools*
Exterior Graffiti	93%	75%	100%	75%
Interior Graffiti	20%	0%	28%	0%
Facility in Working Order	7.2	7.6	6.6	7.1
	N = 12	N = 15	N = 7	N = 12

buildings marked by graffiti. Note too that none of the best performing schools had any interior graffiti, while 20 percent of the worst performing schools did. Similarly, the distribution of graffiti differs between the safest and the most unsafe schools. And, in general, schools that are safe and performing well academically in general appear to be in better working order than low-performing schools.

From these data, one could argue that there are visual cues that can help parents make informed decisions about the schools their children attend by allowing parents to assess relatively easily the conditions about which they care. This argument fits with the growing optimism among political scientists that low-information rationality, the use of heuristics, and ability knowledge may in fact provide citizens with sufficient means to make appropriate electoral choices. One problem with this argument, however, is that these correlations are low. Another problem is that we have no way of actually placing the parents in our sample in the schools—that is, we have no evidence that parents actually have visited the schools and observed these visual conditions. Thus, we leave this explanation for future research.

In the next section we develop an alternative explanation for matching in the absence of general knowledge that is parsimonious and congruent with research on the behavior of consumers in private goods markets. We argue that the match found in table 8.2 may in fact be a function of the behavior of a set of more highly informed shoppers for schools. Thus, while our exploration of visual cues raises the possibility that there are shortcuts to decision making that might help the "average" uninformed parent choose, in the next section we focus on what we call the "marginal" consumer.

The "Average" Consumer versus the "Marginal" Consumer

Studies of competitive private markets show that only a subset of consumers gathers information about their purchases (Katona and Mueller 1955; Newman and Staelin 1972; Claxton, Fry, and Portis 1974; Thorelli and Engledow 1980). Rhoads (1985, 144) argues that in many markets these informed or marginal consumers are the most careful shoppers, and that their actions generate "competitive pressures that help keep prices reasonable for less-informed, non-searching consumers as well." Schwartz and Wilde argue that "*the conventional analysis asks the wrong question. Rather than asking whether an idealized individual is sufficiently informed to maximize his own utility, the appropriate normative inquiry is whether competition among firms* [here, read schools] for *particular groups of searchers* is, in any given market, sufficient to generate optimal prices and terms for *all consumers*" (1979, 638. Emphasis added). Thus, competitive markets require at least some consumers to be sufficiently informed so as to pressure producers to deliver services efficiently.

Empirical studies of private markets often find a group of consumers that search for more information than the average consumer. These consumers are more interested in and more involved with the product (Katona and Mueller 1955; Newman and Staelin 1972; Claxton, Fry, and Portis 1974; Slama and Tashchian 1985; Wilde and Schwartz 1979, 543). Two sets of studies have focused on the critical importance of these informed consumers. Thorelli and Engledow (1980) identify "information seekers" who comprise 10 to 20 percent of the population and help police the market by their comparative shopping. Second, Feick and Price (1987) labeled the upper third of information seekers "market mavens." Slama and Williams (1990) confirmed that market mavens provide comparative product information to others for many products and services.

Teske et al. (1993) extended this work from the private market to the local market for public goods, identifying a set of marginal consumers who are informed about schools and who exert pressure on local schools to be more efficient (see the exchange between Lowery, Lyons, and DeHoog 1995 and Teske et al. 1995; also Dowding, John, and Biggs 1994; John, Dowding, and Biggs 1995). That a small number of parents can influence a school district was made evident in Mesa, Arizona, where the loss of 1,600 students to charter schools was enough to pressure the 70,000-student school district into making reforms (Toch 1998).

These developments in choice districts illustrate a fundamental point that we think has been overlooked in debates about choice. While proponents such as Chubb and Moe and Sugarman and Coons imply that the full competitive benefits of choice at the systemic level will be generated by high levels of information across *all* parents, the response of a smaller group of parents may be sufficient to produce these benefits.

This explanation is related to, but actually quite different from, the two-step flow of information that has long been used to describe voting decisions (e.g., Lazarsfeld, Berelson, and Gaudet 1944; Huckfeldt and Sprague 1995). In both cases, a subset of the population has extensive information about choices. In the two-step model of political decision making however, knowledgeable voters talk to, inform, and influence other "uninformed" citizens. As we have shown however, a large numbers of the parents in our sample do not talk to anyone about their decisions. In our model, the marginal consumer, by making the best choices for herself, provides a positive externality to other consumers by her behavior, even without directly communicating information to less-informed citizens.

The Marginal Consumer in the Market for Education

To investigate the role of the marginal consumer, we replicate the three analyses we presented above for all parents, but now introducing a term for parents who are active choosers. To examine the role of the informed, marginal consumer, we also introduce an interaction term between that active chooser variable and whether or not the parent indicated a particular dimension of education was important. We then rerun the previous models from tables 8.1 and 8.2 with these two terms included. Note that, in contrast to our finding for active choosers in the last chapter, we are now examining accuracy as a function of being an active chooser *and* a parent who considers that dimension of schools to be important.

In table 8.5, we reestimate the effects of parental attributes on knowledge, including the two terms specific to the marginal consumer. In three of the four models, we find that this group of parents is significantly more knowl-

Table 8.5
The Marginal Consumer Knows More about Schools

	Reading	Black %	Hispanic %	Incidents
Asian	6.04	−4.04	−7.47	−1.01
	(7.69)	(5.41)	(5.85)	(2.45)
Black	−5.56	−.46	−7.82(*)	−.00
	(3.96)	(2.92)	(3.04)	(1.47)
Hispanic	−4.35	2.93	−3.03	−.19
	(3.68)	(2.72)	(2.85)	(1.32)
Years of Schooling	−.15	−.01	.10	−.12
	(.28)	(.20)	(.21)	(.10)
Length of Residence	.02	−.19(*)	−.06	−.02
	(.12)	(.09)	(.10)	(.04)
Church Attendance	−.13	−.20	.00	.01
	(.45)	(.30)	(.32)	(.15)
Is Issue Important?	−1.44	.42	.92	−.70
	(1.98)	(2.14)	(2.33)	(.69)
Chooser	10.78(*)	4.37	3.54	−3.81(*)
	(4.28)	(2.46)	(2.62)	(1.57)
Interaction: Chooser*	−16.74(*)	−8.32(*)	−13.01(*)	1.66
Importance	(5.98)	(4.26)	(4.63)	(2.84)
District 4	2.17	−2.09	−1.70	.70
	(1.94)	(1.37)	(1.44)	(.69)
Constant	31.96(*)	17.21(*)	21.71(*)	8.45(*)
	(6.16)	(3.95)	(4.17)	(2.10)
No. of Cases	398	424	452	408
F Statistic	2.05	2.03	1.96	1.34
Probability	.05	.02	.02	.20
Adj. R Squared	.03	.04	.02	.00

Source: Survey of parents in two New York City school districts.

(*) p < = .05

Note: The dependent variable is the distance between the estimate of each condition and the actual objective condition in the school. The number in the first line of each entry is the regression coefficient, while the second number is the standard error of the estimate.

edgeable about schools than other parents. For example, the estimates of reading scores of active choosers who think that high scores are important are almost 17 percentage points closer to the actual reading scores than those estimated by other parents, ceteris paribus. Similarly, choosers who are interested in diversity are 13 points closer to the objective measure of the size of the Hispanic population and 8 points closer to the size of the black population in their children's schools. Thus, for the first time in our analyses of information in the last few chapters, we have identified a group of New York City parents who are significantly more accurate about several elements of schools: those who choose and who care about that dimension.

Note that the one measure where this pattern is not evident is the measure of incidents. Here we find that on average, choosers are more accurate than other parents (there is a main effect), but the interaction effect of *chooser* importance* is not associated with greater accuracy about safety. But as noted above, this may be the result of a measurement problem—we are relying on school building data, not on program data, and hence there may be substantial measurement error in the objective data we are using as the dependent variable.

Do Marginal Consumers Match with Schools?

In table 8.6, we examine the extent to which these marginal consumers have enrolled their children in schools that are high on the dimensions of education they care about. In general, we find evidence of a strong match in the two domains where our data are most reliable. Active choosers who think that diversity is important are in schools that are more than 1 standard deviation above the district average and choosers who care about high scores similarly are in schools that are far above the mean level of performance for schools in the district. Once we introduce the marginal consumer into the model, the match between other parents (the "average consumers") and school performance disappears—that is, the behavior of the marginal consumer solves the puzzle we posed earlier in this chapter.[10]

At this stage, we need to address two important issues. First, it is essential to show that the match between parental preferences and program performance is *not* simply a function of parents choosing alternative schools that are superior on all of these dimensions. As evident in table 8.7, there is no difference in the mean level of performance of alternative schools and neighborhood schools on reading scores and in racial composition. Thus, choosers cannot maximize on all dimensions simply by choosing an alternative school—matching is not an artifact of simply choosing.

Second is the question of whether or not parents who make choices report being more satisfied with the schools they have chosen for their children. We turn next to that issue.

Table 8.6
Does the Marginal Consumer Pick Schools High on the Attributes They Value?

	Reading	Diversity	Incidents
Asian	.63	−.52	−.00
	(.41)	(.30)	(.25)
Black	.16	−.84*	−.04
	(.23)	(.16)	(.14)
Hispanic	.01	−.70*	−.06
	(.22)	(.15)	(.13)
Years of Schooling	−.01	.00	.006
	(.01)	(.01)	(.01)
Length of Residence	.02*	.00	−.00
	(.00)	(.00)	(.00)
Is Issue Important?	.17	−.04	−.14
	(.11)	(.12)	(.07)
Active Chooser	−.09	1.45*	−.34*
	(.26)	(.14)	(.16)
Interaction: Active Chooser*	1.16*	1.09*	−.08
Importance	(.35)	(.23)	(.29)
Accuracy	−.01*	−.007*	−.10*
	(.00)	(.002)	(.005)
Accuracy 2**		−.002	
		(.002)	
Constant	−.04	.44*	−.56*
	(.32)	(.22)	(.21)
No. of Cases	327	397	387
F Statistic	9.17	50.52	46.93
Probability	0.00	0.00	0.00
Adj. R Squared	0.20	0.55	0.53

Source: Survey of parents in two New York City school districts.

(*) p < = .05

(**) Accuracy: The distance measure between the actual score and the score estimated by the respondent. In the diversity equation, there are two measures of knowledge: one the distance score for the percent black (Accuracy), the other for the percent Hispanic (Accuracy 2).

Note: The dependent variable is the z-score of each school on the specific indicator of performance. The number in the first line of each entry is the regression coefficient, while the second number is the standard error of the estimate.

Does Allocative Efficiency Increase Satisfaction with the Schools?

These data demonstrate that allocative efficiency is higher in the option-demand system we study in New York City. It should follow that parents with good matches should be more satisfied with their children's schools than other parents, an argument about consumer sovereignty that dates back at least as far as Milton Friedman in 1955 (see also Coons and Sugarman 1978; Raywid 1981; Levin 1991). To the extent that choice increases the

Table 8.7
Objective Conditions in Alternative versus Neighborhood Schools

	Neighborhood Schools	Alternative Schools/Programs	Significance of difference
% Reading at Grade Level	33	35	.65
Black %	27	34	.12
Hispanic %	65	49	.17

Source: New York City school report cards.

Note: Safety data are available only at the building level and is thus unavailable for alternative schools and programs.

ability of parents to match their preferences for specific values, needs, or pedagogical approaches with the school, the resulting match should lead to higher satisfaction. As Goldring and Shapira observe: "The family sovereignty position suggests choice leads to greater satisfaction in that it accommodates individual family preferences, mainly in the areas of curricula, teaching philosophy, and religion. Parents will be satisfied in exercising their fundamental right of individual choice and freedom of belief about the best education for their children" (1993, 397). We have already shown the first part of this statement to be true—that is, choice does increase the match between what parents want and what their children's schools deliver—does it also lead to higher satisfaction?

Empirical research is nearly unanimous in linking various forms of choice to increased parent satisfaction. McArthur, Colopy, and Schaine (1995, 2) found in a nationwide study that 82 percent of private school parents reported being "very satisfied" with their schools, compared to 61 percent for parents with children in public schools they had chosen, and 52 percent in assigned public schools. Peterson (1998, 17) summarizes results from the Milwaukee, Indianapolis, San Antonio, and Cleveland voucher programs: "If the only thing that counts is consumer satisfaction, school choice is a clear winner." (See also Moe 1995, 30 on vouchers; Vanourek et al. 1998, 193–95; Bierlein 1997, 53 on higher parent satisfaction with charter schools).[11]

Higher levels of parental satisfaction from choice may relate partly to the energy and time that parents put into choice. Some parents may seek to justify their choice and their investment of resources by selectively gathering and interpreting information about performance and by indicating increased satisfaction with their children's schools—viewing the schools through "rose colored glasses" (Erikson 1982; see Festinger 1957 more generally on this phenomenon).

In any case, there are compelling reasons to believe that choice will be associated with higher levels of parent satisfaction. In the analysis that follows, we investigate the extent to which choice affects levels of parent satisfaction with the schools in our study.

Measuring Satisfaction with Schools

We begin by testing empirically the relationship between allocative efficiency and satisfaction, focusing once again on the elementary school parents in our two New York City districts. We employ two indicators of parental satisfaction: (1) has the parent thought of moving her child to a different school? and (2) does the parent think that her child's school is the best in the district? These are both measured as dichotomous variables (1 = agreement). Again, we estimate the effects of allocative efficiency on levels of satisfaction while at the same time controlling for a number of other factors with the following model:

Satisfaction = f (individual characteristics, allocative efficiency, district location)

Where:

Individual characteristics of parents include the set of variables that we have used throughout this book: racial identity, years of schooling, length of time living in the district, and church attendance. We also employ a dummy variable for the district location (District 1 = 1).

In addition, building on the work of previous chapters, we add several other variables to the right-hand side of the model. The first of these reflects the potential importance of parental involvement in the education process and is a scale ranging from 0 to 4, counting the number of educational activities in which the parent reports being involved. Goldring and Shapira in particular emphasize the importance of involvement in parent satisfaction, arguing that parent involvement increases support for schools, which would translate into a higher sense of satisfaction (1993, 398–99).

Second, we add a series of measures to examine how allocative efficiency affects satisfaction. Recall that we are modeling allocative efficiency as a process in which parents match their preferences for specific school attributes to schools high on these attributes, which choice makes possible. Here, however, we are testing the extent to which levels of satisfaction with the schools also increase, as the match between parental preferences and school characteristics increases.

To measure the effects of allocative efficiency, we first create the following two variables:

- Option-demand choosers who think diversity is important * school diversity.
- Option-demand choosers who think high scores are important * reading performance.

While these terms may seem complicated, building on the matching analysis earlier in this chapter, they have a straightforward construction. Focusing on the first interaction term, if a parent is an active chooser who values diversity, then the value of this term is the diversity score of the school in which the parent's child is enrolled, and takes the value of 0 elsewise. The coefficients for this term in the following analysis thus indicate the change in the probability that a parent who is an active chooser and who values diversity will be satisfied with a school as that school becomes more diverse. To create the other interaction term, we substitute high scores for diversity.

Table 8.8 shows the change in levels of satisfaction[12] as a function of these terms. We begin with the likelihood that a parent thought about moving her child to a different school. First note that racial effects are evident—Hispanics and blacks are significantly more likely to have thought about changing their children's schools than are white parents. Also note that dissatisfaction with their children's schools, as measured by an interest in changing schools, increases with the education level of the parent.

The effects of allocative efficiency concern us most—are choosers who locate in the "right" schools less likely to think about moving schools? The answer is yes: choosers who value academic performance are highly sensitive to the academic performance of their schools. If the child of a chooser is in a school that performs 1 standard deviation above the mean of the other schools in the district, the probability of that parent considering a move decreases by 30 percent. Many option-demand choosers are actively seeking high academic performance when they choose schools. The results in table 8.8 indicate that when such choosers do place their children in a school that is performing well, they are more satisfied, as reflected in a much lower probability of considering moving the child to another school.

Next we examine the second measure of satisfaction, the probability of rating the school as the best in the district. Here, we find once again that option-demand choosers who value academic performance and whose children are in high performing schools are much more likely to rank their schools best. Using the same metric as above, an option-demand parent who values academic performance and whose child is in a school that is performing 1 standard deviation better than the average school in the district is 22 percent more likely to think that her child's school is the best school in the district.

Thus, our results consistently point toward a strong relationship between choice and satisfaction. When choice allows parents who care about academic performance to choose schools that are performing well, satisfaction increases, often quite dramatically.

Replicating the Analysis: Shopping for Schools in New Jersey

The obvious question is: is the process we just documented in New York City also evident in New Jersey? We must remember that the environment of choice and information in Montclair is very different from that in New York. First, the number of options is much fewer than in either of the New York districts—there are only two middle schools in Montclair and five schools at

Table 8.8
The Effects of Allocative Efficiency on Parental Satisfaction: New York

	Move	Best School
Black	.25*	−.15
	(.11)	(.11)
Hispanic	.21*	−.07
	(.09)	(.10)
Asian	−.11	−.21
	(.18)	(.19)
Length of Residence	.00	.00
	(.00)	(.00)
Church Attendance	.01	.00
	(.01)	(.01)
Education	.02**	.00
	(.01)	(.00)
District 1	.03	.06
	(.04)	(.05)
Involvement	−.01	.06**
	(.02)	(.02)
Diversity Important	−.04	.01
	(.07)	(.08)
High Scores Important	.01	.02
	(.05)	(.05)
Active Chooser	.09	.01
	(.15)	(.04)
Interaction: Active Public Chooser Interested in Diversity	.06	.12
	(.21)	(.20)
Interaction: Active Chooser Interested in High Scores	−.10	.00
	(.16)	(.18)
Interaction: Active Chooser Reading Important* Reading Score	−.31**	.21*
	(.12)	(.10)
Interaction: Active Chooser Diversity Important* Diversity	−.21	.43
	(.39)	(.47)
Number of Observations	448	437
Chi Square (df = 19)	32.46	23.51
Probability Chi Square	.005	.07
Observed Probability	.38	.58

Note: Coefficients are the change in the probability of a parent saying yes to a dependent variable as a function of a unit change in the independent variable. (Move = the parent has thought of moving her child to a different school; Best = the parent thinks that her child's school is the best in the district.)
*p = .05
**p = .01

the grade 3–5 level. Moreover, Montclair has a strong policy to minimize differences in the performance and demographic composition of its schools. For example, across the two middle schools, the percent of students reading at grade level is within 1 percentage point and there is only about a 5-percentage-point difference in the percent black (the largest racial minority group in Montclair). Across the five schools containing grades 3–5, the percent black ranges from 33 percent to 44 percent and reading scores range from 80 to 95 percent. And, even though there is choice, there is a strong tendency to have children follow established patterns from feeder schools at the pre-K through 2 level into the next level of school and then into intermediate schools. Furthermore, the average Montclair parent is more accurate about several school dimensions than parents in New York City. And finally, very few parents in New Jersey (only 5 percent) ranked diversity or safety as important concerns, reflecting a different environment than New York.

There are several reasons, then, not to expect the matching process to work in exactly the same manner. Yet, when we replicated the New York analysis for reading scores in New Jersey, the results were similar. Montclair parents with children are in grades 3–5, the level at which choice is the most meaningful, who say high scores are important are over 6 points closer to the real reading scores of their schools than other New Jersey parents. In addition, these parents place their children in schools whose performance on reading tests are .67 standard deviations higher than other schools (see table 8.9). Even in this more limited choice environment, there is evidence of a matching process by parents who actively choose their children's schools.

Satisfaction in New Jersey

Our satisfaction models reflect the different structure of choice in New Jersey from New York. Since Montclair supports a system of universal choice, while Morristown relies on strict residential catchment zones, our public school choice variable is a dummy variable for Montclair and our interaction terms are:

- Montclair residents who think diversity is important * diversity.
- Montclair parents who think high scores are important * school reading performance.

In table 8.10 we report the results of our multivariate analysis. First, our model of parent attitudes toward moving their children to another school fails to reach acceptable levels of statistical significance. However, for the second measure of satisfaction, we find confirming evidence that allocative efficiency affects the evaluation of schools: in New Jersey, as in New York, choosers who value high scores and who are in high-performing schools are significantly more likely to believe that their school is the best school than are other parents.

Conclusion

By having greater knowledge about the aspects of the schools they care about and by matching their preferences to appropriate schools, we believe that

Table 8.9
Parental Information and Placement in New Jersey Reading Scores Only

	Accuracy: Reading Scores	Placement Based on Reading Scores
Asian	19.17(*)	−.16
	(5.89)	(.33)
Black	3.28	.26(*)
	(2.53)	(.13)
Hispanic	−8.17	.62
	(7.61)	(.41)
Years of Schooling	−.43	.03
	(.42)	(.02)
Length of Residence	−.04	.01
	(.16)	(.01)
Church Attendance	1.51(*)	−.00
	(.54)	(.03)
Is Issue Important	3.62	−.38(*)
	(2.99)	(.16)
Accuracy(**)		.00
		(.00)
Interaction	−6.38(*)	.67(*)
Montclair* Importance	(3.24)	(.18)
Constant	6.42(*)	−.75
	(7.08)	(.39)
No. of Cases	178	178
F Statistic	3.22	3.27
Probability	.002	.001
Adj. R Squared	.09	.10

Source: Survey of parents in two New Jersey school districts.

(*) $p < = .05$

(**) Accuracy: The distance measure between the actual score and the score estimated by the respondent. This is the dependent variable in the first model, so no coefficient is reported.

The dependent variable is the z-score of each school on reading performance. The number in the first line of each entry is the regression coefficient, while the second number is the standard error of the estimate.

school choosers can play the critically important role of marginal consumers. While we have concentrated on the effects of choice in New York City, the replication of these results in a far different choice environment in New Jersey underlines the robustness of our argument. But the results also indicate some important policy lessons for the implementation of choice.

First, our results suggest that, despite low average information levels, choice can improve allocational efficiency *both* in a low-income, central city environment, as well as in a suburban setting. Second, our best matching results were obtained in a school district marked by a considerable number of schools and a wide range of performance across the dimensions of educa-

Table 8.10
The Effects of Allocative Efficiency on Parental Satisfaction: New Jersey

	Move	Best School
Black	−.11	.13
	(.07)	(.08)
Hispanic	−.04	.01
	(.14)	(.20)
Asian	−.19	.24*
	(.11)	(.11)
Length of Residence	−.009*	.01*
	(.004)	(.005)
Church Attendance	−.01	.00
	(.02)	(.01)
Education	.00	−.02
	(.01)	(.02)
Involvement	−.00	.01
	(.03)	(.04)
High Scores Important	.02	−.11
	(.10)	(.11)
Montclair	.09	.14
	(.09)	(.11)
Interaction: Montclair Reading Important	−.07	.20
	(.12)	(.13)
Interaction: Montclair Reading Important*	.04	.22*
Reading score	(.08)	(.09)
Number of Observations	201	185
Chi Square	11.31	30.25
(df = 19)		
Probability Chi Square	.41	.001
Observed Probability	.25	.62

Note: Coefficients are the change in the probability of a parent saying yes to a dependent variable as a function of a unit change in the independent variable. (Move = the parent has thought of moving her child to a different school. Best = the parent thinks that her child's school is the best in the district.)

*p = .05
**p = .01

tion parents value. The results are somewhat weaker in New Jersey, where parents have limited numbers of choices and where explicit racial-balancing admission policies limit the range of choice.

Thus, our findings may be context dependent—the more a choice system resembles a competitive market with many options and maximum incentives for parents to be involved, the more likely our results are to apply. Ultimately, if voucher programs and, even more importantly, charter school legislation become more common, they will increase the number and range of schools operating in an area. Our data suggest that such an expansion in the number and range of schools in the parent choice set will increase the allocative efficiency that we see evident in the analyses in this chapter.

These results support our argument that public school choice can produce two important benefits. First, at the individual level, choice can allow parents to get more of what they want for their children from the schools. In addition, as parents gain information about the schools they pressure the schools into being more efficient producers of these attributes of education. But how many parents are needed to increase both types of efficiency?

Chubb and Moe, Sugarman and Coons, and other proponents of school choice imply that choice will lead to better schools by creating the conditions under which *all* parents will have incentives to become informed about schools and hence provide competitive pressures on schools. We believe that this overstates not only what we should expect from the average parent, but also what is *necessary* for effective competition. Competitive markets do not need *all* consumers to be informed—competitive pressures can result even if a relatively small subset of consumers engage in informed, self-interested search. Further, in chapter 11, we will show how much more involved these marginal consumers are in school events than average parents, giving them both "voice" and "exit" through which they can pressure schools to perform effectively and efficiently.

We recognize that markets for public goods, such as those created by public school choice, are much more complex than markets for private goods. Many critics of choice (e.g., Rose-Ackerman 1992; Henig 1996) will find themselves in agreement with the part of our analysis showing that some parents will become more informed than others and will match their children with the best schools. However, these critics are concerned that informed parents will make choices that will harm the children of less well-informed parents, in effect creating a zero-sum game and leaving them behind in the worst schools. But this ignores the possibility that competition can force all schools to improve. Thus, a critical question is whether or not these marginal consumers do increase the efficiency of education outcomes for everyone, or just for themselves.

In the next chapter, we turn to the question of productive efficiency. Given that given choice, some parents find the appropriate schools for their children while others do not, the question remains as to whether districts with choice improve student performance overall or only for a small number of students. In chapters 9 and 10, we address this question. In chapter 10 we specifically consider whether improvements in performance are limited to those students whose parents have made informed choices, or whether all schools are influenced positively by the competitive pressures. This chapter gets at the heart of one of the most controversial issues surrounding school choice—the equality of educational opportunity.

Chapter 9

Productive Efficiency: Does School Choice Affect Academic Performance?

In the last chapter, we showed that choice increases allocative efficiency, by allowing parents to better match their preferences with school programs. Here, we examine whether or not choice stimulates improvements in productive efficiency. We do this by asking if schools in our choice district show higher test score performance than districts without choice.

This question shifts the focus of our analysis away from parent preferences and behaviors to the performance of schools and school districts. This shift in analysis also leads us away from the survey data upon which much of the previous analysis was based to a reliance on official reports regarding school performance. As we have noted at several other points in this book, the availability and consistency of such data are serious issues in any study of school performance. For example, we were unable to construct a sufficient database to comprehensively study school performance in New Jersey—and while we do present some performance data for Montclair, our analysis is limited. In contrast, we were able to construct a fairly good cross-sectional database on performance for schools in New York City. And after considerable work, we were able to construct a longitudinal database for District 1 and District 4.

The Effects of Choice in District 4

We are not the first scholars to try to gauge the effects of choice on performance in District 4. There is considerable anecdotal evidence that choice in District 4 has increased the performance of district schools. Because this evidence is based on incomplete data, some scholars argue that the link has not been satisfactorily demonstrated. In addition, some argue that any observed success is attributable to factors besides choice, including administrative leadership and innovation, small school size, and "extra" resources generated from external federal magnet programs and from District 4 exceeding its budget. Since considerable debate remains regarding the factors influencing improvements in District 4, our analysis attempts to isolate the effects of choice from the effects of some of these other factors.

Student Performance in District 4

Some analysts have illustrated improvements in raw reading and math test scores in District 4 after choice was implemented (Fliegel with McGuire

1993; Domanico 1989). These analyses also show that more District 4 students are now accepted into prestigious selective high schools, such as Stuyvesant, Bronx Science, Brooklyn Tech, the LaGuardia School of Music and Performing Arts, than in the past (Fliegel with McGuire 1993; Kirp 1992; Domanico 1989). For example, in 1973, only ten District 4 students were accepted into these schools, compared to nearly three hundred students in the mid-1980s, an acceptance rate twice that of the rest of the city (Fliegel 1992).

According to these studies, several choice schools in District 4 are excellent by any standard. For example, today over 90 percent of graduates from Central Park East Secondary School go on to college, a rate that is nearly double that for the city as a whole (Meier 1995). Currently, the New York City Board of Education reports that the elementary school with the highest reading scores of the city's 670 schools is District 4's Talented and Gifted (TAG) school. Many parents from outside the district have tried to send their children to District 4 schools, in marked contrast to a past pattern of flight from the district, and the continuing pattern of flight from districts with similar demographic characteristics, such as District 1.

However, critics of choice have questioned whether District 4's purported successes are real and whether choice was a major cause. At a minimum, critics note that existing analyses of District 4 are incomplete. As the next section shows, the arguments questioning the effects of choice in District 4 are based on several inter-related issues, most of which we address.

Isolating the Effects of Choice

One set of concerns is the instability of test scores over time. The New York City Board of Education has changed its test several times over the more than two decades that choice has been in effect in District 4. Because the largest improvement in test scores (a gain of 13 percentage points) occurred in 1973 when choice was first getting started, and in 1986 (10 percentage points) when NYC switched to a different test, some have questioned whether District 4's gains were independent of citywide gains (see, e.g., Kirp 1992). To address this issue, in this chapter, we control the extent to which test instruments affect performance by standardizing District 4's test results relative to the citywide average for the tests administered by the city in that year, creating a common baseline for a reliable over-time analysis.

Some scholars argue that while District 4 test scores improved over time, the improvement was the result of bringing in students who are better prepared and of higher socioeconomic status from other districts (Hurwitz 1988; Kirp 1992; Cookson 1992; Henig 1996). They believe that scores improved not because students already in the district improved, but because the schools attracted better students. According to Henig (1996, 131), between 800 and 2,000 students came into District 4 from outside the district.

Moreover, Kirp (1992, 36) posits that "It is largely because of this hidden selection process—which screens for both levels of skills and traits of character, that some very good schools have been created in East Harlem." In response, Fliegel argues that staff in District 4 analyzed these data and found that the profile of incoming students was virtually the same as the District 4 resident students in terms of test score performances. In the analysis in this chapter, we address this issue by controlling for the demographic characteristics of students enrolled in the District schools.

Some scholars have also argued that any improvements in District 4 were driven more by extra money from federal magnet programs and from the district consistently running over-budget during the 1980s (Kirp 1992; Harrington and Cookson 1992). Indeed, at one point District 4 received more per capita federal aid than any other district in the United States (also see Wells 1993, 56). While those who argue that these resources led to improved performance are putting more faith in the effects of resources on test scores than the literature documents (see below), the argument must be addressed. We attempt to do this in our analysis by employing proxy measures (since complete expenditure data are not available), specifically student-teacher ratios, for resources.

Some believe that the creation of smaller schools was the most important factor causing increases in District 4 test scores.[1] Harrington and Cookson (1992, 87) argue that "probably the most important ingredient was school size. Every one of the alternative schools was small. . . . Size alone made these alternative schools nontraditional in New York City, where public schools are about as large and impersonal as you can get, even at the elementary level." In our school level analysis, we control for the possible effects of school size on student test score performance.

Still others argue that any increase in test scores was driven by a small number of elite choice schools (Lee 1993; Henig 1996). According to Young and Clinchy (1992, 25): "East Harlem's practice of allowing individual schools to set admissions criteria and select students aggravates, rather than reduces, such inequities." Given the importance of this issue, in the next chapter, we focus specifically on the performance of students in the non-choice elementary schools, to see if they were indeed "left behind."

Another argument posited by choice skeptics is that the attention focused on District 4 created a "Hawthorne effect" in which teachers, administrators, students, and parents responded to an experimental setting by changing their behavior in the short-run, and that such an effect is unsustainable over time (Henig 1996; Lieberman 1992.) Cookson argues (1994, 55): "Clearly there is something of a Hawthorne effect going on in District 4. . . . It is little wonder that this positive feeling is reflected in student's attitudes . . . Change preceded choice in East Harlem, not the other way around." To address this concern, we examine school performance in District 4 today, when any Hawthorne effect would now be over twenty-five years old.

Finally, many analysts often argue that leadership was more important than choice (e.g., Smith and Meier 1995). As the argument goes, District 4 benefited from outstanding leadership, including Anthony Alvarado, Seymour Fliegel, and Deborah Meier, who have become symbols of successful educational reform. It is very difficult to separate the emergence of strong leaders from the expansion of opportunities spawned by choice. However, it is reasonable to ask why such a concentration of outstanding leaders emerged in District 4 and not in other districts without choice. But more concretely, by examining performance today, when none of the above leaders have been active in District 4 for many years, we can at least partially distinguish the effects of these leaders from the effects of choice.

These multiple concerns about leadership, stratification, extra resources, Hawthorne effects, and small schools cumulate into explanations that rival proponents' arguments that school choice has produced improvements in the performance of District 4 schools and students. Fortunately many of these issues can be addressed with data reported by the New York City Board of Education.

Before presenting our analyses however, we examine briefly the large and often very contentious literature on whether school reforms in general have been shown to improve student performance. This provides guidelines to the size of effects we might expect from a reform such as choice, while at the same time providing evidence about the factors that must be "controlled" to identify the independent effects of choice.

Can Schools Do Anything to Improve Student Performance?

In recent years, scholars in economics, political science, and education have developed a large literature exploring whether and how school resources and institutional arrangements affect student performance. Coleman et al. (1966) initiated much of this research by examining student test score performance as a function of three sets of variables: those related to the family background of students; those related to peer groups; and those related to school resources. Coleman and subsequent studies found little evidence that school resources had any significant impact on test scores, and instead found that family background had the strongest effect on test scores. In perhaps the most widely cited study on school effects after Coleman's work, Hanushek (1986) examined 187 different equations modeling educational "production functions" from 38 publications and found inconclusive evidence that school resources, such as pupil/teacher ratio, teacher education, teacher salary, total expenditure/per pupil, administrative expenditures, and quality of facilities, affect test score performance.

Recently, several researchers have challenged Hanushek's findings. Hedges, Lane, and Greenwald (1994) argue that rather than the simple "vote count" methodology used by Hanushek, a more sophisticated meta-analysis that combines different results shows that resources do affect test scores outcomes. Some analysts argue that test scores are not necessarily the best measure of school performance. For example, Card and Krueger (1992) argue that test scores may be too immediate to be affected much by school resources and that researchers should examine other indicators of longer-term effects, such as income. They find evidence that school resources, such as teacher's salaries, affect future earnings of students (but see Speakman and Welsh 1995; Grogger 1996).

The most hotly contested issue has been the effect of class size. Folger (1992) followed an actual change in some class sizes in Tennessee (the STAR experiment), and found smaller class sizes resulted in higher test scores. Ferguson and Ladd (1996) analyzed test scores in Alabama, using both individual-level, student-level, and district-level data and found that teacher test scores, teacher education, and class size affect student learning. These studies have lead to a growing consensus that small class size, especially in earlier grades, works.

Hanushek (1997), while still not convinced by this recent research showing that smaller classes and better-trained teachers can lead to higher performance, summarizes the current research nicely: "The existing work does not suggest that resources never matter, nor does it suggest that resources could not matter. It only indicates that the current organization and incentives of schools do little to ensure than any added resources will be used effectively" (307).

Of course the literature on school choice has been aimed directly at questions of organization, incentives, and effectiveness. But this work also seeks to link these organizational questions back to performance. Chubb and Moe (1990) argue that school choice provides more autonomy for school-level decision making, which they find is associated with better performance. A heated debate has emerged in the study of Milwaukee's limited experiment with private school vouchers. Witte (1996) found no significant improvements in tests scores over time for the children utilizing vouchers, compared to others, but Peterson, Greene, and Noyes (1996), using a different comparison and methodology, found positive effects on test scores after three years. By the fourth year, Peterson found that among voucher students, math scores increased by 11 points and reading scores increased by 5 points. A recent reanalysis by Rouse (1998) found a result falling between Witte and Peterson—she reported that math scores improved for voucher students in Milwaukee while reading scores did not.

These studies suggest that any test scores improvements from resource or institutional changes should be expected to be moderate rather than overwhelming. They also indicate that while testing school or district effects, analysts must control for student backgrounds as much as possible.

Analyzing District 4 Performance over Time

To test how District 4 has performed over time, we set out to gather longitudinal data on the reading and math scores in both the district and the city as a whole. We quickly discovered why no one else has taken on this task—it was extremely difficult to gather these data going back to the late 1960s, when decentralization first created thirty-two community school districts. However, by combining data from the Board of Education archives at Teacher's College at Columbia University with more recent data held at the New York City Board of Education's headquarters, we were able to put together a time-series.

Based on tests administered by the Board of Education, we examine the percentage of district students reading (or performing math) at or above grade level, averaged for all grades 3–8.[2] One concern noted by critics is that the actual test administered has changed over time. For example, the reading test used from 1974 through 1977 was the 1970 version of the Comprehensive Test of Basic Skills, but from 1978 to 1985 it was the 1977 version of the California Achievement Test; from 1986 to 1988 it was the 1982 version of the Degrees of Reading Power Test; and from 1989 to 1992, it was the 1988 version of the Degrees of Reading Power Test. Thus, students in District 4 might have performed differently over time simply because they were taking different tests, with different nationally normed baselines.

To address concerns that the baseline of tests administered in New York City changed over time, we divided the average District 4 performance by the citywide average figure for grades 3–8. Thus we have a "standardized" measure of performance, reflecting how well District 4 is doing relative to other districts in the city. This is a consistent measure over time that can be used to evaluate changes in District 4.

The results in figure 9.1 show a significant increase over time in both reading and math scores in District 4 relative to the city average. While we were not able to find data tracing all the way back to 1969, when choice started in District 4 in 1974, the district was one of the worst in the city, with its students performing only about half as well as students in the city as a whole. After the implementation of choice, relative scores in District 4 climbed, and by the early- to mid-1980s, District 4's performance nearly reached the city average for reading. There has been a recent decline, but today District 4 schools are working at a level higher than 80 percent of the citywide average—almost twice as high as in 1974. District 4 math scores also climbed, but not quite as high over the time period, and they also showed a leveling off after the late 1980s.[3]

To see if the positive trend is a function of other factors that might affect performance, we created a pooled data set, combining data from all thirty-two New York districts over the years 1974–96. While this does not cover the entire period since decentralization was instituted, it covers most years,

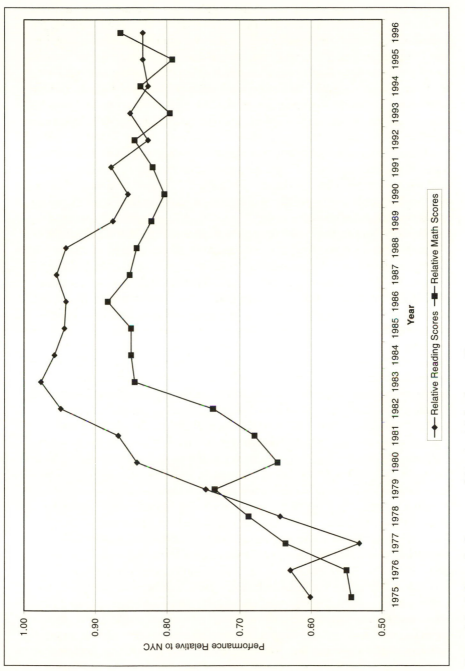

Figure 9.1   Relative Performance of District 4 Schools over Time

and all years for which data are available. Though our major indicator, test scores, was available for the each year in the range, values are missing for certain independent variables. In these cases, we interpolated values to fill in the observations in our time-series. In the cases of demographics, which usually change very slowly over time, these interpolations are reliable. However, we also interpolated values for the teacher variables, which do change more rapidly than demographic conditions. This greater fluctuation leaves us less confident in the reliability of the estimates for those independent variables.

We examined time trends employing the following control variables (measured at the district level): the percentage of students eligible for free lunches (a poverty measure); the percentage of black and Hispanic students; the average pupil/teacher ratio; and the percentage of teachers with more than five years' teaching experience.

The key independent variable in our model measures the expansion of choice in District 4 over time (the percentage of choice schools in the district each year). In District 4, this measure increases from 0 percent in 1973 to 55 percent by 1996, and is set to zero for all other districts in all other years.[4] With these controls in the model, we can assess the extent to which basic underlying factors are responsible for the improvement in scores. In table 9.1 we report the OLS estimates and White's robust standard errors.[5]

These results show a statistically significant relationship between the expansion of choice in District 4 and reading and math test scores. As we estimated a linear model, the coefficient on the percentage of choice schools is easy to interpret: on average, each 10 percent increase in the proportion of choice schools in District 4 increased reading scores by 8.5 percent and math scores 7 percent, relative to the citywide average. For example, if the percentage of District 4 students reading at grade level, relative to the city average, was 60 percent and four new choice schools were opened, out of forty currently operating schools, District 4 reading scores would rise to 68.5 percent of the city average. These are not trivial improvements.

Our findings also show that districts with higher percentages of students in poverty (for reading only) and black and Hispanic students are likely to have lower test scores. And, our results address some of the issues raised in the debate over performance in District 4 by identifying the effects of resources (teacher/pupil ratio) and teacher quality (percent of teachers with more than five years experience, who are assumed to be of higher quality) on student performance. Neither of these variables has a statistically significant effect on relative performance. This lack of effect may result in part from a measurement problem—recall that because of missing data we had to interpolate some of the data. But note, too, that in New York City, budgets are allocated such that low-income and low-performance districts receive more resources—thus reducing the possible effects of resources on performance. Our analysis shows that a higher proportion of higher-socioeconomic status

Table 9.1
District 4 Test Score Performance over Time Compared to Other Districts in New York City

Pooled District-Level Fixed Effects Model of Relative Test Scores as a Function of District Characteristics and District 4 Location: 1974–96

Independent Variable	Reading Scores Coefficient (Robust Standard Error)	Math Scores Coefficient (Robust Standard Error)
Percentage of Schools in District 4 that Are Choice Schools	0.846* (0.094)	0.705* (0.055)
Pupil/Teacher Ratio	0.0009 (0.002)	0.00009 (0.002)
Percent Teachers with More than 5 Years' Experience	−0.0005 (0.0005)	−0.0008 (0.0006)
% of Students Eligible for Free Lunches	−0.0017* (0.0006)	−0.0008 (0.0007)
% of Black Students	−0.0060* (0.0009)	−0.0071* (0.0014)
% of Hispanic Students	−0.0075* (0.0007)	−0.0078* (0.0010)
Constant	1.57* (0.077)	1.59* (0.107)
	N = 715 Adjusted R^2 = 0.91 $p < .000$	N = 683 Adjusted R^2 = 0.87 $p < .000$

*$p < .01$

Note: We also included, but do not report, dummy variables for 31 of the 32 districts.

students, possibly coming into the district from other locations, does not explain District 4's improved performance, since demographic characteristics are controlled in our model.

In table 9.2 we duplicate this analysis for District 1. For reading scores, the District 1 time-counter variable is not significant, meaning that District 1 has not shown any relative improvement in its reading test scores compared to the other thirty-one districts in New York City. All of the other demographic variables are significant in this model and in the expected directions. In the analysis of math scores, we do find a significant (weakly, at 0.09 levels of statistical significance) effect of District 1 on math scores over time. This may reflect the fact that many lower-scoring districts started to score closer to the city average in tests administered in the 1980s. More importantly, however, even though the District 1 time-counter variable is statistically sig-

Table 9.2
District 1 Test Score Performance over Time Compared to Other Districts in New York City

Pooled District-Level Fixed Effects Model of Relative Test Scores as a Function of District Characteristics and District 1 Location: 1974–96

Independent Variable	Reading Scores Coefficient (Robust Standard Error)	Math Scores Coefficient (Robust Standard Error)
District 1 Time Counter	0.0018	0.0046*
	(0.0024)	(0.0027)
Pupil/Teacher Ratio	−0.00002	−0.0002
	(0.002)	(0.0022)
Percent Teachers with More than 5 Years' Experience	−0.0009**	−0.001*
	(0.0004)	(0.0005)
% of Students Eligible for Free Lunches	−0.0022***	−0.0015***
	(0.0006)	(0.0007)
% of Black Students	−0.0064***	−0.0074**
	(0.0005)	(0.0005)
% of Hispanic Students	−0.0079***	−0.0083***
	(0.0006)	(0.0007)
Constant	1.55***	1.60***
	(0.062)	(0.058)
	N = 746	N = 730
	Adjusted R^2 = 0.82	Adjuted R^2 = 0.79
	$p < .000$	$p < .000$

Note: We also included, but do not report, dummy variables for 31 of the 32 districts.

  *significant at 90% level

  **significant at 95% level

***significant at 99% level of confidence

nificant, the substantive effect is small. For every increasing year of the analysis, District 1 math scores improve by 0.002 percentage points, compared to the city average. Over twenty years, this is a relative improvement of only 0.04 percentage points. Thus, while District 1 showed some small improvement in math scores over this period, it was very small, and no improvement in reading scores is evident.

Performance in District 4 Schools Today

From the time of the decentralization decision in 1969 that created thirty-two local school districts responsible for the K–8 education in their areas, the New York City Board of Education has been required to prepare a district-by-district ranking of reading scores. For 1996, the board prepared a more detailed study of reading scores by school, and also conducted its own study of school performance.[6]

Because this study adjusted for the characteristics of schools that may affect performance, it allows for a comparison of student performance across individual schools. In particular, this analysis statistically controlled for the percentage of students eligible for free lunches in the school, a measure of poverty; the percentage of students with limited English proficiency, a measure of academic disadvantage; and the percentage of the students who were in that school for the full year, a measure of population stability.

Controlling for these factors, the board generated predicted performance scores for each school. The board then developed an "honor roll" of high-achieving schools that included those schools where students scored at least 15 points above the predicted value. With seven high-performing schools, District 4 currently has more such schools than any other district in the city. However, with its emphasis on many small schools of choice, District 4 has more individual schools than most other districts. To address this difference, we calculated the percentage of schools in each district that the board of education found to be high-performing schools. In this calculation, District 4 ranks fourth of the thirty-two districts, with 15 percent of its schools listed on this honor roll. Taking this calculation to its logical conclusion, since school sizes vary, we examined how many of the students who took the reading tests in each district are enrolled at schools on this honor roll. Here District 4 regains its top position in New York City, with 20 percent of tested students in high-performing schools. Thus, by whatever measure of high-performing schools used, District 4 is the top, or nearly the top, district in New York City. (District 1 had no honor roll schools.)

In analyzing the current performance of District 4, we are able to go one step further, thanks to the availability of more complete data. We obtained data on school performance for the last three years for each school in the city and analyzed how schools in District 4 today are performing compared to schools across the rest of the city. Because this analysis is at the school level, we can create more refined models than for the district-level analysis. In this analysis, we use the New York state performance tests, which allow us to report school level results for third, sixth, and eighth grade scores.

The results of our analysis for grade six presented in table 9.3 show that, for both math and reading scores, in 1996 schools in District 4 performed significantly better than schools in the rest of the city. This analysis is more refined because it controls for many variables known to affect performance, including demographic composition, school size, poverty, turnover of students, immigration status, and percent of students with limited English proficiency.

Looking at reading scores, the coefficient on the District 4 variable shows that, with other variables held equal, schools in District 4 score nearly 8 points higher in sixth grade reading than other schools: increasing from a

Table 9.3
School Test Score Performance in 1996

Sixth-Grade Test Scores as a Function of School Factors and District 4 Location

Independent Variable	*Reading Scores Co-efficient (Standard Error)*	*Math Scores Coefficient (Standard Error)*
District 4	8.00***	4.64**
	(3.03)	(2.39)
Size of School Population	0.001	0.0009
	(.002)	(0.001)
% Limited English	−0.54***	−0.28***
	(.10)	(0.08)
% Free Lunch	−0.009	0.004
	(0.01)	(0.01)
% Less than 3 Years in USA	−0.11	0.08
	(0.16)	(0.13)
% in School All Year	0.55***	0.26*
	(0.18)	(0.14)
% Black	−0.38***	−0.19***
	(0.04)	(0.03)
% Hispanic	−0.32***	−0.12***
	(0.05)	(0.04)
% Asian	0.09	0.08
	(0.07)	(0.06)
Constant	45.2***	75.1***
	(17.43)	(14.53)
	N = 467	N = 453
	Adjusted R^2 = 0.49	Adjusted R^2 = 0.26
	$p < .001$	$p < .001$

*$p < .10$
**$p < .05$
***$p < .01$

base rate of 45 percent at or above grade level to 53 percent at or above grade level. When it comes to math scores, schools in District 4 again show significantly better performance, with an increase of over 4 points, compared to equivalent schools in other districts.

These results also address some other concerns expressed by scholars who question the effects of choice in District 4: higher District 4 performance is not a function of smaller schools nor is it a function of "imported" higher-socioeconomic status students.

We also ran these same models using test scores from 1995 and 1994, to test whether 1996 was a year of exceptional performance in District 4. Except for math scores in 1994, the District 4 effect is significant and positive in all of these cases. New York City students are also tested in third and eighth grades. We ran these same models, and for third-grade scores, the District 4 variable is significant and positive in half of the six cases (reading and math, over 1994, 1995, and 1996). Students are only tested for reading in eighth grade and here we do not find a District 4 effect.

Thus, we have documented significant district-level improvements in math and reading scores, with the fastest growth happening during the most rapid expansion of choice. Using more-detailed, school-level data, and controlling for student and school characteristics, we have shown a large and significant District 4 effect on sixth grade reading and math scores.

Remember that the size of these improvements in test scores is not trivial. For example, in the literature we reviewed on other school reforms and their effects on test scores, even when researchers can document positive effects, and this happens in fewer than half of the studies, the percentage improvements are rarely larger than those documented here.

However, even with these improvements, District 4 is far from the top district in New York City. Nevertheless, the evidence is clear that test scores have improved and that they are better today in District 4 than in schools in New York City districts with comparable levels of poverty and disadvantage but without choice.

Performance in District 1

To better isolate the independent effects of choice in District 4, we ran similar models as we just presented for District 1 for 1994, 1995, and 1996. In contrast to the District 4 effects we documented, we found no significant effect for schools in District 1. As shown in table 9.4, in 1996, the District 1 dummy variables are insignificant for both math and reading scores. Most of the same demographic control variables are significant for this analysis as they were for the parallel analysis in District 4. Thus, in contrast to District 4's positive performance, we cannot say that District 1 schools perform differently than "predicted," given their demographic characteristics.

Summary: Performance in New York Districts

Previous studies have provided some evidence that choice in District 4 was successful in improving performance. Scholars have attacked this evidence as insufficient and open to multiple interpretations. In this chapter we provide stronger evidence about the success of District 4 students. Where possible, we have shown how these successes are linked to the expansion of school choice in District 4. Moving to a more detailed, school level, we have shown that reading and math scores in District 4 are significantly higher today than in comparable schools in other districts.

Table 9.4
School Test Score Performance in 1996

Sixth-Grade Test Scores as a Function of School Factors and District 1 Location		
Independent Variable	Reading Scores Co-efficient (Standard Error)	Math Scores Coefficient (Standard Error)
District 1	3.17	2.09
	(3.94)	(3.03)
Size of School Population	0.0003	0.0005
	(.002)	(0.001)
% Limited English	−0.42***	−0.22**
	(.13)	(0.10)
% Free Lunch	0.009	0.004
	(0.01)	(0.01)
% Less than 3 Years in USA	−0.12	0.09
	(0.17)	(0.15)
% in School All Year	0.69***	0.33**
	(0.18)	(0.14)
% Black	−0.39***	−0.19***
	(0.04)	(0.03)
% Hispanic	−0.49***	−0.20***
	(0.04)	(0.03)
% Asian	0.031	0.06
	(0.073)	(0.06)
Constant	35.7**	70.1***
	(18.0)	(14.3)
	N = 467	N = 453
	Adjusted R^2 = 0.44	Adjusted R^2 = 0.23
	$p < .001$	$p < .001$

**$p < .05$
***$p < .01$

In our statistical models, we addressed directly some of the concerns that scholars have expressed about District 4. We have controlled for the effects of improved leadership, more school flexibility, access to greater resources, and retention or attraction of better students, and identified an independent effect of choice.

Suburban Analysis: School Performance in Montclair

Ideally, we would like to be able to report a comprehensive analysis of school performance in Montclair, but we are limited by severe data problems. In addition, while District 1 (and the other thirty community districts in New

York) act as a reasonable control group for District 4, the identification of a control group against which to compare Montclair is more complicated. Thus, we present an overview and some basic trends in test score performance in Montclair. We recognize that we cannot produce definitive statements about how the development and expansion of magnet schools into a full choice system affected student test score performance.

While recent New Jersey school report cards include extensive demographic data for students, they do not include test score data for most schools.[7] We were able to gather test score data from 1993 that include scores for all public schools in New Jersey for the state standards in reading, language arts, and math. However, these tests are not as difficult as nationally normed tests and large numbers of schools in Essex County have scores of 100 percent, meaning that all students meet the state standards. In Montclair, 89 percent of third-grade students and 87 percent of sixth-grade students read at a level that meets the state standard. Similarly, 85 percent of Montclair's third-grade students and 80 percent of their sixth-grade students meet the state math standard. While these seem like impressive numbers, comparing third-grade reading scores, eighty-one other schools in Essex County had higher percentages, while fifty-three other schools in Essex County had lower percentages than in Montclair (mostly in Newark). Thus, while Montclair has high percentages of students meeting state standards, a majority of schools in Essex County performed even better. Given the small variance in these reported 1993 state test scores, it is unlikely that a more detailed comparison would allow us better to specify the effects of choice, demographics, and school resources.

Other problems affected our ability to study longitudinal trends. Here we are limited by the most basic problem: a lack of critical pieces of demographic data, school-level resource data and comparable test scores over time. Another issue that makes a rigorous examination of longitudinal trends difficult is pinpointing when Montclair can be said to have implemented choice. In response to pressures for desegregation, Montclair started magnet schools in 1976. By 1985, the town had created its universal choice system, in which all schools had become choice schools. So, we might expect to see some improvements starting after 1977 with perhaps even greater improvements after 1985.

Fortunately, we can utilize some secondary analyses prepared by Clewell and Joy (1990) to document some limited time trends within Montclair. The most detailed data Clewell and Joy provide compare performance in 1974, before any magnet schools were operating, with 1986, just after full choice had been implemented. Fortunately, Montclair had administered the same test, the Iowa Test of Basic Skills (ITBS), throughout this period. For both reading and math, across third, sixth and eighth grades, the range in 1974 was from 43 to 56 percent at or above grade level. By 1986, this performance had increased substantially, to a range of 60 to 81 percent for the same set of scores. We extend the data presented by Clewell and Joy to more recent years, examining the average percentile scores for Montclair students in grades three, six, and eight over this period, after choice was fully implemented and for more recent years. These data show small improvements in all grades from 1984 to 1988. Scores in 1994 and 1995 are also higher, but a different test was used in those years (while the MAT, like the ITBS, is a nationally normed test, changing tests always leads to issues of comparability). Figure 9.2 shows the increases in reading scores over time; these spotty data show an upward trend.

We present a similar graph for Montclair math test scores in figure 9.3. Again, these test scores have increased since the implementation of magnet schools and choice. Unfortunately, since we do not have complete demographics for Montclair students over time, we cannot test whether demographic changes influenced test scores.

Thus, while any analysis of test score performance faces multiple challenges, we have only enough data to present this limited analysis of Montclair. The data we do have, however, suggests that test scores did improve somewhat over the period when the magnet system was implemented and then developed into a full choice system. However, there are many possible explanations for this pattern that cannot be ruled out with the data we have.

Conclusions

While we have presented evidence linking choice to improved performance, we must remember that choice is not a magic bullet that somehow changes schools "automatically." Rather, for schools to improve, there must be pressure from the demand-side of the market-like setting that choice creates. And for choice to work, individual schools, and indeed entire school districts, must respond to that pressure with reforms and improvements. District 4 provides some clues to effective strategies that translate the promise of choice into reality.

By providing choice and information to parents, District 4 encouraged changes on the demand-side, but it also encouraged the schools themselves to change, by experimenting with new teaching ideas and approaches. Administrators hoped that parents would discover the schools that were improving and "vote with their feet." District officials also hoped that competition would stimulate improvements in the nonchoice schools as well, a point we address in the next chapter.

The creation of alternative schools responsive to parent interest inevitably raised the problem of what to do about unsuccessful schools. Many advocates of choice argue that unsuccessful schools must be closed or face some other negative consequences. While everyone recognizes that closing a school is painful, and may be impossible during the school year, advocates of choice argue that the occasional closing of schools should be viewed as nec-

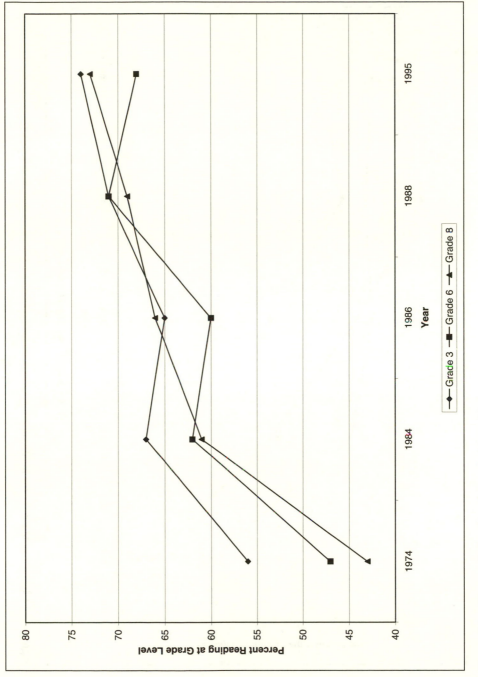

Figure 9.2   Changes in Reading Scores in Montclair

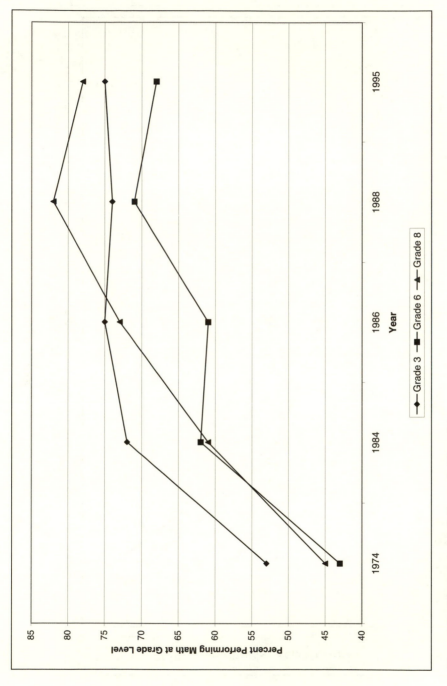

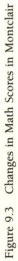

Figure 9.3 Changes in Math Scores in Montclair

essary for improving schools, not as a failure. (Remember that Schumpeter's mainspring of innovation and growth in markets is creative *destruction*.)

If a school is performing poorly, administrators can attempt to change the school's approach or close it down. Closure, while not simple, is often more successful, as school reputations are difficult to change. Indeed, as many as a half-dozen District 4 schools have been closed in the past few years.

Closing unsuccessful schools and developing new schools with different leadership and themes provides dynamism to the supply-side of choice in District 4. While in the 1970s and 1980s ideas for schools came mainly from individual teachers, ideas today are often provided by community-based organizations. Three new schools have been created in District 4 in the last five years. One of these new schools, the Young Woman's Leadership School, has attracted considerable attention in the national media because of its status as a publicly funded, single-sex institution.

Thus, the improvement in performance we linked to choice is not magic. It results from the combination of creating a cadre of informed parents ("marginal consumers") shopping for appropriate schools *and* school-level responses to that competitive pressure.

But for schools actually to improve what they are doing with students on a day-to-day basis, strong leadership must emerge and difficult management decisions may have to be made. Choice can create the systemic conditions that give strong leaders and creative managers the opportunities to produce better schools.

Chapter 10

Does Choice Increase Segregation and Stratification?

In the last chapter we focused on the question of whether choice leads to better educational outcomes. In District 4, in particular, we found improvements in test scores that were above expected levels given the demographics of the district. We argued that these outcomes are largely a product of choice.

Despite growing evidence linking choice to both school performance and allocative efficiency, many scholars, politicians, and educational professionals still oppose choice, often because they are concerned about whose schools are improved and which students get to participate in choice. Many people believe that choice is less about comprehensive educational reform than it is about creating new opportunities for a limited set of parents, students, and schools. Therefore, many critics of choice argue that any improvements associated with choice are a function of a new distribution of students across schools that arises as a result of enhanced parental choice rather than the expansion in the number of better schools.

In other words, critics believe that choice will lead to "skimming"—where the best and brightest students exit traditional neighborhood schools and locate in the newly created and higher performing alternative schools. Related to this concern, some scholars fear that choice will intensify existing disparities in the socioeconomic background of families across schools (Henig 1994; Wells 1993; Tweedie 1990; Riley 1990; Moore and Davenport 1990; Levin 1989). These arguments are based on the claim that choice further expands opportunities for the advantaged while leaving the disadvantaged even further behind. In contrast, some scholars argue that school choice via residential location has always existed for advantaged parents and that public school choice actually expands equity, by giving at least some lower-income parents options previously available only to the wealthy (Rossell 1995; Wong 1992; Coleman 1990).

In this chapter, we examine the effects of choice on the degree of racial segregation and socioeconomic stratification. While we discuss specific issues that arise in testing both the "skimming" and the "stratification" hypothesis in detail later, several general limits must be kept in mind.

First, it is inherently difficult to test the *causal* relationship between school choice and the racial and/or socioeconomic stratification of students using the kinds of data that are available. For example, descriptive analyses of the present distribution of parents and students across choice and nonchoice schools tell us little about the causal processes producing this distribution. Similarly, looking at a distribution of students across schools at only one point in time provides no baseline for comparison. For example, if 80 percent of the population attending alternative schools is white, which schools would these children have attended before school choice was implemented? In many school districts, especially in central cities, we suspect the answer would be either private schools or a small number of neighborhood schools. In this case, the neighborhood schools are highly segregated and the absence of alternative schools does not produce more integrated schools. Indeed, if many of the white students in alternative schools had chosen private schools, the entire school system would be *more* segregated. In short, we have no real way of establishing the counterfactual situation: what the schools in choice districts would look like without choice.

One way to gain analytic leverage on this question would be to study the movement of student populations across schools over time. Such a longitudinal analysis would document the distribution of students before choice was introduced and allow us to measure the extent to which choice may exacerbate stratification or segregation. Unfortunately, in districts with a long history of choice, such as the ones we study, these data are hard to compile. Moreover, even if the longitudinal data existed, our ability to identify how changes in a school or district causally affected parental choice would remain limited.

A second set of research issues relates to how specific institutional arrangements of choice affect the set of options from which parents may choose and how students are actually assigned to schools. In chapter 3, we showed that choice systems vary across the district we study. For example, in Montclair, parent choices are constrained by both district regulations that ensure racially balanced schools and by the relatively limited number of options available. Thus, in Montclair (and many other controlled choice districts), stratification and segregation may occur across classes in a school, via tracking, rather than across schools in the district.

In contrast to controlled choice programs, the option-demand system in place in District 1 and District 4 elementary schools combines a number of features that may make it particularly vulnerable to skimming and stratification. Specifically, the voluntary nature of choice, the potential costs associated with gathering information, and the range of options available to parents all could affect the population of parents participating in choice.

Thus, in evaluating whether and how choice affects the distribution of educational opportunity we must treat choice not as a single uniform reform but as a class of reforms characterized by different design characteristics that may produce different outcomes.

Reexamining Performance in District 4: Skimming, Sorting, or General Improvement?

With these caveats in mind, we begin our study of the relationship between equity and choice by examining whether the increases in test scores in District 4 have been driven primarily by higher-performing alternative schools. We argue that if performance gains are limited to alternative schools, skimming is likely to be at least partly responsible.

Our first, and in some ways, most critical question is whether or not choice has left students in neighborhood schools worse off because the best and brightest students have exited to alternative schools. This is an important question because, despite over twenty-five years of choice, more than three-quarters of elementary school students in District 4 remain in neighborhood schools. To address this issue, we examine the over-time performance of neighborhood elementary schools, since declining performance could signify a skimming process. We analyzed the overall performance of the ten neighborhood elementary schools (out of a total of sixteen) in District 4 that had the lowest reading scores in 1996.[1] If choice in District 4 has led to academic skimming, then as better students enroll in alternative schools, these neighborhood schools should be particularly hard hit. As evident in table 10.1, this does not seem to be the case.

For the ten schools, reading and math scores of students in the two grades were actually *higher* relative to citywide averages in the 1994–96 period than they were in 1974–76. The smallest improvement is for third-grade reading scores, which improved from 57 percent to 69 percent of the city-wide average for the composite of these ten worst schools. Sixth-grade reading scores, and third-and fifth-grade math scores improved at least 22 percentage points in all cases. This evidence strongly suggests that the neighborhood schools have *not* been adversely affected by the creation of alternative schools, but instead have improved over time.

One possible explanation for these results is that by combining all ten schools, we might be overlooking differences among them: for example, per-

Table 10.1
Reading and Math Scores, Relative to Citywide Average, in 10 Lowest Performing District 4 Neighborhood Schools, 1974–76 versus 1995–96

Third Grade Reading Scores		Sixth Grade Reading Scores		Third Grade Math Scores		Fifth Grade Math Scores	
1974–76	*1994–96*	*1974–76*	*1994–96*	*1974–76*	*1994–96*	*1974–76*	*1994–96*
57%	69%	59%	84%	55%	87%	49%	85%

Source: Data compiled by authors of the New York City Board of Education reports. These data combine the scores, relative to the citywide average, for the 10 lowest performing neighborhood schools in the District.

haps a few schools experienced sharp declines in performance over the past two decades while others experienced sharp increases. To test for this, we examined four separate sets of scores,[2] across each of these ten neighborhood schools over time. Of the resulting forty comparisons, thirty showed improvements over time, six showed no change, and only four declined.[3]

In short, there is no evidence that neighborhood schools have been left behind since the institution of choice in District 4.

Although this comparison allows us to see how these neighborhood schools performed relative to the average schools in New York City, it does not assess how well these schools have kept up with the alternative schools in their own district. To test the skimming hypothesis more directly, we compare the performance of neighborhood and alternative schools.

Since the New York City Board of Education did not begin collecting reliable data on alternative schools until the 1993–94 school year, we can compare the performance of students in District 4's alternative and neighborhood schools only over a limited period. In figures 10.1 and 10.2, we report the aggregate differences between alternative and neighborhoods schools on two performance indicators—the percentage of students meeting minimum state requirements on standardized reading and math tests—for the three years in which data were available.[4]

As these figures illustrate, any differences in performance across neighborhood and alternative schools for this period are small. Although aggregate reading scores are consistently higher for alternative schools, these differences are not significant, either substantively or statistically. Similarly, the percentage of students meeting minimum state math requirements is higher

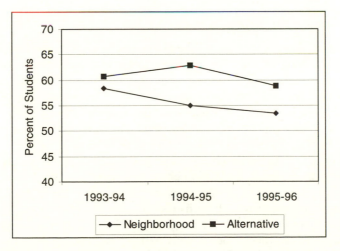

Figure 10.1 Percentage of District 4 Students Meeting Minimum State Reading Requirements

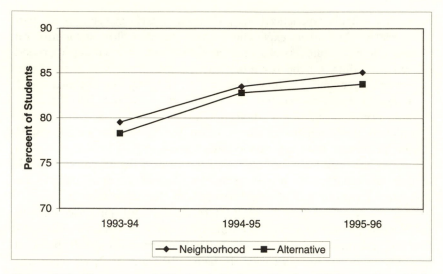

Figure 10.2 Percentage of District 4 Students Meeting Minimum State Math Requirements

across alternative schools than neighborhood schools; however, the differences are even smaller than they were for reading performance. Overall, the data in figures 10.1 and 10.2 show that choice at the elementary school level is not associated with skimming. Instead, as student performance is quite similar across the alternative, choice schools and the neighborhood nonchoice schools, we believe that the evidence is more indicative of a "sorting" process, in which students select schools for programs they want.

School Choice and Performance in District 1

As we noted above, investigating the skimming hypothesis requires that we consider the ways in which the different forms of choice affect equity outcomes, particularly for the option-demand system. Although we did not find the best and brightest students disproportionately concentrated in the alternative schools in District 4's option-demand program, this does not imply that all such programs produce similar results. In particular, some features of District 1's program make it more vulnerable to skimming.

One feature of District 1's choice program that clearly distinguishes it from District 4's is its newness. While choice has been in place for well over twenty-five years in East Harlem, it was first implemented in District 1 in 1990. Consequently, parents have had less exposure to the idea and practice of choice. More importantly, the program in District 1 is much less visible and smaller. At the time of our study, District 1 had only a small number of alternative schools in place: four at the elementary level and one at the intermediate level. Given these small numbers, alternative school students comprise only about 8 percent of the total elementary school population in District 1, compared to more than 25 percent in District 4. And, unlike parents in District 4, who can choose from among ten alternative schools offering an array of pedagogical and thematic approaches, District 1 parents face a very limited choice.

In addition, the level of administrative capacity supporting choice in District 1 is also more limited than in District 4. Of the many differences in capacity, the most important may be the level and availability of information regarding choice in the districts. In our numerous trips to these districts, we found that there was simply less information available about District 1's alternative schools than District 4's. For example, basic information about the programs, sizes, or themes of alternative schools was not included in any of the District 1 publications we were able to locate. And, in conversations we had with various district officials, we were told that the thematic foci of the alternative schools were still being developed. The situation is much different in District 4, where the superintendent and director of options schools annually put together a handbook that describes the choice process and compiles the names, addresses, phone numbers, and important dates relevant to parents.[5]

These differences in the size, scope, and depth of their choice programs and in their information dissemination suggest that different types of parents may be participating in choice across the two districts, which may lead to larger performance differentials in District 1. Focusing on the relative performance of alternative and neighborhood schools in District 1, we investigate evidence of skimming, again relying on school-level data compiled by the New York City Board of Education.

Figures 10.3 and 10.4 show the aggregate comparisons of neighborhood and alternative schools for all years in which data are available.[6] The magnitude of the difference in performance across neighborhood and alternatives schools in District 1 is nearly the same as in District 4. However on average, neighborhood schools in District 1 actually out-perform alternative schools. This finding is contrary to arguments advanced by critics of choice, who often assume that alternative schools are both superior to neighborhood schools and more attractive to higher-performing students.

Performance and Equity Considerations in the Suburbs: Montclair's Controlled Choice Program

While most critics tend to focus on option-demand programs like those at the elementary school level in Districts 1 and 4, controlled choice programs are typically viewed more positively because they are often designed to achieve racial balance across schools. Controlled choice programs should be less prone to stratification and segregation both because all parents *must*

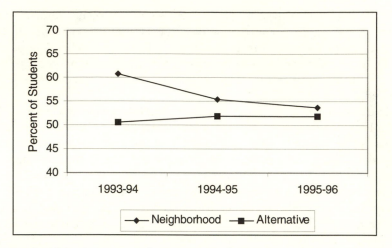

Figure 10.3   Percentage of District 1 Students Meeting Minimum State Reading Requirements

choose, and because district officials regulate parent choices to ensure that all schools have similar racial and/or other demographic characteristics. Thus, there is no distinction between choosers and nonchoosers under controlled choice, nor is there the possibility that parents self-select into schools along racial and socioeconomic lines.

We investigate the question of whether academic skimming is associated with controlled choice programs by considering the range of performance across district schools. As figures 10.5 and 10.6 show, differences in performance on Metropolitan Achievement Tests in math and reading were small

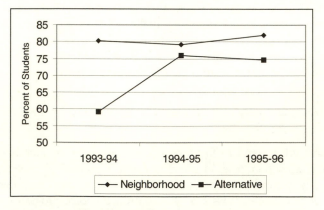

Figure 10.4   Percentage of District 1 Students Meeting Minimum State Math Requirements

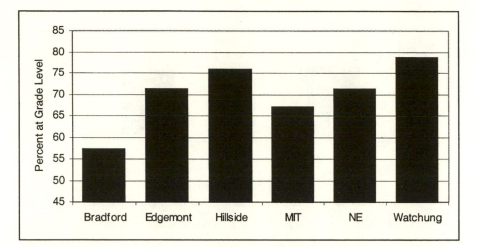

Figure 10.5 Metropolitan Reading Achievement Test Scores for Montclair Elementary Schools, 1994

across all Montclair elementary schools in 1994. The range in reading test scores varied from a low of 57 to a high of 79, while for math tests the range was even more narrow: 65–79. Additionally, as evident in figure 10.7, there are virtually no differences in the average test scores across the two middle schools.

In short, we do not find much evidence of academic skimming in any of the districts that employ choice.

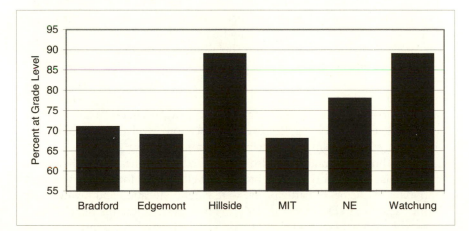

Figure 10.6 Metropolitan Math Achievement Test Scores for Montclair Elementary Schools, 1994

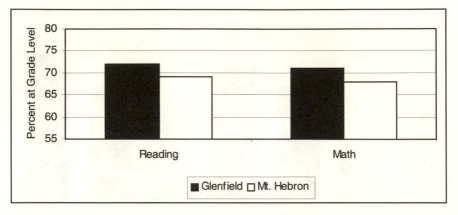

Figure 10.7   Metropolitan Achievement Tests for Montclair Middle Schools, 1994

Skimming along Other Dimensions: Socioeconomic Stratification and Racial Segregation in Schools

Turning now to the second dimension of the equity debate, we consider the extent to which choice programs exacerbate socioeconomic or racial stratification across schools. In terms of racial and socioeconomic stratification, voucher programs are often assumed to produce the greatest inequity. For example, studies of the Alum Rock voucher program of the 1970s found that minorities and parents of lower socioeconomic status were likely to choose less-innovative schools (Bridge and Blackman 1978; Cohen and Farrar 1977, 89; Henig 1994, 119). Studies of Milwaukee's vouchers (Witte, Bailes, and Thorn 1992, 1993) did not find participating students to be among the highest performers, but did find that their parents were more educated, had higher aspirations for their children, and participated more in their children's education than the control group. The Golden Rule voucher program in Indianapolis attracts parents who are somewhat more likely to be white, married, and have fewer children than others in Indianapolis (Heise, Colburn, and Lamberti 1995). Martinez et al. (1995) find that parents using vouchers to send their children to public and private schools in San Antonio are also distinguished by higher levels of education, involvement, and educational expectations than nonparticipating parents.

Public choice programs have also been linked to stratification. In her study of St. Louis's city-county transfer program, Wells (1993) found that the most important predictors of participation were parent education and involvement in their children's education. Similarly, in an analysis of interdistrict choice in Massachusetts, Armor and Peiser (1998) found that students transferring had higher a socioeconomic status, higher achievement on standardized tests, and were more likely to be white than students in their "home" districts.

In contrast, most studies of charter schools find that the percentage of minorities and low-income students is similar to that in the districts or states of these schools. This is partly a function of "lottery" selection mechanisms, but also of the kinds of parents applying to charter schools (Vanourek et al. 1998; Bierlein, Finn, and Manno 1997, 51).

While admitting that some stratification is likely under choice, especially vouchers, Moe (1995, 23–24) argues that it is a mistake to think that stratification is somehow limited to market-like reforms such as choice, as America's present educational system suffers from serious problems with both skimming and racial stratification. As Orfield et al. (1996, 55–61) argue:

> A student in an intensely segregated African American and Latino school was fourteen times more likely to be in a high-poverty school (more than 50 percent poor) than a student in a school that was more than 90 percent white . . . in metropolitan Chicago, the correlation between minority percentage and low-income percentage for elementary schools was .895—so high that, for statistical purposes, the two measures are virtually indistinguishable . . . In the big central cities, fifteen of every sixteen African American and Latino students are in schools where most of the students are nonwhite.

Thus, residential choice and the locally based provision of public schools have resulted in an extreme degree of income and racial stratification, especially in the largest central cities. Thus, in areas like District 4, where racial minorities comprise a majority, the question is whether choice is likely to exacerbate the problem.

Clearly, the relationship between choice arrangements and stratification along racial or sociodemographic lines is complex, difficult to measure, and tricky to evaluate. Many of the findings cited above are based on descriptive studies, which cannot be used to make inferences about the relationship between the choice and stratification. With only a snapshot of the distribution of students across schools, we have a severely limited ability to evaluate whether choice has exacerbated racial or socioeconomic stratification. Finally, looking only at bivariate relations can be misleading since other factors are not explicitly controlled. Many of the studies cited above have paid little or no attention to how program design may contribute to biases in who participates. In addition, they may not take into account parents' preferences—which, as we saw in Chapter 4, vary by race and education level. As Elmore summarizes (1991a, 308): "Offering choice to clients results in some redistribution of opportunities, but the exact nature of this redistribution depends on the institutional structure within which choice occurs, the purposes for which choice is being used, and on client preferences that often have little to do with the content of education."

To evaluate the relationship between racial and socioeconomic stratification, we again begin by considering the two option-demand programs in New York City. We first present descriptive information about the demographic characteristics of students across alternative and neighborhood schools. Shifting our unit of analysis from schools to parents, we then specify and test a model of the choice process. Next, we consider stratification in controlled choice programs by examining Montclair schools.

Stratification and Segregation in Option-Demand Programs

Because the central board of education in New York City only began systematically collecting data for alternative schools in 1993–94, we cannot compare the demographic characteristics or performance of students in these schools until then. Figures 10.8 and 10.9 present data on the percentage of white students in neighborhood and alternative elementary schools in Districts 4 and 1, respectively.

In both districts, the percentage of white students in alternative schools is higher than the percentage in neighborhood schools. For District 4 the differences are marginal—about 4 percentage points. On the other hand, with an average difference of 20 percentage points, the distribution of whites across alternative and neighborhood schools in District 1 is far in excess of what we would expect by chance. We emphasize that this descriptive analysis does not allow us to conclude that school choice has caused or exacerbated the racial segregation apparent in District 1. To determine this we would need to examine the distribution of white students prior to the implementation of their limited choice program.

Turning to the socioeconomic characteristics of students, we consider three indicators for which New York's central board of education collects data: (1) the percentage of students receiving free/reduced lunch, (2) the

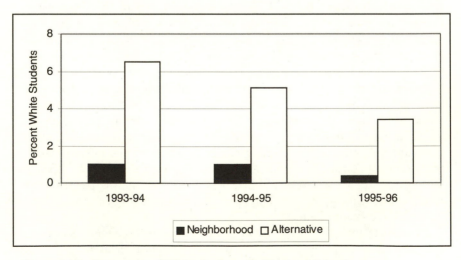

Figure 10.8 Percentage of White Students in District 4 Schools

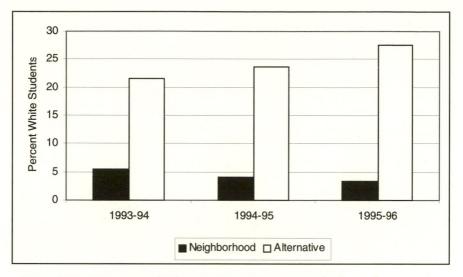

Figure 10.9   Percentage of White Students in District 1 Schools

percentage of students with limited English proficiency, and (3) the percentage of students who are recent immigrants. Because these indicators were not reported for alternative schools until the 1995–96 school year, our comparison is based on only one year of data.

As the figures in table 10.2 suggest, there appears to be no evidence of stratification. In District 1, alternative schools are more advantaged only in terms of their smaller percentage of students with limited English, and in District 4 there are no statistically significant differences for any indicator.

Overall our data show no evidence that alternative schools in these districts are disproportionately comprised of high-socioeconomic status students.

Table 10.2
Indicators of Socioeconomic Status for Neighborhood and Alternative Schools, 1995–96

Indicators	District 4		District 1	
	Neighborhood Schools	*Alternative Schools*	*Neighborhood Schools*	*Alternative Schools*
Free Lunch	89%	82%	87%	100%
Limited English	10%	25%	23%	9%*
Recent Immigrant[a]	2%	5%	5%	3%

Source: New York City Board of Education Annual School Report, 1995–96.

Note: *p ≤ .05, one-tailed t-test.

[a]Measured as having lived less than three years in the United States.

Parental Preferences and Outcomes of Choice

Empirical studies have documented that parents who send their children to alternative rather than neighborhood schools generally have more resources and tend to be more motivated (Martinez, Kemeer, and Godwin 1995; Wells 1993; Witte 1993; Willms and Echols 1992; Bridge and Blackman 1978). Based on these patterns, scholars have argued that choice is driven by demographic and behavioral characteristics of parents. However, as we noted previously, most of these studies are based on bivariate analyses that do not consider how program design, parent preferences, or contextual factors affect the processes and outcomes of school choice.

While option-demand arrangements place greater responsibility on individual parents and students in making schooling decisions, they also increase the importance of institutional and contextual features in determining the outcomes of choice. While some parents will have access to more and better information about schools (Bridge and Blackman 1978; Henig 1994; Wells 1993; Murnane 1986) and some will be more capable of making informed choices (Wells 1993; Witte 1993; Coleman and Hoffer 1987), these processes are not necessarily static. Instead, one should expect the learning curve for certain types of parents to be steeper than for others. Findings from Alum Rock show that while minorities and parents of lower-socioeconomic status started off with poor information about their choice options, over time their information levels improved, reducing the knowledge gap between advantaged and disadvantaged parents (Henig 1994, 119–20; see also Lines 1994).

Based on this evidence, we expect that the length of experience with choice may influence which types of parents participate, as well as socioeconomic factors. In addition to historical experience, since District 4 also devotes more resources to information dissemination, we also expect the potential bias against more disadvantaged parents to be lower in District 4.

Generally, we expect that parents in District 1 who are both more interested and involved in their children's schooling, and more "advantaged" to participate at higher levels than those who are less involved and advantaged. That is, if stratification exists, it is most likely to be in District 1 rather than in District 4.

To examine the factors influencing parents' schooling decisions, we specify a multivariate model that includes the "core" demographic variables used throughout this book and variables reflecting the institutional context of choice as well.

In this analysis, we model whether a parent has chosen a neighborhood school ($Y = 0$) or a public alternative school ($Y = 1$). We expect three key features of the institutional environments of the two choice programs to affect which parents choose alternative schools. These differences reflect (1) the maturity of the choice program; (2) the number and scope of the alternative schools offered; (3) the availability of information about the alternative schools and choice process.

Because there is no way to measure directly program maturity, we measure it indirectly through the size and visibility of both districts' choice programs.[7] Specifically, we expect the accessibility of school choice to increase over time and as the number and range of options increases. We also consider parents' preferences over various attributes of schools. Recall that in our survey, parents were asked to name up to four school attributes they thought were the most important (see chapter 4). Here we include as independent variables four attributes not generally emphasized by traditional public schools, but given more importance by various types of alternative schools: values supported by the school, discipline, high scores, and special programs. Each of these variables is dichotomous and takes the value 1 if the parent included it as one of his/her four most important attributes. To be a significant predictor of whether a parent elects an alternative school, there must be an alternative school representing the attribute and parents must recognize this and be choosing at least partly along this dimension.

The second institutional variable corresponds to the informational environment of the district. We employ two strategies in gauging the effects district outreach and advertising programs have on parents' schooling decisions. First, we utilize a survey question that asked parents whether they thought they had enough information about all the schools and programs in their district when they enrolled their child in school (*Enough Info* = 1 if parents strongly agreed; 0 otherwise). Given the more sophisticated and established outreach programs in District 4, we expect this variable to significantly increase the likelihood of choosing an alternative school in District 4.

Because parents are also likely to get information about schools from noninstitutional sources, we capture these effects with two variables: length of residence in the district and frequency of attendance at religious services. We estimate the model separately in Districts 1 and 4 to control for effects of institutional arrangements on the choice process and because the direction and magnitude of too many variables are expected to differ according to district.

What Affects Parent Choice of Alternative Schools in New York?

The mechanisms underlying the choice process in the two districts are markedly different. In District 1, clearly demographic factors are driving parents' decision to enroll their children in alternative schools (see table 10.3). The coefficients on the *Years of Schooling* and *White* variables are highly significant in this model and their effect on parent behavior substantial. In District 1, white parents are approximately 24 percent more likely to choose alternative schools than are other parents, while each additional year of education increases the probability of choosing an alternative school by 1.6 percent. The

Table 10.3
Factors Affecting Parents' Choice of Alternative Schools

Variables	District 4		District 1	
	Coefficient (Std. Error)	Impact	Coefficient (Std. Error)	Impact
Values Important	.914**	.231	.496	.072
	(.357)		(.410)	
Discipline Important	.104	.017	−.092	−.010
	(.250)		(.307)	
High Scores Important	.265	.042	−.100	−.011
	(.260)		(.295)	
Special Programs	.475*	.090	.049	.005
	(.264)		(.354)	
Black	−.191	−.030	−.002	−.000
	(.292)		(.487)	
White	1.140	.330	1.157**	.236
	(.755)		(.380)	
Other	.638	.150	.526	.082
	(.527)		(.526)	
Years of Schooling	.019	.003	.149**	.016
	(.044)		(.060)	
Employed	.584**	.106	.446	.050
	(.256)		(.308)	
Married	.350	.061	.152	.016
	(.241)		(.283)	
Length of Residence	.034**	.006	.004	.000
	(.016)		(.020)	
Church Attendance	.084	.014	−.019	−.002
	(.057)		(.060)	
Enough Information	.535**	.098	.074	.008
	(.236)		(.281)	
Intercept	−3.273		−3.774	
N	242		229	
χ^2	37.39**		59.06**	
Pseudo R^2	.19		.35	

Note: Impact figures indicate the effect of a change from 0 to 1 for the dummy variables and the effect of a unit change for the continuous variables.

*$p \leq .05$ (one-tailed test).

**$p \leq .01$

fact that neither institutional factor nor any of the variables corresponding to the informational environment were significant provides evidence that the choice process in District 1 is characterized by racial and socioeconomic stratification

The factors affecting choice in District 4 contrast sharply with those in

District 1. First, choice in District 4 is not influenced by race or education. The only demographic variable of consequence is parents' employment status—parents who work are almost 11 percent more likely to enroll their children in alternative schools than parents who do not work. Most importantly, institutional features and the context of choice appear to be driving the choice process in District 4. Two attributes of the alternative schools— values and special programs—were among the most important predictors of choice. In addition, the informational environment plays an important role in the choice process. Parents who have lived longer in the district and parents who felt they had enough information about alternative schools were significantly more likely to enroll their children in alternative schools. This evidence confirms earlier findings by Bridge (1978) and Teske et al. (1993) that parental knowledge about schools increases over time and as a result of experience and exposure to information. In addition, these findings suggest that District 4's efforts to disseminate information have influenced who participates in choice.

These results suggest that school choice is not necessarily associated with racial and socioeconomic stratification. Instead, stratification can be circumvented by creating institutional structures that provide information for parents.

Stratification and Segregation in Montclair

Unlike the two New York districts in our study, choice was not implemented in Montclair because its schools were failing. Indeed, as the Carnegie Foundation Report (1992, 31) notes, Montclair has always been a high-performing district with a motivated parent population. Instead, Montclair adopted school choice in 1976 to voluntarily desegregate schools that were facing a rapidly changing population.

As blacks began moving into the community in larger numbers throughout the 1960s, new housing patterns created a racial imbalance in the zoned schools. Montclair adopted its magnet school plan in 1976 to address segregated schools, and in 1985 expanded the concept by moving to a comprehensive magnet school choice program.

Because Montclair's aim is eliminating segregated schools, in contrast to the programs in New York, it is regulated and not voluntary. As a compromise between parental desire for choice and policymakers' desire for racially balanced schools, stratification takes on a different meaning. Parents who do not choose "opposite-race" schools in sufficient numbers are reassigned to other schools (Rossell 1995). Despite this policy, over 95 percent of Montclair parents get their first-choice school (Clewell and Joy 1990, 7).

In the figures 10.10 and 10.11, we provide over-time data on the racial mix (minority versus non-minority) of several schools in Montclair, demonstrating the effectiveness of controlled choice in achieving racially balanced schools.[8]

The first year of this timeline corresponds to the year immediately prior to the implementation of Montclair's magnet program. In 1975, the district minority population was 43 percent and the racial composition of several schools deviated significantly from that average. For example, both Bradford and Edgemont Elementary Schools had less than 30 percent minority enrollment while Nishuane Elementary School had greater than 60 percent minority enrollment. When choice was implemented in 1976, Montclair closed two schools to help achieve racial balancing. By 1980 Bradford, Edgemont, and Nishuane had made significant strides in achieving this balance. Upon moving to the comprehensive magnet program in 1986, most schools achieved a nearly perfect balance. In 1994, Montclair's schools fluctuated between 45 and 55 percent minority enrollment, a 5-percentage point difference on both sides of the overall minority population, which had increased to 50 percent by 1994.

According to these data, choice appears to have successfully desegregated Montclair's schools over a period of about ten years. However, it is important to remember that racial balance across schools does not necessarily mean that segregation has been eliminated *within* schools—indeed, the issue of resegregation at the classroom level has emerged in many controlled choice districts, including Montclair.

Conclusion

We have shown in this chapter that the institutional mechanisms of choice affect the level of equity found in school choice systems. The controlled choice program in Montclair illustrates some of the ways in which racial

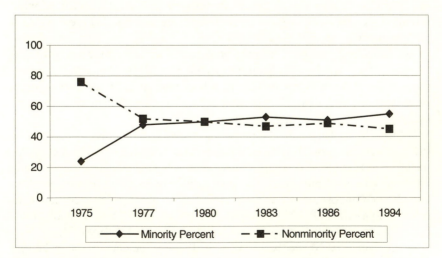

Figure 10.10   The Changing Racial Balance in the Bradford Elementary School, Montclair

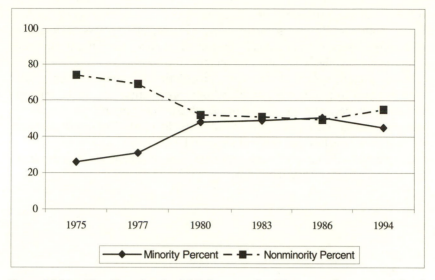

Figure 10.11 The Changing Racial Balance in the Edgemont Elementary School, Montclair

balancing can be established and enforced. But our analysis of the option-demand programs in New York's Districts 1 and 4 demonstrates that while this form of choice may be more prone to stratification along racial and socioeconomic dimensions, these outcomes do not *necessarily* result. The experience of District 4 suggests that all types of parents can change their behavior in response to the new "rules of the game" brought about by choice. However, our comparison of Districts 1 and 4 indicates that we should not expect these behavioral changes to take place overnight.

In addition, even if choice exacerbates stratification in a given district, it would need to be balanced against potential school performance improvements that may ensue from the competitive pressures created by a choice system. Our finding that performance in District 4 neighborhood schools improved over time suggests that the assumption that some students will be "left behind" is not necessarily accurate, as nonchoice schools face pressure from choice schools and work to improve.

This competitive pressure can influence the education marketplace beyond just the public schools. Debates about public school choice and equity often overlook how the development of higher-quality public schools may attract students from private schools and also prevent more students from exiting public schools in the first place (see Hoxby 1998; chapter 12 herein).

Though the effects of choice on stratification will continue to be hotly debated, the questions are complicated and the answers even more difficult. But the debate should clarify what level and type of stratification we are comparing choice systems to, and what aspects of choice are actually related to these patterns. Although the ideal conception of a public school system that is both racially and socioeconomically integrated across each school (and every classroom) may actually exist in some areas, the current American school system is highly stratified by income and race.

In our present system of schooling, jurisdictional boundaries largely dictate who goes to public school with whom. Some argue that racial segregation has been getting worse in recent decades in most metropolitan areas, as previous judicial remedies are repealed (Orfield et al. 1996) and as racial segregation intensifies (Massey and Denton 1993).

Compared to the effect of these processes, does choice really increase stratification significantly? We think not.

Chapter 11

Choosing Together Is Better than Bowling Alone: School Choice and the Creation of Social Capital*

In this chapter, we explore the benefits of school choice beyond those flowing from the consumer behavior that has been the focus of our analysis in previous chapters. Here, we argue that by expanding the options parents have over the choice of schools their children attend, parents not only can become better *consumers* of education, but they can also become better *citizens*. As we explore this issue, we address a fundamental question in the growing literature on social capital: can government create social capital?

Using the example of school choice, we show that the answer is "yes."

Social Capital and Strong Communities

While the concept of social capital has only relatively recently moved to a position of prominence in political science and in contemporary discussions of public policy, the term has been used by sociologists for some time (see, e.g., Loury 1977; Bourdieu 1980). James Coleman (1988) brought the term into wider circulation by identifying several components of social systems that generate social capital, including obligation, trust, more-developed informational channels and networks, and effective sanctions on behavior that violates norms. These concepts are central to almost every analysis of social capital that has followed.

While Coleman must be credited with laying the foundation for the current study of social capital, without question it was Robert Putnam's work, and especially his use of the metaphor of "bowling alone," that propelled the idea of social capital to center stage. In turn, the growing popularity of the term has bred controversy over its definition and over the identification of the factors that nourish it.

There are many dimensions to this still unfolding debate on social capital, and we focus on only one of them: can government institutions create social capital? Before we address this question directly, we begin with a brief review of some of the issues concerning social capital that relate to our study of the relationship between the institution of school choice and the creation of social capital.

One of the first issues that must be addressed is the fundamental nature of

*This chapter is based on earlier work on which Michael Mintrom was a coauthor and we acknowledge his contribution.

social capital. In Coleman's original conception, social capital, like any other form of capital, is important because it helps social groups accomplish other goals, regardless of what those goals may be:

> Just as physical capital and human capital facilitate productive activity, social capital does as well. For example, a group within which there is extensive trustworthiness and extensive trust is able to accomplish much more than a comparable group without that trustworthiness and trust. (Coleman 1988, S101)

Thus in Coleman's view social capital, as it engenders norms of trust, reduces transaction costs, mitigates the intensity of conflicts, and facilitates the emergence of cooperative behavior. This link between social capital and cooperative behavior is also central to Putnam's work. In his study of twenty subnational governments in Italy, Putnam defines social capital as "features of social organization such as networks, norms, and social trust that facilitate coordination and cooperation for mutual benefit" (1993, 67). While Putnam clearly draws on Coleman, his work departs from Coleman in at least one fundamental way: in Coleman's conception, social capital is fundamentally *neutral*—when present, it facilitates the goals of actors, whether those goals be morally or socially desirable (Foley and Edwards 1997; Greeley 1997, 589). In contrast, in Putnam's conception, the quality of democratic politics and the vitality of a country's economic life are highly dependent on the degree to which the citizenry enjoy a rich store of social capital.

Obviously, in this light, social capital is far from neutral and, indeed, Putnam's view of social capital as a *positive* good upon which the strength of democratic institutions is built has become common. Consider Fukuyama's (1995, 356) argument that the "ability to cooperate socially is dependent on prior habits, traditions, and norms, which themselves serve to structure the market. Hence it is more likely that a successful market economy, rather than being the cause of stable democracy, is codetermined by the prior factor of social capital. If the latter is abundant, then both markets and democratic politics will thrive, and the market can in fact play a role as a school of sociability that reinforces democratic institutions."

While Fukuyama emphasizes the importance of social capital in creating strong communities, he does not assign a central role to government in maintaining this link. Similarly, for Putnam, social capital is generated mostly through the quality of secondary associations and not through government action. For Putnam, "civic virtue" comes from experience in associational life because that experience teaches "skills of cooperation as well as a sense of shared responsibility for collective endeavors" (Putnam 1993, 90). In this regard, Putnam's reference to the "amateur soccer clubs, choral societies, hiking clubs, bird-watching groups, literary circles, hunters' associations, Lions Clubs, and the like in each community" (1993, 91) is often cited, and his image of "bowling alone" (Putnam 1995a) summarizes the notion of the decline of such nonpolitical associations in the U.S. as an indicator of the decline in social capital. Thus, central to Putnam's work is the claim that civil societies characterized by a richly variegated associational life will tend to exhibit norms of political equality, trust, tolerance, and active participation in public affairs.

While we agree on the importance of social capital as a foundation for strong communities, we argue that there is a much more central role of government in nourishing the conditions that create social capital. This role also includes providing incentives and opportunities for a rich associational life to flourish, which in turn leads to a debate over the relative importance of bottom-up versus top-down processes in nurturing social capital. In this debate, the importance of associational life in the creation of social capital is agreed upon, but the importance of the broader context within which this associational life either flourishes or starves is at issue.

Bottom-up versus Top-down Creation of Social Capital

Again, Putnam is central to the debate over top-down versus bottom-up routes to social capital. Levi (1996, 52) argues that, Putnam has a "romanticized image of community" and that his concept of social capital is "resolutely society-centered." This view leads him to emphasize a bottom-up approach to the generation of social capital in which social capital is generated by grassroots activity and a vibrant associational life. In contrast, the role of government is largely ignored by Putnam.

Yet there is a clear institutional and social context that defines the boundaries of civic engagement and the extent of citizen involvement in social and political events. That is, there are top-down processes that directly affect the quality of grassroots activity and associational life. In turn, the opportunities for associational groups to generate social capital are affected by the structure and policies of government, and the role of institutions cannot be neglected in the creation of social capital and strong communities (Tarrow 1996, 394–95; Levi 1996; Jackman and Miller 1996a, 1996b).

Much of the work linking the importance of institutions to social capital has been concerned with participation, which should be viewed as a contributor to the creation of social capital, than with social capital itself. Skocpol (1996), for example, argues that civic associations and citizen participation in the United States developed less from the purely local decisions of collections of individuals and more as a consequence of the institutional patterns of federalism, electoral politics, and political parties.

Similarly, Rosenstone and Hansen (1993) provide empirical evidence to support the argument that participation is indeed firmly rooted in institutions and organizations that mobilize individuals and structure their involvement. And Verba, Schlozman, and Brady (1995) have found that networks of recruitment, embedded in institutions and organizations, are critically important for explaining civic volunteerism. But they argue that institutions "incubate the social networks through which solicitations for activity are mediated" (Verba, Schlozman, and Brady 1995, 369).

More recently, Sharp (1998) has focused on local government and its role in the creation of social capital. According to her, local governments can foster the formation of social capital by the institutionalization of participatory structures such as neighborhood organizations or alternative dispute resolution programs. In these programs, local governments can nurture social capital by enriching citizen involvement with associations that emphasize participation. Henig (1998) is also concerned with the role of local government in creating social capital. He argues that the bottom-up approach, as applied to urban neighborhoods and their role in democracy, emphasizes the limited capacity of central authorities to determine the ultimate contents and consequences of the policies they put into motion. But Henig suggests that social capital is more likely to arise, and much more likely to be sustained, in the context of healthy governing institutions.

Not surprisingly, some scholars have also been concerned with the specific role that schools play in the creation of social capital. Indeed, Coleman's classic article on social capital specifically addressed the question of how effective school communities can create social capital (Coleman 1988). Other work has followed this lead. For example, Schneider and Coleman (1993), Lee (1993), and Astone and McLanahan (1991) have examined social capital as a function of the interactions between administrators, teachers, parents, and children.

Our work seeks to merge these disparate strains of research, investigating the extent to which the design of schools can increase levels of social capital. While scholars have recognized the importance of schools in creating social capital for the next generation (see, e.g., Henig 1994, 201–3), for us, schools assume an added importance as arenas in which social capital can be generated among today's parents. In our work, we try to integrate the emphasis on associational life found in other work on social capital with the importance of government structure to develop an approach that helps explain how school choice can help develop social capital.

Thus, while Fukuyama has argued that "social capital is like a ratchet that is more easily turned in one direction than another; it can be dissipated by the actions of governments much more readily than those governments can build it up again" (1995, 62), we argue that government does matter, showing that institutional arrangements that increase parental control over the schools children attend may be able to reverse the "ratcheting down" of social capital.

Measuring Social Capital in the Context of School Choice

We build on the approach of Berry et al. (1993), who emphasize the importance of communities where neighbors talk to each other about politics. In these face-to-face meetings, according to Berry, Portney, and Thomson "democracy moves politics away from its adversarial norm, where interest groups square off in conflict and lobbyists speak for their constituents. Instead, the bonds of friendship and community are forged as neighbors look for common solutions to their problems" (3; also see Mansbridge 1980 on "unitary democracy" and Barber 1984 on "strong democracy"). Berry, Portney, and Thomson's emphasis on "face-to-face" interactions parallels Fukuyama's focus on "spontaneous sociability" and Putnam's emphasis on the role of networks and membership in voluntary and social organizations as supports for representative democracy (also see Diamond 1992). In our analysis we use four measures of social capital, all of which reflect voluntary association with the schools or "spontaneous sociability" central to the creation of social capital.

The first measure is whether or not the parent is a member of the PTA. Membership in such organizations is critical for a variety of reasons. As Putnam argues, "people who join are people who trust . . . the causation flows mainly from joining to trusting" (1995b, 666). Indeed, Putnam uses declining participation in PTAs as one of his indicators of the erosion of social capital.[1] The second measure we analyze is a slightly broader indicator of parental involvement in the schools, asking parents if in the past year they had volunteered for any activities in their children's schools.

The third measure we investigate is the number of other parents our respondents talked with about school matters. We use this measure to reflect the "spontaneous sociability" Fukuyama emphasizes as underlying social capital and the importance of "face-to-face democracy" emphasized by Berry, Portney, and Thomson's. This measure reflects the importance of interactions that teach citizens the civic virtues of compromise, trust, and reciprocity, while enhancing the skills of democratic organization and discourse. As Ostrom puts it (1990, 206): "Networks of civic engagement foster robust norms of reciprocity."

Our final measure reflects the level of trust parents have in their children's teacher to do the "right thing" for their children.[2] Putnam argues that "trust is an essential component of social capital" because it "lubricates cooperation" (Putnam 1993, 170–71). Similarly, for Fukuyama the level of trust in society is *the* most critical dimension of social capital, since it facilitates economic, political, and social transactions. While much work on trust is concerned with general measures of trust in government or interpersonal trust, in this chapter, we concentrate on a single domain-specific dimension of trust (trust in teachers).

Thus, these activities are not only critical to building strong schools, they are also central to building social capital and strong communities.

Is There a Relationship between Choice and Social Capital?

We begin the simple relationship between choice and social capital, looking at the bivariate relationship between chooser type and each of the measures

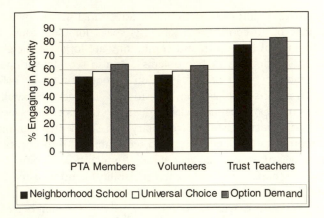

Figure 11.1   Social Capital and School Choice in New York

of social capital we use. We focus first on New York and then replicate the analysis using our New Jersey data. After presenting this simple bivariate data, we then present more complex multivariate models.

Even a quick look at figures 11.1 and 11.2 shows a fairly consistent relationship between parental status as a chooser and our indicators of social capital—hinting immediately at a relationship between the institutions of government and levels of social capital. In particular, note that parents who are choosers are always higher in social capital than parents whose children are enrolled in a neighborhood school. The effects are often quite striking.

Consider first the two measures of the quality of associational life associated with the schools—membership in PTA and participation in voluntary activities. PTA membership is by far the highest among option-demand parents. This is made clear when we look at the pattern of participation in voluntary activity. But note among public school types, option-demand parents are the most likely to be involved in voluntary activities. There is about

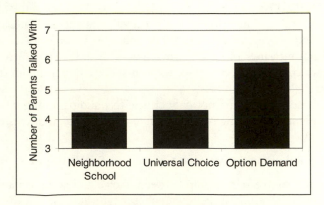

Figure 11.2   "Sociability" in New York

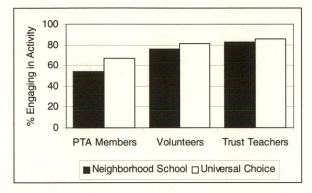

Figure 11.3 Social Capital and School Choice in New Jersey

a 10 percent decline in volunteerism between option-demand and universal choice parents. And, by far, parents with children in neighborhood schools are the least likely to be involved in the associational life of their children's schools. Note too that these parents are over 10 percent less likely to express trust in their children's teachers than are parents who have chosen their children's schools. Finally, as evident in figure 11.2, a similar pattern is evident in patterns of face-to-face interactions among parents: active public school choosers have more extensive interactions with other parents. These

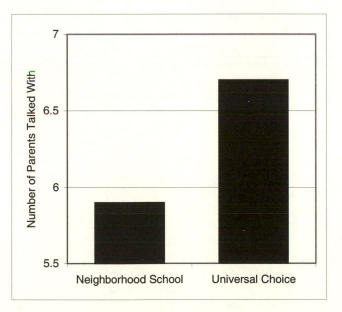

Figure 11.4 "Sociability" in New Jersey

simple patterns all point in the same direction—in New York City, choice is associated with higher levels of social capital.[3]

Figures 11.3 and 11.4 explore the relationship between choice and social capital in New Jersey. In every one of the four measures, virtually repeating the pattern in New York, parents with children in neighborhood schools are lowest in social capital—they are least likely to be members of the PTA, to engage in voluntary school-based activities, and trust their children's teachers. In addition, they engage in fewer face-to-face conversations with other parents than parents who have more choice over their schools.

These are striking patterns. School choice is systematically related to levels of social capital—both in a lower socioeconomic status central city as well as in suburban middle-class communities. However, we need to see if these basic relationships stand up to more rigorous analysis. In the next section, we move from these simple bivariate patterns to more complex explanatory models.

Explaining the Relationship between Choice and Social Capital

While we have already defined our indicators of social capital, we begin this section by explaining our selection of independent variables. In addition to our core explanatory variables, we also use several new variables, which together measure the motivations, resources, time constraints, and school policies that can affect parental involvement in schools (Kerbow and Bernhardt 1993, 116).

As we have discussed throughout this book, three different types of institutional arrangements exist in the two public, central-city districts in our study. The oldest and most traditional form of school organization is the neighborhood model, in which children are assigned to schools based on residential location. The second is universal choice, which characterizes the intermediate school system in District 4. Under this type of arrangement, all parents *must* choose a school for their children (i.e., there is no "default" school). In New York, there is also an option demand system of choice (see Elmore 1991a), that exists in both districts, but that is much more developed in District 4.

Active choosers present us with the same fundamental problem faced by any research on the behavior of parents in school choice settings—parents choosing alternative schools may not be a random selection of all parents in a school district. And, if parents who self-select alternative schools are also high on social capital, then our results will be biased.

While other studies have acknowledged this problem and made various efforts to control for it (Smith and Meier 1995; Chubb and Moe 1990; Coleman, Hoffer, and Kilgore 1982; Coleman and Hoffer 1987), we correct for it by constructing a two-stage nonrandom assignment model, in which the first equation models the assignment process and the second equation the "outcome." The method, described in chapter 3 and based on the work of Achen (1986), corrects for both the nonrandom selection process and other econometric problems associated with the use of dichotomous dependent variables.[4]

By limiting the possibility that parents likely to make active choices are also likely to engage in other activities that we refer to as part of social capital, the use of this methodology is critical to our argument that making an active choice influences parental behavior.

As noted in detail in appendix 1, we begin with an explicit assignment equation:

Assignment equation (Eq. 1): *active choosers* = á + β*[core variables]* + β*[values]* + β*[diversity]* + ε

Where:

Active choosers is a dichotomous variable indicating whether or not a parent has elected an alternative school or program for her child (1 = yes; 0 = no);

Core variables include those we have used throughout this book: a set of dummy variables for racial identification; years of schooling; length of residence in the school district; employment status; gender; and frequency of church attendance.

We have seen the importance of many of these variables on a host of school choice related behaviors, but they may have added importance from a social capital perspective. Most notably, parental education level may be particularly important in the study of social capital—Putnam (1995b, 667) reports that education "is by far the strongest correlate . . . of civic engagement in all its forms." From the social capital perspective, the length of residence variable reflects the argument advanced by Brehm and Rahn (1997) and by Putnam, who argue that mobility decreases social capital.

Church attendance may be a particularly important indicator of alternative forms of interaction and involvement with the local community and the production of social capital. Most notably, Greeley (1997, 590) emphasizes the importance of church attendance in predicting levels of volunteer services. While church attendance is (not surprisingly) strongly related to volunteering for religion-based activities, Greeley shows that religious structures also affected voluntary activity in a wide range of nonreligious activities, including education: "Religion (i.e., religious structures) generated social capital not only for its own projects but for many other kinds of voluntary efforts. It is far and away the strongest resource available to those whom Coleman would have doubtless called 'voluntary actors'" (591).

The *values* and *diversity* variables indicate whether or not a parent thought these attributes of schools were important in their choice of schools. As readers will recall from chapter 4, in our survey parents were asked to name up to four attributes they thought were most important in a school. Two attributes in particular, the values espoused by the school and the diversity of the student body, were considered important by option-demand parents but not by parents of children in neighborhood public schools.[5] We therefore include these variables in the assignment equation for theoretical reasons, as they are important predictors of active school choosers. However, we have no theoretical reason to expect these variables to affect social capital and, indeed, they are not empirically related to the activities we have measured.[6]

Thus, as described in greater detail in appendix 1, we estimate this assignment equation and the predicted value of the active chooser variable is used in estimating the following outcome equation:

Outcome equation (eq. 2): social capital = á + β ["predicted" active choosers] + β [school factors] + β [core variables] + ε

Where:

Core variables are as noted in equation 1 and *values* and *diversity* are excluded.

"Predicted" active choosers is the linear estimates from equation 1 (1964; also see Heckman 1978; Achen 1986). *School factors* measure other aspects of the school environment. These factors include a variable measuring the number of students in the school the child attends, as smaller schools are often considered to be better arenas for building social capital (Harrington and Cookson 1992); a dummy variable (= 1) for universal choosers; and a measure of parental dissatisfaction with children's schools.[7] Previous research (e.g., Witte 1991) has demonstrated that parental dissatisfaction is negatively correlated with levels of parental involvement and participation in school activities.

When the dependent variable in the outcome equation is continuous, as in our analysis of the number of parents with whom a respondent has talked about schools, the two-stage estimation technique is fairly straightforward. However, when the dependent variable is a dichotomous variable another round of corrections is necessary (see appendix 1; also see Achen 1986, 40–47). In our analysis of the other three measures of social capital we report these generalized two-stage least squares (G2SLS) results. Note that since the results are generalized linear probability estimates, the coefficients have a straightforward interpretation: they represent the change in the probability of finding an event given a unit change in the independent variable.

The Effects of Choice in New York City

With these corrections in place, we are now able to estimate the effects of school choice on the behavior of parents controlling for the nonrandom "assignment" across alternative schools[8] The results of this more rigorous analysis, presented in table 11.1, confirm the robustness of the basic relationships we presented in figures 11.1 and 11.2.

Table 11.1
The Effects of Choice on the Formation of Social Capital in New York

	PTA Member	Voluntary Activities	Number of Parents Talked To	Trust Teacher
Active	.128*	.123*	4.053*	.095*
Chooser	(.064)	(.064)	(2.295)	(.049)
Universal	−.035	.025	−.613	.096*
Choice	(.066)	(.062)	(.651)	(.056)
Dissatisfaction	−.042	−.003	.234	−.239***
	(.041)	(.040)	(.404)	(.039)
School Size	.000	.000	.000	.000
	(.000)	(.001)	(.001)	(.000)
Black	.092	.048	−.401	−.057
	(.072)	(.068)	(1.30)	(.044)
Hispanic	−.068	−.021	.419	−.066
	(.066)	(.062)	(1.22)	(.036)
Asian	.041	.149	1.61	.059
	(.187)	(.157)	(2.47)	(.097)
Length of	.005*	.005*	.085**	−.002
Residence	(.003)	(.003)	(.030)	(.002)
Education	.015**	.020**	.148*	−.009*
	(.005)	(.006)	(.063)	(.004)
Employed	−.046	.031	.038	.033
	(.044)	(.042)	(.427)	(.029)
Female	.277***	.110	.370	−.052
	(.056)	(.067)	(.708)	(.036)
Attend	.041***	.023***	.242*	.010
Church	(.009)	(.009)	(.108)	(.006)
Constant	.336**	.327**	.739	1.05
	(.129)	(.135)	(2.34)	(.090)
Test Statistics	N = 580	N = 580	N = 568	N = 578
	F = 66**	F = 107**	F = 44**	F = 43**

Notes: Numbers in parentheses are adjusted standard errors. We do not report R-squared statistics because in the adjustment process necessary to correct for the nonrandom assignment problem, this statistic becomes inappropriate (see Aldrich and Nelson 1994; 14–15).

*p = .05
**p = .01
***p = .001.

Turning first to PTA membership, reported in the first column of table 11.1, we find that ceteris paribus, participation in the PTA among active choosers is 13 percent higher than among nonchoosers ($p < .05$), the largest effect in our model, apart from gender.

The effects of some other variables are worth noting. First, note that as the length of residence increases, so does participation in the PTA ($p < .05$, using a one-tail test). Similarly, frequency of church attendance increases participation in the PTA. These findings confirm empirically the arguments presented by Putnam and Fukuyama, as well as findings by education researchers (Muller and Kerbow 1993; Kerbow and Bernhardt 1993).

The second column of table 11.1 includes the results from the model predicting participation in voluntary events. Here we find that active choosers are over 12 percent more likely to engage in such activities than are nonchoosers. Paralleling the results reported for PTA membership, church going and longer length of residence are associated with volunteering, as is more years of parental education.

We have shown that active participation in school choice increases levels of involvement with voluntary organizations. We turn next to a measure of spontaneous sociability—how many other parents do our respondents engage in discussions about schools? The same cluster of variables emerges as important: ceteris paribus, active choosers talked with four more parents than nonchoosers (see the third column of table 11.1). Again, longer-term residents, respondents with higher education, and frequent church goers talk with more parents than do other respondents.

Finally, as evident in the final column of table 11.1, active choosers are almost 10 percent more likely to trust teachers all or most of the time and universal choosers are 9 percent more likely. In contrast, parents who are dissatisfied with their children's schools are 24 percent less likely to trust their children's teachers.

Taking Advantage of the Quasi-Experimental Design: Replicating the New York Findings in New Jersey

As we have argued, replication is one of the most powerful tools available for validating social scientific findings. In the next stage of our analysis, we take advantage of our quasi-experimental design to replicate the analysis in our pair of New Jersey school districts. This replication allows us to explore the robustness of our findings by testing their sensitivity to changes in the context of choice. In our first comparison, we have demonstrated that school choice fosters behavior that builds social capital among parents in low-income central-city school districts. Given the multitude of problems facing central cities, this is obviously an important finding. However, the next question is obvious: does this relationship hold among middle-income suburban parents who now make up a larger share of the American population than do central-city residents?

School Choice and Social Capital in Suburban Communities

To answer this question we turn to our second paired set of communities, Montclair and Morristown, New Jersey.

Under the universal system of choice in Montclair, all parents are required to choose schools for their children. Therefore, it is not necessary to specify the selection process as we did for the analyses of our New York City parents—that is, no assignment equation is needed and the extensive corrections noted in appendix 1 are not necessary. Thus the results reported in table 11.2 are the results of straightforward multivariate analyses. For comparability with the linear probabilities reported in our analysis of New York, we report the percentage point change for a unit change in the independent variable (for the dummy variable this is the effect of having the characteristic [1] versus not having it [0]). Since all Montclair parents *must* choose their children's school and no one in Morristown public schools can choose (except by moving), the coefficient of the dummy variable for Montclair represents the effects of universal choice, ceteris paribus.

Table 11.2
The Effects of Choice on the Formation of Social Capital in New Jersey

	PTA Member	% Chg.	Volunteer Activity	% Chg.	Parents Talked To	% Chg.	Trust Teachers	% Chg.
Universal	.35**	13%	.21*	6%	1.24**	13%	.28*	6%
Choice	(.11)		(.13)		(.38)		(.14)	
Black	−.55**	−21%	−.48**	−14%	−3.38**	−30%	−.41**	−9%
	(.13)		(.14)		(.44)		(.15)	
Hispanic	−1.24**	−45%	−.96**	−34%	−2.86**	−12%	.34	6%
	(.29)		(.26)		(.91)		(.38)	
Asian	−.57	−22%	.15	4%	−3.49**	−11%	.49	8%
	(.33)		(.39)		(1.17)		(.55)	
Length of	−.01	−.07%	.02**	.6%	.07**	9%	.01	.02%
Residence	(.01)		(.01)		(.03)		(.01)	
Education	.09**	3%	.06**	2%	.31**	16%	.03	.5%
	(.02)		(.02)		(.08)		(.03)	
Employed	−.07	−3%	−.06	−1%	−.78*	−6%	−.27	−5%
	(.14)		(.16)		(.47)		(.18)	
Female	.40**	15%	.52**	16%	1.22***	10%	−.02	−.5%
	(.13)		(.14)		(.44)		(.16)	
Attend	.09**	4%	.06*	2%	.24***	11%	−.01	−.01%
Church	(.03)		(.03)		(.08)		(.03)	
Dissatisfac-	−1.76**	−8%	−.01	−.1%	.51	6%	−.73**	−18%
tion	(.42)		(.14)		(.41)		(.14)	
Constant	−.92		−.45		1.71		1.04	
	(.41)		(.44)		(1.4)		(.49)	
N	629		629		626		622	
χ^2	91***		61***		14***		43***	

Note: Standard errors are in parentheses. In the three probit equations the percentage point change figures indicate the effect of a change from 0 to 1 for the dummy variables and the effect of a unit change for the continuous variables. For the regression equations "Parents Talked To" the percentage changes are calculated from the normalized beta coefficients.

*p = .05
**p = .01
***p = .001

The results in table 11.2 show patterns consistent with those in our New York analysis. Choosers are significantly more likely to engage all measures that build social capital—PTA membership, volunteering for school activities, talking to more people about schools, and trusting teachers—controlling for other important factors.

Conclusion

At the heart of calls for the introduction of market-like reforms into the public sector lies the belief that giving people choices over public goods will increase efficiency. Research into the effects of market-like arrangements in the provision of public goods has established that such competitive mechanisms can in fact pressure the producers of public goods to be more efficient and more responsive (for local public goods, see, e.g., Tiebout 1956; Ostrom 1972; Schneider 1989; Schneider and Teske 1995). Recently, scholars have begun to study the effects of reforms on the demand-side of the market, leading to debates about the level of information held by citizens and the levels necessary for markets for public goods to work (e.g., Lyons, Lowery, and DeHoog 1992; Teske et al. 1993; Lowery, Lyons, and DeHoog 1995, Teske et al. 1995).

This debate has focused on only a limited aspect of the behavior of the citizen/consumer in the market for public goods, revolving around the question of whether or not competition can enhance the behavior of citizens as consumers.

In this chapter, we have broadened the question by asking if government policies that enhance choice over public goods can increase the capacity of the citizen/consumer to act as a responsible, involved citizen. Our results show that in the domain of local public education, the answer is yes.

According to Putnam, societies can evolve two different equilibria as they solve collective action problems. One equilibrium is built on a "virtuous circle" that nurtures healthy norms of reciprocity, cooperation, and mutual trust. The other relies on coercion and creates an environment in which only kin can be trusted. Civic engagement is at the core of Putnam's concept of social capital because it breeds cooperation and facilitates coordination in governing. Public schools constitute a domain in which the virtuous circle is essential for improving the quality of education. Hillary Rodham Clinton has argued (1996) "it takes a village" to raise a child. It may also take a "village" to educate a child: high-quality education is dependent on parental involvement supported by high levels of community involvement. In turn, high-quality education is associated with activities that build social capital—a virtuous circle is created.

Our research shows that the design of the institutions delivering local public goods can influence levels of social capital. No present statistical method can fully correct for problems in estimation introduced by the complex causal linkages that motivate our study. However, our two-stage modeling clearly addresses the biases introduced by the nonrandom "assignment" of parents as active choosers in New York. Our research shows that in both an urban and a suburban setting and under different institutional settings of choice, the act of school choice seems to stimulate parents to become more involved in a wide range of school-related activities that build social capital. Our results support arguments linking participation and urban democracy and, within the domain of schools that we studied, are directly congruent with Berry, Portney, and Thomson (1993, 254) claim that "increased participation does lead to greater sense of community, increased governmental legitimacy, and enhanced status of governmental institutions."

Clearly, many factors affecting the formation of social capital are based on individual-level characteristics effectively beyond the control of government (e.g., social capital increases with church attendance and with length of residence in a community). This fundamentally limits the role that government can play in nurturing the formation of social capital. Despite this, we believe that governmental policies can and do affect the level of social capital.

That school choice can raise levels of social capital hints at at least one aspect of government policies that may be necessary. We believe that government action that supports the creation of effective communities may be the central ingredient to raising social capital. As we have shown, this is clearly true in the domain of schooling, but it is probably just as important in other policy domains as well. In this light, it is the link of choice to the creation and maintenance of such communities that is fundamentally important. In short, the careful design of governmental institutions may be able to reverse the ratchet that Fukuyama believes has only driven social capital down.

Chapter 12

Opting Out of Public Schools: Can Choice Affect the Relationship between Private and Public Schools?

In this book, we have explored the extent to which school choice affects the behavior of parents and schools, studying mostly the behavior of public schools and public school parents. In this chapter, we focus more directly on parents who have opted for the private sector. This change in focus is important, since enrolling a child in a private school is one of the most common forms of choice used by parents: more than 10 percent of American school-age children attend private schools and in many parts of the country, especially in cities in the Northeast, private school enrollment is often much higher.

By gathering data on private schools and including private school parents in our sample, we are better able to study the *entire* choice set available to parents in our research sites. Many scholars believe that private schools interact with public ones to define the local market for education. For example, Borland and Howsen (1992) and Couch, Shughart, and Williams (1993) found that greater competition from private schools was associated with higher public school performance in the southern states they studied. In a nationwide survey, Milliman and Maranto (1996) found that competition from Catholic schools improved public school teachers' perceptions of the performance of the public schools. In perhaps the most comprehensive research on this issue, Hoxby (1994a) found higher public school performance in metropolitan areas with greater private school competition. This evidence suggests that the interaction between these two sectors helps shape a market-like setting for schools. In this chapter, we explore two sets of fundamental questions in this interaction.

First, we explore how the introduction of public school choice has affected the behavior of private school parents (or parents who otherwise might have considered only private schools). Two separate issues here are critical: has public school choice reduced the likelihood that would-be private school parents actually leave the public school system in the first place? Has choice lured private school parents back to the public sector? The second set of questions relates to the extent to which public school choice has narrowed the gap between public and private schools and the parents whose children attend them. While we cannot fully address the first set of questions, we have somewhat more analytic purchase on the second.

Readers should by now have a firm understanding of the theoretical underpinnings for the positive effects of choice: choice exposes public schools to powerful market-like forces built on decentralization, competition, and consumer sovereignty. If public schools respond to these forces, differences between public and private schools should narrow.

These positive responses flow as choice reforms infuse schools with a sense of mission, alter the structure of governance to enhance the voice of both parents and teachers, and create an atmosphere in public schools similar to that found in many private schools. Our analysis of social capital in particular underscored the fact that public schools of choice have changed their culture and restructured their relationship with parents. While these changes may be valuable in and of themselves, in theory they should also produce better outcomes. Many scholars believe that the communal nature of private schools, especially Catholic ones, helps produce academic success (Bryk, Lee, and Holland 1993; Coleman, Hoffer, and Kilgore 1982; Haertel 1987; Hoffer, Greeley, and Coleman 1985), and to the extent that this environment is reproduced in the public sector, better schools should follow (see, for example, Ravitch and Viteritti 1997).

Some Preliminaries: Private School Parents Are Different

In any analysis of the relative performance of private and public schools, we must start with a fundamental fact: private schools tend to enroll more economically and socially advantaged students than do public schools. Given that private schools charge tuition and that a majority of them are religious, it is not surprising that private school students are disproportionately from higher-educated and more affluent families and that they are more likely to be either Catholic or Jewish (Lankford and Wycoff 1992; Gamoran 1996; Goldhaber 1996; Coleman, Hoffer, and Kilgore 1982; Plank et al. 1993). Parent attitudes also differ in fundamentally important ways. Parents who select private schools are more concerned with values, academic quality, and discipline than are other parents (see Hirschoff 1986; Martinez et al. 1995; Smith and Meier 1995).

Thus, students in private schools are better-off economically than public school children and their parents tend to be more concerned about education. Consequently, private schools, on average, spend less time disciplining students and benefit from having students who take their studies more seriously (Coleman, Hoffer, and Kilgore 1982; Haertel 1987).

In turn, difference in outcomes between public and private schools may result in part from who chooses to attend private schools. However, even after controlling for these selection effects, substantial debate remains about the extent to which outcomes between public and private, and especially Catholic, schools still differ. Early studies focusing on test scores found students in private schools did better (e.g., Coleman and Hoffer 1987), and that improvements in performance were higher among low-socioeconomic and minority students than for more advantaged students (Coleman, Hoffer, and Kilgore 1982). Similarly, Greeley (1982) found that the advantages of Catholic schools were strongest for blacks and Hispanics. Recently, however, both Gamoran (1996) and Goldhaber (1996) argue that once differences in the student body are adequately controlled, there are no significant differences in test scores between public and private schools. But, other studies examining graduation rates and college attendance find Catholic school students outperform public school students, ceteris paribus (Evans and Schwab 1995; Chase 1996; Neal 1997; Bryk, Lee, and Holland 1993; Levin 1998).

Obviously this debate will continue. However, we believe that the evidence clearly supports two facts: first, individual and collective student body characteristics play a role in determining school effectiveness; and second, high socioeconomic status is neither a *necessary* nor a *sufficient* condition for high student performance. Indeed, some private schools manage to outperform public schools despite having student bodies comprised primarily of children from low-income families and many schools perform badly despite an advantaged student population.

In short, schools matter. But private schools have advantages over traditional public schools because parents self-select into schools that promote the values, pedagogical approaches, or academic themes they find important. In addition, by their very structure, private schools operate in a much less hierarchical bureaucratic structure than public schools. Under these conditions, private schools can more easily function like communities, fostering higher levels of satisfaction and involvement among parents and higher levels of performance among students.

The Relationship between School Organization and Social Capital

As is frequently noted, private schools are characterized by an organizational structure built around community, while public schools are characterized by bureaucratic structures. These differences may affect levels of social capital. Bryk, Lee, and Holland (1993, 289–99) identify three core features: an extensive array of school activities that provide opportunities for face-to-face interactions and shared experiences among adults and students; a set of distinctive structural components (e.g., a wide scope of teachers' roles and smaller classes) that enable the community to function effectively; and a set of shared beliefs about what students should learn, the proper norms of instruction, and how people should relate to one another. They note the importance of choice in this process: "Trust accrues because school participants, both students and faculty, choose to be there. To be sure, voluntary association does not automatically create social capital, but it is harder to develop such capital in its absence" (314).

In figure 12.1, we build on the results of chapter 11, reporting levels of social capital for all public and private school parents in our sample, using

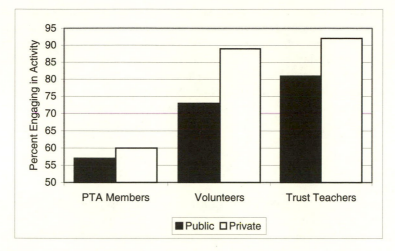

Figure 12.1   Levels of Social Capital across Public and Private School Parents

three of the four dimensions of social capital we studied in the last chapter. Social capital is clearly higher among private school parents. The differences between public and private parents are most striking for the percent of parents who have volunteered (73 percent versus 89 percent) and who trust their children's teachers (81 percent versus 92 percent), while differences in participating in the PTA are marginal (57 percent versus 60 percent). On our fourth measure of social capital, "sociability," private school parents again score higher: on average they spoke to more than 7 other parents from their child's school, compared to only 5.5 for public school parents. Later in this chapter, we attempt to untangle socioeconomic and institutional effects on these differences. First however, we turn to another important dimension of school outcomes—parent satisfaction with schools—and consider differences between public and private school parents

Private Schools and Satisfaction

Several studies have established the link between the act of choosing and resulting satisfaction (McArthur, Colopy, and Schlaine 1995; Friedman 1955; Coons and Sugarman 1978; Raywid 1989; Levin 1991). In chapter 8, we examined the relationship between satisfaction and allocative efficiency, linking satisfaction to the extent to which parents actually get what they want from their schools. We found that public school choice was related to gains in allocative efficiency, which in turn contributed to higher levels of parental satisfaction. We believe that parental satisfaction in private schools is linked not only to the act of choice but is reinforced by the community-based nature of many of these schools. The nongovernmental status and nonbureaucratic organization of private schooling enables parents to realize the approaches to learning they value even more than public school choosers can. In turn, when schools are more tightly linked to parents, families, and students, the quality of the educational experience increases and teachers, parents, and students should be more satisfied.

We examine the aggregate differences between public and private school parents for three measures of satisfaction. Two of these measures were introduced in chapter 8: whether parents had thought about moving their children to a different school (*Change Schools*) and rated their child's school as the best in the district (*Best School*). Here we also include a measure of whether or not a parent believes her child is receiving an excellent education in her school.

Figure 12.2 demonstrates that substantially more private school parents thought their children were receiving excellent educations than did public school parents in our sample (77 percent versus 48 percent). And the difference between public and private school parents for the *Best School* measure, while smaller, is still substantial (11 percentage points). Finally, there are smaller differences in who had considered sending their children to different schools: 14 percent of public school parents had thought about changing schools while only 9 percent of private school parents had.

Taken together, these comparisons point to a consistent pattern: private school parents are more satisfied with their children's schools than are public school parents.

Although these differences have been established in previous research, we

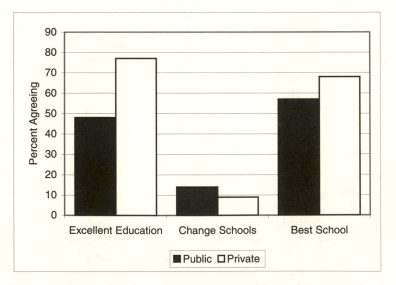

Figure 12.2 Levels of Satisfaction across Public and Private School Parents

present these comparisons to provide the reader with both a preliminary description of our private school parents and a baseline with which to compare differences between parents from the two school sectors. We return to these issues later in the chapter. First however, we address the question of whether public school choice has affected the behavior of private school parents.

The Effects of Public School Choice on the Incentives and Behavior of Private School Parents

We have only limited means by which to address directly the question of how public school choice might affect the behavior of private school parents. In part, these limits stem from the lack of geographically defined catchment zones for private schools. Because many students attend private schools located outside their home districts, to assess whether private school parents return to public sector schools as a result of the introduction of public school choice, we cannot simply compare enrollments in public and private schools within a district.

The best way to analyze whether private school parents are returning to public schools as a result of school choice would be to administer annual surveys to parents residing in a district, asking them about their schooling preferences and decisions. Such surveys could help assess the level of competition between public and private schools by asking whether private school parents were really considering public school choice options.

Unfortunately, our study did not survey our sample of parents over time. Instead, we compiled information from parents at one point in time and supplemented these data with school- and district-level data over a longer period. We therefore cannot directly assess the extent to which public school choice has affected the behavior of private school parents.

However, given our quasi-experimental research design, we can compare public and private school parents across the two sets of matched pairs of school districts.[1] Since the matched pairs share similar demographic characteristics, we expect that, ceteris paribus, roughly the same percentage of parents in each district would elect private schools for their children. If, however, public school choice makes public schools more attractive, the percentage of private school parents should be lower in District 4 and Montclair relative to District 1 and Morristown, respectively.

Table 12.1 shows that private school enrollments are indeed lower in the two districts with developed public school choice programs: nearly twice as many parents in District 1 elect private schools as in District 4, while approximately 25 percent more parents choose private schools in Morristown than Montclair. Clearly, the pattern in table 12.1 is in the predicted direction. However, we lack data on why private school parents chose the schools they did, whether they considered public schools when making their decision,

Table 12.1
Enrollments in Private Schools Are Higher in Nonchoice Districts: Percent of
Parents Enrolled in Private Schools

	Choice	Nonchoice
Central City	9%	15%
Suburbs	19%	26%

Source: School District Data Book Profiles, 1989–90.

and whether public school choice truly influenced would-be private school
parents in District 4 and Montclair to elect public schools over private alternatives. Without these data, the pattern evident in table 12.1 is suggestive,
but far from conclusive.

On the other hand, we can supplement enrollment data with information
from our survey—specifically we asked private school parents if they
thought about moving their children to other schools. Although we did not
ask a follow-up question about why parents considered changing schools or
if public schools were on their list of possible alternatives, this question can
be used as an indicator of the degree to which parents are thinking about
other schooling options.

If public school choice does affect the set of options in parents' choice sets,
we should find that more private school parents in District 4 and Montclair
thought about changing schools than their counterparts in District 1 and
Morristown.

Table 12.2 clearly shows this pattern. While twice as many private school
parents in District 4 considered other schooling options than parents in District 1, private school parents in Montclair were about five times more likely
to have thought about changing schools than parents in Morristown.

Has Public School Choice Narrowed the Gap between Public and Private Spheres of Education?

We know from existing research and our own data that private school parents differ from public school parents along important dimensions. Here we

Table 12.2
Parents in Private Schools Are More Likely to Think about Changing Schools
in Choice Districts

	Choice	Nonchoice
Central City	18%	9%
Suburbs	10%	2%

consider whether the magnitude of these differences is smaller in districts that have instituted public school choice.

We first examine levels of social capital in public and private schools. We then revisit the question of satisfaction, investigating the extent to which public school choice has reduced differences between public and private school parents. Finally, we take a last look at the issue of performance, limiting our analysis to the two New York districts, since data on private schools in New Jersey are unavailable.[2]

We begin with bivariate comparisons of parents across the different types of schools in each district and then use multivariate analyses to sort out more complex patterns. The comparisons reflect differences in the institutional arrangements of choice across our research sites. In Montclair, every parent in our sample is a chooser—thus, we are comparing public school choosers to private school choosers. Similarly, in Morristown we are comparing public nonchoosers to private school choosers. The comparison in New York is more complex since we are comparing private school parents to public school parents, some of whom are choosers and some of whom are nonchoosers. Moreover, public school parents in District 4 face two different systems of choice—option-demand at the elementary school level and universal choice in the middle schools, while District 1 has only a small option-demand program.[3]

Has Choice Reduced the Gap in Social Capital?

In examining the gap between private and public school parents in levels of social capital, we begin with the patterns found in New Jersey. Figure 12.3 reports percentages of parents volunteering, participating in the PTA, and trusting teachers, while figure 12.4 reports means for the sociability variable.

On two variables—trust and sociability—the difference between private and public school parents is smaller in Montclair than in Morristown, and for volunteering the size of the gap is virtually the same. Only for PTA participation is the gap larger in Montclair. However, note that the absolute level of participation in Morristown is substantially lower than it is in Montclair. In fact, public school parents in Montclair participate in the PTA at higher rates than either public or private school parents in Morristown. These bivariate relations present only limited evidence that choice has reduced the gap in social capital in New Jersey.

Turning to patterns in the New York districts, figures 12.5 and 12.6 present the distribution of social capital for parents in District 4. Overall, the evidence does not show a large or consistent gap in favor of private school parents in District 4. Private school parents volunteer at higher rates than any type of public school parent, and have higher levels of sociability, but public school choosers are nearly identical when it comes to levels of trust. Moreover, public choosers are more likely to be members of the PTA than

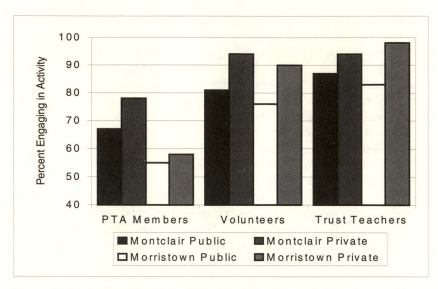

Figure 12.3   Levels of Social Capital across School Types in New Jersey

are their private school counterparts. As we would expect, parents with children in neighborhood schools are lowest in social capital.

As figures 12.5 and 12.6 indicate, levels of social capital among universal choosers generally fall somewhere between those of option-demand choosers and neighborhood school parents. Because the demographics of these parents reflect those of the district overall, the evidence suggests there are indeed effects of choice (rather than selection).

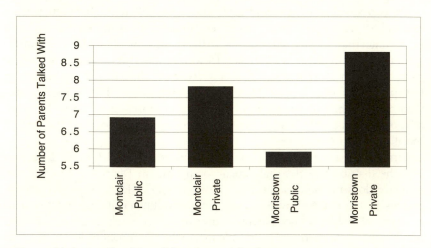

Figure 12.4   Levels of Sociability across School Types in New Jersey Districts

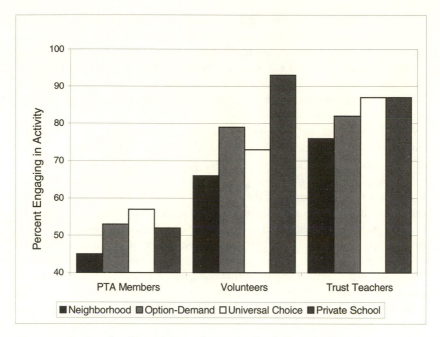

Figure 12.5   Levels of Social Capital across School Types in District 4

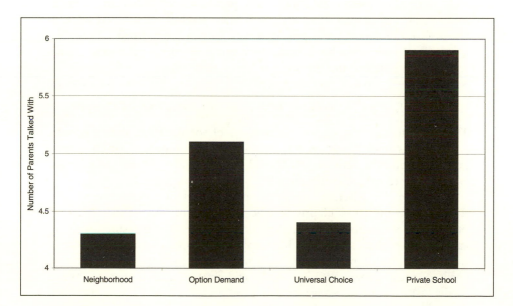

Figure 12.6   Levels of Sociability across School Types in District 4

Turning to District 1 (figures 12.7 and 12.8), a larger percentage of option-demand choosers participate in the PTA, volunteer, and trust teachers than either private school parents or public nonchoosers. They also talk to more parents in their children's schools. In short, in District 1 as in District 4, public school choosers are higher in social capital than nonchoosers. But, in District 1, these parents are also higher in social capital than private school parents.

Why is District 1 so different? While we recognize that we cannot definitively answer this question, we believe the pattern in District 1 is a product of its relatively new and limited choice program. Public schools of choice present the means for concerned parents to identify other parents with similar inclinations and coordinate their behaviors. Under choice, the more concerned and involved District 1 parents have seized these opportunities. The fact that existing alternative schools in District 1 remain unusually small in size and rely rather heavily on parents and staff may also encourage choice parents to form even closer-knit communities than those found in District 4.

The next question is obvious: is this outcome in District 1 better or worse than what would be obtained in the absence of choice? Or, to use the terms from chapter 10, is there evidence of skimming? Clearly, we cannot assume that these parents would exhibit the same levels of social capital had they remained in public schools—indeed our analysis in chapter 11 suggests just the opposite. And perhaps more importantly, we cannot assume that these parents would have remained in public schools absent choice.

At minimum, these data suggest that public school choice can benefit some number of parents by creating a distinctive set of schools and helping them solve the coordination problems they face in large urban school districts. Choice may thereby increase the number of parents choosing public schools—an outcome that we argue is highly desirable.

Has Choice Really Contributed to Differences in Levels of Social Capital?

The discussion of how choice affects levels of social capital among private and public school parents raises the issue of selection bias. Given demographic differences between public and private school parents, should we expect them to exhibit comparable levels of social capital?

We control for selection effects by running a set of multivariate models that measure the effect of private school enrollment (net of the effects of private school parents' demographics) on each of the four measures of social capital. Rather than comparing differences across types of public schools, in these models we simply test whether or not there is a significant difference in levels of social capital between public and private schools parents. These models parallel the two-stage models presented in chapter 11, except that they address the selection effects among private school choosers rather than public school choosers.

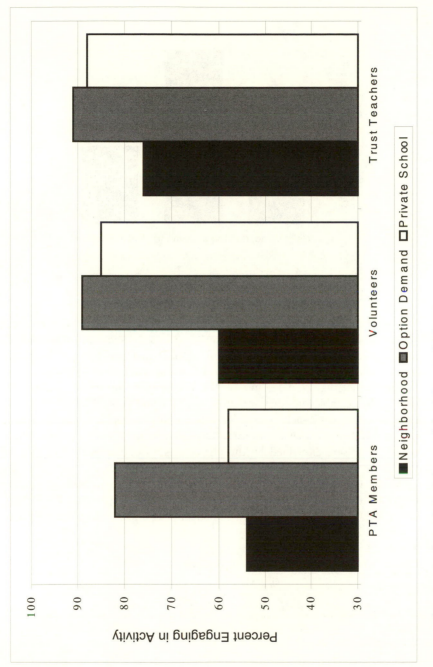

Figure 12.7 Levels of Social Capital across School Types in District 1

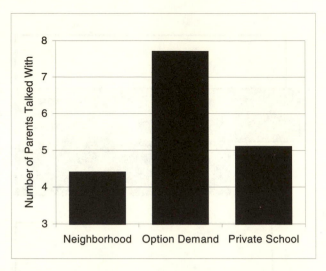

Figure 12.8   Levels of Sociability across School Types in
District 1

If public school choice has narrowed the gap in levels of social capital
across public and private spheres, ceteris paribus we should find nonsignificant coefficients for the private school variable in District 4 and Montclair
and significant coefficients in Morristown and District 1.

The coefficients presented in table 12.3 correspond to the effect of private
school choice, holding other variables constant and controlling for selection
effects.[4] The general lack of significant effects for the private school variable
in this multivariate analysis indicate that many of the differences in levels of
social capital are explained by the characteristics of parents rather than of
schools.

We do not, however, find that choice has reduced the gap between parents
in public and private sectors, ceteris paribus. Although private school attendance does have independent and statistically significant effects for measures

Table 12.3
Effects of Private School Sector Social Capital

| | New York | | New Jersey | |
	District 1	District 4	Morristown	Montclair
PTA	NS	NS	NS	NS
Volunteer	.14**	.12*	.06*	.09**
Trust	NS	NS	.076**	.074*
Sociability	NS	2.59**	NS	NS

Note: denotes nonsignificant difference between public and private school parents.

*p < .05

**p < .01

of social capital, contrary to expectation, these effects are present in both choice and nonchoice districts. And, when comparing across the matched districts, the magnitude of these effects is nearly identical. In short, after controlling for selection, social capital still tends to be higher among private school parents and there is no consistent evidence that public school choice has narrowed that gap.

Has Choice Narrowed the Gap in Satisfaction between Private and Public School Parents?

Turning to parent satisfaction, we employ an approach that again combines bivariate and multivariate methods of analysis. We begin by comparing the percentage of public and private school parents in New Jersey who thought their children were receiving an excellent education at their schools and who thought their children's schools were the best in the district. As evident in figure 12.9, the difference in satisfaction levels between private and public school parents is smaller for both measures in Montclair than in Morristown—confirming our hypothesis.

Satisfaction levels for private and public school parents in New York reveal a similar pattern. In District 4, satisfaction levels among option-demand choosers are nearly equal to private school parents for the *Excellent Education* variable and actually higher than private school parents for the *Best School* variable. Universal choosers also record higher levels of satisfaction than do private school parents on this measure. Overall, there are marginal differences in satisfaction levels across the different types of schools for the *Best*

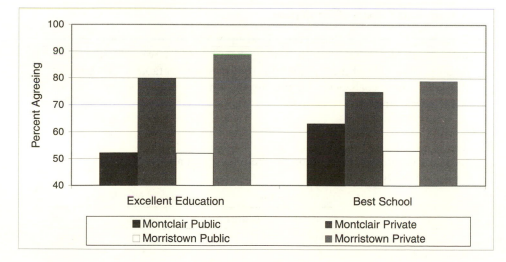

Figure 12.9 Levels of Satisfaction across School Types for Montclair and Morristown

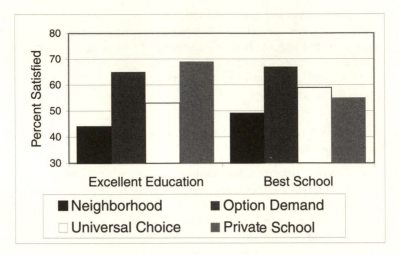

Figure 12.10   Levels of Satisfaction across School Types in District 4

School variable. On the other hand, option-demand and private school choosers are more likely to think their children are receiving an *Excellent Education* than are nonchoosers and universal choosers.

In District 1, private school choosers are clearly more likely to believe that their children are receiving an excellent education, but the gap in satisfaction levels for the *Best School* variable is virtually nonexistent.

A Multivariate Model of Satisfaction

To investigate whether these effects hold up while controlling for other factors, we employ a multivariate probit analysis. While we leave the more detailed discussion of these models for the appendix, in table 12.4 we report the transformed coefficients for the private school variables for each of the models we estimated.

Table 12.4
Impact of Private School Sector on the Probability That a Parent Is Satisfied with His Child's School

	New York		New Jersey	
	District 1	*District 4*	*Morristown*	*Montclair*
Excellent Education	.23**	.13*	.42**	.34**
Best School	NS	NS	.31**	NS

Note: Table entries correspond to the change in the probability of *Y* associated with the difference between being a public and private school parent.

*$p < .05$

**$p < .01$

Similar to the multivariate *Social Capital* models, once again we expect the magnitude of these effects (in absolute terms) to be greater for District 1 and Morristown than for District 4 and Montclair, respectively. A nonsignificant coefficient (represented by *NS*) indicates that there is no difference in levels of satisfaction between public and private school parents.

As an example of how to read this table, consider the coefficients reported for Morristown and Montclair for the *Best School* variable. These coefficients correspond to the change in probability that a private school parent believes her child's school is best, compared to a public school parent in the same district, with other conditions held constant. In Morristown, a private school parent is over 30 percentage points more likely to think her child's school is best compared to a public school parent. However, in Montclair, there are no differences between public and private school parents—that is, on this dimension, both public and private school parents are equally satisfied with their schools.

In general, these results conform relatively closely to the bivariate relationships. Significant differences remain across private and public school parents with respect to the percentage who believe their children are receiving an excellent education. But, most importantly, the magnitude of the effect of private schools is smaller in the two choice districts (District 4 and Montclair) relative to their matched pairs (District 1 and Morristown). This evidence suggests that public school choice has reduced the gap in satisfaction between public and private school parents.

Has Choice Reduced Performance Differentials between Private and Public Schools?

The final issue we consider in this chapter concerns school performance. Here we ask what many would consider as the fundamental question: has choice affected the performance gap between private and public schools?

Chapters 9 and 10 suggest that choice in District 4 not only improved the performance of the students in alternative schools, but also had spillover effects on neighborhood schools. In this section, we compare the performance of District 4's public schools to all private schools within District 4's boundaries.[5] Once again, we distinguish between option-demand choosers in comparing elementary schools. We then conduct a similar analysis for District 1. We cannot replicate this analysis in New Jersey, since private schools do not report performance data to the state and our efforts to gather these data from the schools ourselves were met mostly with refusals and nonresponses.[6]

The question is whether the introduction of public school choice has narrowed any gap in performance between public and private schools. Thus, if choice works, we should find smaller differences between public and private schools in District 4 than in District 1. Our analysis is based on the data presented in table 12.5.

Table 12.5
Performance in Private, Alternative Public, and Neighborhood Schools (Percent Meeting N.Y. State Minimum Standards)

	Elementary Schools		Junior High Schools	
	District 4	District 1	District 4	District 1
Private	69	60	82	83
Alternative	61	52	76	—
Neighborhood	55	57	—	73

Note: The scores are averaged for the years 1994–96. Recall that all of the District 4 junior high schools are choice schools, while none are in District 1.

While this evidence is limited, the results show that in both districts, a considerable gap remains between public and private school performance. As we do not have adequate demographic data on private school students, we can not determine if this gap is driven mainly by the socioeconomic status of students or by the schools themselves. The performance gap is somewhat smaller for District 4's junior high schools than for District 1's, but the effects are inconsistent at the elementary school level. In District 4, alternative elementary schools actually perform at a similar level to the private elementary schools in District 1. In addition, as we showed in chapter 10, neighborhood schools in District 1 perform better than the small number of alternative schools in that district.

Conclusion

The focal question of this chapter concerns the extent to which public school choice has narrowed the gap between public and private spheres of education. Our most consistent finding is that this gap has *not* disappeared. On nearly every measure that we consider, private school parents remain advantaged relative to public school parents. Similarly, the performance gap between private schools and public schools remains.

The differences between public and private schools and the parents and students associated with the two types of schools, have been well documented in other studies, so they are not a huge surprise. And, some of the reasons for this gap are well known. First, private schools attract more advantaged students whose parents have higher educational expectations. Second, since private schools remain outside the authority of public bureaucracies governing public schools, they have more control over the organization, operation, and mission of their schools. In addition, the sectarian basis of many private schools gives them an advantage that stems from the religious beliefs and values that are shared among the community of private school students, parents, and staff.

The results of such institutionalized advantages are evident in the characteristics of public and private school parents in our four research sites. In particular, in chapter 4 we identified differences in the attributes of schools parents find important—most notably the significant proportion of private school parents identifying the values of their children's schools as one of the most important school attributes. Because these preferences are better realized in private schools, private schools are advantaged in terms of allocative efficiency

These differences in preferences and the demographic profile of private school parents lead us to expect the gap between public and private schools to remain. Moreover, we should expect at best modest effects from public school choice.

Our examination of levels of social capital, satisfaction, and performance suggests that public school choice has positively affected parents and schools. Although many of these effects are clearly on the margin and not always consistent, we do find stronger evidence supporting the claim that choice has narrowed the public/private gap with respect to levels of parental satisfaction. On this dimension we find that public school choosers exhibit levels of satisfaction nearly on par with their private school counterparts. Thus, it seems that public school choice has succeeded in replicating some conditions typically found in private schools. When it comes to perceptions of their schools, regardless of sector, parents who choose appear to be more satisfied.

Although we believe the link between choice and satisfaction is important, we emphasize that the strong effects of socioeconomic status, peers, and other organizational factors that work in favor of private schools cannot be overcome by any single reform, including public school choice. Nonetheless, our data suggest that public school choice provides incentives for parents to stay in, or perhaps even return to, the public schools.

However, are all forms of choice equally likely to produce these benefits?

We believe that the answer is clearly no. In this chapter, and indeed throughout the book, we have often found stronger effects for the option-demand system of choice than for universal choice arrangements. In the next and final chapter, we examine the effects of the institutional design of choice more carefully and explain why option-demand systems may be the most effective form of public school choice.

Appendix

The models estimated in tables 12A.1 and 12A.2 are similar to those in chapter 11; however, here we control for selection bias in parents' choice of private schools. For the *PTA*, *Volunteer*, and *Trust* variables, we estimate linear probability models and use Goldberger's method to correct for heteroskedasticity. This correction is not necessary for the *Sociability* model since this variable is continuous.

The two-stage estimation procedure corrects for the nonrandom assignment of parents in public and private schools. This procedure is necessary since the same factors that lead parents to choose private schools also predict levels of social capital. For a lengthier discussion of the issue of selection bias, see chapter 3.

We use maximum likelihood probit to estimate the models in tables 12A.3 and 12A.4. Unlike the social capital models, we do not need to estimate a two-stage selection bias model in order to measure the effects of private schools on levels of parent satisfaction. We discuss the rationale for this in more detail in chapter 3. At issue is whether or not levels of satisfaction are nonrandomly distributed across parents prior to the act of choice or as a result of the kinds of schools parents end up in after they have chosen. In other words, are levels of satisfaction among private school parents likely to be higher because of some innate characteristic of these parents or are levels of satisfaction likely to be the result of characteristics of private schools? We believe satisfaction fundamentally flows from characteristics of schools. Thus, we do not employ the two-stage selection bias models to study these effects.

Table 12A.1
Effects of Private Schools on the Formation of Social Capital: New York

	PTA		Volunteer		Trust		Sociability	
	Dist 4	Dist 1	Dist 4	Dist 1	Dist 4	Dist 1	Dist 4	Dist 1
Private School	−.011 (.067)	−.013 (.062)	.122** (.045)	.143** (.055)	.035 (.041)	−.006 (.028)	2.59** (.946)	−1.382 (1.444)
Black	.014 (.101)	−.109 (.098)	.021 (.048)	−.066 (.089)	.005 (.054)	−.075 (.071)	−1.057 (1.286)	−4.013** (1.312)
Hispanic	−.247* (.096)	−.077 (.070)	−.020 (.050)	−.065 (.062)	−.026 (.042)	.010 (.028)	−.526 (1.190)	−2.852* (1.312)
Asian	−.100 (.195)	−.117 (.125)	.035 (.074)	−.052 (.115)	.079 (.080)	−.370** (.058)	−2.054 (1.825)	−2.977* (1.309)
Length of Residence	−.001 (.003)	.001 (.004)	.001 (.002)	.006* (.003)	−.001 (.002)	.003 (.002)	.019 (.032)	.047 (.042)
Female	.188** (.044)	.215** (.067)	.083 (.059)	.107 (.065)	−.049 (.035)	.040 (.026)	2.19** (.832)	.403 (.711)
Education	.024** (.006)	.009 (.007)	.029** (.007)	.015** (.007)	.004 (.006)	.006 (.004)	.085 (.821)	.171* (.711)
Employed	−.133 (.042)	.016 (.056)	.046 (.041)	.010 (.052)	−.048 (.036)	.022 (.031)	−.296 (.539)	.613 (.643)
Church Attend	.054** (.008)	.038** (.011)	.022** (.009)	.021* (.010)	.007 (.007)	.001 (.005)	.330** (.108)	.334** (.119)
Dissatisfaction	−.007 (.039)	−.035 (.052)	−.055 (.041)	.033 (.046)	−.245** (.047)	−.200** (.041)	.422 (.489)	−.066 (.519)
Constant	.036 (.129)	.195 (.138)	.186 (.123)	.249 (.133)	.880 (.103)	.722 (.068)	−.526 (1.836)	3.577 (1.702)
N	387	386	387	386	386	382	381	376
F(11, 375)	39**	54**	234**	117**	218**	271**	5.66	3.69**

Note: Table entries are estimates from the two-stage selection bias model. Corrected standard errors are in parentheses. Note, *p ≤ .05, **p ≤ .01, two-tailed test.

Table 12A.2
Effects of Private Schools on the Formation of Social Capital: New Jersey

	PTA		Volunteer		Trust		Sociability	
	Mont	Morris	Mont	Morris	Mont	Morris	Mont	Morris
Private School	.081 (.067)	−.034 (.048)	.091** (.031)	.056* (.033)	.074 (.033)	.076* (.026)	.683 (1.780)	.404 (.620)
Black	−.188** (.054)	−.323** (.075)	−.081* (.041)	−.133* (.071)	−.070 (.036)	−.081 (.066)	−2.84** (.615)	−4.24** (.818)
Hispanic	−.283* (.136)	−.543** (.059)	.019 (.079)	−.385** (.100)	.033 (.048)	−.019 (.040)	−.230 (.961)	−2.72** (1.300)
Asian	−.203 (.211)	−.431** (.077)	−.226 (.192)	−.041 (.091)	.063 (.051)	−.008 (.069)	−3.230 (1.983)	−3.81** (1.036)
Length of Residence	.002 (.003)	−.003 (.003)	.006** (.002)	.000 (.002)	−.001 (.002)	.001 (.002)	.063 (.037)	.068 (.037)
Female	.138* (.058)	.084 (.048)	.094** (.035)	.246** (.051)	.035 (.034)	−.016 (.030)	1.462* (.594)	.995 (.556)
Education	.024* (.011)	.009 (.005)	.014 (.010)	.020** (.009)	−.005 (.003)	.005 (.007)	.317** (.113)	.360** (.092)
Employed	.042 (.057)	−.059 (.053)	−.003 (.035)	−.023 (.028)	.054 (.025)	−.031 (.027)	−.952 (.675)	−.639 (.541)
Church Attend	.023* (.010)	.004 (.010)	−.002 (.007)	.010 (.009)	−.001 (.005)	−.006 (.006)	.036 (.117)	.249* (.111)
Dissatisfaction	−.024 (.047)	−.027 (.048)	.015 (.031)	−.032 (.045)	−.153** (.043)	−.120* (.051)	.216 (.532)	.624 (.556)
Constant	.136 (.200)	.546 (.110)	.515 (.167)	.338 (.151)	.960 (.074)	.861 (.129)	1.541 (2.252)	−.236 (1.839)
N	401	392	401	392	396	480	400	390
$F_{(11, 375)}$	107**	59.5**	472**	680**	475**	6.8**	6.8**	10.2**

Note: Table entries are estimates from the two-stage selection bias model. Corrected standard errors are in parentheses. Note, *p ≤ .05, **p ≤ .01, two-tailed test.

Table 12A.3
Effects of Private Schools on Levels of Satisfaction: New York

	Excellent Education		Change Schools		Best School	
	Dist 4	Dist 1	Dist 4	Dist 1	Dist 4	Dist 1
Private School	.136*	.232**	.020	−.127**	−.085	−.028
Parent	(.079)	(.067)	(.056)	(.051)	(.077)	(.064)
Black	−.113	.002	.298**	.169**	−.189*	−.116
	(.110)	(.104)	(.134)	(.095)	(.108)	(.101)
Hispanic	−.097	−.101	.171**	.040	−.107	−.064
	(.106)	(.074)	(.077)	(.050)	(.104)	(.070)
Asian	−.051	−.124	.141	−.087	−.045	−.142
	(.212)	(.130)	(.237)	(.075)	(.201)	(.133)
Length of Resi-	.005	.007*	−.003	.000	.010**	.004
dence	(.004)	(.004)	(.003)	(.003)	(.003)	(.004)
Married	−.044	.077	−.087**	−.060	.054	.112**
	(.055)	(.054)	(.040)	(.040)	(.054)	(.052)
Education	.003	.008	.017**	.015**	−.003	−.002
	(.010)	(.008)	(.008)	(.006)	(.009)	(.007)
Employed	.120**	−.051	−.021	.006	.092	.003
	(.057)	(.060)	(.042)	(.042)	(.057)	(.056)
Involvement	.314**	.144	.003	.034	.258**	.051
	(.106)	(.099)	(.077)	(.070)	(.105)	(.096)
N	393	387	393	387	393	387
Pseudo R^2	.06	.07	.05	.07	.04	.02
χ^2	32.55**	38.65**	19.88*	23.07**	23.83	8.36

Note: Coefficients are the change in the probability that a parent responds favorably to each measure of satisfaction, as a function of a unit change in the independent variable. Note, * $p \leq .05$, ** $p \leq .01$, two-tailed test.

Table 12A.4
Effects of Private Schools on Levels of Satisfaction: New Jersey

	Excellent Education		Change Schools		Best School	
	Mont	Morris	Mont	Morris	Mont	Morris
Private School	.344**	.422**	−.031	−.078**	.091	.314**
	(.088)	(.066)	(.053)	(.030)	(.079)	(.061)
Black	.056	.041	.026	−.050*	.048	.289**
	(.062)	(.082)	(.042)	(.017)	(.058)	(.059)
Hispanic	.148	.089	−.040	−.040	.246**	.043
	(.133)	(.102)	(.081)	(.021)	(.086)	(.109)
Asian	.297	−.046	—	−.026	.247	.139
	(.147)	(.110)		(.030)	(.111)	(.097)
Length of Resi-dence	.001	.004	.000	.000	.013**	.007*
	(.004)	(.004)	(.002)	(.002)	(.004)	(.004)
Married	.029	.134*	−.021	.000	.083	.040
	(.069)	(.076)	(.046)	(.032)	(.067)	(.077)
Education	−.046**	.017	.006	−.005	−.013	.009
	(.014)	(.011)	(.009)	(.004)	(.012)	(.011)
Employed	.011	.009	.021	−.024	.007	−.068
	(.067)	(.059)	(.045)	(.028)	(.063)	(.057)
Involvement	.144	−.002	.061	−.023	.061	−.024
	(.100)	(.102)	(.067)	(.043)	(.095)	(.103)
N	403	394	397	394	403	394
Pseudo R²	.06	.11	.009	.07	.04	.09
χ²	34.43**	59.17**	2.68	13.77	23.45**	45.7**

Note: Coefficients are the change in the probability that a parent responds favorably to each measure of satisfaction, as a function of a unit change in the independent variable. Note, * p ≤ .05, ** p ≤ .01, two-tailed test.

Chapter 13

Myths and Markets: Choice Is No Panacea, But It Does Work

We began this project with a set of what now seem simple expectations, each of which we held with great certainty. We also began with confidence that we would find evidence to support these beliefs. However, after spending years gathering and analyzing data about school choice, we were, as the saying goes, "mugged by reality."

As we immersed ourselves in the world of public school choice and developed more and more information about parents, schools, choice, school officials and the challenges they faced, we began to revise our expectations. In the process, we developed what we hope is a more complex and nuanced understanding of the effects of choice. As we conclude this book, we now try to put some of our most important findings into perspective.

Richard Hofstadter once observed that Americans love to tinker with their local governments, continually seeking to change institutional arrangements in order to improve governmental performance and find a form of government capable of delivering services in an efficient, accountable, and responsive manner. Because no single institutional arrangement can simultaneously satisfy all these demands, reform movements are a perennial feature of local government (see, e.g., Knott and Miller 1987; Kaufman 1969; Ruhil et al. 1999). But this does not mean that the constant reforms that have marked the history of local governments have been for naught. Joseph Schumpeter observed that "creative destruction" is central to the operation of markets—that new ideas can sweep through and destroy existing markets, creating new institutional arrangements that are more productive, more efficient, and more appropriate for changing circumstances. These kinds of radical changes have been found in politics and public policy as well (Baumgartner and Jones 1993; Schneider and Teske 1995).

Given that public education is the most expensive and arguably the most important public good local governments deliver, it is not surprising that throughout this century, school reform has consistently been on the political and policy agenda of governments throughout the United States. Other factors also make schools ripe for reform. For example, despite reams of studies, there is really no known technology that will unquestionably produce high-quality education at a low cost. Moreover, people have legitimately different preferences for different aspects of education and these preferences can change. And given the profound demographic, political, and technological changes taking places in the country at large, it is not surprising that education reform is an enduring part of today's landscape. Indeed, given the rapid expansion of both the theory and the practice of choice, we can even think of schools in the United States as being ripe for "creative destruction" through profound structural and institutional change.

Many of today's reforms seek to empower parents as a means of reducing the monopoly presently held by school bureaucracies. Critics argue that this power has been used to isolate the schools, teachers, and educational administrators from the legitimate demands of the communities supposedly served by the schools. By empowering parents, current reforms seek to increase the accountability of teachers and administrators, thereby improving the performance of schools. In the language we have used throughout this book, choice reforms seek to increase allocative efficiency—allowing parents to better match their children with schools that do what the parents think is best for their children—and productive efficiency—making schools improve the quality of their "product."

To achieve these improvements, many reforms now endorse a market-based approach to schooling. In its archetype, this institutional arrangement provides a limited role for educational officials. School-level actors are given almost total control over the subject matter they teach, how it is taught, who teaches it, and which students are taught. Thus, an education system built around market principles would emphasize decentralization, competition, and consumer sovereignty through choice (Chubb and Moe 1990).

Among today's reforms, vouchers most closely approximate this market approach to education. Chubb and Moe see vouchers as the means of freeing schools from the overly restrictive environment of the stifling bureaucratic structure typical of today's school systems and as a way of creating a publicly funded system of schools that is "almost entirely beyond the reach of public authority" (1990, 216). As they argue, the voucher system would be driven by the intelligence and diligence of parents: "schools are held accountable from below, by parents and students who directly experience their services and are free to choose. The state plays a crucial supporting role here in monitoring the full and honest disclosure of information by the schools— but it is only a supporting role" (216). According to this argument, schools would respond to the needs and interests of students and parents, not central administrators who now control purse strings and rules/regulations. Clearly, other forms of school choice, including the systems we studied, are "less pure" realizations of a market-like model.

But, even in their pure form, neither the bureaucratic model nor even the market model of education we discussed in chapter 1 sufficiently recognizes the critical role parents and communities can and should play in the schooling process. Most importantly, in neither model does parent or community involvement necessarily play a direct role in the learning environment actually created in schools. But the preponderance of evidence suggests that good education is dependent on coproductive links between schools, parents, students, and the larger community.

Thus, we examined a model of education based on the idea that schools are intimately linked to the communities they serve and in which the schools themselves are communities in which stakeholders in the educational process take an active role. In this view, effective schools, high stocks of social capital, and viable communities are linked together in a reinforcing "virtuous circle." Of the many items on the current school reform palette, charter schools seem to be closest to the explicit endorsement of this community-based model. However, the intradistrict choice programs we studied in Montclair and District 4 were built around the idea of increasing parental choice *and* increasing parental involvement in the production of education. Indeed, many of the schools in District 4 resemble charter schools.

We believe that as reform movements continue to transform our schools and to emphasize the role of parents as both consumers and coproducers of quality education, these issues are increasingly central. Our research has focused primarily on the effects of these reforms. We explored in detail several critical issues, including parental values about different aspects of education, the sources of information parents use and the information they possess, the process that matches parental values to appropriate schools, and the incentives parents have to become more involved in their children's education. The empirical work we presented in this book sheds light on the effects of expanded choice.

The two choice districts in our study, District 4 in New York and Montclair, New Jersey, have long histories of choice. While the current school reform movement continues to gain momentum, we know that any large-scale transformation as fundamental as school choice may require years to affect the targeted population. This is one problem with the very promising studies of "controlled" voucher systems and emerging studies of charter schools. Our study allows us to view the effects of fully developed school choice systems.

On the other hand, we recognize that both of the choice districts have implemented choice programs that are limited to public schools within the district. Thus, these programs do not resemble voucher programs, which allow parents with vouchers to attend schools (that increasingly include both sectarian and nonsectarian private schools) throughout a large geographic area.

Moreover, while District 4 did create many mini-schools that emphasize thematic approaches to education, and while both Montclair and District 4 have engaged in extensive outreach efforts to increase parental involvement in the schools, neither of these districts have charter schools. Nonetheless, we believe that many of our findings tell us a great deal about how a broad range of school choice reforms beyond intradistrict choice, including vouchers and charter schools, will affect parental behavior. Thus, in the next section, we highlight some of the most important findings presented in the

book. From there, we develop some more general implications of our findings from the study of school choice.

What Have We Learned?

Throughout this book, we have argued that segregation and stratification are
perennial issues in the study of choice. One of the foundations for this argument is the belief that parents of different racial and socioeconomic status
value different aspects of education. In particular, it is commonly assumed
that low socioeconomic status and minority parents will select schools that
do not emphasize academic performance. Our evidence is to the contrary.
For example, we showed that minority parents and parents who have graduated from high school but have not attended college are significantly *more*
likely to be concerned about strong academic performance in the schools.
We believe that the reason for this is quite simple: test scores act as gatekeepers to success in higher education and the labor market. While higher
status parents know this, their children have more options and alternatives
when considering the future. In addition, higher status parents have a wider
range of expectations from their schools, many of which already function
well academically. Because these parents can take the academic performance
of their schools as a relative "given," they can ask their schools to emphasize
other aspects of education—for example, humanistic approaches to learning.

Given these patterns, we argued that school choice may indeed lead to
differences along class and racial lines in the selection of schools; however,
we argued that the mechanism driving such differentiation is not likely the
one that critics of school choice have decried. Differentiation linked to school
choice may not be so much the product of skimming that results because
parents of higher socioeconomic status strategically identify and then place
their children in the best schools while racial minorities or students of lower
socioeconomic status get left behind in poorly performing schools. Rather,
differences may emerge as the result of "sorting" in which minority or lower
socioeconomic status parents stress a different set of values in education and
choose schools that reflect the fundamental (and different) dimensions of
education they view as important. As we demonstrated, this suggests that
choice can lead to more favorable sorting outcomes rather than the skimming that choice is sometimes accused of encouraging.

In chapters 5 and 6, we looked at how parents search for information, and
whether or not their search patterns changed with the availability of choice.
We were particularly concerned with the way in which parents constructed
networks of information about schools, because previous studies, confirmed
by our own evidence, showed how important talking to parents, neighbors,
and school officials can be in the flow of information. We found some fundamental effects of socioeconomic status on how parents access information
sources, but very little evidence that the design of school choice, at least in

our research sites, affects these socially defined search patterns. It appears that more highly educated parents can rely on their friends, neighbors, and other parents to gather information about the schools, who, not surprisingly, are also highly educated. Since these more highly educated discussants are also somewhat more likely to have better information about certain aspects of the schools, highly educated parents can gather information about the schools as part of their normal daily rounds. In contrast, less educated parents cast their net more widely in the search for information, expending more time and energy seeking out sources of information that are sometimes less reliable.

Henig has argued that in any attempt to make school choice work, the "most important steps could be those that relate to the collection and dissemination of more useful information about how the schools are performing" (1994, 219). We agree that collecting and disseminating such information is critical, but our findings suggest it will be difficult to get such information to parents of lower socioeconomic status. An individual parent's network is so fundamentally defined by the social milieu that the incentives built into school choice may not affect the search procedures of large numbers of parents. Consequently, even the reforms that Henig has in mind may not work. Analysts need to begin to think more carefully and creatively about outreach and information dissemination activities (Schneider 1999).

We continued our study of information by investigating the accuracy of the information parents have about schools and how they use this information to match their preferences with appropriate schools. First we found that, on average, parents, especially those in inner cities, have very little accurate information about the objective conditions in the schools. We then showed that even in the absence of such widespread objective knowledge, parents were able to match their children into schools that are high on the dimensions of education that they think are important. This created an interesting puzzle: how can matching take place in the absence of widespread information?

We found two related answers. First, we showed that it is possible for parents to use a range of visual cues to learn about school performance. But more importantly, we showed that a subset of informed parents who care about the specific dimension they are looking for do indeed make appropriate matching choices. We believe that it is no surprise that we found our strongest matching results in school districts marked by a larger number of schools and with the widest range of performance across the dimensions of education parents value. We also found that parents who match their children with an appropriate school, not surprisingly, are more likely be satisfied with their children's school.

Having found evidence of greater matching and thus allocative efficiency in the choice districts, we then examined school- and district-level data about performance. Although we were unable to get much data for New

Jersey, our analysis showed that schools in District 4 have performed above expectations since initiating choice and that such performance continued through our study period.

We then examined what we now believe may be the most critical question about school choice: what happens to those "left behind"? Our evidence was that nearly all nonchoice neighborhood elementary schools in the option-demand choice system in District 4 have improved their performance, suggesting that competitive responses can counter any tendencies toward stratification of parents and students.

We also demonstrated that parents in choice systems are more likely to become involved in social capital related activities around their children's schools. This finding suggests that choice can have a positive impact on parental behavior, which could then have multiple external benefits for students and schools.

Finally, we examined the complex relationship between public choice and the choice of private schooling. We found that fewer parents pursue private school choice when they have public school choices available. Furthermore, the gap in parent demographics and academic performance between private schools and public schools often is reduced (though certainly not eliminated) when public school choice is available.

Better Answers to Continuing Concerns Surrounding School Choice

With these specific results in place, we address some of the most fundamental, ongoing concerns that both scholars and citizens express about school choice. We recognize that our response is based on a particular sample of parents in a limited number of school districts using a limited range of choice. Nevertheless, we did analyze two experiments with choice that are among the longest lasting in the United States and we did address fundamental processes associated with any form of choice. Therefore we believe that our findings illustrate many of the long-term effects of choice and will contribute to ongoing debates over the multiple forms of choice we described in chapter 1.

Is School Choice a Panacea for American Education?

In the introduction to this book, we quoted Chubb and Moe, who presented the purposefully provocative argument that "choice *is* a panacea . . . [choice] has the capacity *all by itself* to bring about the kind of transformation that, for years, reformers have been seeking to engineer in myriad other ways" (1990, 217).

While we wish this were true, based upon our analysis, it is not.[1] It is clear from our data that public school choice can enhance school performance and that choice can lead many parents (including low-income parents) to change their behavior in a positive manner. However, and this is where we cannot endorse choice as a "silver bullet" to cure the ills of urban education, while these effects are usually (but not always) statistically significant in our analyses, they also tend to be relatively modest in size. And this is in spite of the fact that the public school choice programs we studied have been in place for a long time.

Given our evidence, it is hard for us to characterize public school choice as a cure-all for the many problems of urban education. But, since true panaceas are rare, and especially so in urban districts characterized by poverty and neighborhood blight, we should not lose sight of the many positive gains from public school choice we have documented in this book.

Can Public School Choice Emulate Gains Derived from Market-Like Competition?

Those who support voucher schools as a more market-oriented solution might argue that public school choice can never provide schools with enough autonomy to create market-like processes and the attendant gains. But, we find evidence of these dynamics even in the limited forms of choice we explored. Clearly, public school choice stimulates better performance, a better match between schools and parental preferences, and more parent involvement. We recognize that these effects are not found in every situation we examined and these effects are not always overwhelming, but the gains are nonetheless consistent and important.

We stress that for public school choice to achieve these benefits, both decentralized autonomy for schools and accountability are essential—failing schools must either change or close. Our evidence is that school choice created the conditions and the incentives for school administrators to become more creative leaders and more energetic managers, leading to improvements in the schools.

Moreover, while these managerial and leadership changes are critical outcomes of a system of choice, changes on the demand-side, in the behavior of parents, are also important. Clearly there must a dynamic relationship between the supply- and demand-sides of this quasi-market.

Can Parents Learn Enough about the Schools They Are Asked to Choose Among?

Despite a lack of detailed information about school performance, many of the urban parents we studied were able to use the choice process to place their children into schools that are relatively good at the things they value. We suggested that two phenomena are driving this successful match. First, we believe that some parents are likely using basic heuristics, such as visual cues, to make effective school choices. But more importantly, we argued that a large enough subset of active and informed parents are driving the demand-side of the market-like setting and pressuring schools to compete. In other words, choice has created the conditions for a corps of marginal consumers to emerge and pressure the schools to perform better, a phenomenon that has been documented in many markets for private goods and services.

In turn, we believe that the growing optimism that many social scientists are expressing in their studies of voting behavior may apply equally to the act of choosing schools. "Low information rationality" may be enough to power private markets, voting behavior, *and* school choice. Looking for encyclopedic knowledge on the part of parents may be a futile, unnecessary, and even harmful endeavor, setting the bar higher than necessary and then faulting parents for not being able to clear it.

School Choice May Improve a Few Schools, But Does It Leave Many Behind?

Stratification and concerns about equity are among the most important worries scholars and policy makers express about choice proposals. But any discussion of the effects of school choice on these patterns must begin with a fundamental reality: there are already high levels of income and racial stratification in American public schools, which results from local property tax funding of schools, restrictive zoning laws, and high levels of mobility for middle- and upper-income parents (see for example, Massey and Denton 1993).

Given this demographic reality, stratification cannot mainly be a concern along racial, or even income, lines in many if not most large urban school districts. In these districts, white and middle-class parents have already abandoned the public school system by moving to the suburbs or by placing their children in private schools. In districts such as New York City's District 1 and District 4, the schools are already two-thirds Hispanic, with blacks as the second largest racial group. There are few white or Asian students and nearly all the students in these districts come from low-income families. The question is whether the kinds of public school choice we analyze here actually make stratification and segregation worse than they are now.

We think not. We found little evidence of increased stratification associated with choice. While many analysts have argued that the structural design of option-demand systems is especially prone to stratification, we did not find empirical evidence to support this fear. In this system of choice, parents who have chosen to choose are indeed more likely to place their children in schools that are high on the attributes they value. And, in turn, these parents are more satisfied with their children's schools than are other parents. So these parents are clearly benefiting from choice. The most important question, then, is what happens to those left behind—to those parents who do not choose.

The assumption of many analysts is that these parents will end up in even worse schools that will no longer have a body of alert parents and involved students who will pressure school administrators and teachers to deliver a quality education. While this may be the most critical issue for choice, there is remarkably little evidence in the literature about this issue. In our work, we demonstrated that the neighborhood schools in District 4 were not left behind as choice was instituted and spread through the district. Indeed, the academic performance of neighborhood schools has not declined after more than twenty years of option-demand choice, and in fact has improved, nearly across-the-board. Moreover, in the newly formed and still limited choice program in District 1, the neighborhood schools actually outperform the handful of alternative schools.

We also found that school choice is not necessarily associated with racial and socio-economic stratification. Instead, stratification can be circumvented by expanding the range of options from which parents can choose and by disseminating information about schools to parents.

In controlled choice systems, such as found in Montclair, the potential for racial stratification is vitiated by regulations that require racial balancing. But one cost is evident: the range of choice is limited by these regulations. It is harder to measure whether or not other, more subtle forms of stratification are taking place. There is some evidence that tracking students within schools in Montclair (and in other schools around the country) has partially reproduced segregation by race and class at the classroom level. But, at the school level, choice in Montclair has resulted in all schools in the district being fairly similar in terms of quality.

We recognize that another concern is that public school choice may lead to greater stratification of parents by their involvement and knowledge of schools. But again our empirical evidence does not support this conclusion.

While generalizing from a few successful districts can be a mistake, we believe that public school choice has produced better outcomes for many students, while causing minimal or no harm to others. Economists call such results Pareto-improving, results that meet a very high standard for the outcomes of public policy. Choice seems to meet that standard.

What Effects Does Public School Choice Have on Decisions about Private Schools?

We found that, in districts with public school choice, parents may be less likely to opt for private schools. In part, this is because choice has reduced the gap in performance between public and private schools and in part because choice has created schools that have characteristics that parents value—including, for example, schools with better defined missions and more visible communities.

Not surprisingly, parents who choose private school are different than those whose children are in public schools. That is a finding that many other studies have documented. With our limited data, we were not able to settle the debate about whether or not enhanced performance in private schools is largely a result of this self-selection issue, or something truly different and better about what students experience in private schools. But, our results do point to some interesting theoretical and empirical similarities between option-demand public school choice and private schools.

Since we did not study private schools, per se, we do not want to weigh in directly on the societal debate about whether public funds should be used to support vouchers that children can use at any school, public or private. But we do want to stress that various forms of public school choice—charter schools and vouchers for private or public schools—form a continuum of market-like solutions to the problems of urban education. Specific institutional designs of these systems will have some influence over the outcomes. But choice seems to provide a range of positive effects that should be sought in educational reforms, in whatever form the political process finds most palatable.

Conclusion

For twenty years now, social scientists have been busy showing that institutions do matter to outcomes. It may not be surprising that how school choice is established, and what kinds of institutions are employed, does influence the results that flow from it. For example, we illustrated that the way in which schools and school districts supply information to parents makes a critical difference in how much they learn about their children's schools.

Clearly, other aspects of school choice are dependent upon institutional design. The more a choice system resembles a competitive market with many options and maximum incentives for parents to be involved, the more likely it is that choice will yield beneficial outcomes. Ultimately, as voucher programs and charter schools become more common, the number and range of schools operating in many areas will increase. We believe that this expansion of the parental choice set will increase allocative efficiency.

However, we believe that choice systems need *not* be universal in order to work—that is, school systems can increase the opportunities for many but not necessarily all parents to choose, and still reap many benefits from choice. Competitive markets do not need all consumers to be informed— competitive pressures can result even if a relatively small subset of consumers engage in informed, self-interested search.

This focus on option-demand choice deserves more amplification, since it raises critical institutional design issues. Most of our quantitative findings are as strong, and often stronger, for option-demand choice as they are for universal choice systems. We recognize that this could be partly a function of District 4's successful elementary school choice structure, compared to Montclair and District 4's universal choice systems.[2] Even with the limitations imposed by a small number of research sites, there are theoretical reasons to support these findings.

At first glance, the greater benefits of option-demand choice might seem counterintuitive. If having choice results in good outcomes, then universal choice, with its larger number of choosers, should lead to more of these good outcomes. This would be true if the very act of choice, even when forced upon parents, empowered parents and made them more active participants in their children's education. This demand-side effect would then elicit a more positive competitive response from the schools, as a larger number of choosing parents create more pressure. But, this is not the pattern we found.

As we pondered these results, we came to believe that they are not just anomalies and that there are theoretically important underpinnings for this pattern. Universal choice *requires* all parents and schools to participate. This means that there may be diminishing marginal returns in universal choice systems. In statistical terms, the "passive parents" who are "forced" to make choices may dampen the positive quantitative impacts generated by more active parents.

But we believe something more important than just the statistical results is at play. The option-demand system of choice more closely approximates conditions that exist within private markets for education. Option-demand empowers parents to choose the schools their children will attend, but it does not force all parents to choose. Parents who are not interested in selecting schools for their children or participating more regularly in their children's schooling are free to remain in their "default" neighborhood school. Part of what is so valuable about markets is the noncoercive nature of transactions, which, by definition, means that all participants expect to become better off. And option-demand more closely resembles this aspect of private markets.

Second, option-demand choice may solve what economists often think of as "coordination problems" better than a universal choice system. We know that parental interest in good education and viable school communities is not evenly distributed across the population. Since effective educational processes require coproduction from parents and students, creating a functional educational community may require collecting a sufficient number of more involved parents in one place so that they achieve a critical mass. But, coordinating the behavior of such parents is a problem. We believe that an option-demand system provides a mechanism for solving this coordination problem by signaling that a choice school requires a higher level of commitment to the school and more involvement with the educational process. Similarly, option-demand allows parents who believe in the same particular aspects of education to collect in the same place. In this way, a community of shared values is more likely to be created, and, similar to what happens in private (especially parochial) schools, better education through a stronger school community can result.

The alternative schools in District 4 seem able to send these signals and act as a coordinating "device" for attracting involved and interested parents and creating the conditions in which their behavior mattered. But we have also demonstrated that these newly created schools create a feedback mechanism, building social capital through increasing levels of involvement and commitment. We believe that this evidence supports the underlying philosophy of many charter schools, which even more explicitly than the alternative schools in District 4 act as coordinating mechanisms and emphasize parental involvement in the education process.

Of course, there is a potential downside risk in using this coordination mechanism: by collecting most or all of these parents in a small set of schools, the remaining schools in a district may be weakened. While some of the economic literature on the tradeoffs involved with vouchers (e.g., Epple and Romano 1998) focuses mainly on the peer effects of children in the classroom, there are also concerns about the concentration of active and informed parents in a smaller number of institutions. However, both of these possible negative effects could be counterbalanced by another outcome of choice: if choice schools act as competitors to the neighborhood schools and if they pioneer new methods of teaching or outreach that diffuse to other schools, the benefits of choice schools do not necessarily have a cost for the other schools. In short, choice is not necessarily a zero-sum game.

This is why our evidence on the generally enhanced performance of the nonchoice neighborhood schools in District 4 is critical. While there are other plausible explanations to explain this performance, it is hard to argue against the fact that the schools are competing to attract and retain students and that this has put pressure on them to improve their academic performance. These kinds of school responses to competitive pressure are evident in other systems of choice as well (see, for example, Peterson 1998).

We also showed that the process of option-demand choice has not led to a stratification of schools, or a skimming process in which the best and brightest students are concentrated in the alternative, or choice schools, while the less academically gifted students are left in the traditional neighborhood schools. Instead, we argued that student performance is similar across the alternative, choice schools and the neighborhood, nonchoice schools, suggesting more of a sorting phenomenon, in which students select schools for programs they want.

We believe that the evidence in chapter 12 suggests that alternative public schools thus have replicated *within* the public school system that which sectarian schools have traditionally done within many cities (e.g., Bryk, Lee, and Holland 1993). That is, by providing venues in which parents can signal greater interest and involvement in quality education and where parents with shared values can congregate, alternative public schools, like sectarian schools, provide the milieu in which functional communities can grow and where learning can increase. But unlike the separation between public schools and private schools, the fact that these alternative schools are *public* schools creates more competitive pressure on other public schools than private schools ever could.

Regardless of any questions about stratification within the public school system, before or after choice, these findings indicate an important role of public school choice in maintaining a viable public school system.

Regulation is another institutional design feature that makes public school option-demand, in practice, more similar to a private market than the universal choice systems we examined. These differences relate to the rules that affect the free exchange that typically characterizes transactions in private marketplaces. Specifically, many universal choice programs, such as the one in Montclair, are controlled programs in the sense that the selection process is strictly regulated to ensure that schools are not stratified along racial and ethnic lines. The regulation of the selection process limits somewhat the ability of schools to distinguish their product, while at the same time limiting the ability of parents to choose schools they most prefer, especially since we find some linkage of racial background and preferences for different academic approaches. Even if most parents get their first choice school under such a system, some do not, and this restricts choice. Most option-demand systems, as in District 4, put fewer restraints on the selection and matching process, in part because it is a voluntary and not a coerced system.

Together, the greater regulation of the selection process and the nonvoluntary nature of choice under the universal system weaken the incentives that drive market-like processes, and thus market outcomes. In a fully functioning choice system, parents determine how existing resources will be distributed among schools. When demand exists for some schools, these schools not only receive a direct signal that their product is highly regarded, but less desirable schools (and the parents who select them for their children, or whose children are assigned to them) should also take notice. By forcing parents to choose and by regulating these choices, under universal choice programs, school systems and schools can no longer rely mainly on enrollment decisions as a signal of how the schools are doing. Although some of the parents in the universal choice system certainly select schools on the basis of their preferences for the particular product being offered, many will simply be choosing out of convenience or lack of information. In addition, such a regulated market ensures, to a certain extent, that all schools receive some minimum number of students. This further weakens the allocative function of choice and thus the rationing of resources according to preferences.

On the demand-side, just as schools are unable to rely on enrollments as an indicator of demand, parents also receive little information about the quality of schools by observing enrollments. The problem in universal choice systems is that the feedback mechanism is weakened. This is partly due to regulation of the selection process, which may not allow dissatisfied parents to exercise the exit option, and partly due to the presence of too many inert parents. Under these conditions parents and schools cannot effectively gauge the quality of the product or the real demand that exists among parents.

The presence of too many inert parents constrains the ability of schools to create functional communities, and can also have negative effects on the incentives and behaviors of parents. This is the classic free rider problem in which inert parents benefit from the involvement and engagement of alert parents. However, if these alert parents constitute only a small share of the parent population, the benefits they receive as a result of their vigilance will not be proportional to the amount of time and energy they are expending. This may have a negative effect on their levels of satisfaction and involvement.

Together, these findings suggest many advantages of option-demand choice over universal systems. Quite frankly, this is not a result we expected as we began this research, and we caution that it may not hold in all choice systems—especially since the effects of choice are sensitive to other design issues and to the broader social context in which choice reforms operate. We also note that, even though our data do not confirm a problem with this in District 4, option-demand systems are the most vulnerable to arguments about any stratifying effects of choice, based upon their inherent structure that encourages only voluntary choice.

Since universal choice systems involve more regulation of the choice process, we do not want this argument to be taken to mean that all regulations that limit or constrain school choice are inherently harmful. Indeed, we do not advocate an unconstrained free market for schools. There may be important and legitimate societal reasons to constrain individual choice, for example, to promote integration by race and class. There are also likely to be some necessary supply-side regulations to ensure that taxpayer funding is used to support basic educational goals that members of our society believe are critical for all children. In short, there are compelling reasons to regulate various aspects of schools and of the market-like setting for education. Indeed, as a society we find justifications to regulate products such as cereal, so there would be no reason to justify a completely unregulated educational marketplace.

We recognize that regulation raises a "slippery slope" possibility, where the more supply-side regulations are encouraged in a choice system, the less true choice of differentiated, innovative schools will emerge. The balance between consumer sovereignty and regulation, generated by a combination of democratic and bureaucratic processes, is not an easy one—but like many scholars of education, we believe that the balance has shifted too far toward regulation and bureaucratization.

This brings us back to where we started this book, focusing on Chubb and Moe's concern about democratic constraints becoming structured into bureaucratic regulations that stifle school innovation and creativity. While choice may not be a panacea, and it may not be the only reform needed to address the problems that plague America's system of education, we believe that public school choice clearly improves schools and educational outcomes for parents and students, the players who matter the most in education.

Notes

Introduction
School Choice, Parent Incentives, and the Use of Information

1. Obviously, elementary and secondary schools seek to educate children, who can also be viewed as "consumers" of education. However, many of the fundamental decisions about schools are made by parents, who are the focal point of our analysis.

Chapter 1
Reinventing the Governance Structure of Education

1. It is important to remember that for many parents, private schools have always represented yet another form of choice. Nationwide, over 10 percent of American students are in private schools and in many Northeastern cities, where there is a high concentration of parochial schools, the numbers can be twice that. We recognize that one of the main battles in school choice today is the use of publicly funded vouchers that can be used in sectarian schools. Though we explore private school choice in more detail in chapter 12, throughout most of this book, we concentrate on public school choice.

2. See, for example, Ogawa and Dutton (1994); Ravitch and Viteritti (1997); Henig (1998).

3. We use the term "ideal typical" as developed by Max Weber. That is, we identify the most fundamental aspects of each approach, recognizing that in the real world the "ideal type" may never be realized.

4. These include powerlessness, professional isolation, fragmentation of the workday and educational tasks, and the depersonalized atmosphere of large schools (see Raywid 1989; Darling-Hammond 1997). Indeed, there is empirical evidence that teachers in choice schools are more satisfied with their working conditions and are more supportive of the schools in which they work. See, for example, Peterson (1998) and Vanourek et al. (1998).

Chapter 2
Parent Behavior and the Demand-Side of School Choice

1. At this stage we employ a number of terms that are obviously drawn from the study of markets. However, as this chapter develops, we develop a view of the "market for schools" that is more complex than that used in many discussions of choice.

2. While it is clearly important to consider why parents hold different preferences for various aspects of schooling, that issue is beyond the scope of our analysis.

3. The literature on rationality is voluminous. See Lupia and McCubbins 1998, for a good recent discussion of the issues associated with the use of rationality in politics and public policy.

4. Note too that even though we focus on individual behavior in the context of markets, we are also interested in the aggregate outcomes that can be expected from individual choices in the setting of school choice. Thus, even if some individuals in

our analysis do not always act "rationally," that problem may well be canceled out in the aggregation process.

5. While behavioral decision theorists have discussed a wide set of heuristics for decision making, we note that most political science work has focused on interpersonal cues as shortcuts.

6. This is especially true with regard to schools, where in almost any metropolitan area and indeed in many cities, numerous, often small school districts are the norm, in effect creating submarkets.

7. The field of Behavioral Decision Theory (BDT) is extensive. Among the works we found most useful are: Payne, Bettman and Johnson (1993); Johnson & Payne (1988); Einhorn and Hogarth (1981); Elster (1991); and Taber and Steenbergen (1995).

8. On the importance of the "marginal consumer" in creating efficiency in schools, see Teske et al., 1993.

9. For a review of the growing interest in networks in other social sciences, see especially Wasserman and Galaskiewicz 1994.

Chapter 3
Studying Choice

1. In their survey of parents Clewell and Joy (1990, 7) found that many parents select the school that is closest to them. This is particularly true for the K-2 years, as parents may want to keep their children closer to home while at the same time figuring out which programs might be most appropriate. Quite a bit of "shopping around" takes place at the third grade level.

2. Note that the universal choice program in District 4 has been "open zoned" since the 1970s, meaning that students from all over the city may apply for admission to its schools. Though some critics of District 4's choice program claim that as much as 10 percent of the junior high school population comes from outside the district, we have been unable to verify this figure. We have found no school or district source that reports this information.

3. Recall that high schools in New York are run by the central board of education.

4. Though we will refer to our respondents as "parents" throughout the book, technically we interviewed the person in the households who was responsible for making decisions about the education of children. We use the term parents both for simplicity and because the vast majority of respondents were in fact parents.

5. The considerable disparity between population and sample figures for the employed category stems from the fact that the population figure is calculated on the basis of those individuals actually in the labor force. This obviously excludes homemakers, welfare mothers, and anyone else who is not actively looking for a job.

6. We recognize that at some level there may be a self-selection process in Montclair. This suburb has a long history of choice and has a reputation for good schools in which parent involvement is stressed. Over the years of choice, parents might choose to locate in Montclair because of this reputation—that is, there may be a nonrandom assignment to the Montclair condition based on locational decisions. Unfortunately, we cannot model this locational choice and we recognize that the effects of this "selection process" may introduce some bias into our estimates.

Chapter 4
The Distribution of Preferences

1. If attendance is based on residentially determined zones, parents can indirectly choose schools through locational decisions. However, moving is obviously an expensive solution to this matching problem.

2. Though these concerns are well placed, any skimming resulting from choice needs to be compared to the already large skimming effects evident in the current system. At present, skimming is largely a function of the costs of residential location—higher-income families purchase housing in good communities with good schools, leaving behind those families with fewer resources. In a choice based system, skimming could result from a variety of individual-level characteristics, including values, involvement, information, etc. In later chapters, we investigate this issue more fully.

3. We recognize that parents may be reticent to admit that race is a factor in their decisions and may emphasize more socially acceptable criteria such as educational quality. Consequently there may be some bias in these findings (see Henig 1998). However, there is growing evidence that the actual *behavior* of parents is also motivated by academic quality (see the papers in Peterson and Hassel 1998).

4. This statement is quite literal—the poll asks parents to assign grades of A, B, C, D, and F to the nation's public schools and to the school their oldest child attends. In 1995, only 20 percent of the respondents rated the nation's schools as "A" or "B," while 65 percent gave their own children's schools high marks.

5. In our work, we experimented with various measures of importance: whether or not the respondent indicated a dimension as important on the first reading, on the first or second reading, or on any of the four separate readings. Obviously, the distribution shifts upwards as more possible mentions of importance increase (for example, almost 40 percent of our respondents chose teachers as the most important aspect of education on the first reading. This increased to 61 percent for either of the first two readings and to 84 percent for all four readings). In this chapter, we analyze the pattern of responses for the first reading, but the fundamental patterns that we report here are virtually identical across any measure of importance across the four readings.

6. Note that our survey encompasses inner-city and suburban communities close to a large central city, where safety may be a bigger problem than it is in other types of communities—although the Phi Delta Kappan national surveys often find "lack of discipline" among the biggest school problems parents mention.

7. In addition many more parents refused to report their income than any other demographic information, reducing the number of cases for analysis.

8. Note there are two voucher programs in Milwaukee, PAVE (Partners Advancing Values in Education) and MPCP (Milwaukee Parental Choice Program).The former is a privately funded voucher program started in 1992 by business and religious organizations, while the latter is publicly funded and was implemented in 1990. Both programs target low-income families.

9. In most analyses, especially those using the entire sample, white is the excluded category—because it is the largest. The small number of parents who gave a wide range of other racial identities are excluded from this analysis.

10. In this chapter we use categories of education because of the central importance of this variable in understanding the distribution of the dependent variable. In other chapters, we use a continuous variable measuring the years of schooling.

Chapter 5
How Do Parents Search for Information?

1. The alpha coefficients on these three scales range from .56 for "social" to .60 for the other two scales.

2. Note that we do not include coworkers in any of these scales—for a very simple reason: almost 40 percent of our respondents were not employed. We also did not include children as a source of information in any of the scales.

Chapter 6
Building Social Networks

1. Education is represented by years of schooling completed. "Problems at school" is a dichotomous variable that takes on a 1 if parents report that their child has come home unhappy from school and a value of 0 otherwise. Residence in District 4 is represented by a dichotomous variable that takes on a value of 1 if the parents lives in District 4.

2. We recognize that this may be a function of language, especially for Asians, who represent relatively small populations in both districts, particularly in District 4.

3. Parents were asked how often they talked to a discussant (daily, weekly, monthly, or once a year). In the analyses that follow, we recode this variable to reflect the number of days a year the parent talks to a discussant.

4. A discussant is considered occupying a unique loci when he is the only member in the network who is a coworker, a coreligionist, etc. Thus, we rely on the idea of structural equivalence when creating our measure of structural holes: 28 percent of our respondents with 2 and 3 discussants report talking to a discussant that occupies 1 nonredundant loci, 9 percent reported talking to a discussant that occupies 2 nonredundant loci, 2 percent and .5 percent reported talking to discussants that occupy 3 and 4 nonredundant loci.

5. These percentages can not be summed. 61 percent of the discussants that work in the schools are also members of parent organizations or community school board.

6. The data set is constructed of respondent-discussant dyads. Since the structural hole variable is defined by comparing a discussant to the other discussant(s) in the network, we can not include respondents-discussant dyads from networks consisting of only 1 discussant.

7. In the case of the maximum likelihood models, the estimation procedures provide pseudo-maximum likelihood estimates.

Chapter 7
The Distribution of Knowledge

1. Parents were asked to agree or disagree (on a five-point scale) with the question: "When I enrolled [name of child] in school, I had enough information about all the various schools and programs offered in my district." We recognize that this question may have somewhat different meanings for parents in choice districts versus those in districts without choice. The meaning of this question is most problematic in

Morristown, where parents have no public school options, however, we believe that parents here still want to know about how well their child's school is doing compared to other schools in the district.

2. It was not possible to gather objective data for the child's specific grade level or class, only for the whole school, but since parents choose schools rather than classes, that is probably the most appropriate level of analysis.

3. We computed the absolute distance between the parent estimate and the actual condition, so that in the above example, a parent who estimated the percent reading at grade level at 40 percent would also be assigned a distance score of 10.

4. We recognize that these cut-off points are somewhat arbitrary and we experimented with different ones, but the pattern we report is robust.

5. With five categories, the analysis for the information sufficiency question in column one could employ either Ordinary Least Squares (OLS) or ordered probit. We find that the results are similar in either case, and present the OLS results because they are easier to interpret.

6. In some of the smaller schools, the head is often called a director, not a principal.

7. We did examine whether knowledge of the principal's name is associated with lower distance scores on the other dependent variable measures. It is correlated significantly, but not highly (0.15) with smaller distance scores for class size, but not for the other measures. It may be that knowledge of the principal's name is associated with other forms of school information that we did not specifically ask about in our interviews.

8. A parallel analysis shows that Montclair parents are also significantly more accurate about math test scores. Again, recall that negative coefficients show greater accuracy.

9. Parents in both New Jersey districts are significantly more likely to report finding school district newsletters as useful information sources than are our New York respondents. This may be one way in which New Jersey parents had greater opportunity to access school test score data. School "report cards" with school test scores were introduced in New York City during the period of our survey, but they were very difficult to get.

Chapter 8
Allocational Efficiency

1. In an attempt to explore this issue further while maintaining a sufficient sample size, we combined the two sets of parents into a single sample and introduced dummy variables for level of schooling (intermediate school versus elementary school). We also introduced interaction terms to explore further the questions motivating our research. The results for this pooled analysis are much more complicated because of the additional interaction terms, but are virtually identical to the results we report here. We believe that the right way to study the issue is to have a larger sample of parents in a universal choice system.

2. We did not utilize safety incidents in chapter 7 because the data are not comparable across New York and New Jersey. But, as parents indicated, safety is an important issue in New York schools.

3. Because the dependent variable is standardized by district, we no longer include a dummy variable for district location on the right hand side of the equation—

the standardization procedure corrects for the conditions that the dummy variables would otherwise control.

4. Note that the R-squared statistic for incidents is much lower than for either of the other two dimensions. We believe that this is a function of the level of reporting for this indicator, as well as a measurement problem. We have mapped the school building data onto the programs by noting which buildings the programs are in. However, because most alternative programs are in buildings that also house neighborhood schools, there is no way to compare alternative schools to neighborhood schools or to correlate this indicator with other indicators of program performance.

5. For example, in private markets, only 30 percent of buyers of nondurable products shop at more than one store before making their purchases (Katona and Mueller 1955); for larger items, Claxton, Fry, and Portis (1974) found that only 5 percent of furniture buyers and 8 percent of appliance buyers gathered extensive information.

6. The impact of this work is evident in a whole host of changes in policing practices designed to prevent infractions of "quality of life" issues. For example, in New York City the police acted to stop the infamous "squeegee" men whose "services" (washing windows of stopped cars) many found threatening. Aggressive police action to prevent public urination and panhandling also fit into this category.

7. We wish to thank Rabia Alladin, Ladelle Dutramont, Mark Sutra, and Mark Wilkinson for their help in gathering these data.

8. We believe that the ethnic makeup of the school population is also accessible visually—walking past a school building at the beginning or end of the day, or when warm weather allows use of the school playground, will give parents some visual cues about the ethnic make-up of the school.

9. Note that in this second panel, we shift from data from schools and programs to data that are measured at the school-building level. Because a single building can house multiple programs, the number of observations falls by almost 50 percent.

10. Once again, the pattern for safety is somewhat anomalous. We find that choosers, in general, are in safer schools, but we do not find a significant effect of the interaction term. Again, this result may be driven by the lower quality of the data.

11. For dissent on this issue, see Fuller, Elmore, and Orfield (1996). Rothstein (1998) suggests that schools of choice may have done a better "marketing" job in convincing parents that they have purchased something valuable and Ogawa and Dutton (1994) suggest that satisfaction might be a temporary phenomenon that would change when high expectations were not met over time.

12. To be more precise, we are measuring the change in the probability that a parent reports agreeing with the question related to one of the two measures of satisfaction.

Chapter 9
Productive Efficiency

1. Note that this involves not the creation of smaller classes, which requires greater resources, but the creation of smaller schools through the establishment of mini-schools.

2. Because of limited data availability, we could average only grades 3, 6, and 8 in the years 1974–81. However, this three-grade average is highly correlated with the full 3–8 grade average in years when both averages can be computed.

3. There are two possible problems with the dispersion of these data over time. One is related directly to District 4's performance. It is possible that the rise in District 4 scores reflects regression to the mean—the tendency to converge over time toward an average level—so that the worst districts do better, while the best districts do worse. We tested for this problem by examining District 4's performance in the early days of choice in the mid-1970s. We found that, controlling for race and poverty, District 4 was performing about as predicted at that time. Now, in the 1990s, the district is performing significantly better than predicted by the model. We also found that only one other New York district, District 13, showed a similar increase in test scores over time as in District 4.

A second issue is that the variance in our dependent variable changed somewhat over time. In the mid-1980s, the variance across districts decreased for both reading and math scores, seemingly associated with different tests that were administered at that time. To be sure that the narrowing of variance across districts on the test administered in the 1980s is not a major problem for our analysis, we also ran the models in table 1 excluding those years in which the test variances are greatly collapsed. Our basic results were not changed.

4. While a better measure would be the percentage of students enrolled in choice schools, we were unable to get the information for the last twenty years.

5. When estimating a pooled model, researchers must address a complex set of problems. In this analysis, we follow Beck and Katz (1995) in relying on OLS when estimating our models. Since different districts are likely to perform at different levels, we follow a fixed-effects approach and correct for different levels of the dependent variable across districts by including a dummy variable for each district in both models. We also include a lagged dependent variable in each model in order to control for serial correlation. Finally, we also report White's robust standard errors, which Beck and Katz (1995) demonstrate, are, under most conditions, superior to panel-weighted least squares (PWLS) standard errors but possibly inferior to panel-corrected standard errors.

6. This is the board of education's "Ranking of Schools by Reading Achievement: Overall Comparison of Reading Achievement in Similar Schools, Prepared by the Board's Division of Assessment and Accountability."

7. The New Jersey State Board of Education apparently intends to start releasing test data again in 1999. As we discuss below, we gathered the 1994 and 1995 test score data directly from sources in Montclair, which puts together careful reports of test scores in their district. While these are available from Montclair, they are not available from a central source for all New Jersey schools, limiting analysis.

Chapter 10
Does Choice Increase Segregation and Stratification?

1. These schools are Public Schools 7, 50, 52, 72, 96, 101, 102, 108, 121, and 155.

2. We examine trends for each of four sets of scores: third- and sixth-grade reading and third- and fifth-grade math.

3. Of these four negative trends, two are from PS 155, where reading scores in grades three and six declined—however, over the same time period, math scores improved. Scores for grade three reading in PS 57 declined, but performance on two other tests remained steady and the school improved in one test. The final decline

occurred in PS 96, where performance on grade five math dropped, but the three other comparisons showed improvement over time.

4. Note that we have averaged the third- and sixth-grade scores to give a composite score for the entire elementary school.

5. This handbook is written in both English and Spanish.

6. Since our analysis of District 1's performance over time indicated no relative improvement in test scores in the district compared to the other thirty-one districts (see chapter 9, table 9.2), there is no need to consider the relative performance of District 1 neighborhood schools to citywide averages. Instead, we compare schools within the district.

7. In both districts, the number of alternative schools has increased over time, and in District 4, the commitment of resources to outreach and advertisement has also increased with time.

8. These data for 1975–86 come from Clewell and Joy's (1990) report on Montclair's choice program.

Chapter 11
Choosing Together Is Better than Bowling Alone

1. We recognize a limitation inherent in the cross-sectional nature of our research design. Ideally, research on changes in social capital would employ an interrupted time series analysis. In this ideal research design, data would be collected prior to institutional changes and, by interviewing the same subjects over time, researchers could isolate the specific impact of institutional changes. Unfortunately, few researchers had the foresight or the resources to conduct such a study; trade-offs must inevitably be made. For example, Putnam (1993) used aggregate-level and (some would say) problematic measures of social capital (see, e.g., Jackman and Miller 1996a) and went beyond his data to explore historical differences in the development of Italian regions. The trade-off in our case is that while we cannot gather detailed individual-level data on parents in these districts before they choose a school, we do have detailed individual measures today that our cross-sectional design allows us to test while controlling for individual-level demographic and socioeconomic factors. With replication across four different institutional settings, our quasi-experimental design provides a strong cross-sectional test of the causal relationships postulated in the existing social capital literature.

2. Participation in the PTA and in voluntary activities are dichotomous variables (1 = yes). Fifty-two percent of respondents reported membership in the PTA and 66 percent reported participating in voluntary activities. The number of parents a respondent reported talking with is a continuous variable based on the midpoints of categories presented (mean = 4.5; std.dev. = 4.6). Trust in teachers is operationalized as a dichotomous variable (1 = trusts teachers most of the time or always [77 percent report this level of trust]; 0 = never or only sometimes).

3. Later in our multivariate analysis, we try to isolate the causal mechanisms involved, by controlling for a possible "selection bias"—that is, that active choosers may already be high in social capital.

4. While it is also plausible that there could be a two-way or reciprocal relationship between social capital and school choice, the timing of our research design makes this unlikely: parents made their school choice in spring, 1994. They were not

interviewed until the spring of 1995, during which time they answered questions about activities during the previous school year. Thus, they chose first and engaged in the activities we measured later.

5. Smith and Meier find that religion and race help explain why some parents choose private schools for their children (1995, 71–72). Our values and diversity variables for the public schools are closely related to these concepts. Alternative schools in New York tend to emphasize themes and pedagogical approaches that are based on particular social, educational, or civic values. Diversity has a somewhat different meaning in districts where two-thirds of the children are Hispanic.

6. To estimate two-stage models there must be at least one exclusion in the assignment equation. In other words, we must find at least one variable that significantly influences the assignment but not the outcome (Achen 1986, 38). We use these two variables, diversity and values, as exclusions.

7. Our specific measure, indicating whether or not the parent has often thought about moving her child to another school, is a dummy variable (1 = yes). We expect a negative relationship between this measure and our measures of social capital.

8. While the two-stage results are the technically correct ones, we should also note that these findings are robust with a simpler methodology. Using a one-stage model, the results are essentially the same.

Chapter 12
Opting Out of Public Schools

1. We remind the reader that although District 1 has implemented a limited choice program, it remains largely organized around traditional neighborhood schools.

2. The state of New Jersey requires private schools to submit information solely on their enrollments.

3. The distribution of parents in the District 4 sample is as follows: neighborhood schools (71 percent), option demand schools (10 percent) and universal choice schools (19 percent). In District 1, 12 percent of our sample represent option-demand choosers while the remainder are non-choosers.

4. The full models and discussion of the two-stage estimation procedure are included in the appendix.

5. Though private schools do not recruit students only from the "home" district, they do draw their student bodies heavily from the home and neighboring districts. Thus, we feel that it is most appropriate to compare public schools to the private schools within the district, rather than to the population of private schools in Manhattan or New York City.

6. Though we wrote and called the private schools in New Jersey included in our sample, and even posed as perspective parents asking for information, our efforts to obtain performance information were largely futile.

Chapter 13
Myths and Markets

1. To be fair, Chubb and Moe use these words to be explicitly provocative, when they really mean that choice is probably more important than any other school reform. In addition, they call for a voucher system including private schools, the likes

of which has not yet been implemented. We could imagine a reasonable counterargument that one should not expect dramatic results from a partially implemented system of limited public school choice reforms such as we study.

2. Although Montclair certainly has a well-deserved reputation for excellence.

References

Achen, Chris. 1986. *The Statistical Analysis of Quasi-Experiments*. Chicago: University of Chicago Press.

Akerlof, George. 1970. The Market for Lemons: Quality Uncertainty and the Market Mechanism. *Quarterly Journal of Economics* 84: 488–500.

Aldrich, John, and Forrest Nelson. 1994. *Linear Probability, Logit, and Probit Models*. Newbury Park, Calif.: Sage Publications.

Almond, Gabriel, and Sidney Verba. 1963. *The Civic Culture*. Princeton: Princeton University Press.

Althaus, Scott L. 1995. The Practical Limits of Information Shortcuts: Public Opinion, Political Equality, and the Social Distribution of Knowledge. Paper presented at the annual meetings of the American Political Science Association, Chicago, September 1–3.

Alvarez, R. Michael. 1994. Two-Stage Estimation of Non-Recursive Choice Models. Typescript. California Institute of Technology, Social Science Working Paper 905.

Anderson, Charles. 1990. *Pragmatic Liberalism*. Chicago: University of Chicago Press.

Anhalt, Bari E., Alan DiGaetano, Luis Ricardo Fraga, and Jeffrey R. Henig. 1995. Systematic Reform and Policy Effort in Urban Education. Paper presented at the annual meetings of the Midwest Political Science Association, Chicago, April 6–8.

Anson, Amy, Thomas Cook, Farah Habib, Michael Grady, Norris Haynes, and James Comer. 1991. The Comer School Development Program: A Theoretical Analysis. *Urban Education* 26 (April): 56–82.

Arabie, Phipps, and Yoram Wind. 1994. Marketing and Social Networks. In *Advances in Social Network Analysis*, ed. Stanley Wasserman and Joseph Galaskiewicz. Thousand Oaks, Calif.: Sage Publications.

Archbold, Douglas. 1988. Magnet Schools, Voluntary Desegregation, and Public Choice Theory: Limits and Possibilities in a Big City School System. Madison: University of Wisconsin.

Armor, David J., and Bret M. Peiser. 1998. Interdistrict choice in Massachusetts. In *Learning from School Choice*, ed. Paul E. Peterson, and Bryan C. Hassel. Washington, D.C.: Brookings Institution Press.

Ascher, Carol, Norm Fruchter, and Robert Berne. 1996. *Hard Lessons: Public Schools and Privatization*. New York: Twentieth Century Fund.

Astone, Nan Marie, and Sara McLanahan. 1991. Family Structure, Parental Practices, and High School Completion. *American Sociological Review* 56 (June): 309–20.

Atkins, Charles. 1972. Anticipated Communication and Mass Media Information Seeking. *Public Opinion Quarterly* 36: 188–99.

Axelrod, Robert. 1984. *The Evolution of Cooperation*. New York: Basic Books.

Banarjee, Abhijit. 1992. A Simple Model of Herd Behavior. *Quarterly Journal of Economics* 107: 797–817.

Barber, Benjamin. 1984. *Strong Democracy: Participatory Politics for a New Age*. Berkeley: University of California Press.

Baron, James, and Michael Hannan. 1994. The Impact of Economics on Contemporary Sociology. *Journal of Economic Literature* 2: 1111–46.

Bartels, Larry. 1996. Uninformed Votes: Information Effects in Presidential Elections. *American Journal of Political Science* 40, no. 1: 194–230.

Barzel, Yoram. 1989. *Economic Analysis of Property Rights*. New York: Cambridge University Press.

Bauch, Patricia. 1989. Can Poor Parents Make Wise Educational Choices? In *Private Schools and Public Policy: International Perspectives*, ed. William Boyd and James Cibulka. New York: Falmer Press.

Bauch, Patricia, and Ellen Goldring. 1995. Parent Involvement and School Responsiveness: Facilitating the Home-School Connection in Schools of Choice. *Educational Evaluation and Policy Analysis* 17:1–21.

Baumgartner, Frank, and Bryan Jones. 1993. *Agendas and Instability in American Politics*. Chicago: University of Chicago Press.

Beach, L. R., and T. R. Mitchell. 1978. A Contingency Model for the Selection of Decision Strategies. *Academy of Management Review* 3:439–49.

Beales, Janet R., and Maureen Wahl. 1996. Private Vouchers in Milwaukee: The PAVE Program. In *Private Vouchers*, ed. Terry Moe. Stanford: Hoover Institute Press.

Beatty, Sharon, and Scott Smith. 1987. External Search Effort: An Investigation across Several Product Categories. *Journal of Consumer Research* 14: 83–95.

Beck, Nathaniel, and Jonathon Katz. 1995. Nuisance versus Substance: Specifying and Estimating Time-Series Cross-Section Models. *Political Analysis* 6.

Becker, Gary. 1974. A Theory of Social Interactions. *Journal of Political Economy* 82: 1063–93.

———. 1991. A Note on Restaurant Pricing and Other Examples of Social Influences on Price. *Journal of Political Economy* 99: 1109–16.

Becker, William, and William Baumol, eds. 1996. *Assessing Educational Practices: The Contribution of Economics* Cambridge: M.I.T. Press.

Berelson, Bernard R., Paul F. Lazarsfeld, and William N. McPhee. 1954. *Voting: A Study of Opinion Formation in a Presidential Campaign*. Chicago: University of Chicago Press.

Berry, Jeffrey, Kent Portney, and Ken Thomson. 1993. *The Rebirth of Urban Democracy*. Washington, D.C.: Brookings Institution Press.

Bettman, James. 1986. Consumer Psychology. *Annual Review of Psychology* 37: 257–89.

Bickers, Kenneth and Robert Stein. 1998. The Micro-Foundations of the Tiebout Model. *Urban Affairs Review* 34:76–93.

Biderman, A. D., L. A. Johnson, J. McIntyre and A. W. Weir. 1967. *Report on a Pilot Study in the District of Columbia on Victimization and Attitudes towards Law Enforcement*. Washington, D.C.: Government Printing Office.

Bierlein, Louann. 1997. The Charter School Movement. In *New Schools for a New Century*, ed. by Diane Ravitch and Joseph Viteritti. New Haven: Yale University Press.

Bierlein, Louann, Chester E. Finn, and Bruno V. Manno. 1997. *Charter School Accountability: Findings and Prospects*. Bloomington, Ind.: Phi Delta Kappa Educational Foundation.

Bikchandani, Sushil, David Hirshleifer, and Ivo Welsh. 1992. A Theory of Fads, Fashion, Custom, and Cultural Changes as Informational Cascades. *Journal of Political Economy* 100: 992–1025.

Birnbaum, M. H., and B. A. Mellers. 1983. Bayesian Inference: Combining Base Rates with Opinions of Sources Who Vary in Credibility. *Journal of Personality and Social Psychology* 45: 792–804.

Birnbaum, M. H., and S. E. Stegner. 1979. Source Credibility in Social Judgment: Bias, Expertise, and the Judge's Point of View. *Journal of Personality and Social Psychology* 37: 48–74.

Bishop, John. 1998. Nerd Harassment, Incentives, School Priorities, and Learning. In *Meritocracy and Inequality*, ed. Paul E. Peterson and Susan Mayer. Washington, D.C.: Brookings Institution Press.

Blank, Rolf K. 1990. Educational Effects of Magnet High Schools. In *Choice and Control in American Education.* Vol. 2 of *The Practice of Choice, Decentralization, and School Restructuring*, ed. William H. Clune and John F. Witte. London: Falmer Press.

Blank, Rolf, R. Dentler, C. Balzell, and K. Chabotar. 1983. *Survey of Magnet Schools: Analyzing a Model for Quality Integrated Education.* Prepared by James H. Lowry and Associates and Abt Associates for U.S. Department of Education, Washington, D.C.

Blank, Rolf, Robert Levine, and Laura. Steel. 1996. After Fifteen Years, Magnet Schools in Urban Education. In *Who Chooses? Who Loses? Culture, Institutions and the Unequal Effects of School Choice*, ed. B. Fuller and R. Elmore. New York: Teachers College Press.

Bledoe, Timothy, and Gerry Stoker. 1992. Citizens' Knowledge of Local Government Structures and Representatives in the United States. Paper Presented to the Midwest Political Science Association annual meeting, Chicago.

Bliss, John, William Firestone, and C. Richards. 1991. *Rethinking Effective Schools: Research and Practice.* Englewood Cliffs, N.J.: Prentice Hall.

Bloch, Peter, Daniel Sherrel, and Nancy Ridgway. 1986. Consumer Search: An Extended Framework. *Journal of Consumer Research* 13: 119–26.

Borland, Melvin, and Roy Howsen. 1992. Student Academic Achievement and the Degree of Market Concentration in Education. *Economics of Education Review* 11:1–39.

Bourdieu, Pierre. 1980. *Questions de Sociologie.* Paris: Minuit.

Boxman, Ed A. W., Paul M. De Graaf, and Hendrik D. Flap. 1991. The Impact of Social and Human Capital on the Income Attainment of Dutch Managers. *Social Networks* 13:51–73.

Boyer, Ernest. 1992. *School Choice.* Princeton, N.J.: Carnegie Foundation.

Bracey, Gerald. 1998. Are U. S. Students Behind? *American Prospect* 37: 64–70.

Brandl, John E. 1998. Civic Values in Public and Private Schools. In *Learning from School Choice*, ed. Paul E. Peterson and Bryan C. Hassell. Washington, D.C.: Brooking Institute Press.

Brehm, John, and Wendy Rahn. 1997. Individual Level Evidence for the Causes and Consequences of Social Capital. *American Journal of Political Science* 41 (July): 999–1023.

Bridge, Gary R. 1978. Information Imperfections: The Achilles' Heel of Entitlement Plans. *School Review* 86: 504–29.

Bridge, Gary R., and Julie Blackman. 1978. *A Study of Alternatives in American Education*, Vol. 4 of *Family Choice in Schooling.* Santa Monica: RAND Corporation.

Brudney, Jeffrey L. 1984. Local Coproduction of Services and the Analysis of Municipal Productivity. *Urban Affairs Quarterly* 19, no. 4: 465–84.

Bryk, Anthony S., Valerie E. Lee, and Peter B. Holland. 1993. *Catholic Schools and the Common Good*. Cambridge: Harvard University Press.

Bryk, Anthony S., Penny A. Sebring and Sharon G. Rollow. 1998. *Charting Chicago School Reform: Democratic Localism as a Lever for Change*. Boulder, Colo.: Westview Press.

Burt, Ronald S. 1987. Social Contagion and Innovation: Cohesion versus Structural Equivalence. *American Journal of Sociology* 92:1287–335.

———. 1992. *Structural Holes: The Social Structure of Competition*. Cambridge: Harvard University Press.

Campbell, K. E., P. V. Marsden, and J. Hurlbert. 1986. Social Resources and Socioeconomic Status. *Social Networks* 8: 97–117.

Card, David and Alan Krueger. 1992. Does School Quality Matter? Returns to Education and the Characteristics of Public Schools in the United States. *Journal of Political Economy* 100, no. 1: 1–40.

Carmines, Edward, and James Kuklinski. 1990. Incentives, Opportunities, and the Logic of Public Opinion in American Political Representation. In *Information and Democratic Processes*, ed. John Ferejohn and James Kuklinski. Chicago: University of Illinois Press.

Carnegie Foundation for the Advancement of Teaching. 1992. *School Choice: A Special Report*. Princeton, N.J.: Carnegie Foundation for the Advancement of Teaching.

Carnoy, Martin. 1993. School Improvement: Is Privatization the Answer? In *Decentralization and School Improvement*, ed. Jane Hannaway and Martin Carnoy. San Francisco: Jossey-Bass.

Carroll, John S., and Eric J. Johnson. 1990. *Decision Research: A Field Guide*. Newbury Park, Calif.: Sage Publications.

Cartwright, Desmond. 1965. Influence, Leadership, Control. In *Handbook of Organizations*, ed. James G. March. Chicago: Rand McNally.

Carver, Rebecca L., and Laura H. Salganik. 1991. You Can't Have Choice without Information. *Equity and Choice* (spring): 71–75.

Catterall, James. 1992. Theory and Practice of Family Choice in Education. *Economics of Education Review* 11: 407–16.

Center for Education Reform. 1997. Selected Education Reforms at-a-Glance. *http://www.edreform.com/pubs/glance97.html*

Chaffee, Steven, and Jack McLeon. 1973. Individual versus Social Predictors of Information Seeking. *Journalism Quarterly* 50: 237–46.

Chase, Jennie. 1996. School Choices: How Public and Catholic Schools Influence Their Students. Working paper, Department of Economics, University of North Carolina.

Chriss, Barbara, Greta Nash, and David Stern. 1992. The Rise and Fall of Choice in Richmond, California. *Economics of Education Review* 11: 395–406.

Chubb, John. 1997. Lessons in School Reform from the Edison Project. In *New Schools for a New Century*, ed. by Diane Ravitch and Joseph Viteritti. New Haven: Yale University Press.

Chubb, John, and Terry Moe. 1990a. *Politics, Markets, and America's Schools*. Washington, D.C.: Brookings Institution Press.

———. 1990. Should Market Forces Control Educational Decision Making? *American Political Science Review* 84: 558–67.

Claxton, J., J. Fry, and B. Portis. 1974. A Taxonomy of Prepurchase Information Gathering Patterns. *Journal of Consumer Research*: 35–42.

Clewell, Beatriz C., and Myra F. Joy. 1990. *Choice in Montclair, New Jersey: A Policy Information Paper*. Princeton, N.J.: Educational Testing Service.

Clinton, Hillary Rodham. 1996. *It Takes a Village; and Other Lessons Children Teach Us*. New York: Simon and Schuster.

Clune, William, and John F. Witte, ed. 1990. *Choice and Control in American Education*, Vol. 1–2. London: Falmer Press.

Cohen, David K., and Eleanor Farrar. 1977. Power to the Parents? The Story of Education Vouchers. *The Public Interest* 48 (summer): 72–97.

Cohen, Joel, and Dipankar Chakravarti. 1990. Consumer Psychology. *Annual Review of Psychology* 41: 243–88.

Coleman, James, E. Q. Campbell, C. J. Hobson, J. McPartland, A. M. Mood, F. D. Weinfeld, and R. L. York. 1966. *Equality of Educational Opportunity*. Washington, D.C.: U.S. Government Printing Office.

Coleman, James, and Tomas Hoffer. 1987. *Public and Private High Schools Compared*. New York: Basic Books.

Coleman, James. 1988. Social Capital in the Creation of Human Capital. *American Journal of Sociology* 94 (supplement): S95–120.

———. 1990. *Foundations of Social Theory*. Cambridge: Harvard University Press.

Coleman, James, Thomas Hoffer, and Sally Kilgore. 1982. *High School Achievement: Public, Catholic, and Private Schools Compared*. New York: Basic Books.

Coles, Catherine M., and George L. Kelling. 1996. *Fixing Broken Windows: Restoring Order and Reducing Crime in Our Communities*. New York: Free Press.

Cookson, Peter W., Jr. 1992. *The Choice Controversy*. Newbury Park, Calif.: Corwin Press.

———. 1994. *School Choice: The Struggle for the Soul of American Education*. New Haven: Yale University Press.

Coons, John E. 1992. School Choice as Simple Justice. *First Things* 5: 15–22.

Coons, John E., and Stephen D. Sugarman. 1978. *Education by Choice: The Case for Family Control*. Berkeley: University of California Press.

Cortes, Ernesto J., Jr., 1996. Community Organization and Social Capital. *National Civic Review* 85 (fall): 49–53.

Cosgel, Metin. 1994. Audience Effects in Consumption. *Economics and Philosophy* 10: 19–30.

Couch, J. William Shughart and A. Williams. 1993. Private School Enrollment and Public School Performance. *Public Choice* 76: 301–312.

Crain, Robert. 1993. New York City's Career Magnet High Schools. In *School Choice: Examining the Evidence*, ed. Edith Rasell and Richard Rothstein. Washington, D.C.: Economic Policy Institute.

Cremin, L. A. 1975. Public-Education And Education Of Public. *Teachers College Record* 77, no. 1: 1–12.

Darling-Hammond, Linda. 1997. *The Right to Learn: A Blueprint for Creating Schools that Work*. San Francisco: Jossey-Bass.

Davis, Robert C., Arthur J. Lurigio, and Wesley Skogan. 1996. *Victims of Crime*. Beverly Hills, Calif.: Sage Publications.

Delli Carpini, Michael X., and Scott Keeter. 1996. *What Americans Know about Politics and Why It Matters*. New Haven: Yale University Press.

Delpit, Lisa D. 1995. *Other Peoples' Children: Cultural Conflict in the Classroom*. New York: New Press.

Department of Education, School Finance Project. 1983. *Private Elementary and Secondary Education*. Vol. 2. Washington, D.C.

Diamond, Larry. 1992. Economic Development and Democracy Reconsidered In *Reexamining Democracy,* ed. Gary Marks and Larry Diamond. New York: Sage Publications.

Doherty, Kathryn, and Clarence Stone. 1999. Local Practice in Transition: From Government to Governance. In *Dilemmas of Scale in American Democracy*, ed. Martha Derthick. New York: Cambridge University Press.

Domanico, Raymond. 1989. Model for Choice: A Report on Manhattan's District 4. New York: Manhattan Institute for Policy Research, Center for Educational Innovation, Education Policy Paper no. 1.

Dowding, Keith, Peter John, and Stephen Biggs. 1994. Tiebout: A Survey of the Empirical Literature. *Urban-Studies* 31: 767–97.

Driscoll, Mary. 1993. Choice, Achievement, and School Community. In *School Choice: Examining the Evidence*, ed. Edith Rassell and Richard Rothstein. Washington, D.C.: Economic Policy Institute.

Einhorn, Hillel J., and Robert M. Hogarth. 1981. Behavioral Decision Theory-Processes of Judgment and Choice. *Journal of Accounting Research* 19: 1–31.

Ellison, Glenn, and Drew Fudenberg. 1993. Rules of Thumb for Social Learning. *Journal of Political Economy* 101: 612–43.

Elmore, Richard F. 1991a. Choice as an Instrument of Public Policy: Evidence from Education and Health Care. In *Choice and Control in American Education*, Vol. I, ed. William H. Clune and John F. Witte. New York: Falmer Press.

———. 1991b. Public School Choice as a Policy Issue. In *Privatization and Its Alternatives*, ed. William Gormley. Madison: University of Wisconsin Press.

Elmore, Richard, and Bruce Fuller. 1996. Conclusion: Empirical Research on Educational Choice: What Are the Implications for Policy-Makers? In *Who Chooses? Who Loses? Culture, Institutions, and the Unequal Effects of School Choice*, ed. Bruce Fuller, Richard F. Elmore, and Gary Orfield. New York: Teachers College Press.

Epple, Dennis, and Richard Romano. 1998. Competition between Private and Public Schools, Vouchers, and Peer-Group Effects. *American Economic Review* 88, no. 1: 33–62.

Erickson, Donald. 1982. The British Columbia Story: Antecedents and Consequences of Aid to Private Schools. Los Angeles: Institute for the Study of Private Schools.

———. 1986. Choice and Private Schools: Dynamics of Supply and Demand. In *Private Education: Studies in Choice and Public Policy*, ed. Daniel C. Levy. New York: Oxford University Press.

Evans, William N., and Robert M. Schwab. 1995. Finishing High School and Starting College: Do Catholic Schools Make a Difference? *Quarterly Journal of Economics* 110: 941–74.

Fantini, Mario. D. 1973. *Public Schools of Choice*. New York: Simon and Schuster.

Feick, Lawrence F., and Linda L. Price. 1987. The Market Maven: A Diffuser of Marketplace Information. *Journal of Marketing* 51: 83–97.

Ferguson, Ronald. 1991a. How Professionals in Community-Based Programs Perceive and Respond to the Needs of Black Male Youth. In *Nurturing Young Black Males*, ed. Ronald Miney. Washington, D.C.: Urban Institute Press.

———. 1991b. Paying for Public Education: New Evidence on How and Why Money Matters. *Harvard Journal on Legislation* 28, no. 2: 465–98.

Ferguson, Ronald, and Helen Ladd. 1996. How and Why Money Matters: An Analysis of Alabama Schools. In *Holding Schools Accountable*, ed. Helen Ladd. Washington D.C.: Brookings Institution Press.

Festinger, Leon. 1957. *A Theory of Cognitive Dissonance*. Evanston, Ill.: Row, Peterson.

Finn, Chester, Bruno Manno, Louann Bierlein, and Gregg Vanourek. 1997. *Charter Schools in Action: Final Report*. Washington, D.C.: Hudson Institute.

Fiske, Susan, and Shelley Taylor. 1991. *Social Cognition*. 2d ed. McGraw Hill.

Fliegel, Seymour. 1990. Creative Non-Compliance. In *Choice and Control in American Education*, vol. 2 of *The Practice of Choice, Decentralization, and School Restructuring*, ed. William Clune and John Witte. London: Falmer Press.

Fliegel, Seymour, with James McGuire. 1993. *Miracle in East Harlem*. New York: Times Books.

Foley, Michael W., and Bob Edwards. 1997. Editors Introduction: Escape from Politics? Social Theory and the Social Capital Debate. *American Behavioral Scientist* 40: 550–661.

Folger, J. 1992. Project STAR and Class Size Policy. *Peabody Journal of Education* 67, no. 1.

Fossey, R. 1994. Open Enrollment in Massachusetts: Why Families Choose? *Educational Evaluation and Policy Analysis* 16, no. 3: 320–34.

Friedman, Milton. 1955. The Role of Government in Education. In *Economics and the Public Interest*, ed. R. A. Solo. New Brunswick, N.J.: Rutgers University Press.

———. 1962. *Capitalism and Freedom*. Chicago: University of Chicago Press.

Fukuyama, Francis. 1995. *Trust: Social Virtues and the Creation of Prosperity*. New York: Free Press.

Fuller, Bruce, Richard F. Elmore, and Gary Orfield. 1996a. *Who Chooses? Who Loses? Culture, Institutions, and the Unequal Effects of School Choice*. New York: Teachers College Press.

———. 1996b. Policy-Making in the Dark: Illuminating the School Choice Debate. In *Who Chooses? Who Loses? Culture, Institutions, and the Unequal Effects of School Choice*. New York: Teachers College Press.

Gamoran, Adam. 1996. Student Achievement in Public Magnet, Public Comprehensive, and Private City High Schools. *Educational Evaluation and Policy Analysis* 18 (spring): 1–18.

Gittell, Marilyn. 1973. *School Boards and School Policy: An Evaluation of Decentralization in New York City*. New York: Praeger Publishers.

———. 1980. *Limits to Citizen Participation*. Beverly Hills, Calif.: Sage Publications.

Glenn, Charles, Kahris McLaughlin, and Laura Salganik. 1993. *Parent Information for School Choice: The Case of Massachusetts*. Boston: Center on Families, Communities, Schools, and Children's Learning, Report no. 19.

Goldberger, Arnold. 1964. *Econometric Theory*. New York: John Wiley and Sons.

Goldhaber, Daniel. 1996. Public and Private High Schools: Is School Choice an Answer to the Productivity Problem? *Economics of Education Review* 15: 93–109.

Goldring, Ellen. 1997. Parent Involvement and School Choice: Israel and the U.S. In *Choice and Diversity in Schooling: Perspectives and Prospects*. Ed. Ron Glatter, Philip Woods, and Carl Bagley. London: Routledge.

Graber, Doris A. 1989. Content and Meaning: What's It All about? *The American Behavioral Scientist* 33:144–52.

Granato, Jim, Ronald Inglehart, and David Leblang. 1996a. The Effect of Cultural Values on Economic Development: Theory, Hypotheses, and Some Empirical Tests. *American Journal of Political Science* 40(August): 607–31.

———. 1996b. Cultural Values, Stable Democracy, and Economic Development: A Reply. *American Journal of Political Science* 40 (August): 680–96.

Granovetter, Mark. 1973. The Strength of Weak Ties. *American Journal of Sociology* 78: 1360–80.

———. 1974. *Getting A Job: A Study of Contacts and Careers.* Cambridge: Harvard University Press.

———. 1985. Economic Action and Social Structure: The Problem of Embeddedness. *American Journal of Sociology* 91: 481–510.

Greeley, Andrew M. 1982. *Catholic Schools and Minority Students.* New Brunswick, N.J.: Transaction Books.

———. 1997. The Other Civic America: Religion and Social Capital. *The American Prospect* 32 (May–June): 68–74.

Greene, Jay P. 1998. Civic Values in Public and Private Schools. In *Learning from School Choice*, ed. Paul E. Peterson and Bryan Hassel. Washington, D.C.: Brookings Institution.

Greene, Jay P., William G. Howell, and Paul E. Peterson. 1998. Lessons from the Cleveland Scholarship Program. 1998. *Learning from School Choice*, ed. Paul E. Peterson and Bryan C. Hassel. Washington, D.C.: Brookings Institution Press.

Grogger, Jeff. 1996. Does School Quality Explain the Recent Black/White Wage Trend? *Journal of Labor Economics* 14: 2.

Guttman, Amy. 1987. *Democratic Education.* Princeton: Princeton University Press.

Haertel, Edward H. 1987. Comparing Public and Private Schools Using Longitudinal Data from the HSB Study. In *Comparing Public and Private Schools*, vol. 2 of *School Achievement*, ed. Edward H. Haertel, Thams James, and Henry M. Levin. New York: Falmer Press.

Hagle, Timothy, and Glenn Mitchell. 1992. Goodness-of-Fit Measures for Logit and Probit. *American Journal of Political Science* 36, no. 3: 762–84.

Hallinger, Philip, and Joseph F. Murphy. 1986. The Social Context of Effective Schools. *American Journal of Education* 94 (May): 328–55.

Handler, Joel. 1996. *Down from Bureaucracy: The Ambiguity of Privatization and Empowerment.* Princeton: Princeton University Press.

Hanushek, Eric. 1986. The Economics of Schooling: Production and Efficiency in Public Schools. *Journal of Economic Literature* 24: 1141–77.

———. 1997a. Outcomes, Incentives, and Beliefs: Reflections on Analysis of the Economics of Schools. *Educational Evaluation and Policy Analysis* 19, no. 4: 301–8.

———. 1997b. School Resources and Outcomes. *Journal of Educational Research and Analysis.*

Hassel, Bryan C. 1998. Governance and Educational Equality. In *Learning from School Choice*, ed. Paul E. Peterson and Bryan C. Hassel. Washington, D.C.: Brookings Institute Press.

Harrington, Diane, and Peter Cookson, Jr. 1992. School Reform in East Harlem: Alternative Schools versus Schools of Choice. In *Empowering Teachers and Parents*, ed. G. Alfred Hess. Westport, Conn.: Bergin and Garvey.

Heckman, James. 1978. Dummy Endogenous Variables in a Simultaneous Equation System. *Econometrica* 46 (July): 931–59.

Heckman, James J., V. Joseph Hotz, and Marcelo Dabos. 1987. Do We Need Experimental Data to Evaluate the Impact of Manpower Training on Earnings? *Evaluation Review* 11(August): 395–427.

Hedges, Larry R. Lane, and Rob Greenwald. 1994a. Does Money Matter? A Meta-

Analysis of Studies of the Effects of Differential School Inputs on Student Outcomes. *Educational Researcher* (April) 23: 5–14.

Heise, Michael, Kenneth D. Colburn, Jr., and Joseph F. Lamberti. 1995. Private Vouchers in Indianapolis: The Golden Rule Program. In *Private Vouchers*, ed. Terry Moe. Stanford: Hoover Institute Press.

Henderson, Anne T., ed. 1987. *The Evidence Continues to Grow: Parent Involvement Improves Student Achievement, An Annotated Bibliography*. Columbia, Md.: National Committee for Citizens in Education.

Henig, Jeffrey R. 1994. *Rethinking School Choice: Limits of the Market Metaphor*. Princeton: Princeton University Press.

———. 1996. The Local Dynamics of Choice: Ethnic Preferences and Institutional Responses. In *Who Chooses? Who Loses? Culture, Institutions, and the Unequal Effects of School Choice*, ed. Bruce Fuller, Richard F. Elmore, and Gary Orfield. New York: Teachers College Press.

———. 1998. School Choice Outcomes: A Review of What We Know. Discussion Paper Presented at the Conference on School Choice, Law, and Public Policy, School of Law, University of California, Berkeley, April 17–18.

Hirshleifer, David. 1993. The Blind Leading the Blind: Social Influence, Fads and Information Cascades. University of California, Los Anegels, Anderson School of Management.

Hill, Paul T. 1995. *Reinventing Public Education*. Santa Monica, Calif.: RAND.

Hill, Paul T., and Herbert J. Grover. 1993. Comments and General Discussion. In *School Choice: Examining the Evidence*, ed. Edith Rasell and Richard Rothstein. Washington, D.C.: Economic Policy Institute.

Hill, Paul, Lawrence C. Pierce, and James W. Guthrie. 1997. *Reinventing Public Education*. Chicago: University of Chicago Press.

Hirsch, E. D., Jr. 1996. *The Schools We Need and Why We Don't Have Them*. New York: Doubleday.

Hirschoff, Mary-Michelle Upson. 1986. Public Policy Toward Private Schools: A Focus on Parent Choice. In *Private Education: Studies in Choice and Public Policy*, ed. Daniel C. Levy. New York: Oxford University Press.

Hoffer, Thomas, Andrew M. Greeley, and James S. Coleman. 1985. Achievement Growth in Public and Catholic Schools. *Sociology of Education* 58: 74–97.

Hoxby, Caroline Minter. 1994a. Do Private Schools Provide Competition for Public Schools? National Bureau of Economic Research Working Paper 4978.

———. 1994a. Does Competition among Public Schools Benefit Students and Taxpayers? National Bureau of Economic Research Working Paper 4979.

———. 1996. The Effects of Private School Vouchers on Schools and Students. In *Holding Schools Accountable*, ed. Helen Ladd. Washington, D.C.: Brookings Institution Press.

———. 1998. When Parents Can Choose, What Do They Choose? The Effects of Greater School Choice on Curriculum. In *Meritocracy and Inequality*, ed. Paul E. Peterson and Susan Mayer. Washington, D.C.: Brookings Institution Press.

Huber, P. J. 1967. The Behavior of Maximum Likelihood Estimates under Non-Standard Conditions. In *Proceedings of the Fifth Berkeley Symposium in Mathematical Statistics and Probability*. Berkeley, Calif.: University of California Press.

Huckfeldt, Robert, and John Sprague. 1987a. Networks in Context: The Social Flow of Political Information. *American Political Science Review* 81:1197–1216.

Huckfeldt, Robert, and John Sprague. 1987b. Political Parties and Electoral Mobilization: Political Structure, Social Structure, and the Party Canvass. *American Political Science Review* 86:70–86.

———. 1991. Discussant Effects on Vote Choice: Intimacy, Structure, and Interdependence. *Journal of Politics* 53:122–58.

———. 1995. *Citizens, Politics, and Social Communication: Information and Influence in an Election Campaign.* New York: Cambridge University Press.

Hudson Institute and Butler University. 1992. *First Year Report: Educational Choice Charitable Trust.* Indianapolis: Hudson Institute.

Hurwitz, Howard. 1988. *The Last Angry Principal.* Portland: Halcyon House.

Inglehart, Ronald. 1990. *Culture Shift in Advanced Industrial Society.* Princeton: Princeton University Press.

Iyengar, Shanto. 1989. How Citizens Think about National Issues: A Matter of Responsibility. *American Journal of Political Science* 33: 878–900.

Jackman, Robert, and Ross Miller. 1996a. A Renaissance of Political Culture? *American Journal of Political Science* 40 (August): 632–57.

———. 1996b. The Poverty of Political Culture? *American Journal of Political Science* 40 (August): 697–716.

James, Thomas, and Henry M. Levin. 1987. Introduction. In *Comparing Public and Private Schools*, vol. 1 of *Institutions and Organizations*, ed. Thomas James and Henry M. Levin. New York: The Falmer Press.

Jencks, Christopher. 1966. Is the Public School Obsolete? *The Public Interest* 2 (Winter): 18–27.

John, Peter, Keith Dowding, and Stephen Biggs. 1995. Residential Mobility in London: A Micro-Level Test of the Behavioural Assumptions of the Tiebout Model. *British Journal of Political Science* 25: 379–97.

Johnson, Eric, and John Payne. 1985. Effort and Accuracy in Choice. *Management Science* 31: 395–404.

Kardes, Frank R. 1994. Consumer Judgment and Decision Processes. In *Handbook of Social Cognition*, ed. Robert S. Wyer and Thomas K. Srull. Hillsdale, N.J.: Erlbaum.

Katona, George, and Eva Mueller. 1955. A Study of Purchase Decisions in Consumer Behavior. In *Consumer Behavior*, ed. Lincoln Clark. New York: New York University Press.

Kaufman, Herbert. 1969. Administrative Decentralization and Political Power. *Public Administration Review* 31: 3–15.

Kerbow, David, and Annette Bernhardt. 1993. Parental Intervention in the School: The Context of Minority Involvement. In *Parents, Their Children and Schools*, ed. Barbara Schneider and James S. Coleman. Boulder, Colo.: Westview Press.

King, Gary. 1990. When Not to Use R-Squared. *Political Methodologist* 3, no. 2: 11–12.

King, Gary, Robert O. Keohane, and Sydney Verba. 1994. *Designing Social Inquiry.* Princeton: Princeton University Press.

Kirp, David. 1992. What School Choice Really Means. *Atlantic Monthly* November: 127.

Knoke, David. 1990. *Political Networks: The Structural Perspective.* Cambridge, U.K.: Cambridge University Press.

Knoke, David, and James Kuklinski. 1982. *Network Analysis.* Beverly Hills, Calif.: Sage Publications.

Knott, Jack, and Gary Miller. 1987. *Reforming Bureaucracy: The Politics Of Institutional Choice.* Englewood Cliffs, N.J.: Prentice-Hall.

Kozol, Jonathon. 1991. *Savage Inequalities.* New York: Crown Publishers.

Kranton, Rachel E. 1996. Reciprocal Exchange: A Self-Sustaining System. *American Economic Review* 86, no. 4: 830–51.

Kreps, David M. 1990. Corporate Culture and Economic Theory. In *Perspectives on Positive Political Economy,* ed. James Alt and Kenneth Shepsle. New York: Cambridge University Press.

Kuklinski, James H., Daniel S. Metlay, and W. D. Kay. 1982. Citizen Knowledge and Choices on the Complex Issue of Nuclear Energy. *American Journal of Political Science* 26: 615–42.

Kuklinski, James H., and Norman L. Hurley. 1994. On Hearing and Interpreting Political Messages: A Cautionary Tale of Citizen Cue-Taking. *The Journal of Politics* 56: 729–51.

Kuklinski, James H., Paul J. Quirk, David Schwieder, and Robert F. Rich. 1996. Misinformation and the Currency of Citizenship. Prepared for delivery at the 1996 Annual Meeting of the American Political Science Association, San Francisco, August 29–September 1.

LaLonde, Robert, and Rebecca Maynard. 1987. How Precise Are Evaluations of Employment and Training Programs: Evidence from a Field Experiment. *Evaluation Review* 11(August): 428–51.

Lankford, Hamilton, and James Wycoff. 1992. Primary and Secondary School Choice among Public and Religious Alternatives. *Economics of Education Review* 11: 317–37.

———. 1997. The Effects of School Choice and Residential Location on the Racial Segregation of K–12 Students. Albany: Department of Economics and Public Administration, State University of New York Albany.

LaPierre, Bruce. 1987. Voluntary Interdistrict Desegregation in St. Louis: The Special Master Tale. *Wisconsin Law Review* 44: 971–1040.

Lau, Richard. 1995. Information Search During an Election Campaign. In *Political Judgment,* ed. Milton Lodge and Kathleen McGraw. Ann Arbor: University of Michigan.

Lazarsfeld, Paul F., Bernard Berelson, and Hazel Gaudet. 1944. *The People's Choice: How the Voter Makes up His Mind in a Presidential Campaign.* New York: Duell, Sloan, and Pearce.

Lee, Dwight R. 1991. Vouchers—The Key to Meaningful Reform. In *Privatization and Its Alternatives,* ed. William T. Gormley, Jr. Madison: University of Wisconsin Press.

Lee, Seh-Ahn. 1993. Family Structure Effects on Student Outcomes. In *Parents, Their Children and Schools,* ed. Barbara Schneider and James S. Coleman. Boulder, Colo.: Westview Press.

Lee, Valerie. 1993. Educational Choice: The Stratifying Effects of Selecting Schools and Courses. *Educational Policy* 7: 125–48.

———. 1995. San Antonio School Choice Plans: Rewarding or Creaming? *Social Science Quarterly* 76: 513–21.

Lee, Valerie, Robert Croninger, and Julia Smith. 1996. Equity and Choice in Detroit. In *Who Chooses? Who Losers? Culture, Institutions and the Unequal Effects of School Choice* Ed. Bruce Fuller, Richard F. Elmore, and Gary Orfield. New York: Teachers College Press.

Levy, Mark. 1978. Opinion Leadership and Television News Use. *Public Opinion Quarterly* 42: 402–16.

Leibenstein, Harvey. 1950. Bandwagon, Snob, and Veblen Effects in the Theory of Consumers' Demand. *Quarterly Journal of Economics* 64: 183–207.

Lemann, Nicholas. 1991. A False Panacea. *Atlantic Monthly* (January): 104.

Levi, Margaret. 1996. Social Capital and Unsocial Capital: A Review Essay of Robert Putnam's *Making Democracy Work*. *Politics and Society* 24: 45–55.

Levin, Henry M. 1989. *The Theory of Choice Applied to Education*. Paper no. 89–CERAS-10. Stanford: Stanford University School of Education.

———. 1991. The Economics of Educational Choice. *Economics of Education Review* 10, no. 2: 137–58.

———. 1998. Educational Vouchers: Effectiveness, Choice, and Costs. *Journal of Policy Analysis and Management* 17, no. 3: 373–93.

Levine, Charles. 1984. Citizenship and Service Delivery: The Promise of Coproduction. *Public Administration Review* 44 (March): 178–87.

Lieberman, Myron. 1989. *Privatization and Educational Choice*. New York: St. Martins Press.

Lindeman, Mark. 1996. Studying Informed Preferences: Measures, Models, and Mysteries. Paper presented to the Midwest Political Science Association annual meeting, Chicago.

Lines, Patricia. 1994. Reaching Out to All Parents: The Untold Success at Alum Rock. *Equity and Choice* 10: 56–59.

Lipset, Seymour Martin. 1995. Malaise and Resiliency in America. *Journal of Democracy* (January): 2–16.

Lodge, Milton, and Patrick Stroh. 1993. Inside the Mental Voting Booth: An Impression-Driven Process Model of Candidate Evaluation. In *Explorations in Political Psychology*, ed. Shanto Iyengar and William McGuire. Durham, N.C.: Duke University Press.

Lord, Frederic M. 1967. A Paradox in the Interpretation of Group Comparisons. *Psychological Bulletin* 68 (November): 304–5.

———. 1969. Statistical Adjustments When Comparing Preexisting Groups. *Psychological Bulletin* 72 (November): 336–37.

Loury, Glenn. 1977. A Dynamic Theory of Racial Income Differences. In *Women, Minorities, and Employment Discrimination*, ed. P. A. Wallace and A. LeMund. Lexington, Mass.: Lexington Books.

Lowery, David, William Lyons, and Ruth Hoogland DeHoog. 1995. The Empirical Evidence for Citizen Information and a Local Market for Public Goods. *American Political Science Review* 89 (September): 705–9.

Lupia, Arthur. 1992. Busy Voters, Agenda Control and the Power of Information. *American Political Science Review* 86: 390–404.

———. 1994. Short Cuts versus Encyclopedias: Information and Voting Behavior in California Insurance Reform Election. *American Political Science Review* 88: 63–76.

Lupia, Arthur, and Mathew McCubbins. 1998. *The Democratic Dilemma: Can Citizens Learn What They Need to Know?* Cambridge, U.K.: Cambridge University Press.

Lyons, William, David Lowery, and Ruth Hoogland DeHoog. 1992. *The Politics of Dissatisfaction*. Armonk, N.Y.: M. E. Sharpe.

Mansbridge, Jane. 1980. *Beyond Adversary Democracy*. New York: Basic Books.

Manski, Charles. 1992. Educational Choice (Vouchers) and Social Mobility. *Economics of Education Review* 11:351–69.

Maranto, Robert, Scott Milliman, and Frederick Hess. 1998. Does Public Sector Competition Stimulate Innovation? The Competitive Impacts of Arizona Charter Schools on Traditional Public Schools. Paper presented to the American Political Science Association annual meeting, Boston, September.

Marschall, Melissa. 1996. Skimming versus Sorting: Examining Evidence of Public School Choice. Paper presented at the annual meetings of the Midwest Political Science Association, Chicago, April 18–20.

———. 1998. Urban Renewal, Institutional Reform and Citizen Involvement. Ph.D. Dissertation. SUNY, Stony Brook.

Marsden, Peter V. 1985. Latent Structure Models for Relationally Defined Social Classes. *American Sociological Review* 90, 1002–21.

———. 1987. Core Discussion Networks of Americans. *American Sociological Review* 52: 122–31.

Marsden, Peter V., Cynthia R. Cook, and Arne L. Kalleberg. 1994. Organizational Structures: Coordination And Control. *The American Behavioral Scientist* 37: 911–29.

Martinez, Valerie R., Kenneth Godwin, and Frank Kemerer. 1996. Private Vouchers in San Antonio: The CEO Program. In *Private Vouchers*, ed. Terry Moe. Stanford: Hoover Institute Press.

Martinez, Valerie R., Kenneth Godwin, Frank Kemerer, and Laura Perna. 1995. The Consequences of School Choice: Who Leaves and Who Stays in the Inner-City. *Social Science Quarterly* 76, no. 3: 485–501.

Martinez, Valerie, Frank R. Kemerer, and Kenneth Godwin. 1993. Who Chooses and Why?: Baseline Demographic Data Report, San Antonio School Choice Research Project. Typescript. Center for the Study of Education Reform, College of Education, University of North Texas.

Massey, Douglas S., and Nancy A. Denton. 1993. *American Apartheid: Segregation and the Making of the Underclass.* Cambridge: Harvard University Press.

McArthur, E., K. Colopy, and B. Schlaine. 1995. The Use of School Choice. NCES 95–742R. Washington, D.C.: National Center for Education Statistics, U.S. Department of Education.

McKinney, Joseph. 1995. Public School Choice and Desegregation: A Reality Check. *Journal of Law and Education* 25:649–57.

Mecklenberger, James A., and Richard W. Hostrop, eds. 1972. *Education Vouchers: From Theory to Alum Rock.* Homewood, Ill.: ETC Publications.

Meier, Deborah. 1987. Good Schools Are Still Possible. *Dissent* 34 (fall): 543–49.

1991. Choice Can Save Public Education. *The Nation* 252 (March 4): 265–71.

———. 1995. *The Power of Their Ideas: Lessons for America from a Small School in Harlem.* Boston: Beacon Press.

Miller, Gary J. 1992. *Managerial Dilemmas: The Political Economy of Hierarchy.* New York: Cambridge University Press.

Milliman, Scott, and Robert Maranto. 1996. Competition and the Public Schools: Does the Former Improve the Latter? An Income-Contingent View of Education Markets. Paper presented to the American Political Science Association annual meetings, Sept. 1–5.

———. 1998. Does Competition Harm Public Schools? Family Income and Education Markets. Paper presented to the American Political Science Association annual meetings, Boston, August 29–Sept. 4.

Moe, Terry. 1989. Interest Groups and Structural Politics. In *Can the Government Govern?* Ed. Paul E. Peterson and John Chubb. Washington, D.C.: Brookings Institution Press.

———. 1994. School Choice and the Creaming Problem. In *Midwest Approaches to School Reform*, ed. T. Downes and W. Testa. Chicago: Federal Reserve Bank of Chicago.

———. 1995. Private Vouchers. In *Private Vouchers*, ed. Terry Moe. Stanford: Hoover Institute Press.

———. 1997. Democracy and the Challenge of Education Reform. In *Advances in the Study of Entrepreneurship, Innovation, and Economic Growth*, ed. Gary Libecap. Greenwich, Conn.: JAI Press.

Montgomery, James D. 1990. Is Underclass Behavior Contagious? A Rational-Choice Analysis. Working Paper, Department of Economics, Northwestern University.

Moore, Donald R., and Suzanne Davenport. 1990. School Choice: The New Improved Sorting Machine. In *Choice in Education*, ed. W. Boyd and H. Walberg. Berkeley: McCutchan.

Muller, Chandra, and David Kerbow. 1993. Parental Involvement in the Home, School, and Community. In *Parents, Their Children and Schools*, ed. Barbara Schneider and James S. Coleman. Boulder, Colo.: Westview Press.

Murnane, Richard J. 1986. Comparisons of Private and Public Schools: The Critical Role of Regulations. In *Private Education: Studies in Choice and Public Policy*, ed. Daniel C. Levy. New York: Oxford University Press.

Nathan, Joe. 1989, ed. *Public Schools by Choice*. St. Paul: Institute for Learning and Teaching.

National Center for Education Statistics. 1993. *The Condition of Education 1993*. Washington, D.C.: U.S. Department of Education.

———. 1997. *The Condition of Education 1997*. Washington, D.C.: U.S. Department of Education.

Nault, Richard, and Susan Uchitelle. 1982. School Choice in the Public Sector: A Case Study of Parental Decision-Making. In *Family Choice in Schooling*, ed. Michael Manley-Casimir. Lexington, Mass.: Lexington Books.

Neal, Derek. 1997. The Effect of Catholic Secondary Schooling on Educational Attainment. *Journal of Labor Economics* 15: 98–123.

Nelson, Phillip. 1970. Information and Consumer Behavior. *Journal of Political Economy* 78: 311–29.

Newman, James, and Richard Staelin. 1972. Prepurchase Information Seeking for New Cars and Major Household Appliances. *Journal of Marketing Research* 9: 249–57.

Nie, Norman, Jane Junn, and Kenneth Stehlik-Barry. 1996. *Education and Democratic Citizenship in America*. Chicago: Univeristy of Chicago Press.

North, Douglass. 1990. *Institutions, Institutional Change, and Economic Performance*. New York: Cambridge University Press.

Ogawa, Rodney, and Jo Sargeant Dutton. 1994. Parental Choice in Education: Examining the Underlying Assumptions. *Urban Education* 29: 270–97.

———. 1997. Parent Involvement and School Choice: Exit and Voice in Public Schools. *Urban Education* 32: 333–53.

Okun, Arthur. 1975. *The Big Trade-off: Efficiency and Equity*. Washington, D.C.: Brookings Institution Press.

Olivas, M. 1981. Information Access Inequities: A Fatal Flaw in Educational Voucher Plans. *Journal of Law and Education* 10: 441–65.

Olson, Mancur. 1965. *The Logic of Collective Action.* Cambridge: Harvard University Press.

Orfield, Gary, Susan E. Eaton, and the Harvard Project on Desegregation. 1996. *Dismantling Desegregation: The Quiet Removal of Brown versus Board Education.* New York: New Press.

Osborne, David, and Ted Gaebler. 1992. *Reinventing Government.* New York: Addison-Wesley.

Ostrom, Elinor. 1972. Metropolitan Reform: Propositions Derived from Two Traditions. *Social Science Quarterly* 53 (December): 474–93.

———. 1990. *Governing the Commons: The Evolution of Institutions for Collective Action.* New York: Cambridge University Press.

———. 1996. Crossing the Great Divide: Coproduction, Synergy, and Development. *World Development* 24, no. 6: 1073–87.

Pattison, Philippa. 1994. Social Cognition in Context: Some Applications of Social Network Analysis. In *Advances in Social Network Analysis,* ed. Stanley Wasserman and Joseph Galaskiewicz. Thousand Oaks, Calif.: Sage.

Payne, John W., James R. Bettman, and Eric J. Johnson. 1993. *The Adaptive Decision Maker.* New York: Cambridge University Press.

Percy, Stephen L. 1984. Citizen Participation in the Coproduction of Urban Service. *Urban Affairs Quarterly* 19: 431–46.

Peterson, Paul E. 1998. School Choice: A Report Card. In *Learning from School Choice* ed. Paul E. Peterson, and Bryan Hassel. Washington, D.C.: Brookings Institution Press.

Peterson, Paul E., and Bryan C. Hassel, eds. 1998. *Learning from School Choice.* Washington, D.C.: Brookings Institution Press.

Peterson, Paul E., and Chad Noyes. 1997. School Choice in Milwaukee. In *New Schools for a New Century*, ed. Diane Ravitch and Joseph Viteritti. New Haven: Yale University Press.

Peterson, Paul E., Jay Greene, and Chad Noyes. 1996. School Choice in Milwaukee. *The Public Interest* (fall): 38–56.

Petty, R. E., J. T. Cacioppo, and R. Goldman. 1981. Personal Involvement as a Determinant of Argument-Based Persuasion. *Journal of Personality and Social Psychology* 41: 847–55.

Plank, Stephen, Kathryn Schiller, Barbara Schneider, and James S. Coleman. 1993. Effects of Choice in Education. In *School Choice: Examining the Evidence*, ed. Edith Rasell and Richard Rothstein. Washington, D.C.: Economic Policy Institute.

Popkin, Samuel. 1991. *The Reasoning Voter: Communication and Persuasion in Presidential Campaigns.* Chicago: University of Chicago Press.

Price, Vincent, and John Zaller. 1993. Who Gets the News? Alternative Measures of News Reception and Their Implications for Research. *The Public Opinion Quarterly* 57: 133–64.

Public Agenda. 1997. *Getting By: What American Teenagers Really Think about Their Schools.* New York: Public Agenda.

Purkey, S. C., and M. S. Smith. 1983. Effective Schools: A Review. *The Elementary School Journal* 83, no. 4: 427–54.

Putnam, Robert. 1993. *Making Democracy Work: Civic Traditions in Modern Italy*. Princeton: Princeton University Press.

———. 1995a. Bowling Alone: America's Declining Social Capital. *Journal of Democracy* 6 (January): 65–78.

———. 1995b. Tuning in, Tuning Out: The Strange Disappearance of Social Capital in America. *Political Science and Politics*, 28 (December): 664–83.

Ravitch, Diane. 1994. Somebody's Children: Expanding Educational Opportunities for All America's Children. *Brookings Review* (fall): 1–4.

———. 1996. The Facts About Catholic Education. *The Wall Street Journal*. October 1: 22.

Ravitch, Diane, and Joseph Viteritti. 1996. A New Vision for City Schools. *Public Interest* 122: 3–16.

Ravitch, Diane, and Joseph P. Viteritti, eds. 1997. *New Schools for a New Century: The Redesign of Urban Education*. New Haven: Yale University Press.

Raywid, Mary Anne. 1989. The Mounting Case for Schools of Choice. In *Public Schools by Choice*, ed. Joe Nathan. St. Paul: Institute for Learning and Teaching.

Rhoads, Steven. 1985. *The Economist's View of the World: Government, Markets, and Public Policy*. New York: Cambridge University Press.

Richards, Craig, Rima Shore, and Max Sawicky. 1996. *Risky Business: Private Management of Public Schools*. Washington, D.C.: Economic Policy Institute.

Richmond, Virginia. 1977. The Relationship between Opinion Leadership and Information Acquisition. *Human Communications Research* 4: 38–43.

Riley, Dennis D. 1990. Should Market Forces Control Educational Decision Making? *American Political Science Review* 84 (2): 554–58.

Robinson, John, and Mark Levy. 1986. Interpersonal Communication and News Comprehension. *Public Opinion Quarterly* 50: 160–75.

Rogers, William. 1993. Regression Standard Errors in Clustered Samples. In *Stata Technical Bulletin Reprints*, ed. S. Becketti. College Station, Tex.: Stata Corporation.

Rona, Kenneth, and Mark Schneider. 1996. School Choice: The Role of Expertise, Search Costs, and Cognitive Effort. Presented at the Conference for Judgment and Decision Making. Chicago. April 6–7.

Rose-Ackerman, Susan. 1992. *Rethinking the Progressive Agenda: The Reform of the American Regulatory State*. New York: Free Press.

Rosenstone, Steven, and John Mark Hansen. 1993. *Mobilization, Participation, and Democracy in America*. New York: MacMillian Publishing Company.

Rossell, Christine H. 1995. Controlled-Choice Desegregation Plans Not Enough Choice, Too Much Control? *Urban Affairs Review* 31 (September): 43–76.

Rothstein, Richard. 1998. Charter Conundrum. *The American Prospect* July–August: 46–60.

Rouse, Cecilia. 1998. Private School Vouchers and Student Achievement: An Evaluation of the Milwaukee Parental Choice Program. *Quarterly Journal of Economics* 63:553–602.

Rowan, Brian, Steven T. Bossert and David C. Dwyer. 1983. Research on Effective Schools: A Cautionary Note. *Educational Researcher* 12 (spring): 24–31.

Rubenstein, Michael, and Nancy Adelman. 1994. Public Choice in Minnesota. In *Privatizing Education and Educational Choice: Concepts, Plans, Experience*, ed. Simon Hakim, P. Simon, and G. Bowman. Westport, Conn.: Praeger.

Ruhil, Anirudh V. S., Mark Schneider, Paul Teske, and Byung-Moon Jee. 1999. Institutions and Reform: Reinventing Local Government. *Urban Affairs Review* 34, no. 3: 433–55.

Salganik, Laura Hersh. 1981. *The Fall and Rise of Education Vouchers*. Baltimore: Center for Social Organization of Schools, Johns Hopkins University Press.

Sander, W. 1993. Expenditures and Student Achievement in Illinois. *Journal of Public Economics* 52 (October): 403–16.

Schneider, Barbara, and James. S. Coleman, eds. 1993. *Parents, Their Children and Schools*. Boulder, Colo.: Westview Press.

Schneider, Barbara, Kathryn Schiller, and James S. Coleman. 1996. Public School Choice: Some Evidence from the National Educational Longitudinal Study of 1988. *Educational Evaluation and Policy Analysis* 18: 27–54.

Schneider, Mark. 1989. *The Competitive City*. Pittsburgh: University of Pittsburgh Press.

Schneider, Mark. 1999. Information and Choice in Educational Privatization. Paper presented to the conference on Setting the Agenda for the Study of Privatization of Education. Teacher's College, Columbia University, New York. April 8–10, 1999.

Schneider, Mark, Melissa Marschall, Paul Teske, and Christine Roch. 1998. School Choice and Culture Wars in the Classroom: What Different Parents Seek from Education. *Social Science Quarterly* 79: 489–501.

Schneider, Mark and Paul Teske. 1995. *Public Entrepreneurs: Agents for Change in American Government*. Princeton: Princeton University Press.

Schneider, Mark, Paul Teske, Melissa Marschall, Michael Mintrom, and Christine Roch. 1997. Institutional Arrangements and the Creation of Social Capital: The Effects of School Choice. *American Political Science Review* 91: 82–93.

Schneider, Mark, Paul Teske, Christine Roch, and Melissa Marschall. 1997a. Networks to Nowhere: Segregation and Stratification in Networks of Information about Schools. *American Journal of Political Science* 41: 1201–23.

———. 1997b. School Choice Builds Community. *The Public Interest* 129: 86–90.

———. 1998. Shopping for Schools: In the Land of the Blind, the One-Eyed Parent May Be Enough. *American Journal of Political Science* 42: 769–93.

Schumpeter, Joseph. 1942. *Capitalism, Socialism, and Democracy*. New York: Harper and Row.

Schwartz, Alan, and Louis L. Wilde. 1979. Intervening in Markets on the Basis of Imperfect Information: A Legal and Economic Analysis. *University of Pennsylvania Law Review* 127: 630–82.

Scitovsky, Tibor. 1950. Ignorance as a Source of Oligopoly Power. *American Economic Review* 40: 48–53.

Sharp, Elaine. 1996. Culture Wars and City Politics: Local Government's Role in Social Conflict. *Urban Affairs Review* 31, no. 6: 738–58.

Sharp, Elaine. 1998. Social Capital and Culture Wars. A paper prepared for delivery at the Workshop on Revitalizing Urban Democracy, Russell Sage Foundation, New York, April 2–3.

Shenk, David. 1997. *Data Smog: Surviving the Information Glut*. San Francisco: Harper Press.

Sieber, Sam. 1974. Toward a Theory of Role Acculmation. *American Sociological Review* 39: 567–78.

Simon, Herbert A. 1957. *Models of Man*. John Wiley and Sons: New York.

Simon, Herbert A. 1986. Rationality in Psychology and Economics. In *Rational Choice: The Contrast between Economics and Psychology*, ed. R. M. Hogarth, and M. W. Reder. Chicago: University of Chicago Press.

Skinner, C. J. 1989. Introduction to Part A. In *Analysis of Complex Surveys*, ed. C. J. Skinner, D. Holt, and T. F. Smith. New York: John Wiley and Sons.

Skocpol, Theda. 1996. Unravelling from Above. *The American Prospect* 25 (March–April): 20–25.

Skogan, Wesley G. 1990. *Disorder and Decline: Crime and the Spiral of Urban Decay in American Neighborhoods*. New York: Free Press.

Slama, Mark E., and Armen Tashchian. 1985. Selected Socioeconomic and Demographic Characteristics Associated with Purchasing Involvement. *Journal of Marketing* 49: 72–82.

Slama, Mark E., and Terrell G. Williams. 1990. Generalization of the Market Maven's Information Provision Tendency across Product Categories. *Advances in Consumer Research* 17: 48–52.

Smith, Kevin, and Kenneth Meier. 1995. *Politics, Markets, and Fools*. Armonk, N.Y.: M. E. Sharpe.

Smith, Lones, and Peter Sørensen. 1994a. An Example of Non-Martingale Learning. Typescript. Department of Economics, Massachusetts Institute of Technology.

———. 1994b. Pathological Models of Observational Learning. Typescript. Department of Economics, Massachusetts Institute of Technology

Smrekar, Claire. 1995. *The Impact of School Choice and Community: In the Interest of Families and Schools*. Albany: State University of New York Press.

Sniderman, Paul M., Richard A. Brody, and Philip E. Tetlock. 1991. *Reasoning and Choice: Explorations in Political Psychology*. New York: Cambridge University Press.

Speakman, Robert, and Finis Welsh. 1995. Does School Quality Matter? A Reassessment. Texas A and M University, Department of Economics paper.

Steel, Lauri, and Roger Levine. 1994. *Educational Innovation in Multiracial Contexts: The Growth of Magnet Schools in American Education*. Washington, D.C.: U.S. Department of Education.

Stigler, George. 1961. The Economics of Information. *Journal of Political Economy* 69: 213–25.

Stiglitz, Joseph. 1989. Imperfect Information in the Product Market. In *Handbook of Industrial Organization*, ed. Richard Schmalansee and Robert Willig. Amsterdam: North-Holland.

Strobert, Barbara. 1991. Factors Influencing Parental Choice in Selection of a Magnet School in the Montclair, New Jersey Public Schools. Ph.D. Diss., Columbia University Teachers College.

Swank, Duane. 1996. Culture, Institutions, and Economic Growth: Theory, Recent Evidence, and the Role of Communitarian Polities. *American Journal of Political Science* 40 (August): 660–79.

Taber, Charles, and M. Steenbergen. 1995. Computational Experiments in Electoral Behavior. In *Political Judgment and Process*, ed. Milton Lodge and Kathleen McGraw. Ann Arbor: University of Michigan Press.

Tan, Norma. 1990. The Cambridge Controlled Choice Program: Improving Educational Equity and Integration. New York: Manhattan Institute Center for Education Innovation Policy paper.

Tarrow, Sidney. 1996. Making Social Science Work Across Space and Time: A Critical Reflection on Robert Putnam's *Making Democracy Work. American Political Science Review* 90 (June): 389–97.

Teske, Paul, and Mark Schneider. 1999. What We Know and Don't Know about School Choice. Working manuscript. SUNY Stony Brook.

Teske, Paul, Mark Schneider, Michael Mintrom, and Samuel Best. 1993. Establishing the Micro Foundations of a Macro Theory: Information, Movers, and the Competitive Local Market for Public Goods. *American Political Science Review* 87: 702–13.

Teske, Paul, Mark Schneider, Michael Mintrom, and Samuel Best. 1995. The Empirical Evidence for Citizen Information and a Local Market for Public Goods. *American Political Science Review* 89: 705–9.

Thorelli, Hans, and Jack Engledow. 1980. Information Seekers and Information Systems: A Policy Perspective. *Journal of Marketing* 44: 9–27.

Tiebout, Charles. 1956. A Pure Theory of Local Expenditure. *Journal of Political Economy* 64 (October): 416–24.

Tirole, Jean. 1988. *The Theory Of Industrial Organization.* Cambridge, Mass.: Massachusetts Institute of Technology Press.

Toch, Thomas. 1998. New Education Bazaar: Charter Schools Represent the Free Market in Action—With All Its Problems. *US News and World Report*, April 27.

Tversky, Amos, and Daniel Kahneman. 1986. Rational Choice and the Framing of Decisions. *Journal of Business* 59: S251–78.

Tweedie, Jack. 1990. Should Market Forces Control Educational Decision Making? *American Political Science Review* 84: 549–54.

Tyack, David, and Larry Cuban. 1995. *Tinkering Toward Utopia: A Century of Public School Reform.* Cambridge: Harvard University Press.

Tybout, Alice, and Nancy Artz. 1994. Consumer Psychology. *Annual Review of Psychology* 45: 131–69.

Ubinas, William E., and Rev. Leo Lawrence. 1990. *Community School District One Blueprint for Progress: September 1990–June 1993.* A report issued by Community School District 1, New York.

Valelly, Richard M. 1996. Couch-Potato Democracy? *The American Prospect* 25 (March–April): 25–26.

Van Dunk, Emily. 1998. Evaluating School Choice: Views from Parents in Cleveland and Milwaukee. Paper presented to the Midwest Political Science Association annual meetings, Chicago, April 17–20.

Vanourek, Gregg, Bruno V. Manno, Chester E. Finn, Jr., and Louann A. Bierlin. 1998. Charter Schools as Seen by Students, Teachers, and Parents. In *Learning from School Choice*, ed. Paul E. Peterson and Bryan C. Hassel. Washington, D.C.: Brookings Institution Press.

Verba, Sidney, Kay Lehman Schlozman, and Henry Brady. 1995. *Voice and Equality: Civic Voluntarism in American Politics.* Cambridge: Harvard University Press.

Wasserman, S., and J. Galaskiewicz, eds. 1994. *Advances in Social Network Analysis: Research from the Social and Behavioral Sciences.* Newbury Park, Calif.: Sage Publications.

Weimer, David L., and Aidan R. Vining. 1992. *Policy Analysis: Concepts and Practice.* 2d ed. Englewood Cliffs, N.J.: Prentice-Hall.

Wells, Amy Stuart. 1993a. *Time to Choose: America at the Crossroads of School Choice Policy.* New York: Hill and Wang.

Wells, Amy Stuart. 1993b. The Sociology of School Choice: Why Some Win and Others Lose in the Educational Marketplace. In *School Choice: Examining the Evidence*, ed. Edith Rassell and Richard Rothstein. Washington, D.C.: Economic Policy Institute.

White, H. 1980. A Heteroskedasticity-Consistent Covariance Matrix Estimator and a Direct Test for Heteroskedasticity. *Econometrica* 48: 817–30.

Wilde, Louis L. 1981. Information Costs, Duration of Search, and Turnover: Theory and Applications. *Journal of Political Economy* 89: 1122–41.

Wilde, Louis L., and Alan Schwartz. 1979. Equilibrium Comparison Shopping. *Review of Economic Studies* 55: 543–53.

Willms, Douglas J. 1996. School Choice and Community Segregation: Findings from Scotland. In *Generating Social Stratification: Toward a New Researsch Agenda*, ed. Alan Kerchkoff. Boulder, Colo.: Westview Press.

Willms, Douglas J., and Frank Echols. 1992. Alert and Inert Clients: The Scottish Experience of Parental Choice of Schools. *Economics of Education Review* 11, no. 4: 339–50.

Williamson, Oliver. 1985. *The Economic Institutions of Capitalism*. New York: Free Press.

Wilson, James Q. 1989. *Bureaucracy: What Government Agencies Do and Why They Do It*. New York: Basic Books.

Wilson, James Q., and George L. Kelling. 1982. The Police and Neighborhood Safety. *The Atlantic* (March): 29–38.

Wilson, Steven F. 1992. *Reinventing the Schools: A Radical Plan for Boston*. Boston: Pioneer Institute.

Wilson, William Julius. 1987. *The Truly Disadvantaged: The Inner City, the Underclass, and Public Policy*. Chicago: University of Chicago Press.

Witte, John F. 1991b. *First Year Report: Milwaukee Parental Choice Program*. Madison: University of Wisconsin, Robert M. LaFollette Institute of Public Affairs.

Witte, John. F. 1993. The Milwaukee Parental Choice Program. In *School Choice: Examining the Evidence*, ed. Edith Rassell and Richard Rothstein. Washington, D.C.: Economic Policy Institute.

Witte, John. 1996. Evaluation of Choice in Milwaukee. In *Who Chooses? Who Loses? Culture, Institutions, and the Unequal Effects of School Choice*, eds. Bruce Fuller, Richard F. Elmore, and Gary Orfield. New York: Teachers College Press.

Witte, John F., Andrea B. Bailey, and Christopher A. Thorn. 1992. *Second Year Report: Milwaukee Parental Choice Program*. Madison: University of Wisconsin, Robert M. LaFollette Institute of Public Affairs

———. 1993. *Third Year Report: Milwaukee Parental Choice Program*. Madison: University of Wisconsin, Robert M. LaFollette Institute of Public Affairs.

Witte, John F., and Mark E. Rigdon. 1993. Education Choice Reforms: Will They Change American Schools? *Publius: The Journal of Federalism* 23 (summer): 95–114.

Witte, John F., and Christopher A. Thorn. 1994. Who Chooses? Voucher and Interdistrict Choice Programs in Milwaukee. In *Midwest Approaches to School Reform*, ed. Thomas A. Downes and William A. Testa. Chicago: Federal Reserve Bank of Chicago.

Wohlstetter, Priscilla, Richard Wenning, and Kerri L. Briggs. 1995. Charter Schools in the United States: The Question of Autonomy. Working paper, University of Southern California's Center on Educational Governance.

Wong, Kenneth K. 1992. Choice in Public Schools: Their Institutional Functions and Distributive Consequences." *Research in Urban Policy* 4: 175–98.

Young, Timothy, and Evans Clinchy. 1992. *Choice in Public Education.* New York: Teachers College Press.

Zaller, John. 1992. *The Nature And Origins of Mass Opinion.* Cambridge, U.K.: Cambridge University Press.

Index